What to do for a Grade A

Top class AO1	Top class AO1 ... includes details and specialist terms. For example: • This is good → Siffre (in the 1960s) described how his circadian rhythms changed ... • This isn't good → One study found that people's daily rhythms became different ... You don't need to write *more*, you just need to include specific *bits* of information such as specialist terms, researchers' names, percentages and so on.
Top class AO2	Top class AO2 ... uses text or quotes from the stem of the question. For example (answer to the question about Cheryl on the facing page): • This is good → Cheryl may have developed a secure attachment with her adoptive parents as she was adopted early, before the end of the sensitive period for attachment development. • This isn't good → Strong attachments are most likely to form during a sensitive period in development which may be true in early adoptions, like Cheryl. It's not enough to just mention a few key words – you must really *engage* with the stem. This is a skill that needs practice.

Top class AO3	Top class AO3 ... is elaborated and therefore effective. For example:
	
	❶ **Beginner** level: State your **point**: One limitation is ... This theory is supported by ... One strength is ....
	
	❷ **Intermediate** level: Add some **context**.
	
	  • This is good → One limitation is that artificial materials were used. The study by the Petersons used consonant syllables.
	
	  • This isn't good → One limitation is that artificial materials were used. This doesn't tell us about everyday life.
	
	  The second example is **generic** – it could be used anywhere.
	
	  Context is king.
	
	❸ **Higher** level: Add further **explanation** to make the point **thorough**.
	
	❹ Finish with a **conclusion** e.g. 'This shows that ...'
	
	  Read the criticisms throughout this book as examples of higher level. We have provided further elaboration and a conclusion for each one.
	
	If you find higher level difficult then just do intermediate. In a 16-mark A level essay there are 10 marks for AO2, four intermediate-level criticisms should be sufficient or three higher-level.
	
	Whatever you do AVOID a list of beginner-level criticisms with no context.

Top class essays	Make it organised – it helps the examiner see the separate elements of your answer. Use paragraphs. There is more advice on essay (extended writing) questions on the next page ...

Describe **FEWER** studies but describe them in detail.

Identify **FEWER** evaluation points, but explain each one thoroughly.

ALL I WANT FOR CHRISTMAS

List-like is bad.

It's actually quite easy to list lots of points – explaining them is challenging.

Context is king.

Good evaluation points must contain evidence.

Your point may be well-elaborated but, if the same elaborated point can be placed in many different essays then it is too **EASY**.

Good evaluation points must have **CONTEXT**.

Introduction

The term 'research' refers to theories, explanations or studies.

Knowledge Check

The Knowledge Check questions throughout this book should help you identify many of the different ways that questions will be asked in the exam.

Each A level paper has 96 marks and it is a 2-hour exam (120 minutes) which gives you 1¼ minutes for each mark.

Just because you have written lots doesn't mean you will get high marks.

Students who write a long answer often do poorly.

- Such answers tend to ramble and may not answer the question.
- Spending too much time on one question means less time elsewhere.
- Your answer may lack detail – lists of studies and lists of evaluation points don't get high marks.
- Long essays are often very descriptive and there are never more than 6 marks for description.

Download suggested answers to the Knowledge Check questions from **tinyurl.com/yd3ezhkb**

More information if you can bear it

There are lots of little rules

One or more Two or more	*Discuss* **one or more** *explanations of obedience.* (16 marks)
	Means you can potentially gain full marks for just one explanation (gives you time to describe and evaluate it fully, which is important to show detail).
	Or you can elect to do more explanations – but too many explanations is not good because your answer becomes list-like (no details and no elaboration).
Difference between	*Explain the difference between electroencephalograms (EEGs) and event-related potentials (ERPs).* (4 marks)
	The danger is that you will simply describe each item. You must find a way to contrast them both, for example considering the data produced by each one.
Questions with extra information	*Describe* **and** *evaluate the cognitive approach. Refer to* **one** *other approach in your answer.* (16 marks)
	Describe **one** *animal study of attachment. Include details of what the researcher(s) did* **and** *what they found.* (4 marks)
	Make sure you satisfy the demands of ALL parts of the question.

How much should I write?

	In general 25–30 words per mark is a good rule – as long as the answer is focused on the topic.
	For an A level essay of 16 marks you might therefore write:
	AO1 150–200 words AO3 250–300 words

Here are two ways to produce top class AL essays:

Route 1	Route 2
6 marks AO1	*6 marks AO1*
Six paragraphs/points, write about 150 words.	*Six* paragraphs/points, write about 150 words.
10 marks AO3	*10 marks AO3*
Four paragraphs/evaluations at *intermediate* level, write about 300 words.	*Three* paragraphs/discussions at *higher* level, write about 300 words.
	Doing just three gives you time to elaborate and produce more of a **discussion** (offering a contrasting view– A level AO3 is more about discussion than just evaluation).

AQA
PSYCHOLOGY
For A Level
Year 2
Revision Guide
2nd Ed

Cara Flanagan

Michael Griffin

Jo Haycock

Matt Jarvis

Rob Liddle

Arwa Mohamedbhai

Illuminate
Publishing

Published in 2020 by Illuminate Publishing Ltd,
P.O. Box 1160, Cheltenham, Gloucestershire GL50 9RW

Orders: Please visit www.illuminatepublishing.com
or email sales@illuminatepublishing.com

British Library Cataloguing in Publication Data

A catalogue record for this book is available from the
British Library

ISBN 978-1-912820-47-4

Printed in the UK by Cambrian Printers, Aberystwyth

03.21

The publisher's policy is to use papers that are natural,
renewable and recyclable products made from
wood grown in sustainable forests. The logging and
manufacturing processes are expected to conform to the
environmental regulations of the country of origin.

Every effort has been made to contact copyright holders
of material produced in this book. If notified, the publisher
will be pleased to rectify any errors or omissions at the
earliest opportunity.

Editor: Nic Watson

Cover design: Nigel Harriss

Text design: Nigel Harriss

Layout: Sarah Clifford and Stephanie White

Front cover photographer: Jason Duda

Model: Madeline Rae Mason

Unsung heroes

This wonderful little book is the product of the five authors but we owe considerable gratitude to Arwa Mohamedbhai for writing the suggested answers to the Knowledge Check feature (see p.6 for details) and above all those who manage the whole production – first of all our mentor and most wonderful publisher, Rick Jackman and the very special team at Illuminate (Clare Jackman, Peter Burton and Saskia Burton).

Second to Nigel Harriss, supreme designer, who is responsible for the unique and spectacular design, and Sarah Clifford and Stephanie White who have gone above and beyond in working wonders adapting the design where needed and getting all our material to fit on the page.

And finally to Nic Watson who is our editor but that doesn't begin to describe what she does – she has our backs and makes sure that everything that needs to be checked is checked, and does all of this with enormous patience, kindness and fanatical attention to detail.

About the authors

Cara is author of many books for A level students and a conference organiser and speaker, she is also senior editor of *Psychology Review*. She is looking forward to spending more time lying on a beach or climbing mountains.

Michael is a teacher of psychology, Assistant Headteacher and previous Head of Sixth Form. He is an author of resources for the delivery of psychology lessons and provides CPD for other psychology teachers.

Jo is Head of Psychology at Sir John Talbot's School, Shropshire and has set up a network group for local psychology teachers. Her first degree is in psychology and she also has a Masters in Education. For 16 years she was an Associate Lecturer and consultant for the Open University on their psychology degree. Spare time is about enjoying engaging in sports after avoiding it for most of the first 45 years of her life.

Matt is a Chartered Psychologist and Associate Fellow of the British Psychological Society. He taught psychology for 25 years and is currently Learning Technology and Innovation Manager for a Social Justice and Education charity. Matt is also an editor of *Psychology Review*. When not working or writing Matt DJs and loves live music and festivals.

Rob was an A level teacher for more than 20 years and would like to give a big shout out to his ex-colleagues at Winstanley College. In his spare moments, he likes nothing more than to pluck away tunelessly at his guitar, ideally in the Lake District. He plans to ask Matt how you become a Chartered Psychologist.

Arwa is a teacher of psychology and is Head of Year 12 at Bacup and Rawtenstall Grammar School, Lancashire. Arwa is an experienced examiner with a major awarding body.

Contents

For a free download of suggested answers to the Knowledge Check feature visit
www.illuminatepublishing.com/2edpsychrganswers2

Revision Guides

Flashbooks

Revision Apps

=

An unbeatable combination for revision!
Visit www.illuminatepublishing.com/aqapsych

Introduction

AO stands for 'assessment objective'.

Apply it

The 'Apply it' questions throughout this book aim to help you practise AO2 skills – 30% of the marks in the exam are AO2.

In the A level exam there are three papers:

Paper 1
A: Social influence (24 marks)
B: Memory (24 marks)
C: Attachment (24 marks)
D: Psychopathology (24 marks)

Paper 2
A: Approaches in Psychology (24 marks)
B: Biopsychology (24 marks)
C: Research methods (48 marks)

Paper 3
A: Issues and debates in Psychology (24 marks)
B: Relationships OR Gender OR Cognition and development (24 marks)
C: Schizophrenia OR Eating behaviour OR Stress (24 marks)
D: Aggression OR Forensic psychology OR Addiction (24 marks)

On all sections of the exam the type of question is unpredictable (i.e. any of those on the right).

Research methods questions will be in every section in addition to the Research methods section on Paper 2.

25%

About 25% of the marks for your A level exam will come from questions on research methods.

Types of exam questions

AO1	Identify, define, outline, describe, explain	Identify **one** emotional characteristic of depression. (*1 mark*) Outline the multi-store model of memory. (*4 marks*) Explain what is meant by 'reductionism'. (*4 marks*)
AO2	Application	[Stem] Siddik was in a car accident and since then he has had difficulty producing speech fluently. He speaks very slowly and it takes a lot of effort to produce sentences, which often lack fluency. [Question] Using your knowledge of localisation of function suggest which area of Siddik's brain was damaged in the car accident. Explain your answer. (*4 marks*)
AO3	One criticism	Explain **one** limitation of Milgram's research on obedience. (*4 marks*)
	Evaluation	Evaluate humanistic psychology. (*8 marks*)
AO1 + AO3	Mini-essays	Outline **and** evaluate research into **one** biological rhythm. (*8 marks*)
	Extended writing	Discuss gender bias in psychological research. (*16 marks*)
AO1 + AO2 + AO3	Extended writing + application	[Stem] Billy's wife, Cheryl, was adopted as a child. Billy has read about attachment and wonders if Cheryl's early experiences will affect her relationship with their children. However, she was adopted very early and had a close relationship with her adoptive parents. [Question] Discuss the influence of early attachment on childhood and adult relationships. Refer to Billy's concerns in your answer. (*16 marks*)

Research methods questions

AO1	Explain	Explain what is meant by a 'critical value' when using inferential statistics. (*2 marks*)
AO2	Application	[Stem] In a study on memory the researcher wanted to ensure that the memory abilities of participants would not act as a confounding variable. [Question] Explain how a matched pairs design could have been used in this experiment. (*2 marks*)
AO3	Evaluate	Explain **one** limitation of qualitative data. (*2 marks*) Below are five statements about the limitations of questionnaires compared with interviews. Which **two** statements are correct? A. Answers may be inaccurate because people portray themselves in a good light. B. People who cannot read will be unable to take part. C. It is difficult to get a large number of people to respond. D. There are only closed questions. E. People may misunderstand a question and can't ask for help. (*2 marks*)

Effective revision

Create revision cards.	For the **description** the maximum you need is about 200 words.

- Identify 6 points on the topic.
- Record a trigger phrase in the left-hand column.
- Record about 25–30 words in the right-hand column.

For example, for a description of the psychodynamic approach:

AO1 trigger phrase	Description
Unconscious	We are aware of our conscious mind, we can be aware of pre-conscious thinking in dreams and the unconscious is beyond awareness. It stores biological drives and instincts.
Tripartite	The Id is the primitive part driven by the pleasure principle. The Ego mediates between the Id and the Superego, driven by the reality principle. The Superego is driven by the morality principle.
Psychosexual stages	Each stage is marked by a different conflict that the child must resolve to move on to the next stage. Unresolved conflicts lead to fixations.

Reduce your cards to the minimum for revision:

AO1 trigger phrase	Description
Unconscious	Conscious, pre-conscious (e.g. dreams), unconscious (beyond awareness).
Tripartite	Id (primitive, pleasure principle), Ego (mediator, reality), Superego (morality).
Psychosexual stages	Each stage has conflict to resolve or leads to fixations.

For the **evaluation** the maximum you need is about 300 words.

- Identify 3 or more evaluation points (remember LESS IS MORE).
- Record a trigger phrase in the left-hand column.
- For intermediate level, record evidence or explanation in the next column.
- If you are doing higher level, add further evidence/explanation and end with a conclusion (link back).
- A well-elaborated evaluation point should be about 60 words.

For example, for criticisms of the psychodynamic approach, read what is in this book...

Trigger phrase	Intermediate level	Higher level	Conclusion
One strength is that the psychodynamic approach has explanatory power.	Although Freud's theory is controversial and often bizarre, it has had huge influence on Western contemporary thought.	It has been used to explain a wide range of behaviours (moral, mental disorders) and drew attention to the influence of childhood on adult personality.	This suggests that the approach has had a positive influence on modern-day thinking.

... and reduce your cards to the minimum for revision:

Trigger phrase	Intermediate	Higher	Conclusion
Explanatory power.	Influence on Western thought.	Wide range of behaviours (moral, mental disorders), influence of childhood.	Positive influence in psychology.

Rehearse the content.	Cover up all columns except the left-hand one and try to recall what is there using the trigger phrase.
Rehearse the trigger phrases.	When you are standing at a bus stop, see if you can remember all the trigger phrases for one topic.
Practise writing timed answers.	Write an essay answer with your trigger phrases in front of you. Give yourself 20 minutes for a 16-mark answer.

If you learn too much you will just try to squeeze it into the exam and you don't have time.

Focus on fewer points and make sure you *explain* them in detail. That's where the marks are.

In this book we have aimed to provide six points of AO1 for each topic, consisting of a trigger phrase (left-hand column) and explanations (right-hand column). For example, on page 20:

Key features of the psychodynamic approach	
Tripartite structure of personality. Dynamic interaction between the three parts.	Freud saw personality as having three parts: • Id – primitive part of the personality operates on the *pleasure principle*, demands instant gratification. • Ego – works on the *reality principle* and is the mediator between the Id and Superego. • Superego – internalised sense of right and wrong, based on *morality principle*. Punishes the Ego through guilt. Appears age 5.
Five *psychosexual stages* determine adult personality.	Each stage is marked by a different conflict that the child must resolve to move on to the next. Any conflict that is unresolved leads to fixation where the child becomes 'stuck' and carries behaviours associated with that stage through to adult life.

On the facing page (page 21) there are evaluation points. Each evaluation point has a trigger phrase across the top and there are three boxes below with suggested elaboration.

No athlete would dream of running a race without doing many practice runs of the right distance and within a set time.

Introduction

Understanding marking

AO1 question: Outline the cognitive approach to psychology. *(4 marks)*

Answer The cognitive approach is one of a number of approaches that psychologists use. It focuses especially on the mind and internal thought processes. Cognitive basically means thinking.

Computer-processing models are used to look at these as it is believed that information processing within the mind works much like a computer does. One example of this is Atkinson and Shiffrin's multi-store model of memory which shows how the brain processes memory step-by-step in a similar way to how a computer works. It uses the ideas of input and output like a computer does. *(94 words)*

AO2 question: [Stem] Asif is studying psychology and tells his mother about biological rhythms: 'We learned about a part of the brain that sets a constant rhythm for the body so you wake and fall asleep at about the same time every day. It's so cool.'

His mother is interested and responds: 'That doesn't explain why I wake up a lot earlier in summer when it gets light at 5 am. If there is a constant rhythm why would this change?'

[Question] With reference to the conversation above, explain how the sleep/wake cycle is controlled by biological factors. *(6 marks)*

Answer Your sleep/wake cycle is the phrase that is used to describe when you go to sleep and when you wake up. All people all over the world go to sleep and wake up and so do animals. It is very important for their well-being. Well, what is it that determines when you go to sleep? There is a small part of your brain that sets a constant rhythm. This is the biological pacemaker. It sets the pace for the processes in your body and makes everything work in tune. This is what Asif was talking about.

However, Asif's mother is right too because this is reset by light. The biological rhythms in your body are tuned into biological factors and also the world outside. It is important for both of these to be in tune. *(137 words)*

AO3 question: Discuss one criticism of the behaviourist approach in psychology. *(4 marks)*

Answer A strength of the behaviourist approach is that it focused on observable behaviour and therefore was an objective approach. This objectivity gave psychology scientific credibility. Behaviourists made careful measurements in controlled lab settings. The controlled settings meant they could replicate the research and demonstrate that their findings were valid. However, it might be pointed out that the validity might not extend to humans, nevertheless the scientific approach did increase the status of psychology in the eyes of other scientists. *(79 words)*

Examiner comments

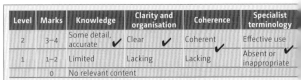

Level	Marks	Knowledge	Clarity and organisation	Coherence	Specialist terminology
2	3–4	Some detail, accurate ✔	Clear ✔	Coherent ✔	Effective use
1	1–2	Limited	Lacking	Lacking	Absent or inappropriate ✔
	0	No relevant content			

Comments The length of this answer (94 words) is a little short for 4 marks. A 4-mark question probably requires two aspects, each with some detail – which means there should be four 'things' in the answer (aspect 1 + detail, aspect 2 + detail). In this answer, aspect 1 (thinking) lacks detail. The answer is a mixture of level 1 and 2 criteria but the detail for aspect 2 tips the balance = 3 marks. Note that 2 out of 4 marks would be 50% (probably a Grade C) whereas 3 out of 4 marks would be 75% (probably a Grade A answer).

Level	Marks	Knowledge	Application	Effectiveness	Clarity and coherence	Specialist terminology
3	5–6	Well-detailed	Clear	Effective	Generally coherent	Appropriate
2	3–4	Evident ✔	Evident	Some effectiveness	Sometimes lacking ✔	On occasions
1	1–2	Inaccuracies	Limited ✔	Limited ✔	Lacking	Absent or inappropriate ✔
	0	No relevant content				

Comments There is good and bad in this answer. There is some engagement with the stem, for example, 'This is what Asif was talking about', and the answer addresses some specific aspects of the stem, e.g. 'constant rhythm'. However, the answer reads more like a prepared answer than an answer to Asif's mother's question.

There are a number of missed opportunities for specialist terms, for example, 'biological pacemaker' should be 'endogenous pacemaker' or even better 'suprachiasmatic nucleus', and there is no link between light and exogenous zeitgebers.

The answer is Level 2 but clearly we would be tempted to the band below, so 3 out of 6 marks (Grade C answer).

Level	Marks	Evaluation/ discussion	Explanation	Focus	Coherence	Specialist terminology
2	3–4	Relevant, not generic ✔	Well-explained ✔	Focused ✔	Mostly coherent ✔	Used appropriately ✔
1	1–2	Outlined only	Limited	Muddled	Muddled	Absent or inappropriate
	0	No relevant content				

Comments For the most part critical points are embedded in essays rather than a stand-alone question requiring only one criticism. However, it is good to practise these as a way of developing your skills of effective evaluation. This answer fulfils all of the top level criteria and, as we are not tempted by any Level 1 criteria, it is worth 4 out of 4 marks. Notice also the *discussion* – a counterpoint is introduced. It's not all one criticism.

Understanding marking

AO1 + AO3 question: Discuss reductionism in psychology.

(16 marks)

Answer Reductionism is the attempt to reduce concepts and explanations to simpler components so that it is easier to understand behaviour. It also refers to reducing things to the simplest level – the physical basis for behaviour. Psychological and social explanations are at higher levels. Biological and chemical explanations are at lower levels.

Psychologists who are reductionists, such as behaviourists, think that reductionism enables us to better understand behaviour. Behaviourists conduct experiments, such as pigeons learning in a Skinner box, and apply the same principles to human behaviour. For example the learning theory of attachment suggests that the love between a baby and its mother happens as a result of conditioning. However this may be an oversimplification as attachment is more related to sensitive responding rather than feeding. So in this case reductionism may not be relevant.

Another example of reductionism in psychology is the biological approach, where behaviour is reduced to the activity of the nervous system and hormones. An example of this is OCD where it has been shown that drugs that increase serotonin levels are successfully used to treat OCD. Therefore this suggests that abnormal levels of serotonin might be a cause of OCD. Therefore we have reduced the experience of OCD to the action of a neurotransmitter, which may not fully represent the complexity of the disorder.

In contrast with the reductionist approach in psychology the holistic approach suggests that reductionism represents complex systems too simply. Gestalt psychologists took a holistic perspective and suggested that the whole thing does not equal the sum of the parts. An example of the holistic approach is humanistic psychologists who saw successful therapy as bringing together all aspects of the 'whole person'. The problem with holistic explanations is they tend not to lend themselves to rigorous scientific testing. For example, humanistic psychology tends to be criticised for its lack of empirical evidence, and is instead seen as a rather loose set of concepts.

One solution would be to combine holistic and reductionist approaches. However, if you do that, for example when trying to explain depression, it becomes difficult to establish which one to use as a basis for therapy. This suggests, when it comes to finding solutions for real-world problems, lower level explanations may be more appropriate.

The reductionist approach has strengths and limitations. Its strengths are that many successful approaches in psychology have conducted reductionist research and provided reductionist theories. Without this research we would know far less. On the other hand some psychologists question whether such research really does give us any useful insights. (427 words)

Level	Marks	Knowledge	Accuracy	Discussion	Focus	Clarity and organisation	Specialist terminology
4	13–16	Generally well-detailed	Accurate ✔	Thorough, effective	Focused	Clear, coherent	Effective use
3	9–12	Evident	Occasional inaccuracies/ omissions	Mostly effective	Lacks focus	Mostly clear and organised ✔	Mostly used effectively ✔
2	5–8	Limited	Lacking in places	Limited effectiveness ✔	Mainly descriptive ✔	Lacking in places	Occasionally inappropriate
1	1–4	Very limited	Many inaccuracies	Limited or absent	Poor	Lacking clarity, poor organisation	Absent or inappropriate
	0	No relevant content					

Examiner comments

The introduction starts with a lengthy definition, which was not required by the question. It is scene-setting but not an especially good use of time.

A useful AO1 example of reductionism in psychology followed by a reasonably effective counterpoint about why reductionism doesn't work. In contrast with the first paragraph, the second paragraph *is* focused on reductionism *in psychology*, as required by the question.

There is a second example of reductionism (the biological approach) which is described with some detail and extended to drug therapies, using some specialist terminology and another example from across the specification. The paragraph ends with a very brief evaluation (AO3) point.

The holistic approach is described – however, that is not the subject of the essay. This is largely a wasted paragraph as a description and evaluation of holism is largely irrelevant. A mistake like this is all too easy to make without careful planning. If the same material had been phrased as an evaluation of reductionism then it would have been creditworthy.

This penultimate paragraph *is* using holism as a commentary on reductionism (AO3).

The final paragraph appears to be intended as a conclusion but in fact is little more than a summary of points already made and therefore does not add much.

Overall comments

Knowledge: reasonably detailed, evident.

Accuracy: accurate.

Discussion: some effective points but limited in quantity and quality for an A level essay.

Focus: lacks focus on the demands of the question. If we consider the creditworthy material only then there is more description and one good plus two weak discussion points.

Clarity and organisation: mostly clear and organised.

Specialist terminology: mostly used appropriately but not extensive use of specialist terms.

Overall the level that best describes this answer is Level 3 but the discussion (AO3) is poor and counts for a significant part of the mark, so overall this is near the top of level 2 – 7 or 8 out of 16, Grade C or D.

Origins of Psychology

Chapter 1: Approaches in Psychology

Spec spotlight

Origins of Psychology: Wundt, introspection and the emergence of Psychology as a science.

If you're not sure what is meant by 'introspection', you need to take a long hard look at yourself.

Science is defined as a means of acquiring knowledge through *systematic and objective* investigation. The aim is to discover general laws. Experiments are the ideal of science but not the only scientific method used by psychologists.

Apply it

Two students are discussing whether or not psychology can really be considered a science. Tara thinks it can and argues that Wundt made a significant contribution to the development of Psychology as a science. Max accepts that behaviourism is quite scientific but reckons that many approaches in psychology are not scientific at all.

Can psychology be regarded as a science? Explain your answer, referring to Tara's and Max's views.

Wundt and introspection

Wilhelm Wundt established the first psychology lab.	Opened in Leipzig, Germany in 1879. The aim was to describe the nature of human consciousness (the 'mind') in a carefully controlled and scientific environment – a lab.
Introspection.	Wundt pioneered introspection, the first systematic experimental attempt to study the mind.
Controlled procedures.	The same **standardised** instructions were given to all participants and stimuli (objects or sounds) were presented in the same order (standardised procedures).
	For instance, participants were given a ticking metronome and they would report their thoughts, images and sensations, which were then recorded.
Structuralism.	Introspection led to identifying the structure of consciousness by breaking it up into the basic structures: thoughts, images and sensations.
	This marked the beginning of scientific psychology, separating it from its broader philosophical roots.

Emergence of Psychology as a science

1900s Early behaviourists rejected introspection.	Watson (1913) argued that introspection was subjective, in that it is influenced by a personal perspective. According to the **behaviourist** approach, 'scientific' psychology should only study phenomena that can be observed and measured.
1930s Behaviourist scientific approach dominated psychology.	Skinner (1953) brought the language and rigour of the natural sciences into psychology. The behaviourists' focus on learning, and the use of carefully controlled lab studies, would dominate psychology for 50 years.
1950s Cognitive approach studied mental processes scientifically.	Following the computer revolution of the 1950s, the study of mental processes was seen as legitimate within psychology.
	Cognitive psychologists likened the mind to a computer and tested their predictions about memory and attention using **experiments**.
1980s The biological approach introduced technological advances.	**Biological** psychologists have taken advantage of recent advances in technology, including recording brain activity, using scanning techniques such as **fMRI** and **EEG**, and advanced genetic research.

One strength is that aspects of Wundt's work are scientific.

For instance, he recorded the introspections within a controlled lab environment.

He also standardised his procedures so that all participants received the same information and were tested in the same way.

Therefore Wundt's research can be considered a forerunner to the later scientific approaches in psychology that were to come.

One limitation is that other aspects of Wundt's research are subjective.

Wundt relied on participants self-reporting their 'private' mental processes. Such data is subjective. Participants may also have hidden some of their thoughts.

This makes it difficult to establish meaningful 'laws of behaviour', one of the aims of science.

Therefore Wundt's early efforts to study the mind were naïve and would not meet the criteria of scientific enquiry.

Evaluation extra: Wundt's contribution.

Wundt produced the first academic journal for psychological research and wrote the first textbook. He is often referred to as the 'father' of modern psychology.

His pioneering research set the foundation for approaches that were to come, particularly the behaviourist approach and cognitive psychology.

This shows that, despite the flaws in his early experimental research, Wundt made a significant contribution to psychology.

One strength is that research in modern psychology can claim to be scientific.

Psychology has the same aims as the natural sciences – to describe, understand, predict and control behaviour.

Learning, cognitive and biological approaches all use scientific methods e.g. lab studies are controlled and unbiased.

Throughout the 20th century and beyond, psychology has established itself as a scientific discipline.

One limitation of psychology is that some approaches use subjective data.

Humanistic approach does not formulate general laws of behaviour. **Psychodynamic** approach uses **case studies** with unrepresentative samples.

Psychologists study humans who are active participants and therefore respond to **demand characteristics**.

Therefore a scientific approach to the study of human thought and experience is not desirable or possible.

Evaluation extra: Paradigm.

Kuhn said that any science must have a paradigm: a set of principles, assumptions and methods that all people who work within that subject agree on.

Psychology does not have a paradigm. However, most would agree it is the study of mind and behaviour.

This suggests that the question of whether psychology is a science remains unanswered.

Do you agree with this conclusion?

Revision BOOSTER

An essay on Wundt's work alone is perhaps less likely than other areas in the Approaches section. One possibility is that you might be asked to 'outline and briefly evaluate the work of Wundt' or 'briefly discuss the contribution of Wundt to the emergence of Psychology as a science'. In both of these questions evaluative points would be required so these are included here.

Similarly, it is debatable whether an essay would be set on the *emergence of Psychology as a science*, but for evaluation, you could consider which approaches in psychology would meet scientific criteria and which would not.

I ♥ PSYCHOLOGY

Yes of course you do – but the question of whether Psychology is a science is not one that has a straightforward answer...

Download suggested answers to the Knowledge Check questions from tinyurl.com/yd3ezhkb

Knowledge Check

1. Explain what Wundt meant by 'introspection'. *(2 marks)*
2. Outline **and** briefly evaluate the work of Wundt. *(8 marks)*
3. Briefly discuss the emergence of Psychology as a science. *(6 marks)*

Learning approaches: The behaviourist approach

Spec spotlight

Learning approaches:
i) The behaviourist approach, including classical conditioning and Pavlov's research, operant conditioning, types of reinforcement and Skinner's research.

'Conditioning' means 'learning'.

'Have you heard of a bloke called Ivan Pavlov?'

'I must admit, the name rings a bell.'

Apply it

Joel is addicted to online fruit machine gambling. He spends a lot of time and money on this and other forms of online gambling.

1. Explain Joel's gambling addiction in terms of operant conditioning. Use the concepts of positive and negative reinforcement in your explanation.

2. Explain a feature of operant conditioning that might lead to a reduction in his gambling behaviour.

Rat presses lever in Skinner box and receives food – positive reinforcement for the lever-pressing behaviour.

Key features of the behaviourist approach

Focus on observable behaviour only.	The **behaviourist** approach is only concerned with studying behaviour that can be observed and measured. It is not concerned with mental processes of the mind. *Introspection* was rejected by behaviourists as its concepts were vague and difficult to measure.
Controlled lab studies.	Behaviourists tried to maintain more control and objectivity within their research and relied on lab studies to achieve this.
Use of non-human animals.	Behaviourists suggest the processes that govern learning are the same in all species, so animals (e.g. rats, cats, dogs and pigeons) can replace humans as experimental subjects.

Classical conditioning. *Pavlov's research.*	**Classical conditioning** refers to learning by *association*. UCS → UCR NS → no response NS + UCS CS → CR	**Pavlov's research** – conditioning dogs to salivate when a bell rings: *Before conditioning:* **UCS** = food, **UCR** = salivation, **NS** = bell *During conditioning:* Bell and food occur at same time. *After conditioning:* **CS** = bell, **CR** = salivation Pavlov showed how a neutral stimulus (bell) can come to elicit a new learned response (**conditioned response**, CR) through association.
Operant conditioning. *Skinner's research.*	**Operant conditioning** refers to learning as an active process whereby humans and animals *operate* on their environment. Behaviour is shaped and maintained by its *consequences*.	**Skinner's research** – rats and pigeons, in specially designed cages (Skinner boxes). When a rat activated a lever (or a pigeon pecked a disc) it was *rewarded* with a food pellet. A desirable consequence led to behaviour being repeated. If pressing a lever meant an animal avoided an electric shock, the behaviour would also be repeated.
Three types of consequences of behaviour.	**Positive reinforcement** – receiving a reward when behaviour is performed. **Negative reinforcement** – avoiding something unpleasant when a behaviour is performed. **Punishment** – an unpleasant consequence of behaviour. Positive reinforcement and negative reinforcement increase the likelihood that behaviour will be repeated. Punishment decreases it.	

One strength of behaviourism is that it uses well-controlled research.

The approach has focused on the careful measurement of observable behaviour within controlled lab settings.

Behaviourists have broken behaviour down into stimulus–response units and studied causal relationships.

This suggests that behaviourist **experiments** have scientific credibility.

Counterpoint

However this approach may oversimplify learning and ignore important influences on behaviour (e.g. thought). Other approaches (e.g. **social learning** and **cognitive**) incorporate mental processes.

This suggests learning is more complex than just what we can observe.

One strength is behaviourist laws of learning have real-world application.

The principles of conditioning have been applied to a broad range of real-world behaviours and problems.

Token economy systems reward appropriate behaviour with tokens that are exchanged for privileges (operant conditioning). Successfully used in prisons and psychiatric wards.

This increases the value of the behaviourist approach because it has widespread application.

One limitation is behaviourism is a form of environmental determinism.

The approach sees all behaviour as determined by past experiences that have been conditioned and ignores any influence that **free will** may have on behaviour.

Skinner suggested that free will was an illusion. When something happens we may think 'I made the decision to do that' but our past conditioning determined the outcome.

This is an extreme position and ignores the influence of conscious decision-making processes on behaviour (as suggested by the cognitive approach).

Evaluation extra: Ethical issues.

Procedures such as the Skinner box allowed behaviourists to maintain a high degree of control over their experimental 'subjects'.

However the animals were housed in harsh, cramped conditions and deliberately kept below their natural weight so they were always hungry.

Therefore there is a question of benefits versus costs – some would argue that there have been enormous benefits (e.g. application to therapy) which offsets the harm the animals experienced.

Revision BOOSTER

When writing critical points it is desirable to explain them thoroughly.

- Always start with a statement of your point (P).
- Provide further explanation (E) using examples (E) and/or evidence (E).
- If you can, end your evaluation with a T statement (This shows that..., Therefore ...).

CRAIG SWANSON © WWW.PERSPICUITY.COM

A former participant in the Skinner box studies struggles to find work.

Knowledge Check

1. Explain what is meant by 'classical conditioning'.
   (2 marks)
2. Outline Skinner's research into operant conditioning.
   (4 marks)
3. Explain how **two** types of reinforcement could be used by a parent to encourage their child to come home by 9pm on a school night.
   (4 marks)
4. Discuss the behaviourist approach. Refer to the research of both Pavlov and Skinner in your answer.
   (16 marks)

Learning approaches: Social learning theory

Spec spotlight

Learning approaches: ii) Social learning theory including imitation, identification, modelling, vicarious reinforcement, the role of mediational processes and Bandura's research.

Imitation – the sincerest form of flattery apparently.

Apply it

Faz is an eight-year-old boy. Although he has never been bullied at his primary school, Faz often sees an older boy bullying other children. The older boy is physically aggressive, sometimes to get money or sweets, or just to show everyone who's boss.

1. Explain the social learning processes which may lead to Faz becoming a bully himself. Refer in your explanation to the roles of imitation, identification, modelling and vicarious reinforcement.

2. In terms of mediational processes, explain **three** ways in which Faz is unlikely to become a bully.

Note that modelling is a named term on the specification that can be used in two subtly different ways. From the observer's perspective, 'modelling' is imitating the behaviour of a role model. From the role model's perspective, it is demonstrating behaviour that may be imitated.

Key features of social learning theory (SLT)

Learning that occurs indirectly.	Albert Bandura agreed with the **behaviourist** approach that learning occurs through experience.
	However, he also proposed that learning takes place in a social context through *observation* and *imitation* of others' behaviour.
Learning related to consequences of behaviour – *vicarious reinforcement*.	Children (and adults) observe other people's behaviour and take note of its consequences. Behaviour that is seen to be rewarded (reinforced) is more likely to be copied = vicarious reinforcement.
Mediational (cognitive) processes play a crucial role in learning.	There are four mediational processes in learning:
	1. *Attention* – whether behaviour is noticed.
	2. *Retention* – whether behaviour is remembered.
	3. *Motor reproduction* – being able to do it.
	4. *Motivation* – the will to perform the behaviour.
	The first two relate to the learning, the last two to the performance (so, unlike behaviourism, learning and performance do not have to occur together).
Identification with role models is important.	People are more likely to imitate the behaviour of those with whom they identify. Such role models are similar to the observer, attractive and have high status.

Bandura's research

	Bandura et al. (1961)	**Bandura and Walters (1963)**
PROCEDURES	Children watched either:	Children saw adult who was:
	• An adult behaving aggressively towards a Bobo doll.	• Rewarded.
	• An adult behaving non-aggressively towards a Bobo doll.	• Punished.
		• There was no consequence.
FINDINGS AND CONCLUSIONS	When given their own doll to play with, the children who had seen aggression were much more aggressive towards the doll.	When given their own doll, the children who saw the aggression *rewarded* were much more aggressive themselves.

The Bobo doll studies suggest that children are likely to imitate (model) acts of violence if they observe these in an adult role model.

It is also the case that **modelling** aggressive behaviour is more likely if such behaviour is seen to be rewarded (vicarious reinforcement).

One strength is SLT emphasises the importance of cognitive factors.

Neither **classical conditioning** nor **operant conditioning** can offer a comprehensive account of human learning on their own because cognitive factors are omitted.

Humans and animals store information about the behaviour of others and use this to make judgements about when it is appropriate to perform certain actions.

This shows that SLT provides a more complete explanation of human learning than the behaviourist approach by recognising the role of mediational processes.

Counterpoint

Recent research suggests that observational learning is controlled by mirror neurons in the brain, which allow us to empathise with and imitate other people.

This suggests that SLT may make too little reference to the influence of biological factors on social learning.

One limitation is SLT relies too heavily on evidence from contrived lab studies.

Many of Bandura's ideas were developed through observation of children's behaviour in lab settings and this raises the problem of **demand characteristics**.

The main purpose of a Bobo doll is to hit it. So the children in those studies may have been behaving as they thought was expected.

Thus the research may tell us little about how children actually learn aggression in everyday life.

Another strength is SLT has real-world application.

Social learning principles can account for how children learn from other people around them, as well as through the media, and this can explain how cultural norms are transmitted.

This has proved useful in understanding a range of behaviours such as how children come to understand their gender role by imitating role models in the media.

This increases the value of SLT as it can account for real-world behaviour.

Evaluation extra: Reciprocal determinism.

Bandura emphasised *reciprocal determinism* – we are influenced by our environment, but we also exert an influence upon it through the behaviours we choose to perform.

This element of choice suggests there is some **free will** in the way we behave.

This is a more realistic and flexible position than is suggested by the behaviourist approach as it recognises the role we play in shaping our own environment.

Revision BOOSTER

Evaluation points like these do not just come in handy for longer essay-style questions. It is possible you might be asked for a single strength or limitation as part of a short-answer question. Also, some questions ask for a 'brief discussion' of particular approaches. For such questions, our counterpoints would do the job nicely.

The word 'bobo' is Spanish for 'clown'. The word 'doll' is English for 'doll'.

The specification for this topic includes the terms: imitation, identification, modelling, vicarious reinforcement, the role of mediational processes and Bandura's research.

This means that exam questions may include any of these.

Knowledge Check

1. Explain what is meant by 'identification' in social learning theory. *(2 marks)*
2. Outline Bandura's research into social learning. *(4 marks)*
3. With reference to mediational processes in social learning, explain how a child might learn to bake a cake by watching his mother. *(6 marks)*
4. Describe **and** evaluate the social learning approach. *(16 marks)*

The cognitive approach

Spec spotlight

The cognitive approach: the study of internal mental processes, the role of schema, the use of theoretical and computer models to explain and make inferences about mental processes. The emergence of cognitive neuroscience.

Revision BOOSTER

Note the difference between a theoretical model and a computer model. Both are named on the specification so you need to be able to provide an explanation and an example of each.

Also note the other terms that you can be examined on: internal mental processes, schema, inferences and the emergence of cognitive neuroscience.

**PARIS
IN THE
THE SPRING**

Did you spot the second 'the'? If not, that'll be your schema then.

Key features of the cognitive approach

Scientific study of mental processes.	In direct contrast to the **behaviourist** approach, the **cognitive** approach argues that mental processes should be studied, e.g. studying perception and memory.
Role of *inference* in the study of mental processes.	Mental processes are 'private' and cannot be observed, so cognitive psychologists study them indirectly by making inferences (assumptions) about what is going on inside people's heads on the basis of their behaviour.
The idea of *schema* is central to the cognitive approach.	• **Schema** are packages of information developed through experience. • They act as a 'mental framework' for the interpretation of incoming information received by the cognitive system. • Babies are born with simple motor schema for innate behaviours such as sucking and grasping. • As we get older, our schema become more detailed and sophisticated.
Theoretical models to explain mental processes.	The information processing approach suggests that information flows through a sequence of stages that include input, storage and retrieval, as in the *multi-store model* (see page 32 of our Year 1 revision guide).
Computer models to explain mental processes.	Computer models refer to programmes that can be run on a computer to imitate the human mind (e.g. conversational machines to deal with consumer enquiries). By running such a programme psychologists can test their ideas about information processing.
The emergence of *cognitive neuroscience*.	• Cognitive neuroscience is the scientific study of the influence of brain structures *(neuro)* on mental processes *(cognition)*. • With advances in brain scanning technology in the last twenty years, scientists have been able to describe the neurological basis of mental processing. • This includes research in memory that has linked *episodic* and *semantic memories* to opposite sides of the **prefrontal cortex** in the brain (Tulving *et al.* 1994). • Scanning techniques have also proved useful in establishing the neurological basis of some disorders, e.g. the *parahippocampal gyrus* and OCD.

One strength is the cognitive approach uses scientific and objective methods.

Cognitive psychologists have always employed controlled and rigorous methods of study, e.g. lab studies, in order to infer cognitive processes at work.

In addition the two fields of biology and cognitive psychology come together (cognitive neuroscience) to enhance the scientific basis of study.

This means that the study of the mind has established a credible, scientific basis.

Counterpoint

The use of inference means cognitive psychology can occasionally be too abstract and theoretical. Also, research often uses artificial stimuli (such as word lists).

Therefore, research on cognitive processes may lack **external validity** and not represent everyday experience.

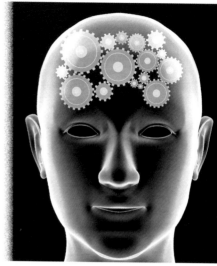

Probably why they call it 'cog psychology'.

Another strength of the approach is the application to everyday life.

The cognitive approach is dominant in psychology today and has been applied to a wide range of practical and theoretical contexts.

For instance, *artificial intelligence* (AI) and the development of robots, the treatment of depression and improving eyewitness testimony.

This supports the value of the cognitive approach.

One limitation is that the approach is based on machine reductionism.

Although there are similarities between the operations of the human mind and computers (inputs-outputs, central processor, storage systems), the computer analogy has been criticised.

For instance, emotion and motivation have been shown to influence accuracy of recall, e.g. in eyewitness accounts. These factors are not considered within the computer analogy.

This suggests that machine reductionism may weaken the **validity** of the cognitive approach.

Not everyone agrees with this conclusion. What do you think?

Evaluation extra: Soft determinism.

The cognitive approach recognises that our cognitive system operates within certain limits, but we are free to make decisions before responding to a stimulus (**soft determinism**).

This is in contrast to the behaviourist approach which suggests we are passive to the environment and lack free choice in our behaviour.

This suggests that the cognitive approach takes a more flexible middle-ground position and is more in line with our subjective sense of **free will**.

Apply it

Amber is two years old. Her parents have noticed that her play behaviour is not random, but seems to demonstrate certain patterns. For example, she is obsessed with Russian dolls and loves to get adults to remove each doll one at a time, then replace them over and over again. She really enjoys putting smaller objects inside larger ones and making dens and sitting in them.

Explain how the concept of a schema can help us understand such patterns of play.

Knowledge Check

1. Outline what cognitive psychologists mean by 'schema'. *(3 marks)*
2. Briefly explain how theoretical models are used in cognitive psychology to make inferences about mental processes. *(4 marks)*
3. Outline the emergence of cognitive neuroscience in psychology. *(6 marks)*
4. Discuss the cognitive approach. *(8 marks)*
5. Describe **and** evaluate the cognitive approach. *(16 marks)*

The biological approach

Spec spotlight

The biological approach: the influence of genes, biological structures and neurochemistry on behaviour. Genotype and phenotype, genetic basis of behaviour, evolution and behaviour.

Yeah they look cute now but wait until they wake up.

Apply it

Wilson's disease is a rare genetic disorder which can affect several of the body's systems, including the brain. This results in symptoms such as clumsiness, speech problems, difficulty in concentrating, depression and anxiety. It is caused by the body storing too much copper, a mineral which we need in just tiny amounts. There is no cure. But the disorder can be managed by reducing the amount of copper in the person's diet, and carefully monitoring blood and urine, so the individual can develop normally.

Using Wilson's disease as an example, explain the difference between genotype and phenotype.

Key features of the biological approach

Everything psychological is at first biological.	If we want to fully understand human behaviour we must look to biological structures and processes within the body, such as *genes* and *neurochemistry*.
The mind and body are one and the same.	From the **biological** approach, the mind lives in the brain – meaning that all thoughts, feelings and behaviour ultimately have a physical basis. This is in contrast to the **cognitive** approach which sees the mind as separate from the brain.
Neurochemical basis of behaviour.	Neurochemistry refers to the action of chemicals in the brain – neurotransmitters transmit messages. An imbalance of neurotransmitters may be a cause of some mental disorders, e.g. underproduction of **serotonin** in OCD.
Genetic basis of behaviour.	Psychological characteristics (e.g. intelligence) are inherited. Twin studies are used to investigate genetic influences. **Concordance rates** between twins are calculated – the extent to which twins share the same characteristic. Higher concordance rates among identical (monozygotic, **MZ**) twins (genetically 100% the same) than non-identical (dizygotic, **DZ**) twins (about 50% the same) is evidence of a genetic basis.
The difference between *genotype* and *phenotype*.	• A person's genotype is their actual genetic make-up. • Phenotype is the way that genes are expressed through physical, behavioural and psychological characteristics. • The expression of genotype (phenotype) is influenced by environmental factors. • For example, *phenylketonuria (PKU)* is a genetic disorder that can be prevented by a restricted diet. • This suggests that much of human behaviour depends on the interaction of nature and nurture.
Theory of evolution is used by the biological approach to explain behaviour.	• Darwin (1859) proposed the theory of natural selection. • Any genetically determined behaviour that enhances survival *and* reproduction will be passed on to future generations. • Such genes are described as **adaptive** and give the possessor and their offspring advantages. • For instance, attachment behaviours in newborns promote survival and are therefore adaptive and naturally selected.

One strength of the biological approach is its real-world application.

Understanding of neurochemical processes in the brain has led to the use of psychoactive drugs to treat serious mental disorders.

For example, drugs that treat clinical depression increase levels of the neurotransmitter serotonin at the synapse and reduce depressive symptoms.

This means that people with depression are able to manage their condition and live a relatively normal life, rather than being confined to hospital.

Counterpoint

However, antidepressant drugs do not work for everyone. Cipriani *et al.* (2018) compared 21 antidepressant drugs and found wide variations in their effectiveness.

This challenges the value of the biological approach as it suggests that brain chemistry alone may not account for all cases of depression.

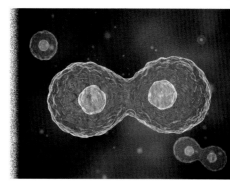

Biology is the only science in which multiplication is the same thing as division.

Another strength is the biological approach uses scientific methods.

In order to investigate both genetic and neurochemical factors, the biological approach makes use of a range of precise and objective methods.

These include scanning techniques (e.g. **fMRI**), which assess biological processes in ways that are not open to bias.

This means that the biological approach is based on objective and reliable data.

One limitation is that biological explanations are determinist.

Biological explanations tend to be determinist in that they see human behaviour as governed by internal, genetic causes over which we have no control.

However, the way genotype is expressed (phenotype) is heavily influenced by the environment. Not even genetically identical twins look and think exactly the same.

This suggests that the biological view is too simplistic and ignores the mediating effects of the environment.

Evaluation extra: Natural selection.

Critics of Darwin's work, such as Popper, claim it is not possible to show evolution happening, only that it has taken place (unfalsifiable).

However, others argue that natural selection is supported by fossil records (e.g. gradually changing forms from dinosaurs to birds).

This suggests that although natural selection is not able to tell us what species will evolve into, it provides an adequate account of past development.

Apply it

Biological psychologists believe that behaviours have evolved because they provide some advantage, in terms of allowing us to adapt to our environments. Examples from our Year 1 book include:
(1) conforming to the behaviour of other members of a group,
(2) having both long-term and short-term memories,
(3) experiencing OCD (which many psychologists believe has a genetic basis).

For each of these examples, explain what the adaptive advantages could be.

Knowledge Check

1. Outline **two** key features of the biological approach in psychology. *(6 marks)*
2. Explain the difference between genotype and phenotype. *(4 marks)*
3. Explain the process of evolution. Include an example in your answer. *(4 marks)*
4. Describe **and** evaluate the biological approach in psychology. *(16 marks)*

The psychodynamic approach

Spec spotlight

The psychodynamic approach: the role of the unconscious, the structure of personality, that is Id, Ego and Superego, defence mechanisms including repression, denial and displacement, psychosexual stages.

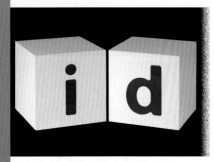

Id. A handy word to know if you're running out of tiles in Scrabble.

Revision BOOSTER

The psychodynamic approach is complex and wide-ranging. It would be easy to overdo the AO1 content in an essay on this approach. Keep description of things like Freud's psychosexual stages to a minimum and only select a few examples.

Apply it

Gregory got his girlfriend's and his mum's names mixed up the other day. Felix is only interested in satisfying his own desires. Lisbeth feels guilty all the time over the smallest things. Heathcliffe's parents are having trouble getting him potty-trained. Alanis is five and wants to marry her daddy when she grows up. There are holes in Brynn's bedroom door where he punches it when he comes in from work.

Identify the psychodynamic concepts on this page that could apply to these people. Explain your choices.

Key features of the psychodynamic approach

Unconscious mind has important influence on behaviour.	Sigmund Freud suggested the mind is made up of: • Conscious – what we are aware of ('tip of the iceberg'). • Preconscious – thoughts we may become aware of through dreams and 'slips of the tongue'. • Unconscious – a vast storehouse of biological drives and instincts that influence our behaviour.
Tripartite structure of personality. Dynamic interaction between the three parts.	Freud saw personality as having three parts: • *Id* – primitive part of the personality operates on the *pleasure principle*, demands instant gratification. • *Ego* – works on the *reality principle* and is the mediator between the Id and Superego. • *Superego* – internalised sense of right and wrong, based on *morality principle*. Punishes the Ego through guilt. Appears age 5.
Five *psychosexual stages* determine adult personality.	Each stage is marked by a different conflict that the child must resolve to move on to the next. Any conflict that is unresolved leads to fixation where the child becomes 'stuck' and carries behaviours associated with that stage through to adult life.
Sequence of stages is fixed.	Oral (0–1 years) – pleasure focus = mouth, the mother's breast is the object of desire. Anal (1–3 years) – pleasure focus = anus, the child gains pleasure from withholding and eliminating faeces. Phallic (3–6 years) – pleasure focus = genital area. Latency – earlier conflicts are repressed. Genital (puberty) – sexual desires become conscious.
Oedipus complex is a *psychosexual conflict* at the phallic stage.	In the phallic stage, little boys develop incestuous feelings towards their mother and a murderous hatred for their father. Later boys repress their feelings for their mother and identify with their father, taking on his gender role and moral values. Girls of the same age experience penis envy.
Defence mechanisms used by Ego to reduce anxiety.	Unconscious strategies used by the Ego, for example: • *Repression* – forcing a distressing memory out of the conscious mind. • *Denial* – refusing to acknowledge reality. • *Displacement* – transferring feelings from their true source onto a substitute target.

One strength of the psychodynamic approach is it introduced psychotherapy.

Freud's psychoanalysis was the first attempt to treat mental disorders psychologically rather than physically.

Psychoanalysis claims to help clients deal with everyday problems by providing access to their unconscious, employing techniques such as dream analysis.

Therefore psychoanalysis is the forerunner to many modern-day 'talking therapies' (e.g. counselling).

Counterpoint

Although psychoanalysis is claimed successful for clients with mild **neuroses**, it is inappropriate, even harmful, for more serious mental disorders (such as **schizophrenia**).

Therefore Freudian therapy (and theory) may not apply to mental disorders where a client has lost touch with reality.

Another strength is the psychodynamic approach has explanatory power.

Freud's theory is controversial and often bizarre, but it has had huge influence on Western contemporary thought.

It has been used to explain a wide range of behaviours (moral, mental disorders) and drew attention to the influence of childhood on adult personality.

This suggests that, overall, the psychodynamic approach has had a positive influence on psychology and modern-day thinking.

One limitation is the psychodynamic approach includes untestable concepts.

Karl Popper (philosopher of science) argued that the psychodynamic approach does not meet the scientific criterion of *falsification*, in the sense that it cannot be disproved.

Many of Freud's concepts, such as the Id or the Oedipus complex, occur at an unconscious level making them difficult, if not impossible, to test.

This means that Freud's ideas lack scientific rigour, the theory is pseudoscience ('fake' science) rather than real science.

Evaluation extra: Psychic determinism.

The psychodynamic approach suggests that much of our behaviour is determined by unconscious conflicts. Freud believed there was no such thing as an 'accident'.

However, few psychologists would accept this view as it leaves no room for **free will** beyond early childhood.

This suggests that Freud's views were too extreme as most people do have a sense of control over their behaviour.

Freudian slip joke: Sigmund Freud walked into a bra...

Knowledge Check

1. The psychodynamic approach places emphasis on the role of the unconscious in behaviour. Explain the role of the unconscious in behaviour.
   (4 marks)
2. Explain how **one** defence mechanism might help someone cope with the anxiety of losing their job.
   (2 marks)
3. Name **and** explain **one** of Freud's psychosexual stages of development. *(3 marks)*
4. Discuss the psychodynamic approach. In your answer outline **one or more** differences between the psychodynamic approach **and** the humanistic approach.
   (16 marks)

Humanistic psychology

Spec spotlight

Humanistic psychology: free will, self-actualisation and Maslow's hierarchy of needs, focus on the self, congruence, the role of conditions of worth. The influence on counselling psychology.

Self-actualisation

Self-esteem

Love and belongingness

Safety and security

Physiological needs

Maslow's hierarchy of needs – the lower needs must be met first, before a person can move on to the higher needs.

Apply it

Anika feels depressed because she feels that her life is empty and worthless. There were so many things she wanted to do and be but now she thinks it's just too late. She sees a person-centred therapist for counselling.

Referring to both Maslow's hierarchy of needs **and** *Rogers' concept of congruence, explain how Anika could be helped to recover from depression.*

Key features of the humanistic approach

Concept of *free will* is central.	**Humanistic** psychologists see humans as affected by external and internal influences but self-determining (have **free will**).
	Psychology should concern itself with subjective experience rather than general laws as we are all unqiue – a person-centred approach.
Hierarchy of needs has *self-actualisation* at the top.	In Maslow's hierarchy of needs the four lower levels (deficiency needs such as food, water and safety) must be met before the individual (baby, child or adult) can work towards self-actualisation – a growth need.
	Self-actualisation refers to the innate tendency that each of us has to want to achieve our full potential and become the best we can possibly be.
Focus on the self.	The *self* refers to the ideas and values that characterise 'I' and 'me' and includes perception of 'what I am' and 'what I can do'.
Aim of therapy is to establish *congruence*.	Rogers argued that personal growth requires an individual's concept of self to be congruent with their ideal self (the person they want to be).
	If too big a gap, the person will experience a state of incongruence and self-actualisation isn't possible.
Parents who impose *conditions of worth* may prevent personal growth.	Issues such as worthlessness and low self-esteem have their roots in childhood and are due to a lack of *unconditional positive regard* from our parents.
	A parent who sets boundaries on their love for their child (conditions of worth) by claiming 'I will only love you if...' is storing up psychological problems for that child in future.
Humanistic approach has had a lasting influence on *counselling psychology*.	In Rogers' client-centred therapy (counselling) an effective therapist should provide the client with three things:
	• Genuineness.
	• Empathy.
	• Unconditional positive regard.
	The aim is to increase feelings of self-worth and reduce incongruence between the self-concept and the ideal self.
	Rogers work transformed psychotherapy. 'Non-directive' counselling techniques are practised, not only in clinical settings, but throughout education, health, social work and industry.

One strength is that humanistic psychology is anti-reductionist.

Humanistic psychologists reject any attempt to break up behaviour and experience into smaller components.	They advocate **holism** – the idea that subjective experience can only be understood by considering the whole person (their relationships, past, present and future, etc.).	This approach may have more **validity** than its alternatives by considering meaningful human behaviour within its real-world context.

Counterpoint

However, humanistic psychology, unlike behaviourism, has relatively few concepts that can be reduced to single variables and measured.

This means that humanistic psychology in general is short on empirical evidence to support its claims.

Another strength is the approach is a positive one.

Humanistic psychologists have been praised for promoting a positive image of the human condition – seeing people as in control of their lives and having the freedom to change.	Freud saw human beings as prisoners of their past and claimed all of us existed somewhere between 'common unhappiness and absolute despair'.	Therefore humanistic psychology offers a refreshing and optimistic alternative.

One limitation is that the approach may be guilty of a cultural bias.

Many humanistic ideas (e.g. self-actualisation), would be more associated with **individualist** cultures such as the United States.	**Collectivist** cultures such as India, which emphasise the needs of the group, may not identify so easily with the ideals and values of humanistic psychology.	Therefore, it is possible that the approach does not apply universally and is a product of the cultural context within which it was developed.

Evaluation extra: Limited application.

Critics argue that, compared to other approaches, humanistic psychology has had limited impact within psychology, or practical application in the real world.	However, Rogerian therapy revolutionised counselling techniques and Maslow's hierarchy of needs has been used to explain motivation, particularly in the workplace.	This suggests that the approach does have value, despite the fact that (unlike other approaches), it is resolutely 'anti-scientific'.

Humanistic psychologists believe we have 'free will' – a philosophical position which suggests we are able to reject internal and external influences. Not to be confused with 'Free Willy', which is a film about a whale.

Knowledge Check

1. Explain what humanistic psychologists mean by 'conditions of worth'. *(2 marks)*
2. Briefly discuss the concept of self-actualisation. *(4 marks)*
3. Briefly evaluate humanistic psychology. *(6 marks)*
4. Discuss Maslow's hierarchy of needs. Refer to self-actualisation in your answer. *(8 marks)*
5. Describe **and** evaluate the humanistic approach in psychology. *(16 marks)*

Comparison of approaches

Spec spotlight

Comparison of approaches.

Comparing apples is somewhat easier than comparing psychological approaches....

Revision BOOSTER

The phrase 'comparison of approaches' is one that only appears on the A Level specification, not the AS. This means you cannot be explicitly asked to do this on the AS exam paper.

Having said that, comparing approaches is a good way of getting AO3 evaluation marks in an essay – as long as you make it clear how the comparison highlights a strength or limitation of the approach you have been asked about.

Apply it

This spread presents several important issues in psychology. The various approaches have unique perspectives on each one, for example nature versus nurture.

1. Which approach do you think most emphasises nature, and which most emphasises nurture? Explain how they differ.

2. Now choose **two** approaches which take a similar line on this issue (i.e. both nature or both nurture). How are they similar?

(You could answer the same questions for the other issues, such as determinism and reductionism.)

Approach	Behaviourist	Social learning	Cognitive
Views on development	The processes that underpin learning are continuous, occurring at any age.	Same as behaviourist approach.	Stage theories of child development, particularly the idea of increasingly complex **schema** as child gets older.
Nature versus nurture	Babies are 'blank slates' at birth. All behaviour comes about through learned associations and reinforcements.	As for behaviourist approach with additional processes of observation and imitation.	Many of our information-processing abilities and schema are innate, but are constantly refined by experience.
Reductionism	Reduces complex learning into stimulus–response units for ease of testing in a controlled lab environment.	Recognises how cognitive factors interact with the external environment.	Use of the computer analogy which ignores the role of human emotion (*machine reductionism*).
Determinism	All behaviour is environmentally determined by external forces that we cannot control, e.g. **operant conditioning** (**hard determinism**).	We are influenced by our environment and also exert some influence upon it (*reciprocal determinism*).	Suggests we are the 'choosers' of our own behaviour, but only within the limits of what we know (**soft determinism**).
Explanation and treatment of abnormal/ atypical behaviour	Abnormality arises from faulty learning. Behavioural therapies aim to condition new more healthy behaviours.	Principles such as **modelling** have been used to explain (and reduce) for example aggressive behaviour.	Cognitive therapies such as **cognitive behaviour therapy** (**CBT**) used in the treatment of depression, aim to eradicate faulty thinking.

Biological	Psychodynamic	Humanistic
Genetically determined maturational changes influence behaviour, e.g. cognitive/intellectual development.	The most coherent theory of development, tying concepts and processes to age-related stages. No change after genital stage.	The development of the self is ongoing throughout life. Childhood is particularly important period e.g. parents provide unconditional positive regard.
Behaviour stems from the genetic blueprint we inherit from our parents (genotype), though expression of this is influenced by the environment (phenotype).	Much of our behaviour is driven by biological drives and instincts, but also a child's relationships with its parents are crucial.	Parents, friends and wider society have a critical impact on the person's self-concept.
Reduces and explains human behaviour at the level of the gene or neuron.	Reduces behaviour to the influence of biological drives, although also sees personality as a dynamic, **holistic** interaction between Id, Ego and Superego.	Anti-reductionist, based on holistic investigation of all aspects of the individual.
Much of our behaviour is directed by innate influences (*genetic determinism*).	Unconscious forces drive our behaviour (*psychic determinism*) and these are rationalised by our conscious minds.	Human beings have **free will** and are active agents who determine their own development.
Psychoactive drugs that regulate chemical imbalances in the brain have revolutionised the treatment of mental disorders.	Anxiety disorders emerge from unconscious conflicts and overuse of defence mechanisms. Psychoanalysis aims to put people in touch with their unconscious thoughts.	Humanistic therapy, or counselling, is based on the idea that reducing incongruence will stimulate personal growth.

The TV usually does what we tell it to – but to what extent are we in control of our thoughts and behaviour?

Eclecticism

Worth noting that most modern psychologists would take an eclectic (multidisciplinary) approach to the study of human behaviour. Very few researchers work entirely within one approach.

Eclecticism refers to combining of several approaches and/or methods to provide a more comprehensive account.

For example, the **diathesis-stress model** suggests that many mental disorders are a complex interaction of genetic predisposition and environmental triggers.

Combining treatment options from several different perspectives, e.g. drugs, cognitive therapy, family therapy, has led to more effective outcomes for patients and lower relapse rates.

Knowledge Check

1. Outline **one** way in which the psychodynamic approach **and** humanistic psychology are similar. *(4 marks)*
2. Briefly discuss **one** difference between the social learning approach **and** the behaviourist approach. *(4 marks)*
3. Outline the cognitive approach. Compare the cognitive approach with the biological approach. *(16 marks)*

The nervous system

Spec spotlight

The divisions of the nervous system: central and peripheral (somatic and autonomic).

The function of the endocrine system: glands and hormones.

The fight or flight response including the role of adrenaline.

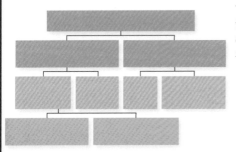

You might have to label a diagram in the exam. Nervous..?

The nervous system acts more rapidly than the endocrine system but they are both very fast. The nervous system's average response time is 0.25 seconds but may be as quick as 100 milliseconds. The endocrine responses are slower because hormones have to travel through the bloodstream (about 2 or 3 seconds) but last longer.

Apply it

Leah is being interviewed for a job. It's really important to her and everything is going fine, until one interviewer asks her a question and she suddenly realises she doesn't know the answer. She tries hard to remember the information she needs but can't concentrate. She can hear her heart beating faster, her face is reddening, her hands are shaking and she feels sick.

Explain the roles of (1) the CNS, (2) the ANS, and (3) the endocrine system in Leah's behaviour.

The nervous system

The key features of the *nervous system*.	The nervous system is a specialised network of cells and our primary communication system. It is based on electrical (and chemical) signals whereas the endocrine system (facing page) is based on hormones.

The nervous system has two main functions:

1. To collect, process and respond to information in the environment;
2. To co-ordinate the working of different organs and cells in the body.

The structure and function of the *central nervous system* (CNS).	• CNS is made up of the brain and the spinal cord.

- The brain is the centre of conscious awareness.
- The outer layer of the brain, the cerebral cortex (3 mm thick), is highly developed in humans and is what distinguishes our higher mental functions from those of animals.
- The brain is divided into two hemispheres.

- The spinal cord is an extension of the brain and is responsible for reflex actions.
- It passes messages to and from the brain and connects nerves to the PNS.

The structure and function of the *peripheral nervous system* (PNS).	• The PNS transmits messages, via millions of neurons, to and from the nervous system.

- The PNS is further subdivided into:
  - **Autonomic nervous system (ANS)** governs vital functions in the body such as breathing, heart rate, digestion, sexual arousal and stress responses.
  - **Somatic nervous system (SNS)** governs muscle movement and receives information from sensory receptors.

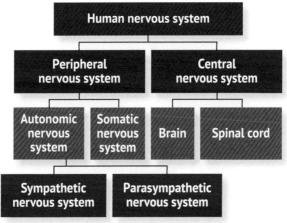

The major subdivisions of the human nervous system.

The endocrine system

The key features of the *endocrine system*.	The endocrine system works alongside the nervous system to control vital functions in the body through the action of hormones.

It works more slowly than the nervous system (seconds instead of milliseconds) but has widespread and powerful effects. |
| *Glands*. | Glands are organs in the body that produce hormones.

The key endocrine gland is the *pituitary gland*, located in the brain. It is called the 'master gland' because it controls the release of hormones from all the other endocrine glands in the body. |
| *Hormones*. | Hormones are secreted in the bloodstream and affect any cell in the body that has a receptor for that particular hormone.

For example, *thyroxine* produced by the thyroid gland affects cells in the heart and also cells throughout the body which increase metabolic rates. This in turn affects growth rates. |
| The endocrine system and the ANS work together.

For example, the *fight or flight response*. | Often the endocrine system and the ANS work in parallel, for instance during a *stressful event*.

• Stressor perceived by *hypothalamus* which activates the *pituitary*.

• The **sympathetic nervous system** is now aroused.

• *Adrenaline* (the stress hormone) is released from the *adrenal medulla* into the bloodstream. This delivers the aroused state causing changes in target organs in the body e.g. increased heart rate, dilation of pupils, decreased production of saliva. This is called the fight or flight response.

• Immediate and automatic – this response happens the instant a threat is perceived.

• **Parasympathetic nervous system** (rest and digest) takes over once the threat has passed. This returns the body to its resting state. This acts as a 'brake' and reduces the activities of the body that were increased by the actions of the sympathetic branch (rest and digest). |

© Mike Baldwin / Cornered

SURVIVAL GUIDES

FIGHT

FLIGHT

Revision BOOSTER

Questions in this section are likely to be either descriptive or application. There is very little scope for evaluation/discussion in this section so an essay in biopsychology is very unlikely.

Sympathetic state	Parasympathetic state
Increases heart rate	Decreases heart rate
Increases breathing rate	Decreases breathing rate
Dilates pupils	Constricts pupils
Inhibits digestion	Stimulates digestion
Inhibits saliva production	Stimulates saliva production
Contracts rectum	Relaxes rectum

Knowledge Check

1. Using an example, explain what is meant by the 'fight or flight response'. *(4 marks)*
2. Identify **and** outline **two** divisions of the peripheral nervous system. *(4 marks)*
3. Describe **two** glands of the endocrine system. *(4 marks)*
4. Explain the difference between the nervous system **and** the endocrine system. *(4 marks)*

Spec spotlight

The structure and function of sensory, relay and motor neurons.

The process of synaptic transmission including reference to neurotransmitters, excitation and inhibition.

CNS = central nervous system.

PNS = peripheral nervous system.

The structure and function of neurons

Types of *neurons*.

There are 100 billion nerve cells (neurons) in the human nervous system, 80% of which are located in the brain.

By transmitting signals *electrically* and *chemically*, these provide the nervous system with its primary means of communication.

There are three types of neuron:

1. *Sensory neurons* carry messages from the PNS to the CNS. They have long dendrites and short axons. Located in the PNS in clusters called ganglias.
2. *Relay neurons* connect sensory neurons to motor or other relay neurons. They have short dendrites and short axons. Of all neurons, 97% are relay neurons and most are in the brain and visual system.
3. *Motor neurons* connect the CNS to effectors such as muscles and glands. They have short dendrites and long axons. Cell bodies may be in the CNS but long axons form part of PNS.

The structure of a neuron.

Neurons vary in size but all share the same basic structure:

cell body
sensory neuron
direction of conduction
nodes of Ranvier
myelin sheath
dendrites
relay neuron
axon
cell body
axon
motor neuron

- *Cell body* (or soma) – includes a nucleus which contains the genetic material of the cell.

- *Dendrites* – branchlike structures that protrude from the cell body. These carry nerve impulses from neighbouring neurons towards the cell body.

- *Axon* – carries the electrical impulse away from the cell body down the length of the neuron.

  ○ It is covered in a fatty layer of *myelin sheath* that protects the axon.

  ○ Gaps in the axon called *nodes of Ranvier* speed up the transmission of the impulse.

- *Terminal buttons* at the end of the axon communicate with the next neuron in the chain across a gap called the *synapse*.

Yeah, my heart stood still, a neuron ron yeah a neuron ron.

Ask your parents...

Revision BOOSTER

It is important that you can describe the structure and function of each of the three types of neuron as these are specifically named on the specification.

Electrical transmission.

The firing of a neuron.

When a neuron is in a resting state the inside of the cell is *negatively charged* compared to the outside.

When a neuron is activated, the inside of the cell becomes *positively charged* for a split second causing an *action potential* to occur.

This creates an electrical impulse that travels down the axon towards the end of the neuron.

Synaptic transmission

A *synapse*.	Each neuron is separated from the next by an extremely tiny gap called the synapse.
Chemical transmission. The events that occur at the synapse.	Signals within neurons are transmitted electrically, but signals between neurons are transmitted chemically across the synapse. When the electrical impulse reaches the end of the neuron (the *presynaptic terminal*) it triggers the release of *neurotransmitter* from tiny sacs called *synaptic vesicles*. Once a neurotransmitter crosses the gap, it is taken up by a *postsynaptic receptor site* on the next neuron, so the impulse only ever travels in one direction. The chemical message is converted back into an electrical impulse and the process of electrical transmission begins.
Neurotransmitters.	Neurotransmitters are chemicals that diffuse across the synapse to the next neuron in the chain. Many neurotransmitters have been identified. Each has its own specific molecular structure that fits perfectly into a postsynaptic receptor site, like a lock and key. Each has specific functions. For example: • *Acetylcholine* (ACh) found where a motor neuron meets a muscle, causing muscles to contract. • **Serotonin** affects mood and social behaviour (among other things) which is why it has been implicated as a cause of depression.
Excitation and inhibition.	Neurotransmitters generally have either an excitatory or inhibitory effect on the neighbouring neuron. • *Adrenaline* – generally excitatory, increasing the positive charge of the postsynaptic neuron, making it more likely the postsynaptic neuron will fire. • *Serotonin* – generally inhibitory, increasing the negative charge of the postsynaptic neuron, making it less likely the postsynaptic neuron will fire. • **Dopamine** is an unusual neurotransmitter as it is equally likely to have excitatory or inhibitory effects on the postsynaptic neuron.
Summation.	Excitatory and inhibitory influences are summed and must reach a certain threshold in order for the action potential of the postsynaptic neuron to be triggered. If the net effect of the neurotransmitters is inhibitory then the postsynaptic neuron is less likely to fire (i.e. no electrical signal is transmitted). It is more likely to fire if the net effect is excitatory.

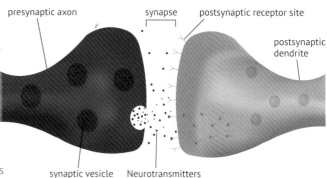

presynaptic axon · synapse · postsynaptic receptor site · postsynaptic dendrite · synaptic vesicle · Neurotransmitters in the synapse

My friend just burst into my room and asked me what an electrical synapse in the human body was.

The nerve.

Apply it

Sabiha loves chocolate. She eats it all the time and really believes that it gives her a 'boost' and makes her feel happier. Her friend Bev tells her that's probably because chocolate contains chemicals that have a real effect on the neurotransmitters of the nervous system.

Use your knowledge of synaptic transmission to explain what is happening at Sabiha's synapses.

Knowledge Check

1. Explain the difference between a motor neuron and a relay neuron. *(2 marks)*
2. Briefly describe the structure of a neuron. *(3 marks)*
3. Briefly outline how excitation **and** inhibition are involved in synaptic transmission. *(4 marks)*
4. Briefly explain the sequence of events that take place at the synapse. *(4 marks)*

Localisation of function in the brain

Spec spotlight

Localisation of function in the brain: motor, somatosensory, visual, auditory and language centres; Broca's and Wernicke's areas.

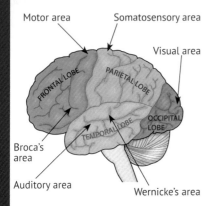

Motor area
Somatosensory area
Visual area
FRONTAL LOBE
PARIETAL LOBE
OCCIPITAL LOBE
TEMPORAL LOBE
Broca's area
Auditory area
Wernicke's area

Apply it

Melvin had a stroke (a burst blood vessel caused damage to part of his brain). He has problems walking because his right arm and leg are partly paralysed. He experiences numbness down his right side and also has trouble speaking, although he can understand what people are saying to him.

Use your knowledge of localisation of brain function to explain Melvin's experience and symptoms.

Revision BOOSTER

You will improve your exam marks if you use specialist terms wherever possible.

Localisation of function

Holistic theory replaced by localisation theory.	In the early 19th century **holistic** theory suggested that all parts of the brain were involved in processing thought and action.
	But specific areas of the brain were later linked with specific physical and psychological functions (localisation theory).
	If an area of the brain is damaged through illness or injury, the function associated with that area is also affected.
Brain is divided into two *hemispheres* and *lateralised.*	Lateralisation – some physical and psychological functions are controlled by a particular hemisphere.
	Generally, the left side of the body is controlled by the right hemisphere, the right side of the body by the left hemisphere.
Outer layer of brain is called the *cerebral cortex.*	The cerebral cortex is like a 'tea cosy' covering the inner parts of the brain. It is about 3 mm thick and is what separates us from lower animals as it is highly developed.
	The cortex appears grey due to the location of cell bodies – hence the phrase 'grey matter'.
Cerebral cortex of both hemispheres is divided into *four lobes* (frontal, parietal, occipital and temporal).	*Motor area* – at the back of the frontal lobe (both hemispheres). Controls voluntary movement. Damage may result in loss of control over fine motor movements.
	Somatosensory area – at the front of the parietal lobes. Processes sensory information from the skin (touch, heat, pressure, etc.). The amount of somatosensory area devoted to a particular body part denotes its sensitivity.
	Visual area – in the occipital lobe at the back of the brain. Each eye sends information from the right visual field to the left visual cortex, and from the left visual field to the right visual cortex.
	Auditory area – in the temporal lobe. Analyses speech-based information. Damage may produce partial hearing loss – the more extensive the damage, the more serious the loss.

The language centres

Broca's area Speech production.	Identified by Broca in the 1880s, in the left frontal lobe.
	Damage to this area causes Broca's aphasia which is characterised by speech that is slow, laborious and lacking in fluency. Broca's patients may have difficulty finding words and naming certain objects.
	People with Broca's aphasia have difficulty with prepositions and conjunctions (e.g. 'a', 'the', 'and').
Wernicke's area Language understanding.	Identified by Wernicke in the 1880s, in the left temporal lobe.
	People with Wernicke's aphasia produce language but have problems understanding it, so they produce fluent but meaningless speech.
	They will often produce nonsense words (neologisms) as part of the content of their speech.

One strength of localisation theory is support from neurosurgery.

Neurosurgery is used to treat mental disorders e.g. *cingulotomy* involves isolating the *cingulate gyrus* – dysfunction of this area may be a cause of OCD.

Dougherty *et al.* (2002) studied 44 people with OCD who had a cingulotomy. At follow-up, 30% met the criteria for successful response and 14% for partial response.

The success of such procedures strongly suggests that behaviours associated with serious mental disorders may be localised.

Another strength of localisation theory is brain scan evidence to support it.

Petersen *et al.* (1988) used brain scans to show activity in Wernicke's area during a listening task and in Broca's area during a reading task.

Also, a study of long-term memory by Tulving *et al.* (1994) revealed semantic and episodic memories are located in different parts of the prefrontal cortex.

There now exists a number of sophisticated and objective methods for measuring activity in the brain, providing sound scientific evidence of localisation of function.

Counterpoint

Lashley removed areas of the cortex (up to 50%) in rats learning the route through a maze. Learning required all of the cortex rather than being confined to a particular area.

This suggests that higher **cognitive** processes (e.g. learning) are not localised but distributed in a more holistic way in the brain.

Phineas Gage was working on a railroad when a tamping iron shot through his cheek taking a chunk of his frontal lobe with it. Now we've all had some bad days, but that takes the biscuit.

One limitation is the language localisation model has been questioned.

Dick and Tremblay (2016) found that very few researchers still believe language is only in Broca's and Wernicke's area.

Advanced techniques (e.g. **fMRI**) have identified regions in the right hemisphere and the thalamus.

This suggests that, rather than being confined to a couple of key areas, language may be organised more holistically in the brain, which contradicts localisation theory.

Evaluation extra: Case study evidence.

Unique cases of neurological damage support localisation theory, e.g. Phineas Gage who lost some of his brain in an explosion and his personality changed.

However it is difficult to make meaningful **generalisations** based on a single individual and conclusions may depend on the subjective interpretation of the researcher.

This suggests that some evidence supporting localisation may lack **validity**, oversimplifying brain processes, and undermining the theory.

Knowledge Check

1. Select **three** specific areas of the brain that you have studied **and** briefly outline the functions of each.
   (2 marks + 2 marks + 2 marks)

2. Outline research into localisation of function in the brain. *(6 marks)*

3. Discuss **two** criticisms of research into localisation of function in the brain.
   (3 marks + 3 marks)

4. A clinical psychologist's report on a client with a brain injury concludes that the client had damage to the motor, somatosensory and language areas of her brain.

   Discuss localisation of function in the brain. Refer to the **three** brain areas mentioned in the psychologist's report. *(16 marks)*

Hemispheric lateralisation and split-brain research

Spec spotlight

Hemispheric lateralisation; split-brain research.

The next time you describe yourself as having a 'splitting headache', spare a thought for Sperry's split-brain participants.

Getting it right (or left)

RVF = right visual field.
LVF = left visual field.
RH = right hemisphere.
LH = left hemisphere.

Testing a split-brain participant.

Hemispheric lateralisation

Hemispheric lateralisation	The brain is *lateralised* i.e. two sides (*hemispheres*).
Localised	Some functions are localised and appear in both left and right hemispheres (LH and RH).
	e.g. auditory, visual, motor, somatosensory areas.
Localised and lateralised	Two main language centres are in the LH (for most people) – Broca's area (left frontal lobe), Wernicke's area (left temporal lobe).
	RH produces rudimentary words but provides emotional context. LH may be the analyser, RH the synthesiser.
Contralateral	In the motor area, the right hemisphere controls the left side of the body and vice versa (cross-wired).
Contralateral and ipsilateral	Left visual field (LVF) of both eyes is connected to the RH and right visual field (RVF) of both eyes is connected to the LH.
	Enables the visual areas to compare the slightly different perspective from each eye and aids depth perception.
	Same arrangement for auditory areas.

Sperry (1968) Split-brain research

PROCEDURE	'Split-brain' = two hemispheres surgically separated by cutting the connections e.g. the *corpus callosum*.
	Used to treat severe epilepsy to reduce the 'electrical storm' across hemispheres.
	Eleven split-brain participants were studied using the set-up shown on the left. Image or word projected to RVF (processed by LH), and same, or different, image could be projected to the LVF (processed by RH).
	Presenting the image to one hemisphere meant that the information could not be conveyed from that hemisphere to the other.
FINDINGS AND CONCLUSIONS	Object shown to RVF:
	• Participant can describe what is seen (language centres in LH).
	Object shown to LVF:
	• Cannot name object (no language centres in RH).
	• Can select matching object behind screen using left hand.
	• Can select object closely associated with picture (e.g. ashtray if picture of cigarette).
	• Pinup picture shown to LVF, participant giggled but reported seeing nothing.
	Demonstrates how certain functions are lateralised in the brain, shows that LH is verbal and the RH is 'silent' but emotional.

One strength is evidence of lateralised brain functions in 'normal' brains.

PET scans show when 'normal' participants attend to global elements of an image, the RH is more active.

When required to focus on finer detail the specific areas of the LH tend to dominate (Fink *et al.* 1996).

This suggests that hemispheric lateralisation is a feature of the normal brain as well as the split-brain.

One limitation is the idea of analyser versus synthesiser brain may be wrong.

There may be different functions in the RH and LH but research suggests people do not have a dominant side, creating a different personality.

Nielsen *et al.* (2013) analysed 1000 brain scans, finding people did use certain hemispheres for certain tasks but no dominance.

This suggests that the notion of right- or left-brained people is wrong (e.g. 'artist' brain).

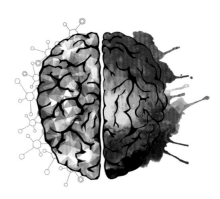

If we're talking hemispheres of the brain, it would seem that opposites attract.

Evaluation extra: Lateralisation versus plasticity.

Lateralisation is **adaptive**, enabling two simultaneous tasks with greater efficiency, e.g. only lateralised chickens better at finding food while watching for predators (Rogers *et al.* 2004).

On the other hand, neural plasticity is also adaptive. After damage to brain, language function can 'switch sides' (Holland *et al.* 1996).

This seems to suggest that lateralisation is first preference but ultimately plasticity is more important because it deals with loss of lateralisation.

One strength is support from more recent split-brain studies.

Luck *et al.* (1989) showed that split-brain participants are *better* than normal controls e.g. twice as fast at identifying the odd one out in an array of similar objects.

In the normal brain, the LH's superior processing abilities are 'watered down' by the inferior right hemisphere (Kingstone *et al.* 1995).

This supports Sperry's earlier findings that the 'left brain' and 'right brain' are distinct in terms of functions and abilities.

One limitation is that causal relationships are hard to establish.

In Sperry's research the behaviour of the split-brain participants was compared to a *neurotypical* **control group**.

However, none of the control group had epilepsy. Any differences between the groups may be due to epilepsy not the split-brain (a **confounding variable**).

This means that some of the unique features of the split-brain participants' **cognitive** abilities might have been due to their epilepsy.

Evaluation extra: Ethics.

Sperry's participants were not deliberately harmed and procedures were explained in advance to gain **informed consent**.

However, participants may not have understood they would be tested for many years, and participation was stressful.

This suggests that there was no deliberate harm but the negative consequences make the study unethical.

Apply it

Daisy had a split-brain operation to treat her severe epilepsy. Most of the time it doesn't seem to affect her everyday life. But some psychologists have asked her to take part in research to test her visual and language abilities. She knows you are studying psychology, so has asked you to explain what she can expect.

Use your knowledge of split-brain research to outline what Daisy might experience as a research participant.

Knowledge Check

1. Outline research into hemispheric lateralisation.
   (6 marks)

2. Describe **one** spilt-brain study. In your answer explain what the researcher(s) did **and** what they found. *(6 marks)*

3. Discuss **one** criticism of research into hemispheric lateralisation. *(4 marks)*

4. Describe **and** evaluate split-brain research. *(16 marks)*

Plasticity and functional recovery of the brain

Spec spotlight

Plasticity and functional recovery of the brain after trauma.

The brain is plastic, not rubber.

Apply it

Michael Schumacher won the world Formula One racing championship seven times. In 2013 he sustained a serious head injury during a skiing accident. He was in a medically-induced coma for several months. Schumacher's condition slowly improved. He began to learn to walk and speak again, but continued to have memory problems.

Using Michael Schumacher's experience as an example, explain what psychologists have discovered about plasticity of the brain and its functional recovery after trauma.

Revision BOOSTER

On these AO1 pages (left-hand side of the spread), there are nearly always six key points for each topic. This easily covers the descriptive content you would need for any essay – because description is worth 6 marks. Don't be tempted to over-describe. Just try to say a few sentences for each of the six points.

Plasticity

The brain is *'plastic'* – synaptic connections form and are pruned.	During infancy, the brain experiences a rapid growth in synaptic connections, peaking at about 15,000 at age 2–3 years (Gopnik *et al.* 1999). As we age, rarely-used connections are deleted and frequently-used connections are strengthened – *synaptic pruning*. It was once thought these changes were limited to childhood. But recent research suggests neural connections can change or be formed at any time, due to learning and experience.
The concept of plasticity is supported by a taxi driver study.	Maguire *et al.* (2000) found significantly more volume of grey matter in the posterior hippocampus in London taxi drivers than in a matched **control group**. This part of the brain is linked with the development of spatial and navigational skills. As part of their training, London cabbies take a complex test called 'The Knowledge' to assess their recall of city streets and possible routes. This learning experience appears to alter the structure of the taxi drivers' brains! The longer they had been in the job, the more pronounced was the structural difference.
Plasticity is also supported by research on learning.	Draganski *et al.* (2006) imaged the brains of medical students three months before and after final exams. Learning-induced changes were seen in the posterior hippocampus and the parietal cortex, presumably as a result of learning for the exam.

Functional recovery of the brain after trauma

Following trauma unaffected areas of the brain take over *lost functions*.	Functional recovery of the brain after trauma is an important example of neural plasticity – healthy brain areas take over functions of areas damaged, destroyed or even missing. Neuroscientists suggest this process occurs quickly after trauma (spontaneous recovery) and then slows down – at which point the person may require rehabilitative therapy.
The brain 'rewires' itself by forming new synaptic connections.	The brain is able to rewire and reorganise itself by forming new synaptic connections close to the area of damage. *Secondary neural pathways* that would not typically be used to carry out certain functions are activated or 'unmasked' to enable functioning to continue.
Structural changes in the brain.	Further structural changes may include: • *Axonal sprouting* – growth of new nerve endings which connect with other undamaged cells to form new neuronal pathways. • *Denervation supersensitivity* – axons that do a similar job become aroused to a higher level to compensate for the ones that are lost. • *Recruitment of homologous (similar) areas* – the opposite side of the brain takes over specific tasks e.g. language production.

One limitation of plasticity is possible negative behavioural consequences.

The brain's adaptation to prolonged drug use leads to poorer **cognitive** functioning in later life, as well as an increased risk of dementia (Medina et al. 2007).

60–80% of amputees have phantom limb syndrome (experience sensations in missing limb due to changes in *somatosensory cortex*).

This suggests that the brain's ability to adapt to damage is not always beneficial and may lead to physical and psychological problems.

One strength of plasticity is that it may not decline sharply with age.

Ladina Bezzola et al. (2012) demonstrated how 40 hours of golf training produced changes in the neural representations in participants aged 40–60.

Using **fMRI**, motor cortex activity in the novice golfers increased compared to a control group, suggesting positive effects after training.

This shows that neural plasticity can continue throughout the lifespan.

Evaluation extra: Seasonal brain changes.

Seasonal plasticity occurs in response to environmental changes, e.g. the suprachiasmatic nucleus (SCN) shrinks in spring and expands in autumn (Tramontin and Brenowitz 2000).

However, much of the work on seasonal plasticity has been done on animals, most notably songbirds. Human behaviour may be controlled differently.

This suggests that animal research may be a useful starting point but can't simply be **generalised** to humans.

One strength of functional recovery is its real-world application.

Understanding plasticity has led to neurorehabilitation. Understanding axonal growth encourages new therapies.

For example, constraint-induced movement therapy involves massed practice with an affected arm while unaffected arm is restrained.

This shows that research into functional recovery helps medical professionals know when interventions can be made.

One limitation is neural plasticity may be related to cognitive reserve.

Schneider et al. (2014) looked at the time brain injury patients had spent in education (indicated their *cognitive reserve*) and their chances of a disability-free recovery (DFR).

40% of patients who achieved DFR had more than 16 years' education compared to about 10% of patients who had less than 12 years' education.

This suggests that cognitive reserve is a crucial factor in determining how well the brain adapts after trauma.

Evaluation extra: Small samples.

Research on new treatments e.g. Banerjee et al. (2014) showed total recovery from stroke using stem cell treatment compared to normal 4% recovery.

However this study drew conclusions based on just five participants and no control group, typical of research on functional recovery.

This research may lack **validity**, but waiting for larger samples may prevent the development of valuable treatments.

Name the four coloured areas below (see lobes of the brain on page 30).

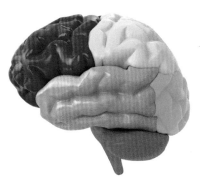

Not that kind of plastic. And not those colours either.

Funny word, plastic

Here's a definition of the word plastic: materials easily shaped or moulded.

Revision BOOSTER

Have you checked out our revision advice on pages 4 to 9?

Knowledge Check

1. Explain what is meant by 'plasticity' in relation to the brain. *(2 marks)*
2. Outline research (theories and/or studies) into functional recovery of the brain after trauma. *(6 marks)*
3. Evaluate research into functional recovery of the brain after trauma. *(6 marks)*
4. A newspaper recently carried the following headline and story: 'Knowledge changes the brain, claim psychologists. Brain scans show that taxi drivers who have to learn hundreds of London routes have bigger brain areas than the rest of us.'

   Describe **and** evaluate research into plasticity of the brain. Refer to the newspaper report in your answer. *(16 marks)*

Spec spotlight

Ways of studying the brain:
scanning techniques,
including functional magnetic
resonance imaging (fMRI);
electroencephalograms (EEGs)
and event-related potentials
(ERPs); post-mortem
examinations.

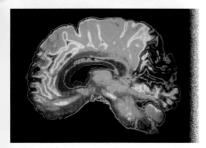

*Even though your brain is only about
2% of your weight, it uses 20–30%
of the calories you consume. So go
on, have that dessert... your brain
needs it.*

Psychology and fMRI

Psychologists typically study brain
activity by getting participants
to have their brains scanned while
they perform a task involving mental
processing (e.g. memory, language).
The assumption is that brain
areas active during the task must
be correlated with that mental
process.

Apply it

*Danny has frequent seizures. It
appears he may have epilepsy
and is going to have some tests to
diagnose the disorder. He has been
told he will have an EEG and an
fMRI scan.*

Referring to Danny's case, explain
what is involved in these **two** ways of
studying the brain, **and** what they tell
us about brain functioning.

Scanning and other techniques

Psychologists use *medical techniques* to investigate brain localisation.	Techniques for investigating the brain are often used for medical purposes in the diagnosis of illness. The purpose of scanning in psychological research is often to investigate localisation – to determine which parts of the brain do what.
fMRI Highlights active areas of the brain.	Functional magnetic resonance imaging (**fMRI**) detects changes in both blood oxygenation and flow that occur due to neural activity in specific brain areas. When a brain area is more active it consumes more oxygen and blood flow is directed to the active area (*haemodynamic response*). fMRI produces a 3D image showing which parts of the brain are active and therefore must be involved in particular mental processes.
EEG Shows overall electrical activity.	Electroencephalogram (**EEG**) measures electrical activity within the brain via electrodes using a skull cap (looks a bit like a swimming cap with the electrodes attached). The scan recording represents the brainwave patterns generated from thousands of neurons. This shows overall brain activity. EEG is often used as a diagnostic tool. For example unusual arrhythmic patterns of brain activity may indicate abnormalities such as epilepsy, tumours or sleep disorders.
ERPs Brainwaves related to particular events.	Event-related potentials (ERPs) are what is left when all extraneous brain activity from an EEG recording is filtered out. This is done using a statistical technique, leaving only those responses that relate to the presentation of a specific stimulus (for example). ERPs are types of brainwave that are triggered by particular events. Research has revealed many different forms of ERP and how these are linked to **cognitive** processes (e.g. perception and attention).
Post-mortem examinations.	A technique involving the analysis of a person's brain following their death. Areas of the brain are examined to establish the likely cause of a deficit or disorder that the person experienced in life. This may also involve comparison with a *neurotypical* brain in order to assess the extent of the difference.

Strengths of fMRI are that it is risk-free and high spatial resolution.

Unlike other scanning techniques (e.g. PET), fMRI does not rely on the use of radiation and is safe.	It also produces images with high spatial resolution, showing detail by the millimetre.	This means fMRI can safely provide a clear picture of how brain activity is localised.

Limitations of fMRI are that it is expensive and poor temporal resolution.

fMRI is expensive compared to other techniques.	It has poor temporal resolution because of 5-second lag between initial neural activity and image.	This means fMRI may not truly represent moment-to-moment brain activity.

Strengths of EEG are practical uses and high temporal resolution.

EEG has contributed to our understanding of the stages of sleep.	It has high temporal resolution – brain activity in one millisecond.	This shows the real-world usefulness of the technique.

Limitations of EEG are information is generalised and source not pinpointed.

The EEG produces a generalised signal from thousands of neurons.	It is difficult to know the exact source of neural activity.	Therefore EEG can't distinguish the activity of different but adjacent neurons.

Strengths of ERP are specificity and good temporal resolution.

Measures of neural processes more specific with ERPs than EEGs.	ERPs have excellent temporal resolution, better than fMRI.	This means that ERPs are frequently used in cognitive research.

Limitations of ERPs are lack of standardisation and background 'noise'.

Lack of standardisation makes it difficult to confirm findings in studies involving ERPs.	Background 'noise' and extraneous material must be completely eliminated.	These issues are a problem because they may not always be easy to achieve.

Strengths of post-mortems are in localisation and medical research.

Broca and Wernicke both relied on post-mortem studies.	Used to link HM's memory deficits to damage in his brain.	This means they continue to provide useful information.

Limitations of post-mortems are knowing causation and ethics.

Observed damage in the brain may not be linked to the deficits under review.	Post-mortem studies raise ethical issues of consent after death (e.g. HM).	This challenges their usefulness in psychological research.

The skull cap. Part of the Lady Gaga summer collection.

Revision BOOSTER

On this page we have identified EIGHT evaluation points. For each of these, we have included THREE levels of elaboration. As evaluation is worth up to 10 marks, this amount of expansion is just what you need to produce great answers.

Knowledge Check

1. Explain **two** differences between functional magnetic resonance imaging (fMRI) and post-mortem examinations as ways of studying the brain.
   (2 marks + 2 marks)

2. Briefly outline electroencephalograms (EEGs) **and** event-related potentials (ERPs) as ways of studying the brain. *(6 marks)*

3. Discuss **two** criticisms of any **one** way of studying the brain. *(3 marks + 3 marks)*

4. Discuss **two or more** ways psychologists study the brain.
   (16 marks)

Biological rhythms: Circadian rhythms

Spec spotlight

Biological rhythms: circadian rhythms.

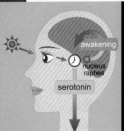 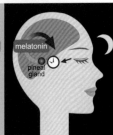

Biorhythms are not the same as biological rhythms. Biorhythms are a pseudoscientific idea that we perform better when certain biological cycles are aligned – 'pseudoscientific' because there is no valid evidence to support the idea.

Circadian rhythms (about one cycle every 24 hours)

Biological rhythms governed by *endogenous pacemakers* and *exogenous zeitgebers*.	Biological rhythms are periodic activity, governed by: 1. Internal biological 'clocks' (endogenous pacemakers). 2. External changes in the environment (exogenous zeitgebers). Some of these rhythms occur many times a day (*ultradian rhythms*). Others take more than a day to complete (*infradian rhythms*).
The *circadian rhythm* lasts for about 24 hours.	*Circa* meaning 'about' and *diem* meaning 'day'. There are several important types of circadian rhythm such as the sleep/wake cycle.
Sleep/wake cycle governed by internal and external mechanisms.	*Exogenous zeitgebers* – the fact we feel drowsy when it's night-time and alert during the day shows the effect of daylight. *Endogenous pacemakers* – a biological clock 'left to its own devices' without the influence of external stimuli (e.g. light) is called 'free-running'. The basic rhythm is governed by the *suprachiasmatic nucleus* (SCN). The SCN lies just above the optic chiasm which provides information from the eyes about light. Exogenous zeitgebers (light) can reset the SCN.
Siffre demonstrated a free-running circadian rhythm of about 25 hours.	French caver Siffre spent long periods in dark caves to examine the effects of free-running biological rhythms – two months (in 1962) and six months (in the 1970s). In each **case study**, Siffre's free-running circadian rhythm settled down to about 25 hours. Importantly, he did have a regular sleep/wake cycle.
Aschoff and Wever also found a similar circadian rhythm.	A group of participants spent four weeks in a World War 2 bunker deprived of natural light (Aschoff and Wever 1976). All but one (whose sleep/wake cycle extended to 29 hours) displayed a circadian rhythm between 24 and 25 hours. Siffre's experience and the bunker study suggest that the 'natural' sleep/wake cycle may be slightly longer than 24 hours but is entrained by exogenous zeitgebers associated with our 24-hour day (e.g. daylight hours, mealtimes, etc.).
Folkard *et al.* showed *endogenous pacemakers* stronger than *exogenous zeitgebers*.	Folkard *et al.* (1985) studied a group of 12 people who lived in a dark cave for three weeks, going to bed when the clock said 11.45 pm and waking when it said 7.45 am. The researchers gradually speeded up the clock (unbeknown to the participants) to a 22-hour day. Only one participant comfortably adjusted to the new regime. This suggests the existence of a strong free-running circadian rhythm not controlled by exogenous zeitgebers.

Apply it

Tameka is a nurse who works in the accident and emergency department of a large hospital. She works different shifts over a period of time. Whenever her shift changes she feels tired and less alert than usual. Tameka feels anxious and worries that she could make a mistake at work. She is also worried about her health.

Explain what psychologists have discovered about circadian rhythms. Refer to Tameka's experience in your answer.

One strength of circadian rhythm research is application to shift work.

Shift work creates desynchronisation of biological rhythms. Boivin et al. (1996) found shift workers experience a lapse of concentration around 6 am (a *circadian trough*) so accidents are more likely.

Research also suggests a link between shift work and poor health, with shift workers three times more likely to develop heart disease (Knutsson 2003).

Thus, research into the sleep/wake cycle may have economic implications in terms of how best to manage shift work.

Counterpoint

The research is **correlational**, therefore desynchronisation may not be the cause of observed difficulties. For example, Solomon (1993) concluded that high divorce rates in shift workers might be due to missing out on important family events.

This suggests that it may not be biological factors that create the adverse consequences associated with shiftwork.

Another strength is real-world application to medical treatment.

Circadian rhythms co-ordinate the body's basic processes (e.g. heart rate, hormone levels) with implications for *chronotherapeutics* (timing medication to maximise effects on the body).

Aspirin reduces heart attacks, which are most likely in the morning. Bonten et al. (2015) found taking aspirin is most effective last thing at night.

This shows that circadian rhythm research can help increase the effectiveness of drug treatments.

One limitation is that generalisations are difficult to make.

Studies of the sleep/wake cycle often use small groups of participants (e.g. Aschoff and Wever), or even single individuals (e.g. Siffre).

Participants may not be representative of the wider population and this limits making meaningful **generalisations**. Siffre observed that his internal clock ticked much more slowly at 60 than when he was younger.

This suggests that, even when the same person is involved, there are factors that may prevent general conclusions being drawn.

Not everyone agrees with this conclusion. What do you think?

Evaluation extra: Shifting the school day.

Research shows benefits for teenagers' academic and behavioural performance when lessons start later in the day (Adolescent Sleep Working Group 2014).

However, a later start is disruptive for parents and teachers, and teenagers may simply stay up later and still be exhausted.

This suggests changing the school day may not be practical even though it may be desirable.

Owls go to bed late and wake up late, very much the teenagers of the bird world. Larks go to bed early and are at their best in the mornings. The scientific name for larks is 'annoying'.

Getting it right

Confused about exogenous and endogenous? Try this: the prefix 'exo' means 'external'. The first two letters tell you everything you need to remember.

Revision BOOSTER

Evidence is key in psychology. But whether it's description (AO1) or evaluation (AO3) depends on how you use it. The studies here are descriptive – so focus on procedures and findings, and what they tell us about circadian rhythms.

Knowledge Check

1. Explain what is meant by 'circadian rhythms'. *(2 marks)*
2. Explain what research has shown about circadian rhythms. *(4 marks)*
3. Evaluate research into circadian rhythms. *(6 marks)*
4. Discuss research into circadian rhythms. *(16 marks)*

Biological rhythms: Infradian and ultradian rhythms

Spec spotlight

Biological rhythms: infradian and ultradian rhythms.

The Stern and McClintock study. It's the pits.

Apply it

Naga and Claudia are talking about living in female-only halls of residence back in the 1980s. Naga says, 'All of us on the same corridor used to have the same menstrual cycles.' Claudia agrees, 'Yes, when we first arrived we all had different cycles, but it didn't take long for us to synchronise.'

Outline what psychologists have discovered about **infradian rhythms**. Refer to Naga's and Claudia's conversation in your answer.

Here's an example of alpha waves and sleep spindles:

Revision BOOSTER

Write very brief essay plans for each possible essay and then practise writing the essay out in full from these. Time yourself – 20 minutes for a 16-mark essay.

Infradian rhythms (less than one cycle in 24 hours)

The *female menstrual cycle* is an infradian rhythm.	The human female menstrual cycle is about 28 days (i.e. less than one cycle in 24 hours – *infra diem* meaning 'below' a day).
	Rising levels of **oestrogen** cause the ovary to release an egg (ovulation). Then *progesterone* helps the womb lining to thicken, readying the womb for pregnancy. If pregnancy does not occur, the egg is absorbed and the womb lining comes away (menstrual flow).
Exogenous zeitgebers may synchronise menstrual cycles.	Stern and McClintock (1998) studied 29 women with irregular periods. Pheromones were taken from some at different stages of their cycles, via a cotton pad under their armpits. These pads were cleaned with alcohol and later rubbed on the upper lips of the other participants.
	68% of women experienced changes to their cycle which brought them closer to the cycle of their 'odour donor'.
SAD is another infradian rhythm.	*Seasonal affective disorder* (SAD) is a depressive disorder (low mood, lack of activity) with a seasonal pattern.
	Often called the 'winter blues' because the symptoms are triggered during the winter months when the number of daylight hours becomes shorter.
SAD may be caused by the hormone *melatonin*.	During the night, the pineal gland secretes melatonin until dawn when there is an increase in light.
	In winter, less light means secretion goes on for longer.
	This has a knock-on effect on the production of **serotonin** in the brain (low serotonin is linked to depressive symptoms).

Ultradian rhythms (more than one cycle in 24 hours)

Stages of sleep are an ultradian rhythm.	Sleep pattern occurs in 90-minute periods (i.e. more than one cycle in 24 hours – *ultra diem* meaning 'beyond' a day).
	Divided into five stages, each characterised by a different level of brainwave activity (monitored using **EEG**).
Five stages of sleep have been identified.	**Stages 1 and 2** Light sleep where a person may be easily woken. In stage 1, brain waves are high frequency and have a short amplitude. These are *alpha waves*. In stage 2, the alpha waves continue but there are occasional random changes in pattern called *sleep spindles* (see diagram on left).
	Stages 3 and 4 This is known as deep sleep or *slow wave sleep* (SWS). The individual waves now have lower frequency and higher amplitude. It is difficult to wake someone at this point.
	Stage 5 (REM sleep) The body is paralysed yet brain activity closely resembles that of the awake brain. During this time, the brain produces *theta waves* and the eyes occasionally move around, thus *rapid eye movement* (REM). Dreams most often experienced during REM sleep, but may also occur in deep sleep.

One strength is research on the menstrual cycle shows its **evolutionary basis.**

For our distant ancestors it may have been advantageous for females to menstruate together and become pregnant at the same time.

In a social group, this would allow babies who had lost their mothers to have access to breast milk, thereby improving their chances of survival.

This suggests that synchronisation is an **adaptive** strategy.

One limitation is the methodology used in synchronisation studies.

There are many factors that may change a woman's menstrual cycle and act as **confounding variables** (e.g. stress, changes in diet, etc.).

Any supposed pattern may occur by chance. This may be why other studies (e.g. Trevathan et al. 1993) have not **replicated** Stern and McClintock's original findings.

This suggests that menstrual synchrony studies are flawed.

Do you agree with this conclusion?

Evaluation extra: Real-world application.

Light therapy reduces the debilitating effects of SAD (e.g. excessive sleepiness) in around 80% of people (Sanassi 2014). It is also safer than using antidepressants.

However, Rohan et al. (2009) recorded a relapse rate of 46% over successive winters, compared to 27% in a comparison group receiving **CBT**.

This suggests that light therapy may be an effective short-term treatment but additional treatments may be required if benefits are to be maintained.

One strength is understanding age-related changes in sleep.

SWS reduces with age. Growth hormone is produced during SWS so this becomes deficient in older people.

van Cauter et al. (2000) suggest the reduced sleep may explain impairments in old age. SWS sleep can be improved using relaxation and medication.

This suggests that knowledge of ultradian rhythms has practical value.

One limitation is individual differences in sleep stages.

Tucker et al. (2007) found large differences between participants in the duration of stages 3 and 4.

They suggest that these differences are biologically determined.

This makes it difficult to describe 'normal sleep' in any meaningful way.

Evaluation extra: The sleep lab.

One of the benefits of conducting studies of sleep in lab settings is control of **extraneous variables**, such as noise or temperature that may affect sleep.

However, lab studies involve participants being attached to complicated machinery, so their sleep does not represent their ordinary sleep patterns.

This dilemma means it might be best to conduct some studies in people's own homes and compare patterns with records made in lab settings.

One treatment for seasonal affective disorder is using a light box to increase exposure to strong light which may affect melatonin levels.

Brainwaves are called 'waves' because they rise and fall. There are two features of waves. First is the time between each peak (described as the frequency of the wave) and second is the height of each peak which represents amount of electrical activity (described as amplitude).

Revision BOOSTER

Most of the AO3 points on all of these pages include a summary sentence to round off each criticism (in the third column). They usually begin with a phrase such as, 'This suggests that...' or 'This means that...' Try to get into the habit of doing likewise. You don't have to use this exact wording. But the benefits of this kind of language are that it's definitely evaluative and it makes your critical points crystal clear.

Knowledge Check

1. Explain what is meant by 'infradian rhythms' **and** 'ultradian rhythms'.
   (2 marks + 2 marks)

2. Outline research into **either** infradian rhythms **or** ultradian rhythms. *(6 marks)*

3. Evaluate research into infradian rhythms. *(6 marks)*

4. Describe **and** evaluate research into infradian rhythms **and** ultradian rhythms. *(16 marks)*

Endogenous pacemakers and exogenous zeitgebers

Spec spotlight

The effect of endogenous pacemakers and exogenous zeitgebers on the sleep/wake cycle.

Even though the SCN connections have been altered in my brain, a milky drink before bedtime and I'm out like a light.

Apply it

Will is a teenager with a sleep problem. He finds it very hard to get to sleep at night and wakes after a short time, getting only about two hours' sleep each night. He feels very tired during the day and his college work and health are suffering. Will has a chaotic lifestyle with no regular routines. He has irregular mealtimes and goes to bed at different times. He spends a lot of time before sleeping working on his tablet.

Using Will's experience as an example, explain the effects of both endogenous pacemakers **and** exogenous zeitgebers on the sleep/wake cycle.

SCN goes to Hollywood

Who remembers the film 'Mary Poppins'? You must remember that great song about endogenous pacemakers and the sleep/wake cycle. All together now: Superchiasmaticnucleusexpialidocious…

Chapter 2: Biopsychology

Endogenous pacemakers and the sleep/wake cycle

SCN is a primary endogenous pacemaker.	The *suprachiasmatic nucleus* (SCN) is a tiny bundle of nerve cells in the *hypothalamus* which helps maintain circadian rhythms (e.g. sleep/wake cycle).
	Nerve fibres from the eye cross at the *optic chiasm* on their way to the right and left visual areas. The SCN lies just above the optic chiasm and receives information about light from this structure.
Influence of SCN on the sleep/wake cycle demonstrated with chipmunks and hamsters.	DeCoursey *et al.* (2000) destroyed SCN connections in the brains of 30 chipmunks which were returned to their natural habitat and observed for 80 days. Their sleep/wake cycle disappeared and many were killed by predators.
	Ralph *et al.* (1990) bred 'mutant' hamsters with a 20-hour sleep/wake cycle. SCN cells were transplanted from the foetal tissue of these hamsters into the brains of normal hamsters, which then developed cycles of 20 hours.
Pineal gland and melatonin are endogenous mechanisms.	The SCN passes information on day length to the pineal gland which increases production of melatonin during the night.
	Melatonin is a hormone that induces sleep and is inhibited during periods of wakefulness. It has also been suggested as a causal factor in *seasonal affective disorder*.

Exogenous zeitgebers and the sleep/wake cycle

External environmental factors that reset biological clocks.	The German word *zeitgeber* means 'time giver'.
	Resetting biological clocks is a process known as *entrainment*.
	Without external cues, the free-running biological clock continues to 'tick' in a cyclical pattern. Zeitgebers reset the sleep/wake cycle (interaction of internal and external factors).
Light is a key exogeneous zeitgeber that influences the sleep/wake cycle.	Light can reset the body's main endogenous pacemaker (SCN), and also has an indirect influence on key processes in the body controlling hormone secretion, blood circulation, etc.
	Campbell and Murphy (1998) woke 15 participants at various times and shone a light on the backs of their knees – producing a deviation in the sleep/wake cycle of up to three hours. Light does not necessarily rely on the eyes to influence the SCN.
Social cues also have an important influence on the sleep/wake cycle.	The sleep/wake cycle is fairly random in human newborns, but most babies are entrained by about 16 weeks. Schedules imposed by parents are a key influence, including adult-determined mealtimes and bedtimes.
	Research on jet lag shows adapting to local times for eating and sleeping (not responding to one's own feelings of hunger and fatigue) entrains circadian rhythms and tackles jet lag.

One limitation of SCN research is that it may obscure other body clocks.

Body clocks (*peripheral oscillators*) are found in many organs and cells (e.g. lungs, skin). They are highly influenced by the actions of the SCN but can act independently.

Damiola *et al.* (2000) showed how changing feeding patterns in mice altered circadian rhythms of cells in the liver for up to 12 hours, leaving the SCN unaffected.

This suggests there may be many other complex influences on the sleep/wake cycle, aside from the master clock (SCN).

Another limitation is endogenous pacemakers cannot be studied in isolation.

Only in exceptional circumstances are endogenous pacemakers 'free running' and unaffected by the influence of exogenous zeitgebers.

Total isolation studies (e.g. Siffre's cave study) are rare. In everyday life, pacemakers and zeitgebers interact so it may make little sense to separate the two.

This suggests the more researchers attempt to isolate the influence of internal pacemakers, the lower the **validity** of the research.

Evaluation extra: Ethics.

Animal studies of the sleep/wake cycle are justified because there are similar mechanisms in all mammals, so **generalisations** can be made to the human brain.

However, a disturbing issue is the ethics involved. Animals were exposed to considerable risk in the Decoursey *et al.* study and most died as a result.

This suggests that studies like these cannot be justified and researchers should find alternative ways of studying endogenous pacemakers.

One limitation is effects of exogenous zeitgebers differ in different environments.

Exogenous zeitgebers do not have the same effect on people who live in places where there is very little darkness in summer and very little light in winter.

For instance, the Innuit Indians of the Arctic Circle have similar sleep patterns all-year round, despite spending around six months in almost total darkness.

This suggests the sleep/wake cycle is primarily controlled by endogenous pacemakers that can override environmental changes in light.

Another limitation is **case study** evidence undermines effects of exogenous cues.

Miles *et al.* (1977) reported the case of a man, blind from birth, with an abnormal circadian rhythm of 24.9 hours.

Despite exposure to social cues, such as mealtimes, his sleep/wake cycle could not be adjusted.

This suggests that social cues alone are not effective in resetting the biological rhythm and the natural body clock is stronger.

Evaluation extra: Age-related insomnia.

Natural changes in circadian rhythms mean older people fall asleep early and have poorer quality sleep (Duffy *et al.* 2015).

However, Hood *et al.* (2004) found that management of insomnia improved if elderly people were more active and had more exposure to natural light during the day.

This suggests that exogenous changes in lifestyle may be just as likely to cause age-related insomnia as internal, biological changes.

'Oh how embarrassing, being caught without my nightshirt on...'

Download suggested answers to the Knowledge Check questions from **tinyurl.com/yd3ezhkb**

Knowledge Check

1. Outline what is meant by 'endogenous pacemakers' **and** 'exogenous zeitgebers'.
   (2 marks + 2 marks)

2. Describe **one** study into the effect of endogenous pacemakers on the sleep/wake cycle. *(6 marks)*

3. Explain what research (theories and/or studies) has shown about the effect of exogenous zeitgebers on the sleep/wake cycle. *(6 marks)*

4. Describe **and** evaluate research into the effects of endogenous pacemakers **and** exogenous zeitgebers on the sleep/wake cycle. *(16 marks)*

Specification content for AS and Year 1

Spec spotlight

For A level you need to know everything in the AS specification (listed on right) plus the topics covered on this and the next five spreads.

Remember

Overall, at least 25% of the marks in assessments for AS/A level Psychology will be based on assessment of research methods.

On Paper 2 at A level there is a section of the exam on research methods – worth 48 marks (that's a lot of questions).

But research methods are also assessed on any other topic on any other paper!

It's not what you do... it's the way that you do it.

Knowledge Check

1. Explain the difference between an aim and a hypothesis. **(2 marks)**
2. Explain what is meant by 'quasi-experiment'. Give an example in your answer. **(3 marks)**
3. Explain **one** strength **and one** limitation of using a repeated measures design. **(2 marks + 2 marks)**
4. Explain how a psychologist could select a stratified sample of participants. **(3 marks)**
5. Explain the difference between a naturalistic and controlled observation. **(4 marks)**
6. Briefly discuss the use of **one** self-report technique in psychology. **(4 marks)**

AS and Year 1 Specification content

The A level exam includes all you have learned already in Year 1. The list below indicates what that is!

Tick off what you already know and would feel confident answering questions on in the exam. Revisit concepts if necessary.

Aims: stating aims, the differences between aims and hypotheses. ☐

Hypotheses: directional and non-directional. ☐

Variables: manipulation and control of variables, including independent, dependent, extraneous, confounding; operationalisation of variables. Control: random allocation and counterbalancing, randomisation and standardisation. Demand characteristics and investigator effects. ☐

Experimental method. Types of experiment, laboratory and field experiments; natural and quasi-experiments. Experimental designs: repeated measures, independent groups, matched pairs. ☐

Sampling: the difference between population and sample; sampling techniques including: random, systematic, stratified, opportunity and volunteer; implications of sampling techniques, including bias and generalisation. ☐

Ethics, including the role of the British Psychological Society's code of ethics; ethical issues in the design and conduct of psychological studies; dealing with ethical issues in research. ☐

Pilot studies and the aims of piloting. ☐

Observational techniques. Types of observation: naturalistic and controlled observation; covert and overt observation; participant and non-participant observation. Observational design: behavioural categories; event sampling; time sampling. ☐

Self-report techniques. Questionnaires; interviews, structured and unstructured. Questionnaire construction, including use of open and closed questions; design of interviews. ☐

Correlations. Analysis of the relationship between co-variables. The difference between correlations and experiments. Positive, negative and zero correlations. ☐

Quantitative and qualitative data; the distinction between qualitative and quantitative data collection techniques. Primary and secondary data, including meta-analysis. ☐

Descriptive statistics: measures of central tendency – mean, median, mode; calculation of mean, median and mode; measures of dispersion: range and standard deviation; calculation of range. ☐

Presentation and display of quantitative data: graphs, tables, scattergrams, bar charts, histograms. Distributions: normal and skewed distributions; characteristics of normal and skewed distributions. ☐

Mathematical content: calculation of percentages, converting a percentage to a decimal, decimal places, converting a decimal to a fraction, using ratios, estimates, significant figures, standard form, order of magnitude calculations, mathematical symbols, substituting values. ☐

Introduction to statistical testing; the sign test; probability; when to use the sign test; calculation of the sign test. ☐

The role of peer review in the scientific process. ☐

The implications of psychological research for the economy. ☐

Analysis and interpretation of correlations	
An association between two *co-variables*.	**Correlation** refers to a mathematical technique which measures the relationship or association between two continuous variables (co-variables). These are plotted on a scattergram where each axis represents one of the variables being investigated.
Correlation coefficient represents the strength of the correlation.	Statistical tests of correlation produce a numerical value somewhere between −1 and +1. This is the correlation coefficient. This value tells us the strength of the relationship between the two variables. The closer the coefficient is to 1 (+1 or −1), the stronger the relationship between the co-variables. The closer to zero, the weaker the relationship is. However, it should be noted that coefficients that appear to indicate weak correlations (e.g. .30) can still be statistically significant – it depends on the size of the data set.
Correlation coefficient represents the direction of the correlation.	Value of +1 represents a perfect positive correlation. Value of −1 represents a perfect negative correlation. Note that a correlation coefficient of +.50 is as strong as −.50. The sign just informs us of the direction. Correlation coefficients are calculated using an inferential test, such as Pearson's (for interval level data) or Spearman's.

Scattergrams showing various correlation coefficients.

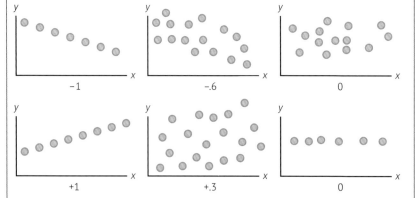

Note that both graphs on the right represent zero correlation even though the distribution of scores is quite different.

Spec spotlight

Analysis and interpretation of correlation, including correlation coefficients.

An understanding of correlation as a method of research is covered in the Year 1 book, including the strengths and limitations. The A level specification adds a bit more on this topic.

Correlations are all about how two (or more) things are related.

Knowledge Check

A psychologist measured the correlation between accuracy of memory recall and age using 20 participants. He found a significant negative correlation of −.72.

1. Sketch an appropriate graph that approximately represents this finding. Label your graph carefully. *(4 marks)*

2. Describe the nature of the relationship between memory and age. *(4 marks)*

3. Explain what is meant by 'correlation coefficient'. *(2 marks)*

4. Explain what a correlation of −.72 means. *(2 marks)*

Case studies

Spec spotlight

Case studies.

Gavin had taken his psychology teacher's suggestion that he should 'study a case' a little too literally.

Case study versus case history

A case history is the record of information that is collected about a person or group. It is something that a doctor or social worker might prepare but it also is an important component of a case study.

The term 'case study' refers to the research methods used to collect information about the case being studied – observation, interviews, psychological tests. It is the methods that are used for data collection and analysis.

Apply it

A cognitive psychologist investigates a person (RL) with severe amnesia. She interviews RL about his distant past, recent past and present to find out how much he can and cannot remember. She also observes RL's day-to-day behaviour and asks family members to complete questionnaires. She does this over a period of one year to detect any changes in his amnesia.

Explain **two** strengths **and two** limitations of this case study as an investigation into amnesia.

Case studies	
Detailed, in-depth and longitudinal.	To study a 'case' in psychology is to provide a detailed and in-depth analysis of an individual, group, institution or event. **Case studies** tend to take place over a long period of time (**longitudinal**) and may involve gathering data from family and friends of the individual as well as the person themselves.
Unusual and also typical cases.	Case studies often involve analysis of unusual individuals or events, such as a person with a rare disorder or the sequence of events that led to the 2011 London riots. Case studies may also concentrate on more 'typical' cases, such as an elderly person's recollections of their childhood.
Usually involve *qualitative* data.	Researchers will construct a case history of the individual or event concerned, perhaps using interviews, observations, questionnaires or a combination of all of these. The data collected is mainly qualitative. Psychological tests may also be used to assess, for example, intelligence or personality. These are likely to produce quantitative data.

Evaluation		
⊕ Rich, detailed insight.	Preferred to the more 'superficial' forms of data that might be collected (e.g. from an **experiment** assessing one aspect of behaviour at one moment in time).	Such detail is likely to increase the **validity** of the data collected.
⊕ Enables study of unusual behaviour.	Some behaviours/ conditions are very rare (e.g. HM) and cannot be studied using other methods.	In addition some cases can help understanding of 'typical' functioning.
⊖ Prone to **researcher bias**.	Conclusions are based on the subjective interpretation of the researcher and personal accounts.	This may reduce the validity of the study.
⊖ Small samples.	Sample may be one individual/event with unique characteristics.	This makes it difficult to make **generalisations** (low **external validity**).

Content analysis

People are studied *indirectly* through their communications.	Content analysis is a type of observational research. People are studied indirectly via the communications they have produced. This may include: • Spoken interaction (e.g. a speech or conversation). • Written forms (e.g. texts or email). • Examples from the media (e.g. books, magazines, TV).	
Coding may produce quantitative data.	Coding is the first stage of content analysis. Some data sets may be extremely large (such as the transcripts of several dozen lengthy interviews). So information needs to be categorised into meaningful units. This may involve counting up the number of times a particular word or phrase appears in the text to produce quantitative data. For instance, newspaper reports may be analysed for the number of times derogatory terms for people with mental health problems are used, such as 'crazy' or 'mad'.	
Thematic analysis produces qualitative data.	Thematic analysis is similar to content analysis but is more qualitative, and aims to produce themes rather than, e.g. word counts. These themes are more descriptive than the coding units. For instance, people with mental health problems may be represented in newspapers as a 'threat to our children' or as a 'drain on the NHS'. Such themes may then be developed into broader categories, such as 'control' or 'stereotyping' of people with mental health problems.	
⊕ Many ethical issues may not apply.	The material to study (e.g. TV adverts, films, etc.) may already be in the public domain.	So there are no issues with obtaining consent, for example.
⊕ A flexible method.	Content analysis can produce both quantitative and qualitative data as required.	This means it is a flexible approach that can be adapted to suit the aims of the research.
⊖ Communication is studied out of context.	The researcher may attribute motivations to the speaker or writer that were not intended.	This is likely to reduce the validity of the conclusions drawn.
⊖ May lack objectivity.	Content analysis may lack objectivity, especially when more descriptive forms of thematic analysis are used.	Such bias may threaten the validity of the findings and conclusions. However, *reflexivity* is a method of addressing the lack of objectivity. Personal viewpoints are seen as an important part of the data collected.

Spec spotlight

Content analysis and coding. Thematic analysis.

The content of some communication doesn't need that much analysis.

Apply it

A researcher investigates the degree of aggression exhibited in online communications. She has to collect examples of online communication and decides to use content analysis to test her hypothesis.

Bearing in mind the aim of the study, explain how the researcher could code her data.

Knowledge Check

1. A researcher intends to investigate one father's role in parenting. Explain how the researcher might conduct this case study. *(4 marks)*

2. Explain the difference between content analysis and thematic analysis. *(4 marks)*

Reliability

Spec spotlight

Reliability across all methods of investigation. Ways of assessing reliability: test-retest and inter-observer; improving reliability.

'What do I love about him?' mused Duck. 'It's his reliability I suppose. He doesn't say much and he never buys me flowers – but no matter where I go, and however long I go for, he'll never be far from where I left him.'

Reliability: it ain't great unless it's ...

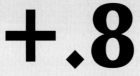

Statisticians don't write correlations with a leading zero and in reality they always write it as two decimal places but +.80 kinda spoils the rhyme!

Apply it

A clinical psychologist constructed a questionnaire to measure the amount of stress experienced by sixth-form students.

1. She decided to check the reliability of her questionnaire. Explain how she could have done this.

2. The psychologist discovered that the reliability of her questionnaire was low. Explain **one** way in which she could have improved the reliability of the questionnaire.

Reliability

Reliability is a measure of *consistency*.	If a particular measurement is repeated and the same result is obtained then that measurement is described as being reliable. Reliability = consistency.

Ways of assessing reliability

Test–retest. Test the same person twice.	The same test or questionnaire is given to the same person on two or more different occasions.
	If the test or questionnaire is reliable the results should be the same (or very similar) each time it is administered.
Inter-observer. Compares observations from different observers.	In an observation, two or more observers compare their data by conducting a *pilot study* – a small-scale trial run of the observation to check that observers are applying behavioural categories in the same way.
	Observers should watch the same event, or sequence of events, but record their data independently.
Reliability is measured using a **correlation**.	In test–retest and inter-observer reliability, the two sets of scores are correlated. The correlation coefficient should exceed +.80 for reliability.

Improving reliability

Questionnaires. Rewrite questions.	A questionnaire that produces low test–retest reliability may need some items to be deselected or rewritten.
	The researcher may replace some open questions (which respondents interpret inconsistently) with closed, fixed-choice alternatives which may be less ambiguous.
Interviews. Improved training.	The best way of ensuring reliability in an interview is to use the same interviewer each time.
	If this is not possible, all interviewers must be trained (e.g. so they avoid questions that are leading or ambiguous).
Observations. Operationalisation of behavioural categories.	Behavioural categories should be **operationalised** and measurable (e.g. 'pushing' is less open to interpretation than 'aggression').
	Categories should not overlap (e.g. 'hugging' and 'cuddling'), all possible behaviours should be included.
	If categories are overlapping or absent, different observers have to use their own judgement in deciding what to record and where, and may end up with inconsistent records.
Experiments. Standardised procedures.	In order to compare the performance of different participants, the procedures must be the same (consistent) every time. Therefore **standardised procedures** are the experimenter's concern.

Types of validity

Validity = is the result *legitimate*?	Whether an observed effect is genuine and represents what is actually 'out there' in the real world.
Data can be reliable but not valid.	e.g. an IQ test may produce the same result every time when the same people are tested but not measure what it is designed to.
Internal validity	Control within a study e.g. reduce **demand characteristics**.
External validity	Generalising to other settings, populations or eras.
Ecological validity Do findings generalise to other settings?	Ecological validity refers to whether findings can be **generalised** from one setting to another, most particularly generalised to everyday life. This may not relate to the setting (e.g. a lab) but more to the realism of the participants' task.
Temporal validity Do findings remain true over time?	Findings should be consistent over time. e.g. Asch's study may lack temporal validity because it was conducted during a conformist era in US history.

Ways of assessing validity

Face validity A test looks like it measures what it claims to.	A basic method to assess validity – does the test measure what it's supposed to measure 'on the face of it'? This is achieved by simply 'eyeballing' the measuring instrument or by passing it to an expert to check.
Concurrent validity Whether findings are similar to those on a well-established test.	A new intelligence test, for instance, may be administered to a group of participants. Their scores are then compared with performance on a well-established test (correlation should exceed +.80 for validity).

Improving validity

Experiments. Control group and standardisation.	A **control group** means that a researcher is more sure that changes in the DV were due to the effect of the IV. Standardised procedures and single-/double-blind minimise impact of participant reactivity and investigator effects.
Questionnaires. Lie scale and confidentiality.	Lie scales control for the effects of **social desirability bias**. Respondents are assured that all data submitted is confidential.
Observations. Good categories.	Behavioural categories that are well-defined, thoroughly operationalised and not ambiguous or overlapping.
Qualitative research. Interpretive validity and triangulation.	Interpretive validity shown through the coherence of narrative and direct quotes from participants. Triangulation involves using a number of different sources as evidence (e.g. interview data, personal diaries, etc.).

Does it do what it says on the tin? If the answer's yes, then it's got validity.

Knowledge Check

1. In the context of any research method, explain the difference between reliability and validity. *(4 marks)*

2. Two psychologists conducted an observational study of behaviour at a pedestrian crossing. Explain how inter-observer reliability could be established **and** what could be done to improve it if it was low. *(4 marks)*

3. A psychologist conducted an experiment in which he measured attachment behaviour in young children. Explain **two** ways in which he could have assessed the validity of this experiment. *(2 marks + 2 marks)*

Statistical testing

Spec spotlight

Factors affecting the choice of statistical test, including level of measurement (nominal, ordinal and interval) and experimental design. When to use the following tests: Spearman's *rho*, Pearson's *r*, Wilcoxon, Mann–Whitney, related *t*-test, unrelated *t*-test and Chi-Squared test.

Luck is when people take probability personally.

Knowledge Check

1. A psychologist investigated whether older people (over 50) or younger people (under 30) were more likely to binge-drink alcohol. Which statistical test should the psychologist use to analyse the data? Give **three** reasons for your choice. *(1 mark + 3 marks)*

2. Give **three** reasons why a researcher would use a Wilcoxon test to analyse data from a research study. *(3 marks)*

3. A psychologist compared the number of people working day shifts and night shifts who reported being depressed or happy. Which statistical test should the psychologist use to analyse the data? Give **three** reasons for your choice. *(1 mark + 3 marks)*

Statistical testing

Statistical tests are used to see if results are due to *chance*.

A statistical test is used to determine whether a difference or association/**correlation** found in a particular investigation is statistically significant (i.e. whether the result could have occurred by chance or there is a real effect).

Criteria for statistical (inferential) tests

Three criteria.

1. Looking for a difference or a correlation/association?
2. Is experimental design related (repeated measures/matched pairs) or unrelated (independent groups)?
3. What is the level of measurement? See below.

Choosing a statistical test.

	Test of difference		Test of association or correlation
	Unrelated design	Related design	
Nominal data	Chi-Squared	Sign test	Chi-Squared
Ordinal data	Mann–Whitney	Wilcoxon	Spearman's *rho*
Interval data	Unrelated *t*-test	Related *t*-test	Pearson's *r*

Note that Chi-Squared is a test of both difference and association/correlation. Data items must be unrelated.

Also note that the three tests on the blue background are parametric tests (the two forms of *t*-test and Pearson's *r*). The criteria for a parametric test are – interval level data, normal distribution expected and homogeneity of variance (standard deviation squared).

Levels of measurement

Nominal data.

Categories.

Each item can only appear in one category. There is no order.

For example, people naming their favourite football team.

Ordinal data.

Placed in order, intervals are subjective.

Data is collected on a numerical, ordered scale but intervals are variable, so that a score of 8 is not twice as much as a score of 4.

Ordinal data lacks precision because it is based on subjective opinion rather than objective measures.

For example, asking someone to rate how much they like psychology on a scale of 1 to 10.

Interval data.

Units of equal, precisely defined size.

Interval data is based on numerical scales that include units of equal, precisely defined size.

This includes counting observations in an observational study (8 tallies is twice as much as 4 tallies) or any 'public' unit of measurement (e.g. time, temperature).

Interval data is 'better' than ordinal data because more detail is preserved.

Probability and significance

If the statistical test is not significant the *null hypothesis* is accepted.	The null hypothesis states there is 'no difference' or 'no correlation' between the conditions.
	The statistical test determines which hypothesis (null or alternative) is 'true' and thus which we accept and reject.
The null hypothesis is accepted or rejected at a particular level of *probability*.	*Probability* is a measure of the likelihood that a particular event will occur, where 0 is a statistical impossibility and 1 a statistical certainty.
	There are no statistical certainties in psychology but there is a *significance level* – the point at which the null hypothesis is accepted or rejected.

Use of statistical tables

The *calculated* and *critical* values.	To check for statistical significance the calculated value (result of the statistical test) is compared with a critical value in a table of critical values based on probabilities.
Using *tables of critical values*.	To find the correct critical value, there are three criteria:
	• Hypothesis one-tailed (directional) or two-tailed (non-directional).
	• Number (*N*) of participants or degrees of freedom (*df*).
	• Level of significance (or *p* value).
The usual *level of significance* is 0.05 (or 5%).	This means there is a 5% chance that the results of a particular study sample occurred even if there was no real difference in the population (i.e. the null hypothesis is true).
	Sometimes a more stringent (1%) level is used, e.g. drug trials.

Type I and Type II errors

Type I error.	The null hypothesis is rejected and the alternative hypothesis is accepted when the null hypothesis is 'true'.
	This is an optimistic error or false positive as a significant difference or correlation is found when one does not exist.
Type II error.	The null hypothesis is accepted but, in reality, the alternative hypothesis is 'true'.
	This is a pessimistic error or false negative.
What makes each error more likely?	A Type I error is more likely to be made if the significance level is too lenient (too high, e.g. 0.1 or 10%).
	A Type II error is more likely if the significance level is too stringent (too low, e.g. 0.01 or 1%), as potentially significant values may be missed.

There are 7.5 billion people on the planet. So even if you are one in a million, there are still 7,500 people like you. Sobering thought.

The rule of R

Some statistical tests require the calculated value to be equal to or more *than* the critical value for statistical significance. For other tests, the calculated value must be equal to or less than the critical value.

The rule of R can help with this. Those statistical tests with a letter 'R' in their name are those where the calculated value must be equal to or more than the critical value (note that there is also an 'r' in 'more' which is a further clue!).

Knowledge Check

1. A psychologist collected data in a study and analysed it with a statistical test. The result of the test was significant at $p \leq 0.05$. What is meant by the phrase 'the result of the test was significant at $p \leq 0.05$'? *(2 marks)*

2. In relation to statistical testing, explain what is meant by 'probability'. *(2 marks)*

3. In relation to statistical testing, explain the difference between a Type I and Type II error. *(4 marks)*

Inferential tests

Spec spotlight

Students should demonstrate knowledge and understanding of inferential testing and be familiar with the use of inferential tests.

An *inferential test* is another term for a *statistical test*.

The sign test is the only test you may be asked to calculate in an exam.

It is expected that you will be familiar with the use of the other inferential tests named in the specification.

Apply it

1. A researcher uses the Wilcoxon test to analyse his data. The results are shown in the table below. Fill in the column 'Rank' by ranking the differences.

Participant	Difference between condition A and B	Rank
1	6	
2	3	
3	16	
4	6	
5	4	
6	19	
7	12	
8	6	
9	4	

2. A class of psychology students want to assess whether 8-year-old children are better than 5-year-old children at solving logical puzzles.

Here are their findings:

Six of the 5-year-olds could solve the puzzle but 27 couldn't.

28 of the 8-year-olds could solve the puzzle but 9 couldn't.

Add this data to the contingency table below, including the row and column totals and the overall total.

	5-year-olds	8-year-olds	Column total
Could solve puzzle			
Could not solve puzzle			
Row total			

Inferential tests

Sign test	**Step 1** Enter pairs of related data in a table.
	Step 2 For each pair, score plus or minus (*plus* if item 1 > item 2 or if the items are the same, *minus* if item 1 < item 2 or if the items are different).
	Step 3 S = the number of less frequent sign (plus or minus).
	Step 4 Compare calculated value (S) with critical value.

Mann–Whitney test	**Step 1** Rank all data.
	• List all the data from lowest to highest. Lowest number has a rank of 1.
	• Where two data items are the same, add up the ranks they would get and use the mean for those ranks.
	Step 2 Work out the calculated value of U.
	• Add total ranks for Group A (R_A) and total for Group B (R_B)
	• Use the smaller value of R to calculate either U_A or U_B.
	• $U_A = R_A - \dfrac{[N_A (N_A + 1)]}{2}$ (N_A = number of participants in Group A)
	Step 3 Compare calculated value (U_A or U_B) with critical value.

Wilcoxon test	**Step 1** Calculate the difference between each pair of data. And then rank the differences.
	Step 2 Work out the calculated value of T. T is the sum of the less frequent sign.
	Step 3 Compare calculated value (T) with critical value.

Spearman's rho	**Step 1** Rank each set of scores separately.
	Step 2 Find the difference (d) between each pair of ranks, square it and add them up ($\sum d^2$).
	Step 3 Work out the calculated value of *rho*.
	$rho = 1 - \dfrac{6\sum d^2}{N(N^2 - 1)}$ Where $\sum$ = 'sum of'
	Step 4 Compare calculated value (*rho*) with critical value.

You might be asked to substitute values in a formula.

If $\sum d^2 = 43$ and $N = 14$

$rho = 1 - [(6 \times 43) / (14 \times (14 \times 14 - 1))]$

$= 1 - [258 / 2730]$ = .91 (answer to 2 decimal places)

Chi-Squared	**Step 1** Fill data (observed values, O) in a contingency table (see left).
	Step 2 Calculate expected frequencies (E) for each cell (row total × column total and divide by overall total).
	Step 3 Work out the calculated value of χ^2. $\chi^2 = \sum (O - E)^2 / E$.
	Step 4 Compare calculated value (χ^2) with critical value.

Inferential tests

Pearson's r Unrelated and related t-test	The formula for these tests is very complex and very unlikely to be used in an exam. You might be required to calculate the degrees of freedom (df): Pearson's r $df = N - 2$ Related t-test $df = N - 1$ Unrelated t-test $df = N_A + N_B - 2$ (N_A is the number of participants in Condition A and N_B is the number of participants in Condition B).

Checking a table of critical values.	For all inferential tests, after you have worked out the calculated value, this is then compared with values in the table of critical values, and a statement made about whether the null hypothesis must be accepted or can be rejected. This is the table of critical values for the Wilcoxon test:

Level of significance for a one-tailed test	0.05	0.025	0.01
Level of significance for a two-tailed test	0.10	0.05	0.02
$N =$ 5	0		
6	2	0	
7	3	2	0
8	5	3	1
9	8	5	3
10	11	8	5

In the exam you may be asked to check whether a particular calculated value is significant using a table of critical values.

Calculated value of T must be EQUAL TO or LESS THAN the critical value in this table for significance to be shown.

In an exam you will be given a table similar to this.

Step 1   Select the one-tailed row or the two-tailed row depending on whether the hypothesis was directional or non-directional.

Step 2   Select the row that represents the number of participants in your study. For example, if your study had 9 participants, select the row $N = 9$

Step 3   Determine significance.

Look at your calculated value, let's say $T = 6$. At the bottom of the table, the instructions say the calculated value must be EQUAL TO or LESS THAN the critical value for significance to be shown. Our value is less than 8 but not less than 5.

Therefore,

- One-tailed test – result is significant at the 5% level.
- Two-tailed test – result is not significant at the 5% level.

Step 4   For a one-tailed test we can reject the null hypothesis ($p \le 0.05$) and accept the alternative hypothesis. But for a two-tailed test we would have to accept the null hypothesis ($p \le 0.05$).

NO to learning FORMULA

You do NOT have to learn any formula.

The mathematical skills section says 'Substitute numerical values into algebraic equations using appropriate units for physical quantities. Solve simple algebraic equations'.

A possible YES to substitution

You MIGHT be asked to substitute values in a formula but you would be given the formula. You just need to be familiar with the abbreviations.

Knowledge Check

1. A psychologist used an unrelated t-test. Group A has 12 participants. Group B has 16 participants. Calculate the degrees of freedom (df) using this formula:
$df = N_A + N_B - 2$ *(2 marks)*

2. A correlational study has ordinal data so Spearman's *rho* is used to analyse the results. The formula for this statistic is:
$$1 - \frac{6\sum d^2}{N(N^2 - 1)}$$
The researcher works out that $\sum d^2 = 309$ and $N = 20$.
Calculate the value of *rho* to 2 decimal places.   *(3 marks)*

3. State the level of significance for your result using the critical values below (directional hypothesis). *(2 marks)*

Level of significance for a one-tailed test	0.05	0.025
Level of significance for a two-tailed test	0.10	0.05
$N = 20$	.380	.447

Reporting psychological investigations

Spec spotlight

Reporting psychological investigations. Sections of a scientific report: abstract, introduction, method, results, discussion and referencing.

Experimental psychologist's Valentine's poem:

Roses are red,
Violets are blue,
If you were a null hypothesis,
I would fail to reject you.

Apply it

A researcher conducted an experiment, collected and analysed data and drew conclusions. He now has to write a report of the experiment.

1. Identify **six** sections that he should include.

2. Choose **one** of these sections and briefly explain what information he should include.

Knowledge Check

1. In relation to reporting psychological investigations, explain what is meant by the 'abstract'. *(2 marks)*

2. Identify **two** sections of a report of a psychological investigation. *(2 marks)*

3. Explain what information should be included in the method section of a report of a psychological investigation. *(4 marks)*

Sections of a scientific report

Abstract. A summary of the study.	A short summary (about 150–200 words in length) that includes all the major elements: the aims and hypotheses, method/procedure, results and conclusions.
Introduction. A literature review.	A look at relevant theories, concepts and studies. The research review should follow a logical progression – beginning broadly and becoming more specific until the aims and hypotheses are presented.
Method. Detailed enough for replication.	The method should include sufficient detail so that other researchers are able to **replicate** the study: <ul><li>Design (e.g. independent groups, naturalistic observation, etc.), and reasons/justification given for the choice.</li><li>Sample – how many participants, biographical/demographic information (as long as this does not compromise anonymity), the sampling method and target population.</li><li>Apparatus/materials – detail of any assessment instruments used and other relevant materials.</li><li>Procedure – a 'recipe-style' list of everything that happened, includes briefing, **standardised instructions** and debriefing.</li><li>Ethics – how these were addressed within the study.</li></ul>
Results. Descriptive and inferential statistics.	A summary of key findings from the investigation. <ul><li>Descriptive statistics such as tables, graphs and charts, measures of central tendency and measures of dispersion.</li><li>Inferential statistics including reference to the choice of statistical test, calculated and critical values, level of significance and final outcome (i.e. which hypothesis was rejected).</li><li>Any raw data and any calculations appear in an appendix rather than the main body of the report.</li></ul>
Discussion. Evaluating the outcome.	There are several elements: <ul><li>Summary of findings in verbal, rather than statistical, form.</li><li>Relationship of the results to previous research (this research may have been presented in the introduction).</li><li>Limitations of the study, plus suggestions of how these might be addressed in a future study.</li><li>Wider real-world implications of the research.</li></ul>
Referencing.	Journal articles – author(s), date, article title, journal name (in italics), volume(issue), page numbers. e.g. Flanagan, C. (2016) Experiments in psychology. *Psychology Review, 23*(2), 23–25. Books: author(s), date, title of book (in italics), place of publication, publisher. e.g. Flanagan, C. and Berry, D. (2016) *A Level Psychology*, Cheltenham: Illuminate Publishing. Web references: source, date, title, weblink and date accessed. NHS (2018) Phobias: https://www.nhs.uk/conditions/phobias/ [Accessed May 2020].

Features of science

Paradigms and *paradigm shifts.*	Kuhn (1962) said that what distinguishes scientific disciplines from non-scientific disciplines is a shared set of assumptions and methods – a paradigm.
	Kuhn argued that social sciences (including psychology) lack a universally accepted paradigm and are best seen as 'pre-science', unlike natural sciences (e.g. biology).
	Paradigm shifts occur when there is a scientific revolution. A handful of researchers question the accepted paradigm when there is too much contradictory evidence to ignore.
Theory construction.	A theory is a set of general laws or principles that have the ability to explain particular events or behaviours.
	Testing a theory depends on being able to make clear and precise statements (hypotheses) on the basis of the theory.
	A hypothesis can then be tested using scientific methods to determine whether it will be supported or refuted.
	The process of deriving a new hypothesis from an existing theory is known as deduction.
Falsifiability. Proof is not possible. *Hypothesis testing.*	Popper (1934) argued that the key criterion of a scientific theory is its falsifiability.
	Genuine scientific theories should hold themselves up for hypothesis testing and the possibility of being proved false.
	Popper distinguished between theories which can be tested and falsified, and what he called 'pseudosciences' which couldn't be falsified.
Replicability. Testing the **validity** of research results.	If a scientific theory is to be 'trusted', the findings from it must be shown to be repeatable across a number of different contexts.
	By repeating a study, as Popper suggested, we can see the extent to which the findings can be **generalised**.
Objectivity. To reduce bias in research.	Scientific researchers must keep a 'critical distance' during research. They must not allow their personal opinions or biases to 'discolour' the data or influence the behaviour of participants.
	As a general rule, those methods in psychology that are associated with the greatest level of control (such as lab **experiments**) tend to be the most objective.
Empirical method. Direct experience.	Empirical methods emphasise the importance of data collection based on direct, sensory experience.
	The experimental method and the observational method are good examples of the empirical method in psychology.
	Early empiricists (such as Locke) saw knowledge as determined only by experience and sense perception. A theory cannot claim to be scientific unless it has been empirically tested.

Spec spotlight

Features of science: objectivity and the empirical method; replicability and falsifiability; theory construction and hypothesis testing; paradigms and paradigm shifts.

Falsification is about never having to say you're right.

Knowledge Check

1. Outline **two** features of science. *(2 marks + 2 marks)*
2. Explain the importance of the empirical method in science. *(4 marks)*
3. In relation to features of science, explain what is meant by 'hypothesis testing' **and** 'paradigm shifts'. *(2 marks + 2 marks)*
4. Explain the difference between replicability and falsifiability in relation to features of science. *(4 marks)*

Spec spotlight

Gender and culture in Psychology – universality and bias. Gender bias including androcentrism and alpha and beta bias.

The burden of gender bias may have hampered the progress of women in psychology in the past. It's certainly not helping here...

Apply it

Two psychology students were discussing the issue of gender bias. Ed says, 'I think a lot of psychological theories suggest males are superior to females.' Louise replies, 'That's funny, because I think psychological research assumes males and females are basically the same.'

Referring to Ed and Louise's points of view, explain how gender bias might operate in psychology.

Links across the specification

In this chapter on issues and debates it is expected that you will draw on examples from your own studies of psychology. We have provided some examples but you should constantly be thinking of others as you read through this chapter.

The issue of gender bias

Universality and *bias*.	Psychologists possess beliefs and values influenced by the social and historical context within which they live. This may undermine psychologists' claims to discover *facts* about human behaviour that are objective, value-free and consistent across time and culture (universality).
	Bias is a leaning towards a personal view that doesn't reflect reality. Psychological theory and research may not accurately represent the experience and behaviour of men and women (= **gender bias**).
Alpha bias exaggerates differences.	Differences between the sexes are usually presented as fixed and inevitable.
	These differences occasionally heighten the value of women, but are more likely to devalue females in relation to males.
Examples of alpha bias. *Psychodynamic theory.*	Alpha bias favouring males – Freud (1905) claimed children, in the phallic stage, desire their opposite-sex parent. This is resolved by identification with their same-sex parent. But a girl's identification is weaker, creating a weaker Superego and weaker moral development.
	Alpha bias favouring females – Chodorow (1968) said that daughters and mothers are more connected than sons and mothers because of biological similarities – so women develop better bonds and empathy for others.
Beta bias minimises differences.	Ignoring or underestimating differences between men and women often occurs when female participants are not included in the research process but it is assumed that research findings apply equally to both sexes.
Examples of beta bias. *Fight or flight, tend and befriend.*	Early research into fight or flight was based on male animals (because female hormones fluctuate). Fight or flight was assumed to be a universal response to threat.
	Taylor *et al.* (2000) suggest that females exhibit a *tend and befriend* response governed by the hormone **oxytocin** which is more plentiful in women (but also present in small quantities in men) and reduces the fight or flight response. It is an evolved response for caring for young (see page 180).
Androcentrism. Male-centred.	Alpha and beta bias are consequences of androcentrism. Psychology has traditionally been a subject dominated by males – list of 100 famous psychologists contained 6 females.
	This leads to female behaviour being misunderstood and even pathologised (taken as a sign of illness).
	For example, feminists object to the category of *premenstrual syndrome* (PMS) because it medicalises female emotions (e.g. anger) by explaining these in hormonal terms. But male anger is often seen as a rational response to external pressures (Brescoll and Uhlmann 2008).

One limitation is that gender differences are given as fixed and enduring.

Maccoby and Jacklin (1974) concluded that girls have better verbal ability and boys better spatial ability – due to hardwired biological brain differences.

Joel *et al.* (2015) used brain scanning and found no such gender differences.

This suggests that we should be wary of accepting research as biological facts when it might be explained better as social stereotypes.

Counterpoint

Ingalhalikar *et al.* (2014) suggests the popular social stereotype that females are better at multitasking may have some biological truth to it – their hemispheres are better connected.

This suggests that there may be biological differences but we still should be wary of exaggerating the effect they may have on behaviour.

Another limitation is that gender bias promotes sexism in the research process.

Women are underrepresented in university departments (Murphy *et al.* 2014). Research is more likely to be conducted by males which may disadvantage females.

For example, a male researcher may expect female participants to be irrational and unable to complete complex tasks (Nicolson 1995), which may mean they underperform.

This means that the institutional structures and methods of psychology may produce findings that are gender-biased.

Is there a 'glass ceiling' in psychology, denying women opportunities at senior research level?

A further limitation is research challenging bias may not be published.

Formanowicz *et al.* (2018) analysed 1000 articles relating to gender bias – such research is funded less often and is published by less prestigious journals.

This still held true when gender bias was compared to ethnic bias, and when other factors were controlled (e.g. the gender of the author(s) and methodology).

This suggests that gender bias in psychological research may not be taken as seriously as other forms of bias.

Do you agree with this conclusion?

Evaluation extra: Good or bad?

Gender-biased research creates misleading assumptions about female behaviour, fails to challenge negative stereotypes and validates discriminatory practices.

However, modern researchers recognise the effect assumptions have on their work (*reflexivity*) and embrace them as a crucial aspect of the research process.

This suggests that gender bias may add an extra dimension to research if psychologists are up front about it in their work.

Knowledge Check

1. Explain what is meant by 'universality' **and** 'bias' in relation to gender.
   (2 marks + 2 marks)

2. Outline gender bias in psychology. Include in your answer reference to androcentrism. *(6 marks)*

3. In relation to gender bias in psychology, evaluate the roles of alpha bias **and** beta bias. *(6 marks)*

4. A news website carried this item: 'It's official! Men and women are different. Men really are better at maths and women really are better at talking, psychologists claimed yesterday'.

   With reference to this item, describe **and** evaluate the role of gender bias in psychology. *(16 marks)*

Gender and culture in Psychology: Cultural bias

Spec spotlight

Gender and culture in Psychology – universality and bias. Cultural bias, including ethnocentrism and cultural relativism.

This is Norm. People don't mess with Norm. Over the years, the norms of psychology may have created cultural bias.

Apply it

Lesley is a psychologist who replicates Milgram's obedience study in Japan. She finds that the levels of obedience are higher than in Milgram's study. She concludes that people are generally more obedient than Milgram believed.

Explain how Lesley's research and conclusion might involve cultural bias.

Revision BOOSTER

A word of warning. By all means use (for example) conformity studies (discussed at top of facing page) but the key word here is 'use'. Remember that the question you are answering is about cultural bias, not conformity as such.

So don't be sidetracked into describing Asch's conformity studies (which you will probably know a lot about, so it's tempting). Keep your focus on cultural bias.

Cultural bias	
Americans and students over-represented in research.	A review found that 68% of research participants came from the United States, and 96% from industrialised nations (Henrich *et al.* 2010). Another review found that 80% of research participants were undergraduates studying psychology (Arnett 2008).
WEIRD people set standard.	What we know about human behaviour has a strong **cultural bias**. Henrich *et al.* coined the term WEIRD to describe the group of people most likely to be studied by psychologists – Westernised, Educated people from Industrialised, Rich Democracies. If the norm or standard for a particular behaviour is set by WEIRD people, then the behaviour of people from non-Western, less educated, agricultural and poorer cultures are inevitably seen as 'abnormal', 'inferior' or 'unusual'.
Ethnocentrism. Superiority of own culture.	A form of cultural bias. In psychological research this may be communicated through a view that any behaviour that does not conform to a European/American standard is somehow deficient or underdeveloped.
Example of ethnocentrism – the *Strange Situation.*	Ainsworth and Bell's (1970) research on attachment type reflected the norms of US culture. They suggested that ideal (secure) attachment was defined as a baby showing moderate distress when left alone by the mother figure. This has led to misinterpretation of child-rearing practices in other countries which deviated from the US norm, e.g. Japanese babies rarely left on own, more likely to be classed as insecurely attached as they showed distress on separation (Takahashi 1986).
Cultural relativism helps to avoid cultural bias.	The 'facts' that psychologists discover may only make sense from the perspective of the culture within which they were discovered. Being able to recognise this is one way of avoiding cultural bias in research.
Universality versus cultural relativism (*etic* and *emic* approaches).	Berry (1969) argues that: • An etic approach looks at behaviour from outside a given culture and identifies behaviours that are universal. • An emic approach functions from inside a culture and identifies behaviours that are specific to that culture. Ainsworth and Bell's research illustrates an *imposed etic* – they studied behaviours inside a single culture (America) and then assumed their ideal attachment type could be applied universally.

One limitation is many classic studies are culturally-biased.

Both Asch's and Milgram's original studies were conducted with white middle-class US participants. **Replications** of these studies in different countries produced rather different results.

Asch-type **experiments** in **collectivist** cultures found significantly higher rates of conformity than the original studies in the US, an **individualist** culture (e.g. Smith and Bond 1993).

This suggests our understanding of topics such as social influence should only be applied to individualist cultures.

Counterpoint

Individualism–collectivism distinction may no longer apply due to increasing global media, e.g. Takano and Osaka (1999) found that 14 of 15 studies comparing the US and Japan found no evidence of individualist versus collectivist differences.

This suggests that cultural bias in research may be less of an issue in more recent psychological research.

One strength is the emergence of cultural psychology.

Cultural psychology is the study of how people shape and are shaped by their cultural experience (Cohen 2017). It is an emerging field that takes an emic approach.

Research is conducted from inside a culture, often alongside local researchers using culturally-based techniques. Fewer cultures are considered when comparing differences (usually just two).

This suggests that modern psychologists are mindful of the dangers of cultural bias and are taking steps to avoid it.

Another limitation is ethnic stereotyping.

Gould (1981) explained how the first intelligence tests led to eugenic social policies in America. During WWI psychologists gave IQ tests to 1.75 million army recruits.

Many test items were ethnocentric (e.g. name US presidents) so recruits from south-eastern Europe and African-Americans scored lowest and were deemed genetically inferior.

This illustrates how cultural bias can be used to justify prejudice and discrimination towards ethnic and cultural groups.

Evaluation extra: Relativism versus universality.

Cross-cultural research can challenge dominant individualist ways of thinking and viewing the world. This may provide us with a better understanding of human nature.

However, research (e.g. Ekman 1989) suggests that facial expressions for emotions (such as disgust) are the same all over the world, so some behaviours are universal.

This suggests a full understanding of human behaviour requires both, but for too long the universal view dominated.

Evidence suggests that some emotions, such as disgust, are universal in the way they are expressed. I'm no expert but I reckon this lass isn't a huge broccoli fan...

Revision BOOSTER

What's the Number One route to evaluating an explanation or concept? The answer is – THINK LINK. You've probably noticed that the evaluation sections of this Revision Guide are chock-full of research studies. You need to make sure you use them effectively.

Knowledge Check

1. In relation to culture in psychology, explain what is meant by 'bias' **and** 'universality'. *(2 marks + 2 marks)*

2. Using an example, outline the effect of ethnocentrism on psychology. *(4 marks)*

3. Discuss the role of cultural relativism in psychology. *(6 marks)*

4. Some psychological research has been criticised for studying behaviour in one culture and assuming the findings apply to all cultures.

   Discuss cultural bias in psychology. *(16 marks)*

Free will and determinism

Spec spotlight

Free will and determinism: hard determinism and soft determinism; biological, environmental and psychic determinism. The scientific emphasis on causal explanations.

Not everyone succumbs to environmental determinism.

Apply it

Sanj has a serious mental disorder. His dad and other members of his family also have the disorder. Sanj experienced a great deal of trauma and stress as he was growing up. He spent little time at school and eventually turned to crime and drugs.

Using Sanj's experience as an example, explain what is meant by determinism. Refer to **three** types of determinism in your answer.

Revision BOOSTER

There are some things you just have to remember. Quite a lot of things, actually. So try this. Once you've thoroughly familiarised yourself with what's on a page, close the book. But wait, there's more. Then, write down everything you can remember about what you've just read. Organise it, structure it, focus on headings and key words. Start with the 'big picture'. Then fill in the details.

The free will–determinism debate

The debate.	Is our behaviour a matter of **free will** or are we the product of internal and/or external influences?
	Most approaches in psychology are **determinist** but disagree on the causes of human behaviour.

Key concepts of the debate

Free will. Self-determining.	The notion of free will suggests humans are free to make choices.
	There are biological and environmental influences on our behaviour – but free will implies we can reject them.
	This is the view of the **humanistic** approach.
Determinism.	**Hard determinism** (*fatalism*) suggests that all human action has a cause, and it should be possible to identify these causes.
	Soft determinism suggests that all human action has a cause but people have freedom to make choices within a restricted range of options.
Types of determinism.	**Biological determinism** The **biological** approach describes many causes of behaviour, e.g. the influence of the **autonomic nervous system** on stress or the influence of genes on mental health.
	Modern biological psychologists would recognise the mediating influence of the environment on our biological structures (another determinist influence).
	Environmental determinism Skinner described free will as 'an illusion' and all behaviour as the result of conditioning.
	Our experience of 'choice' is the sum total of reinforcement contingencies that have acted upon us throughout our lives.
	Psychic determinism Freud emphasised the influence of biological drives and unconscious conflicts repressed in childhood.
	Even something as seemingly random as a 'slip of the tongue' can be explained by the unconscious.
Science seeks to find *causal explanations* where one thing is determined by another.	A basic principle of science is that every event has a cause and these can be explained with general laws. Knowledge of these allows scientists to predict and control events.
	In psychology, the laboratory **experiment** allows researchers to simulate the conditions of the test tube and remove all other **extraneous variables** to demonstrate a causal effect.

One strength of free will is it has practical value.

Roberts *et al.* (2000) looked at adolescents who had a strong belief in fatalism – that their lives were 'decided' by events outside of their control.

They were at greater risk of developing depression. People who exhibit an internal, rather than external, *locus of control* are more likely to be optimistic.

This suggests that, even if we do not have free will, the fact that we believe we do may have a positive impact on mind and behaviour.

'I cannot be held responsible for this crime, your Honour. A combination of psychic, biological and environmental determinism made me do it.'

Dave's carefully researched defence was starting to fall apart.

One limitation is evidence doesn't support free will, it supports determinism.

Libet *et al.* (1983) asked participants to randomly flick their wrist and say when they felt the will to move. Brain activity was also measured.

The *unconscious* brain activity leading up to the *conscious* decision to move came half a second *before* the participant's conscious decision to move.

This may be interpreted as meaning that even our most basic experiences of free will are actually determined by our brain before we are aware of them.

Counterpoint

The fact that people consciously become aware of decisions milliseconds after they had begun to enact the decision still means they may have made the decision to act. Our consciousness of the decision is a 'read-out' of our sometimes unconscious decision-making.

This suggests this evidence is not appropriate as a challenge to free will.

One limitation of determinism is the role of responsibility in law.

The hard determinist stance is not consistent with the way in which our legal system operates. In court, offenders are held responsible for their actions.

Indeed, the main principle of our legal system is that the defendant exercised their free will in committing the crime.

This suggests that, in the real world, determinist arguments do not work.

Herr Professor Sigismund Schlomo Freud.

Evaluation extra: Do we want determinism?

Determinism places psychology on equal footing with other more established sciences and has led to valuable real-world applications, such as therapies.

However free will has intuitive appeal. Most of us see ourselves as making our own choices rather than being 'pushed' by forces we cannot control. Some people (e.g. child of a criminal parent) prefer to think that they are free to self-determine.

This suggests that if psychology wants to position itself alongside the natural sciences, determinist accounts are likely to be preferred. However, common-sense experience may be better understood by an analysis of free will.

Knowledge Check

1. Explain the difference between hard determinism and soft determinism. *(4 marks)*

2. Briefly outline **three** types of determinism. *(2 marks + 2 marks + 2 marks)*

3. Briefly discuss the strengths **and/or** limitations of taking a determinist approach in psychology. *(8 marks)*

4. Discuss free will **and** determinism in psychology. *(16 marks)*

The nature–nurture debate

Spec spotlight

The nature–nurture debate: the relative importance of heredity and environment in determining behaviour; the interactionist approach.

'It says in here that genetic similarity may cause people to behave, think and dress in the same way,' said Len. 'Sounds like baloney to me,' replied Ken.

Twin studies

MZ twins share 100% of genes but **DZ twins** only 50% (on average) – so we would expect a greater likelihood of both MZ twins developing the same behaviour if it is mostly genetic.

This is because both MZ and DZ twins are raised together in the same environment, but MZ twins have a greater degree of genetic similarity than DZs.

Revision BOOSTER

IQ is mentioned as an example on the right. But lots of other characteristics, such as schizophrenia or depression, have a heritability coefficient around 50%. So all of them are good examples to use to illustrate an interactionist approach to the nature–nurture debate.

The nature–nurture debate

Interactionist approach.	It is not really a debate because all characteristics combine nature and nurture (even eye colour is only .80 heritable).
	For example attachment can be explained in terms of quality of parental love (Bowlby 1958) or child's temperament (Kagan 1984). Environment and heredity interact.
Diathesis-stress model.	In the **diathesis-stress model** behaviour is caused by a biological/environmental vulnerability (diathesis) which is only expressed when coupled with a biological/ environmental trigger (stressor).
	For example, a person who inherits a genetic vulnerability for OCD may not develop the disorder. But, combined with a psychological trigger (e.g. a traumatic experience) this may result in the disorder appearing.
Epigenetics.	Epigenetics is a change in genetic activity without changing the genetic code.
	Lifestyle and events we encounter (e.g. smoking, diet, trauma, war) leave 'marks' on our DNA (genes) – switching genes on or off.
	This has a lifelong influence and can be passed on to future generations.

Key concepts of the debate

Nature. Inherited influences (e.g. genes).	Early nativists (e.g. Descartes, 17th century) argued that human characteristics are innate – the result of our genes.
	Psychological characteristics (e.g. intelligence or personality) are determined by biological factors, just like eye colour or height.
Nurture. Environmental influences.	Empiricists (e.g. Locke, 17th century) argued the mind is a blank slate at birth, and is shaped by interaction with the environment e.g. the **behaviourist** approach.
	Lerner (1986) identified different levels of the environment: • Prenatal terms, e.g. mother smoking or hearing music. • Postnatal experiences, e.g. the social conditions a child grows up in.
Measuring nature and nurture.	*Concordance* – the degree to which two people are similar on a particular trait.
	Heritability – proportion of differences between individuals in a population, with regards to a particular trait, due to genes. 0.01 (1%) is very little contribution, 1.0 (100%) means genes are the only reason.
	The figure for heritability in IQ is about 0.5 (Plomin 1994).

One strength in nature–nurture research is adoption studies.

If adopted children are more similar to their adoptive parents, suggests environmental influence, if more similar to biological parents, suggests genetic influence.

Rhee and Waldman (2002) found in a **meta-analysis** of adoption studies that genetic influences accounted for 41% of variance in aggression.

This shows how research can separate nature and nurture influences.

Counterpoint

Children create their own nurture by selecting environments appropriate to their nature – a naturally aggressive child will choose aggressive friends and become more aggressive (niche-picking, Plomin).

This suggests that it does not make sense to look at evidence of either nature or nurture.

Father passing on his love of 'music' to his daughter. Hmmm... those hair colours look familiar...

Another strength of the nature–nurture debate is support for epigenetics.

In 1944, the Nazis blocked the distribution of food to the Dutch people and 22,000 died of starvation (the *Dutch Hunger Winter*).

Susser and Lin (1992) found that women who became pregnant during the famine had low birth weight babies who were twice as likely to develop schizophrenia.

This suggests that the life experiences of previous generations can leave epigenetic 'markers' that influence the health of their offspring.

A further strength is the debate can have real-world application.

Nestadt *et al.* (2010) put the heritability rate at .76 for OCD i.e. it is highly heritable. Such understanding can inform *genetic counselling*.

People who have a high genetic risk of OCD because of their family background can receive education about inheritance, management and prevention of the disorder.

This shows that the debate is not just theoretical but that it is also important, at a practical level, to understand the interaction between nature and nurture.

Evaluation extra: Implications of the debate.

The extreme nativist stance is **determinist** and has led to controversy, e.g. linking ethnicity, genetics and intelligence, and eugenic policies.

Empiricists suggest that any behaviour can be changed by altering environmental conditions (e.g. **aversion therapy**). This may lead to a society that controls and manipulates its citizens.

This shows that both positions, taken to extremes, may have dangerous consequences for society so a moderate, interactionist position is preferred.

Apply it

Most psychologists agree that both heredity and environment play a role in determining behaviour. But they disagree on how important their contributions are.

1. Choose a specific behaviour that is familiar to you from your Year 1 studies (e.g. OCD). Use your knowledge of the nature–nurture debate to explain how heredity and environment determine the behaviour.

2. Outline how the interactionist approach tries to resolve the debate.

Knowledge Check

1. Explain what is meant by the 'nature–nurture debate'. *(4 marks)*

2. Briefly discuss the relative importance of heredity and environment in determining behaviour. *(8 marks)*

3. In relation to the nature–nurture debate, briefly evaluate the interactionist approach. *(4 marks)*

4. This article appeared on a magazine's website: 'The way we behave comes down to a combination of factors. People are shaped by their experiences, families and upbringing. But they are also born with characteristics that contribute to who they are'.

   With reference to the issues raised above, discuss the nature–nurture debate in psychology. *(16 marks)*

Holism and reductionism

Spec spotlight

Holism and reductionism: levels of explanation in psychology. Biological reductionism and environmental (stimulus-response) reductionism.

'The whole is greater than the sum of its parts.' Where cake is concerned, she's inclined to agree.

Apply it

Brendan and Stacey both have obsessive-compulsive disorder (OCD) and have been learning more about their condition. Brendan says, 'I think it's a psychological thing really because it's mainly about the obsessive thoughts.' But Stacey disagrees: 'For me it's more to do with biological factors because I find that medication helps.'

Explain the role of reductionism in psychology. Address both Brendan's and Stacey's arguments in your answer.

Revision BOOSTER

Reductionism – it can be a tricky one. Students often misunderstand it and therefore misuse the concept in exam answers. Examiners frequently read that a reductionist approach is one that 'ignores other factors'. Try to avoid this very general point. Instead, consider that reductionism is more to do with explaining particular behaviours or phenomena at the simplest level possible. Oh, and don't forget about holism.

The holism–reductionism debate

Not a continuum.	Debate over which position is preferable for psychology – study the whole person (**holism**) or study component parts (**reductionism**).
	As soon as you break down the 'whole' it isn't holistic. Reductionism can be broken down into *levels of explanation*.

Key concepts of the debate

Holism. The whole.	Holism proposes that it only makes sense to study a whole system – the whole is greater than the sum of its parts (Gestalt psychology).
	For example **humanistic** psychology focuses on experience which can't be reduced to biological units, qualitative methods investigate themes.
Reductionism. Breaking into parts.	Reductionism is based on the scientific principle of *parsimony* – that all phenomena should be explained using the simplest (lowest level) principles.
Levels of explanation from highest to lowest.	For example, OCD may be understood in different ways: • Socio-cultural level – behaviour most people would regard as odd (e.g. repetitive handwashing). • Psychological level – the individual's experience of having obsessive thoughts. • Physical level – the sequence of movements involved in washing one's hands. • Environmental/behavioural level – learning experiences (conditioning). • Physiological level – abnormal functioning in the frontal lobes. • Neurochemical level – underproduction of **serotonin**. Can argue about which is the 'best' explanation of OCD, but each level is more reductionist than the one before.
Biological reductionism.	**Biological reductionism** suggests all behaviour can be explained through neurochemical, physiological, **evolutionary** and/or **genetic** influences. For example, drugs that increase serotonin are used to treat OCD. Therefore low serotonin may be a cause of OCD. We have reduced OCD to the level of neurotransmitter activity.
Environmental reductionism.	**Environmental reductionism** proposes that all behaviour is acquired through interactions with the environment, e.g. the **behaviourist** approach (stimulus–response links). For example, the learning theory of attachment reduces the idea of love (between baby and mother) to a learned association between the mother (neutral stimulus) and food (unconditioned stimulus) resulting in pleasure (conditioned response).

One limitation of holism is that it may lack practical value.

Holistic accounts of human behaviour become hard to use as they become more complex which presents researchers with a practical dilemma.

If many different factors contribute to, say, depression, then it becomes difficult to know which is most influential and which to prioritise for treatment.

This suggests that holistic accounts may lack practical value (whereas reductionist account may be better).

Some behaviours only emerge within a group context. It would take a brave person to do this on their own...

One strength of reductionism is its scientific status.

In order to conduct well-controlled research variables need to **operationalised** – target behaviours broken down into constituent parts.

This makes it possible to conduct **experiments** or record observations (behavioural categories) in a way that is objective and reliable.

This scientific approach gives psychology greater credibility, placing it on equal terms with the natural sciences.

Counterpoint

Reductionist explanations at the level of the gene or neurotransmitter do not include an analysis of the context within which behaviour occurs and therefore lack meaning.

This suggests that reductionist explanations can only ever form part of an explanation.

Revision BOOSTER

You have just over a minute to spend writing for each mark in the exam – but make sure you give that amount of time to the short-answer questions. It's probably easier to boost your marks on these rather than on essay questions.

One limitation of reductionism is the need for higher level explanations.

There are aspects of social behaviour that only emerge within a group context and cannot be understood in terms of the individual group members.

For example, the Stanford prison study could not be understood by observing the participants as individuals, it was the behaviour of the group that was important.

This shows that, for some behaviours, higher (or even holistic) level explanations provide a more valid account.

Not everyone agrees with this conclusion. What do you think?

Knowledge Check

1. Explain what is meant by 'levels of explanation in psychology'. *(4 marks)*

2. Outline biological reductionism **and** environmental (stimulus-response) reductionism in psychology. *(6 marks)*

3. Evaluate reductionism in psychology. *(6 marks)*

4. Some psychologists believe that behaviour can only be fully understood by considering the whole person. Other psychologists believe behaviour has to be broken up into its constituent parts for a complete understanding.

   With reference to these **two** positions, discuss holism **and** reductionism in psychology. *(16 marks)*

Evaluation extra: Brain and mind.

A reductionist account of consciousness would argue that we are thinking machines – that **cognitive** processes are associated with physical processes in the brain.

On the other hand, neuroscientists struggle to explain the subjective experience of the same neural process. This is referred to as the 'explanatory gap' in brain science.

This suggests that not all aspects of consciousness, particularly individual differences in experience, can be explained by brain activity.

Idiographic and nomothetic approaches

Spec spotlight

Idiographic and nomothetic approaches to psychological investigation.

There's always one isn't there – trying to make a point.

Point. Pencil. Geddit? Never mind.

Apply it

Sabiha, a teacher, decides to set up a classroom debate. She arranges it so half the class have to support the idiographic approach to psychological investigation and the other half have to support the nomothetic approach. Each side has to come up with: an example of their approach from an area of psychological research, an outline of their chosen example and in what way it is idiographic/nomothetic, two strengths of their example, one limitation of their example.

Outline each of the above for each side of the debate.

Revision BOOSTER

Note that the specification says '...approaches to psychological investigation', so keep your focus on research studies.

The idiographic–nomothetic debate

Two approaches.	Debate over which position is preferable for psychology: <ul><li>Detailed study of one individual or one group to provide in-depth understanding (*idiographic*), or</li><li>Study of larger groups with the aim of discovering norms, universal principles or 'laws' of behaviour (*nomothetic*).</li></ul> The two approaches may both have a place within a scientific study of the person.

Key concepts of the debate

Idiographic approach and *qualitative* research.	The number of participants is small, often a single individual/group. Research might include others e.g. family, friends. The initial focus is about understanding the individual, but **generalisations** may be made based on findings. Qualitative research e.g. individual with depression might be interviewed, emergent themes identified and conclusions formed. This might help inform mental health professionals determine best practice.
Examples in psychology.	Rogers' concept of counselling (page 22) was based on his work as a therapist. His 'theory' on the role of *unconditional positive regard* in self-development was based on his in-depth study of his clients. Freud's explanation of phobia was based on the detailed **case study** of Little Hans over many years (page 102).
Nomothetic approach and *quantitative* research.	General principles of behaviour (laws) are developed which are then applied in individual situations, such as in therapy. Quantitative research – hypotheses are formulated, samples of people (or animals) are gathered and data analysed for its statistical significance. Nomothetic approaches seek to quantify (count) human behaviour.
Examples in psychology.	Skinner studied animals to develop the general laws of learning (page 12). Sperry's split-brain research involved repeated testing and was, in part, the basis for understanding hemispheric lateralisation (page 32).
Objective versus subjective.	The nomothetic approach seeks **standardised** methods of assessing people. This ensures true **replication** occurs across samples of behaviour and removes the contaminating influence of bias. The idiographic approach tends *not* to believe that objectivity is possible in psychological research. It is people's individual experience of their unique context that is important.

One strength is idiographic and nomothetic approaches work together.

The idiographic approach uses in-depth qualitative methods which complements the nomothetic approach by providing detail.

In-depth **case studies** such as HM (damaged memory) may reveal insights about normal functioning which contribute to our overall understanding.

This suggests that even though the focus is on fewer individuals, the idiographic approach may help form 'scientific' laws of behaviour.

Counterpoint

Idiographic approach on own is restricted, no baseline for comparison, also unscientific and subjective.

This suggests that it is difficult to build effective general theories of human behaviour in the complete absence of nomothetic research.

Teri knew she was different. Very few other people would have paired a brown jacket with a grey scarf.

One strength is both approaches fit with the aims of science.

Nomothetic research (like natural sciences) seeks objectivity through standardisation, control and statistical testing.

Idiographic research also seeks objectivity through triangulation (comparing a range of studies), and reflexivity (researchers examine own biases).

This suggests that both the nomothetic and idiographic approaches raise psychology's status as a science.

Revision BOOSTER

This is where a thorough understanding of research methods is so useful. The idiographic–nomothetic debate is closely linked to choice of methodology (much less so about theory). Your understanding of the debate can only be improved by looking again at research methods.

One limitation of the nomothetic approach is the individual experience is lost.

Nomothetic approach focuses on general laws and may 'lose the whole person' within psychology.

For example, knowing about a 1% lifetime risk of schizophrenia says little about having the disorder – which might be useful for therapeutic ideas.

This means, in its search for generalities, the nomothetic approach may sometimes fail to relate to 'experience'.

Evaluation extra: Distinct or complementary?

Each approach is distinct and appropriate for different situations, e.g. Schaffer described general stages of attachment (nomothetic) whereas case studies of extreme neglect highlight subjective experience (idiographic).

However, they may be two ends of a continuum, e.g. when diagnosing personality disorders, clinicians begin with general nomothetic criteria, then focus on the individual unique needs (Millon 1995).

This suggests that these approaches are not either/or, we can consider the same topic from both perspectives.

Knowledge Check

1. Outline idiographic **and** nomothetic approaches to psychological investigation.
   (2 marks + 2 marks)
2. Explain **two** differences between idiographic and nomothetic approaches to psychological investigation.
   (2 marks + 2 marks)
3. Explain **one** limitation of nomothetic approaches to psychological investigation.
   (4 marks)
4. Describe **and** evaluate idiographic **and/or** nomothetic approaches to psychological investigation.
   (16 marks)

Ethical implications of research studies and theory

Spec spotlight

Ethical implications of research studies and theory, including reference to social sensitivity.

No one could accuse Janet of being 'socially sensitive'.

Apply it

A group of university researchers carried out a study of the academic abilities of primary school-aged children. Their participants came from several schools within a short distance of the university. They found that children from European backgrounds on average showed the lowest academic ability. Children from far-east Asian backgrounds had the highest ability.

Explain the ways in which this research could be considered socially sensitive.

Three essays

Note that for this topic there are a number of 16-mark essays that could be set, such as:

Discuss ethical implications of research studies.

Discuss ethical implications of research.

Discuss social sensitivity in psychological theory.

In all of these, socially sensitive issues in research studies would be creditworthy. So focus your revision on that. If the essay is just on socially sensitive research, then general ethical implications would not be creditworthy.

Ethical implications and social sensitivity

Ethical issues, guidelines and implications.	Ethical issues arise because of conflict between the need for valid research findings and preserving the rights of participants.
	Ethical guidelines protect participants and guide researchers.
	Guidelines are also related to the ethical *implications* (consequences) of research.
Socially sensitive research (SSR).	Psychologists must be aware of the consequences of research for the research participants or for the group of people represented by the research.
	Some research is more socially sensitive (e.g. studying depression) but even seemingly innocuous research (e.g. long-term memory in a student population) may have consequences (e.g. for exam policy).
Implications for the research processes.	Consequences should be considered at all stages of the research process.
Research question.	The phrasing of the research question influences how the findings are interpreted.
	For example, if a research study is looking at 'alternative relationships' this is likely to focus on homosexual relationships and may overlook heterosexual ones because 'alternative' suggests alternative to heterosexual relationships (Kitzinger and Coyle 1995).
Dealing with participants.	For example, **informed consent**, confidentiality and psychological harm.
	For example, when interviewing victims of domestic abuse, participants may worry about an ex-partner finding out what they said and also participants may find the experience of talking about abusive experiences stressful.
The way findings are used.	Need to consider in advance how findings might be used, especially because findings may give scientific credence to prejudices. For example the use of early (flawed) IQ tests in America during World War I led to prejudice against Eastern Europeans and lower immigration quota (see page 59).
	The media may be especially interested in sensitive findings, e.g. research on patients in a minimally conscious state who appeared to be responsive (Cyranoski 2012).

One strength of SSR is benefits for the group studied.

The **DSM**-1 listed homosexuality as a 'sociopathic personality disorder' but finally removed it in 1973, as a result of the Kinsey report (Kinsey *et al.* 1948).

Anonymous interviews with over 5000 men about their sexual behaviour concluded that homosexuality is a normal variant of human sexual behaviour.

This illustrates the importance of researchers tackling topics that are sensitive.

Counterpoint

However there may be negative consequences that could have been anticipated, e.g. research on the 'criminal gene' (see page 210). Implies that people can't be held responsible for their wrongdoing.

This suggests that, when researching socially sensitive topics, there is a need for very careful consideration of the possible outcomes and their consequences.

As the only Accrington Stanley supporter, Brian (5th row, 3rd from the left) felt very much in the minority. Was he being too sensitive?

Another strength is that policymakers rely on SSR.

Government needs research when developing social policy related to child care, education, mental health provision, crime etc. Better to base such policies on scientific research rather than politically-motivated views.

For example the ONS (Office for National Statistics) are responsible for collecting, analysing and disseminating objective statistics about the UK's economy, society and population.

This means that psychologists also have an important role to play in providing high quality research on socially sensitive topics.

Revision BOOSTER

Issues and debates essays cry out for examples of psychological studies and theories. You'll get more marks if you can provide relevant examples to illustrate the points you are making about ethical implications. Don't forget to explain exactly how the examples illustrate your points.

One limitation is that poor research design may have a long-term impact.

For example, Burt's (1955) research on IQ showed it is genetic, fixed and apparent by age 11. Led to the 11+ exam which meant not all children had the same educational opportunities.

Research later shown to be based on invented evidence but the system didn't change and continues in parts of the UK today (e.g. Kent and Belfast).

Therefore any SSR needs to be planned with the greatest care to ensure the findings are valid because of the enduring effects on particular groups of people.

Download suggested answers to the Knowledge Check questions from tinyurl.com/yd3ezhkb

Evaluation extra: To do or not to do.

We could avoid SSR, in fact that's what people seem to be doing. The APA (2001) claimed that 95% of non-sensitive proposals are approved but only 50% of SSR.

However, Sieber and Stanley advised that ignoring such topics is not responsible. Researchers could use a more reflexive approach (as in qualitative research).

This suggests that SSR can be ethical if researchers' biases form part of the findings.

Knowledge Check

1. Explain what is meant by 'ethical implications'. *(2 marks)*
2. Outline **one or more** ethical implication(s) of research studies in psychology. *(4 marks)*
3. Outline **two** ethical implications of theories in psychology. *(2 marks + 2 marks)*
4. Discuss the ethical implications of research studies **and/or** theories in psychology. Refer in your answer to social sensitivity. *(16 marks)*

Evolutionary explanations for partner preferences

Spec spotlight

The evolutionary explanations for partner preferences, including the relationship between sexual selection and human reproductive behaviour.

Cute, but pretty dangerous. That's love for you.

Sexual selection

Darwin's (1871) concept of sexual selection concerns the selection of those characteristics that aid successful reproduction (rather than survival). Attributes or behaviours that increase reproductive success are passed on and may become exaggerated over succeeding generations of offspring.

Apply it

Michael is a 65-year-old businessman who owns a big yacht and a massive house. He has just married Catherine who is 22. She is Michael's fourth wife. As he gets older he seems to marry younger and younger women. Catherine wants four children, but Michael has a history of having affairs outside marriage. Catherine told him if she ever caught him doing that to her, she'd take 'appropriate physical action'.

How does evolutionary theory for partner preferences explain **both** Michael's **and** Catherine's behaviour?

Sexual selection

Natural and *sexual selection*.	Any genes which are advantageous for survival are naturally selected. In addition any genes that promote successful reproduction are selected (= sexual selection).
Anisogamy related to mating strategies.	Anisogamy refers to the difference between male and female sex cells. Male cells (sperm) are plentiful because they are relatively 'cheap', whereas female cells (ova) are 'expensive' because they require more energy to produce them. A consequence of anisogamy is that there are plenty of fertile males but fertile females are a rarer 'resource'. This gives rise to two different mating strategies – inter-sexual and intra-sexual.

Inter-sexual selection

Selection of mates between sexes (i.e. females select males/males select females).

Female strategy quality over quantity.	Females make a greater investment of time, commitment etc. before, during and after birth (Trivers 1972). Therefore, the female's optimum mating strategy is to select a genetically-fit partner who is able to provide resources.
Impact on partner preference.	Preferences of both sexes determine attributes that are passed on, e.g. if height is considered an attractive male trait, it increases in the male population over generations because females choose the tallest males – the trait becomes exaggerated. Over time this leads to taller and taller men being selected (*runaway process*), Fisher's (1930) *sexy sons hypothesis*.

Intra-sexual selection

Selection of mates within sexes (e.g. males compete with other males for mates).

Male strategy quantity over quality.	Males compete for access to females as sperm is plentiful but fertile females are a limited resource and are choosy. Males who 'win' pass on their genes to the next generation so the traits that contributed to their victory (e.g. height, cunning) are perpetuated.
Impact on partner preference.	Intra-sexual selection pressures lead to certain patterns of human reproductive behaviour: • Physical consequences – males who are bigger win competitions for mates, so size is selected in males. Signs of fertility are selected (e.g. narrow waist in humans indicates youthfulness). • Behavioural consequences – male aggressiveness also helps win competitions.

One strength is research support for inter-sexual selection.

In one study (Clark and Hatfield 1989) students asked other students: 'I have been noticing you around campus. I find you to be very attractive. Would you go to bed with me tonight?'

No female students agreed in response to requests from males. But 75% of males agreed to the females' requests.

This supports the view that females are choosier than males in partner preferences and that males have evolved a different strategy to ensure reproductive success.

Counterpoint

Buss and Schmitt (2016) claim sexual selection theory is simplistic because it suggests that one strategy is **adaptive** for all males and another is adaptive for all females. Instead, both have similar preferences when seeking long-term relationships (e.g. loyalty, love, kindness, etc.).

This is a more complex and nuanced **evolutionary** view of partner preferences – it takes account of the context of reproductive behaviour.

Another strength is research support for intra-sexual selection.

Buss (1989) surveyed over 10,000 adults in 33 countries asking about those attributes predicted to be important in partner preferences.

He found that females valued resource-related characteristics more than males did (e.g. good financial prospects). Males seek signs of reproductive capacity (e.g. physical attractiveness and youth).

These findings reflect consistent sex difference in preferences, supporting predictions from sexual selection theory.

One limitation is that social and cultural influences are underestimated.

Partner preferences have been influenced by changing social norms and cultural practices. These have occurred too rapidly to be explained in evolutionary terms.

The wider availability of contraception and changing roles in the workplace mean women's partner preferences are no longer resource-oriented (Bereczkei et al. 1997).

This suggests that partner preferences today are likely to be due to both evolutionary and cultural influences – a theory which fails to explain both is limited.

Evaluation extra: Sexual selection and homosexuality.

Sexual selection theory explains partner choice in heterosexual men (fertility/attractiveness) and women (resources/ambition) but what about homosexual mate choice (not for reproduction)?

Research into 'personal ads' shows that homosexual men and women use different strategies from each other that are in line with their heterosexual counterparts (Lawson et al. 2014).

This shows that gay men and lesbian women use selection strategies that evolved to promote successful reproduction even though these are not relevant for their choices, supporting evolutionary theory.

Revision BOOSTER

What are your evaluations like? Why not try and make them more like ours? Start with your initial point – a strength or a limitation in most cases. Then... elaborate using three more steps, just as we've done on all of these AO3 pages.

Which of the tiny two-dimensional men should Rebecca choose?

Knowledge Check

1. In relation to evolutionary explanations for partner preference, explain what is meant by 'sexual selection'. *(3 marks)*

2. Outline the evolutionary explanation for partner preference. *(6 marks)*

3. Evaluate the relationship between sexual selection and human reproductive behaviour. *(6 marks)*

4. 'To put it bluntly,' says Donald, 'women want to settle down with a man to provide for her and men just want to spread their seed around as much as possible.'

   With reference to evolutionary explanations for partner preferences, describe **and** evaluate the relationship between sexual selection and human reproductive behaviour. *(16 marks)*

Factors affecting attraction: Self-disclosure

Spec spotlight

Factors affecting attraction in romantic relationships: self-disclosure.

They were at a fairly advanced stage in their relationship, but this was the first time Alice revealed she had five kids.

Apply it

Marina is talking about her marriage to Jacob. 'We make time to talk to each other every day. We take it in turns, no interruptions. We used to talk about how our days had been, what we had been doing, that sort of thing. But these days we talk about stuff that really matters, how we feel about things. And we talk about everything; there are no secrets between us.'

Explain how Marina's and Jacob's experience illustrates the role of self-disclosure in romantic relationships.

Know your onions

Altman and Taylor used a metaphor to explain deepening self-disclosures. It's like an onion – we 'peel away' layers of ourselves from the surface down to our inner core. A useful way of thinking about the process.

Self-disclosure

Important early in a relationship.	Self-disclosure refers to revealing intimate information to another person.
	For example, revealing your likes and dislikes, hopes and fears, interests and attitudes. We share what really matters to us.
	Most people are careful about disclosing too much too soon.
	Self-disclosure plays an important role in developing a relationship beyond initial attraction.

Social penetration theory

Self-disclosure limited at start.	Altman and Taylor (1973) suggest it is a gradual process of revealing your inner self to someone else.
	Revealing personal information is a sign of trust.
	Partner then has to reciprocate and reveal personal information.
Penetration leads to development.	As romantic partners increasingly disclose more information they 'penetrate' more deeply into each other's lives.
	Depenetration describes how dissatisfied partners self-disclose less as they disengage from the relationship.
Breadth is narrow to begin with.	Both breadth and depth of self-disclosure are key according to the social penetration theory ('layers of an onion' metaphor).
	Breadth is narrow at the start of a relationship because if too much information is revealed this may be off-putting and one partner may decide to quit the relationship.
Depth increases.	As a relationship develops more layers are gradually revealed.
	We are likely to reveal more intimate information including painful memories, secrets, etc.

Reciprocity of self-disclosure

Need for *reciprocity* for a relationship to develop.	Reis and Shaver (1988) suggest that, in addition to a broadening and deepening of self-disclosure, there must be reciprocity.
	Successful relationships will involve disclosure from one partner which is received sensitively by the other partner.
	In turn this should then lead to further self-disclosure from the other partner.

One strength is support for self-disclosure from research studies.

Sprecher and Hendrick (2004) found strong **correlations** between several measures of satisfaction and self-disclosure in heterosexual couples.

Men and women who used self-disclosure (and believed their partners also disclosed) were more satisfied with and committed to their romantic relationship.

This supports the **validity** of the view that reciprocated self-disclosure is a key part of a satisfying romantic relationship.

Counterpoint

Sprecher and Hendrick found strong positive correlations but this does not mean that self-disclosure causes relationships to be satisfying. It may be that satisfied partners disclose more, or both caused by time spent together.

This suggests that self-disclosures may not cause satisfaction directly, which reduces the validity of social penetration theory.

Another strength is real-world application to improve communication.

Hass and Stafford (1998) found that 57% of homosexual men and women reported they used open and honest self-disclosure as a relationship maintenance strategy.

Couples who limit communication to 'small talk' can be encouraged to increase self-disclosure in order to deepen their own relationships.

This highlights the importance of self-disclosure and suggests the theory can be used to support people having relationship problems.

One limitation is that self-disclosure is not satisfying in all cultures.

Tang et al. (2013) concluded that people in the US (**individualist** culture) self-disclose significantly more sexual thoughts and feelings than people in China (**collectivist** culture).

Even though the level of disclosure was lower in China, relationship satisfaction was no different from that in the US.

Therefore social penetration theory is a limited explanation of romantic relationships because it is not necessarily **generalisable** to other cultures.

Evaluation extra: Self-disclosure and breakdown.

Social penetration theory claims (and research shows) that self-disclosure in relationships is associated with satisfaction.

However, when a relationship breaks down partners often disclose more often and more deeply to increase their satisfaction, but this often does not save the relationship (Duck 2007).

This challenges social penetration theory because deeper self-disclosure does not lead to a deeper relationship (and may contribute to its breakdown).

After an ill-advised game of cat's cradle, Tim and Amanda had been entangled for nearly seven hours.

Revision BOOSTER

On every spread we provide fairly equal amounts of AO1 and AO3 but in an extended writing 16-mark question you need more of the latter. We have given you lots of AO1 so you can answer specific description questions – but take care not to include too much in any 16-mark question.

Knowledge Check

1. Explain what is meant by 'self-disclosure' in relation to factors affecting attraction in romantic relationships. *(2 marks)*

2. In relation to factors affecting attraction in romantic relationships, outline research into self-disclosure. *(6 marks)*

3. Explain **one** criticism of research into self-disclosure as a factor affecting attraction in romantic relationships. *(4 marks)*

4. Asad fancied Sabiha and asked her out on a date. Halfway into a lovely evening he said, 'I really want to get married and have lots of kids as soon as possible – it's really important to me.' Sabiha decided not to go on a second date.

   With reference to Asad and Sabiha's experience, describe **and** evaluate research into self-disclosure as a factor affecting attraction in romantic relationships. *(16 marks)*

Factors affecting attraction: Physical attractiveness

Spec spotlight

Factors affecting attraction in romantic relationships: physical attractiveness, including the matching hypothesis.

Sure he looks angelic now but imagine that face screaming at 4 in the morning.

Apply it

Most people agree that Gaby is very physically attractive. They think she comes across as a very nice and kind person too. When people wonder why she is single, Gaby replies it's because she hasn't found anyone in her league yet!

Explain how Gaby's experience illustrates the role of physical attractiveness in romantic relationships.

It's all about attraction

It helps to remember that this topic is not a theory of how romantic relationships start. It is about factors affecting attraction in relationships of any duration.

Physical attractiveness

Explaining importance of attractiveness: *symmetry.*	Shackelford and Larsen (1997) found that people with symmetrical faces are rated as more attractive.
	It is thought that this is a signal of genetic fitness that cannot be faked (which makes it an 'honest' signal).
	Explanations based on physical attractiveness are **evolutionary** ones – attributes that signal high quality are naturally selected.
Baby face features seen as attractive.	Neotenous (baby face) features are thought to trigger protective and caring instincts, related to the formation of attachment in infancy.
	This is also an evolutionary explanation because features that strengthen attachment are **naturally selected**.
Halo effect describes how physical attractiveness is generalised.	We hold preconceived ideas about the attributes of physically attractive people. We believe that all their other attributes are overwhelmingly positive.
	For example, Dion *et al.* (1972) found that physically attractive people are consistently rated as kind, strong, sociable and successful compared with unattractive people.

Walster *et al.* (1966) Matching hypothesis

We choose partners who match us in attractiveness (physical attractiveness, intelligence etc.)

PROCEDURE	Computer dance – students rated on physical attractiveness by objective observers and completed questionnaires.
	Told questionnaire data used to pair partners, but in fact randomly paired with partners.
FINDINGS AND CONCLUSIONS	Physically attractive partners were liked the most and more likely to be asked on another date – hypothesis not supported.
	But Berscheid *et al.* (1971) **replicated** study and students selected partners themselves. This time they chose partners of similar physical attractiveness.
	This suggests that we tend to seek and choose partners whose physical attractiveness matches our own. Partner choice is a compromise – we avoid rejection by the most physically attractive and settle for those in our 'league'.

One strength is research support for the halo effect.

Palmer and Peterson (2012) found that physically attractive people were rated more politically knowledgeable and competent than unattractive people.

This halo effect persisted even when participants were told the 'knowledgeable' people actually had no expertise.

This suggests dangers for democracy if politicians are elected just because they are considered physically attractive by enough voters.

Another strength is research support for evolutionary processes.

Cunningham *et al.* (1995) found large eyes and small nose in females were rated as attractive by white, Asian and Hispanic males.

What is considered physically attractive is consistent across cultures – attractive features (symmetry) are a sign of genetic fitness and therefore perpetuated (sexual selection).

Therefore the importance of physical attractiveness makes sense in evolutionary terms.

Touching to think that their shared love of repulsive yellow jackets had brought them together.

One limitation is real-world research does not support matching hypothesis.

Taylor *et al.* (2011) studied online dating activity logs, which measured actual dating choices and not fantasy preferences.

This real-world test of the hypothesis found that people sought dates with partners who were more physically attractive than themselves.

This contradicts the central prediction that real couples seek to match attractiveness.

Counterpoint

Choosing people for dating is different from real-world romance. Feingold's (1988) **meta-analysis** found a significant **correlation** in ratings of physical attractiveness between romantic partners. People may express ideals in dating selection and also in lab research.

This shows there is support for the matching hypothesis from real-world studies.

Evaluation extra: Individual differences.

A lot of evidence indicates the important role of physical attractiveness in relationship formation (e.g. sexual selection).

But some people are not affected by attractiveness e.g. Touhey (1979) found that people with non-sexist attitudes were uninfluenced by physical attraction when judging the likeability of potential partners.

This shows that the impact of physical attractiveness is moderated by other factors.

Revision BOOSTER

Your own experience of relationships is useful here. Have you found yourself subject to the halo effect? How valid do you think it really is? Do you assume that attractive people are also kind, honest, helpful and so on? If you can apply a psychological theory to your own experience, that's a kind of revision. It could help you to understand the information and retain it. And you'll be thinking about psychology – always a good thing!

... however, don't include such anecdotal material in an exam answer. It is unlikely to gain marks.

Knowledge Check

1. Outline research into physical attractiveness as a factor in romantic relationships. *(6 marks)*

2. In relation to factors affecting attraction in romantic relationships, outline the matching hypothesis. *(6 marks)*

3. Explain **one** criticism of the matching hypothesis. *(4 marks)*

4. Discuss **two** factors affecting attraction in romantic relationships. *(16 marks)*

Factors affecting attraction: Filter theory

Spec spotlight

Factors affecting attraction in romantic relationships: filter theory, including social demography, similarity in attitudes and complementarity.

You've got two minutes my friend – impress me! Speed dating: the ultimate filtering opportunity.

Apply it

Yusuf and Ayla first met at university where they were on the same corridor in halls of residence.

Yuan and Xia met on a demonstration against fox-hunting.

Gurmeet and Debina married 20 years ago. They enjoy telling each other about their different hobbies and interests.

Explain how the experiences of each of these couples illustrates elements of the filter theory of romantic relationships.

Revision BOOSTER

Always think 'less is more' – writing about fewer things gives you the opportunity to demonstrate your detailed understanding.

Filter theory

Field of availables and *field of desirables*.	Kerckhoff and Davis (1962) explain attraction in terms of attitudes and personalities. 1. First we consider the *field of availables* (pool of potential partners who are accessible to us). 2. From this we select the *field of desirables* via three *filters* of varying importance at different stages of a relationship.

1st filter: Social demography

Factors that influence chances of meeting e.g. age, education.	Demographics are features that describe populations. Social demographics include geographical location and social class. You are more likely to meet and have meaningful encounters with people who are physically close and share other features with yourself (e.g. same social class). Anyone who is too 'different' (e.g. too far away, too middle class) is not a potential partner and is 'filtered out' before the next stage – outcome is *homogamy* (partner is similar to you, shares your background).

2nd filter: Similarity in attitudes

Sharing beliefs and values.	Important for couples who have been together less than 18 months. In early stages of a relationship agreeing on basic values promotes better communication and self-disclosure.
Law of attraction.	Byrne (1997) found that similarity in attitudes causes mutual attraction. Where such similarity does not exist it is found that often the relationship fades after only a few dates.

3rd filter: Complementarity

Partners meet each other's needs.	Partners complement each other when they have traits that the other lacks. For example, one partner may enjoy making the other laugh, and in turn this partner enjoys being made to laugh.
Important in longer term/ later stages of a relationship.	Complementarity is thought to give the romantic partners a feeling of togetherness and 'making a whole'. For example, partners will feel like they are meeting each other's needs if one likes caring and the other enjoys being cared for ('opposites attract').

One strength is support from Kerckhoff and Davis's original study.

Dating couples completed questionnaires to measure similarity of attitudes/values, complementarity of needs and relationship 'closeness'.

Closeness was linked to similarity of values only for partners together less than 18 months. Complementarity of needs was more important in longer relationships.

This is evidence that similarity is important in the early stages of a relationship, but complementarity becomes more important later.

Counterpoint

Original findings not **replicated** (Levinger 1974), perhaps due to social changes and assumption that partners together more than 18 months must be more committed.

This assumption is questionable so filter theory is based on research evidence that lacks **validity**.

One limitation is that complementarity does not always predict satisfaction.

Filter theory predicts high levels of satisfaction in a relationship with complementarity, e.g. where one partner needs to be dominant and the other submissive.

But Markey and Markey (2013) found that long-term lesbian romantic partners were most satisfied when both partners were equally dominant.

Therefore similarity of needs rather than complementarity may be associated with long-term satisfaction, at least in some couples.

Another limitation is that *perceived* similarity matters more.

Actual similarity is linked to attraction only in very brief lab-based interactions. Perceived similarity found more important in real-world relationships (Montoya et al.).

One interpretation is that romantic partners perceive they have more similarities as they become more attracted to each other.

This means that perceived similarity may be an effect of attraction and not a cause – not predicted by filter theory.

Evaluation extra: Social change.

Filter theory claims physical location and other demographic factors initially filter the field of availables down to people similar to ourselves (homogamy).

However, the role of filters has changed – online dating increases the field of availables beyond location. Such social changes increase relationships between people from different backgrounds.

This means filter theory needs to be adapted to explain modern relationships by completely revising the features of the 1st level filter.

Revision BOOSTER

In an exam everyone feels some measure of anxiety – when you are anxious, you forget those things which are not well learned or well practised. So practise, practise, practise!

Aw – how lovely, sharing a special moment. Who would have thought less than three years later they'd be arguing over who gets custody of the goldfish?

Knowledge Check

1. In relation to factors affecting attraction in romantic relationships, explain what is meant by 'social demography', 'similarity in attitudes' **and** 'complementarity'.
   (2 marks + 2 marks + 2 marks)

2. Outline **two or more** factors affecting attraction in romantic relationships. *(6 marks)*

3. Discuss strengths **and/or** limitations of filter theory as an explanation of factors affecting attraction in romantic relationships.
   (10 marks)

4. When it comes to relationships, some people believe 'opposites attract' and others think 'birds of a feather flock together'.

   With reference to both these points of view, describe **and** evaluate filter theory. *(16 marks)*

Spec spotlight

Theories of romantic relationships: social exchange theory.

Little did he know the box contained nothing but a post-it and written upon it was the single phrase, 'You're dumped'.

Apply it

Two counselling psychologists are writing a report on what makes a good relationship. They conclude that both partners know what they want from a relationship and have to get at least that out of it, otherwise they start wondering if they'd be happier elsewhere. A relationship is all about rewards and costs – if it is not profitable then it will not last.

How does the social exchange theory of relationships explain the psychologists' conclusions?

Social exchange theory (SET)

SET assumes relationships are guided by the *minimax principle*.	Thibault and Kelley (1959) proposed that relationships could be explained in terms of economics – an exchange of goods or less tangible things (e.g. favours). Satisfaction is judged in terms of profit (the perceived value of costs minus the value of rewards). Partners are motivated to minimise the costs to themselves whilst maximising rewards. Profitable relationships continue, unprofitable relationships fail.
Nature of costs and rewards.	Costs may include loss of time or stress. Rewards may include sex, praise or companionship. Opportunity cost also needs to be accounted for (i.e. the recognition that investment in a given relationship is at the 'cost' of expending those resources elsewhere).
CL is a measure of profit.	Comparison level (CL) is a judgement of the reward level we believe we deserve in a relationship, determined by relationship experiences and social norms. We will generally pursue a relationship where the CL is high but some people (e.g. with low self-esteem) may have low CLs.
CLalt is an additional measure of profit.	Comparison level for alternatives (CLalt) – we consider whether we might gain more rewards and endure fewer costs in a different relationship (or none). We stay in a relationship, despite available alternatives, when we consider it is more rewarding than the alternatives. If relationship is satisfying, alternatives not noticed.
CLalt depends on our current relationship.	Duck (1994) suggests that there are always alternatives around. If the costs of our current relationship outweigh the rewards, then alternatives become more attractive.
Four stages of relationships.	• *Sampling* stage involves exploring rewards and costs by experimenting in our relationships (not just romantic ones) and observing others. • *Bargaining* stage occurs at start of a relationship where romantic partners negotiate around costs and rewards. • *Commitment* stage is where relationships become more stable. Costs reduce and rewards increase. • *Institutionalisation* stage is when partners become settled because the norms of the relationship are established.

One strength of SET is research supporting some of its concepts.

Kurdeck (1995) interviewed homo- and heterosexual couples, committed partners perceived they had most rewards and fewest costs and also viewed alternatives as unattractive.

The study also showed that the main SET concepts predicting commitment are independent of each other (so they individually have an effect).

The findings confirmed predictions of SET, supporting the **validity** of the theory in gay and lesbian as well as heterosexual couples.

Counterpoint

Studies into SET (including Kurdek's) ignore the role of equity (see next spread). What matters in a romantic relationship is not the balance of rewards and costs but the partners' perceptions that this is fair.

Therefore SET is a limited explanation because it cannot account for a significant proportion of research findings that confirm the importance of equity.

Rory tried to convince himself that he would rather watch football – but actually, he loved Bake Off.

One limitation of SET is the direction of cause and effect.

SET claims that we become dissatisfied *after* we perceive costs outweigh rewards or alternatives seem more attractive.

But Argyle (1987) argues dissatisfaction comes first, then we start to perceive costs and alternatives – committed partners do not even notice alternatives.

Therefore considering costs/alternatives is caused by dissatisfaction rather than the reverse – a direction not predicted by SET.

Another limitation is that SET concepts are vague.

Unlike in research, real-world rewards/costs are subjective and hard to define because they vary, e.g. 'having your partner's loyalty' is not rewarding for everyone.

Also comparison levels are problematic – it is unclear what the values of CL and CLalt need to be before individuals feel dissatisfied.

This means SET is difficult to test in a valid way.

Evaluation extra: Inappropriate central assumptions.

SET assumes that all relationships are based on costs and rewards, profit and loss, constant monitoring of satisfaction.

However, Clark and Mills (2011) argue that romantic relationships are not exchange-based but *communal*-based. Partners do not 'keep score' (would question commitment if they did).

This suggests that quite a few relationships might not be exchange-based e.g. those where trust is a fundamental component.

Knowledge Check

1. Outline the social exchange theory of romantic relationships. *(6 marks)*
2. Outline any **one** theory of romantic relationships. *(6 marks)*
3. Explain **two** criticisms of the social exchange theory of romantic relationships. *(3 marks + 3 marks)*
4. Dom has been going out with Shelley for one month. He tells his friend, 'She keeps buying me presents and doing nice things – it's hard work keeping up with her!'

   Discuss the social exchange theory of romantic relationships. Refer to Dom and Shelley in your answer. *(16 marks)*

Theories of romantic relationships: Equity theory

Spec spotlight

Theories of romantic relationships: equity theory.

In the see-saw of life, the best relationships are all about balance.

Apply it

Dan is explaining to Mike the secret of his long relationship with his girlfriend. 'You both have to feel you're getting something good out of it,' he says. 'Things don't have to be equal, but they do have to be fair. And you have to talk together about how to make things fair.'

Explain how Dan's wise advice supports the equity theory of romantic relationships.

Equity and exchange

It is easy to feel muddled about the difference between these two. In social exchange theory contentment is about what you get, even though there is an exchange of 'goods'. In equity theory it isn't about what you get, it's about a feeling of fairness. You might be getting the best deal but still feel unsatisfied.

The role of equity

Most people have a *need for equity* in relationships.	*Social exchange theory* suggests that partners aim to maximise the rewards and minimise the costs of a relationship.
	In contrast Walster *et al.* (1978) propose that equity is more important where both partners' level of profit (rewards minus costs) should be roughly the same.
Underbenefitting and *overbenefitting* can lead to dissatisfaction.	The underbenefitted partner is likely to be the least satisfied and their feelings may be evident in anger and resentment.
	The overbenefitted partner may feel less dissatisfied but is still likely to feel discomfort and shame.
Equity is about the *fairness* of the ratios.	It's not the size or amount of the rewards and costs that matters – it's the ratio of the two to each other.
	For example, if one partner is disabled they may not be able to do certain chores but compensate in other areas, so both partners still feel a sense of fairness.

Consequences of inequity

Sense of inequity impacts negatively on relationships.	The greater the perceived inequity, the greater the dissatisfaction – equity theory predicts a strong positive **correlation** between the two.
	This applies to both the overbenefitted and underbenefitted partner.
Changes in equity occur during a relationship.	At the start of a relationship it may feel perfectly natural to contribute more than you receive.
	If that situation carries on as the relationship develops (one person continues to put more in and get less out), then dissatisfaction will set in.
Dealing with inequity.	The underbenefitted partner is motivated to make the relationship more equitable if they believe the relationship is salvageable. The greater the inequity the harder it is to restore equity.
	The change could be **cognitive** rather than behavioural. A dissatisfied partner might revise their perceptions of rewards and costs so the relationship feels more equitable even if nothing changes.
	What was once perceived as a cost (e.g. abuse) can become accepted as the norm for the relationship.

One strength is that equity theory has research support.

Utne *et al.* (1984) conducted a survey with recently-married couples who had been together more than two years before marrying.

Those who thought their relationship equitable were more satisfied than those who saw themselves as over- or underbenefitting.

This study supports the central predictions of equity theory that equity is a major concern of couples and is linked with satisfaction.

Counterpoint

Berg and McQuinn (1986) found that equity did not distinguish between relationships which ended and those that continued – other variables (e.g. self-disclosure) were more important.

This means the **validity** of the theory is in doubt because the predictions of the theory are not supported by research.

Newlyweds don't consider profit when judging their relationship – though it obviously helped that Lionel was the son of a millionaire.

One limitation is that equity theory may not be valid in all cultures.

Aumer-Ryan *et al.* (2007) found that couples in an **individualist** culture (US) were most satisfied when their relationship was equitable.

However, partners in a **collectivist** culture (Jamaica) were most satisfied when overbenefitting (both men and women, so not explained by gender differences).

This suggests that the theory is limited because it only applies to some cultures.

Revision BOOSTER

Ironically, there is an intimate relationship (see what we did there?) between equity theory and SET. That's no surprise because equity theory developed in response to perceived limitations of SET. But this means that it would be a great idea to revise these two theories together. You could even use equity theory (carefully) to evaluate SET in an essay.

On the other hand, don't get them mixed up. In short, make sure you know the similarities and differences between them.

Another limitation is that there are individual differences.

Huseman *et al.* (1987) suggest that not all partners are concerned about equity. *Benevolents* are happy to contribute more than they get (underbenefit).

Entitleds believe they deserve to overbenefit and accept it without feeling distressed or guilty.

This shows that a desire for equity varies from one individual to another and is not a universal feature of romantic relationships.

Evaluation extra: Equity – cause or effect?

Some research shows inequity may cause dissatisfaction (e.g. Utne *et al.*, above).

Other research shows dissatisfaction causes inequity. Dissatisfaction leads to noticing inequities, then more dissatisfaction – 'cycle of misery' (Grote and Clark 2001).

Therefore inequity may be a cause and an effect of dissatisfaction – equity theory is just a partial explanation of this process.

Knowledge Check

1. Outline the equity theory of romantic relationships. *(6 marks)*
2. Briefly outline **two** theories of romantic relationships. *(6 marks)*
3. Discuss **one** criticism of the equity theory of romantic relationships. *(4 marks)*
4. Describe **and** evaluate the equity theory of romantic relationships. *(16 marks)*

Spec spotlight

Theories of romantic relationships: Rusbult's investment model of commitment, satisfaction, comparison with alternatives and investment.

Rusbult's investment model.

Apply it

Hana is in a relationship but her commitment is wavering. In the past, she did a lot to keep things going but now she wonders if she would get more out of a relationship with someone else, or be better on her own. But she thinks of all the good times she has had and everything she has put into her current relationship.

Explain how Hana's experience illustrates the elements of Rusbult's investment model of romantic relationships.

Revision BOOSTER

Write very brief essay plans for each possible essay and then practise writing the essay out in full from these skeleton plans. Time yourself – 20 minutes for a 16-mark essay.

The investment model

An extension of SET.	Rusbult's investment model (2011) further developed social exchange theory (SET).
	A satisfying relationship is one where the partners are getting more out of the relationship than they expect, given social norms and their previous experiences.
Commitment results from 3 factors.	Factor 1: *Satisfaction* – the extent to which partners feel the rewards of the romantic relationship exceed the costs (comparison level, CL).
	Factor 2: *Comparison with alternatives* (CLalt) – a judgement about whether a relationship with a different partner would increase rewards and reduce costs.
	Factor 3: *Investment* – the resources associated with a romantic relationship which would be lost if the relationship ended.
Two types of investment: *intrinsic* and *extrinsic*.	Intrinsic – any resources put directly into the relationship (e.g. money, energy and self-disclosures).
	Extrinsic – investments that previously did not feature in the relationship (i.e. were external to it) which are now closely associated with it (e.g. a jointly-purchased house, children, shared memories).
Commitment determined by satisfaction + alternatives + investment.	High levels of satisfaction (more rewards with few costs) + the alternatives are less attractive + the sizes of their investment are increasing = partners will be committed to the relationship.
Satisfaction versus commitment.	Commitment is the main factor that causes people to stay in romantic relationships, satisfaction contributes to commitment.
	This explains why, for example, a dissatisfied partner stays in a relationship when their level of investment is high. They will be willing to work hard to repair problems in the relationship so their investment is not wasted.
Relationship maintenance mechanisms.	Committed partners use maintenance behaviours to keep the relationship going, for example:

- Promoting the relationship (accommodation).
- Putting their partner's interests first (willingness to sacrifice).
- Forgiving them for any serious transgressions (forgiveness).

One strength of the model is research support from a meta-analysis.

Le and Agnew's (2003) review found that satisfaction, CLalt and investment size all predicted commitment – commitment linked with greater stability and longevity.

The outcomes were true for both men and women, across all cultures and for homosexual and heterosexual relationships.

This suggests that the model's claim that these factors are universally important in relationships is valid.

Counterpoint

Research studies show strong **correlations** between factors. But it does not follow that these factors cause commitment (e.g. perhaps commitment comes before investment).

Therefore it is not clear that the model has identified the *causes* of commitment rather than factors that are associated with it.

Another strength is it can explain why people stay in abusive relationships.

Rusbult and Martz (1995) studied abused women staying at a shelter. Those reporting the greatest investment and fewest alternatives were the most likely to return to abusive partners.

The women in this study were dissatisfied with their relationships but returned to their partners because they were committed to them.

Therefore the model shows that satisfaction on its own cannot explain why people stay in relationships – commitment and investment are also factors.

One limitation of the model is that it oversimplifies investment.

Goodfriend and Agnew (2008) argue that there is more to investment than just the resources you have already put into a relationship.

Early in a relationship partners make very few actual investments but they do invest in future plans – these motivate partners to commit.

This means the original model is a limited explanation as it fails to consider the true complexity of investment.

Evaluation extra: Perception versus reality.

The investment model is supported by studies using self-report methods such as questionnaires – these are affected by subjective biases and beliefs.

But what may matter more is a person's *perception* about how much investment they have made or how attractive their alternatives are.

Therefore the use of self-report measures is appropriate because they assess partners' subjective perceptions about relationships, which are the most important influences on commitment.

Doting parents Rick and Tanya would make their kids run around for 11 hours a day. It was the only way they'd be guaranteed any sleep.

Knowledge Check

1. In relation to theories of romantic relationships, explain what is meant by 'commitment', 'satisfaction' **and** 'investment'.
   (2 marks + 2 marks + 2 marks)

2. Briefly outline **two** theories of romantic relationships. *(6 marks)*

3. Briefly evaluate Rusbult's investment model of romantic relationships. *(6 marks)*

4. Cath and Katie are discussing what is important in a successful relationship. Cath says, 'The more satisfied you are in a relationship, the more committed you will be to it.' Katie disagrees: 'I think if you commit to a relationship and work at it, that makes it more satisfying.'

   Discuss Rusbult's investment model of romantic relationships. Refer to Cath's **and** Katie's comments in your answer. *(16 marks)*

Theories of romantic relationships: Duck's phase model

Spec spotlight

Theories of romantic relationships: Duck's phase model of relationship breakdown: intra-psychic, dyadic, social and grave dressing phases.

It had seemed like hours since she last spoke. Aaron was beginning to regret asking if he could go on a fortnight's holiday to Ibiza with 'the lads'.

Apply it

Adam is brooding on his unhappiness in his relationship with his girlfriend.

Ramona and Giles are both unhappy and have started discussing what they are going to do next.

Kelvin and Pieter have told their friends and family that they are getting relationship counselling.

1. Identify which stage of Duck's model each couple is experiencing. Briefly summarise the main features of these stages. Relate your summaries to the couples above.

2. There is another stage in Duck's model – identify it and write an example of your own. Also write a brief statement about the main feature(s) of the stage.

Duck's phase model

Breakdown is a *process*.	Duck (2007) proposed a phase model of relationship breakdown.
	He argued that the ending of a relationship is not a one-off event but a process that takes time and goes through four distinct phases.
Each phase has a *threshold*.	Each phase is characterised by one partner reaching a threshold where their perception of the relationship changes.
	This dissatisfied partner may reassess and decide the relationship isn't so bad, halting the process of breakdown.
	Or they cross the threshold and move on to the next stage.
Intra-psychic phase.	Threshold – *'I can't stand this anymore'*, indicating a determination that something has to change.
	A partner becomes dissatisfied with the relationship in its current form. They then worry about the reasons for this and this will usually focus on their partner's shortcomings.
	The dissatisfied partner tends to keep this to themselves but may share their thoughts with a trusted friend, weighing up the pros and cons of continuing.
Dyadic phase.	Threshold – *'I would be justified in withdrawing'*.
	Once a partner concludes that they are justified in ending the relationship they have to discuss this with their partner. Dissatisfactions about equity, commitment, etc. are aired.
	Ironically, self-disclosures may be more frequent as partners feel they can reveal true feelings.
Social phase.	Threshold – the dissatisfied partner concludes, *'I mean it'*.
	Once a partner wants to end the relationship they will seek support particularly from joint friends.
	These friends may choose a side but others may try and prevent the break-up by acting as a go-between.
	Once the news is public though this is usually the point of no return.
Grave dressing phase.	Threshold – *'It's now inevitable'*.
	Once the end becomes inevitable then a suitable story of the relationship and its end is prepared for wider consumption.
	This is likely to include an attempt to ensure that the storyteller will be judged most favourably.
	This creation of a personal story in addition to the public one is necessary so the partner can 'move on'.
	Final threshold – *'Time to get a new life'*.

One strength is its application to real-world relationship breakdown.

The model suggests that some repair strategies might be more effective at one stage of relationship breakdown rather than another.

For example, in the intra-psychic stage partners could worry more positively about each other. Improving communication skills is beneficial in the dyadic phase.

This suggests that the model can provide supportive insights to help people through difficult times in their lives.

Counterpoint

Moghaddam *et al.* (1993) argue the model is based on breakdown in **individualist** cultures where relationships are mostly voluntary and often end. Relationships in **collectivist** cultures are often 'obligatory' and less easy to end – the whole concept of romantic relationship differs between cultures.

Therefore the model's application to reverse breakdown can only be applied in some cultures.

One limitation is that the model is incomplete.

Rollie and Duck (2006) added a *resurrection phase* in which ex-partners apply to future relationships what they have learned from the recent past.

Also, partners may return to earlier phases at any point and processes are more important than linear movement through phases.

This means the original model does not take account of the complexity of breakdown and its dynamic nature.

Another limitation is that the early phases are less well explained.

Research participants recall relationship breakdown retrospectively, so report may not be accurate (especially recalling the early phases).

The intra-psychic phase happens 'longer ago' and partners may spend a long time in it, so recall of what happened could be especially distorted.

Therefore the model does not explain the early part of the breakdown process as well as later phases.

Do you agree with this conclusion?

Evaluation extra: Description rather than explanation.

Duck's model describes the *what* in the various phases with no consideration of causal factors.

In contrast, Felmlee's (1995) fatal attraction hypothesis explains *why* – qualities that were attractive eventually produce dissatisfaction.

Therefore Duck's model might be improved by adding some of Felmlee's approach.

Revision BOOSTER

In a 16-mark essay you don't have to write everything on this spread. What is here is actually more than 700 words!! For a 16-mark essay you probably only have time to write 500 words – but don't cut down the elaboration of the AO3 points. Better to do three elaborated points rather than four briefer ones. Better to write points with counterpoints. And always do more evaluation.

They weren't talking since Simon had refused to take back his comment that Jonathan's vest was 'garish'.

Knowledge Check

1. Briefly outline the intra-psychic **and** social phases of Duck's phase model of relationship breakdown.
   (2 marks + 2 marks)

2. Outline Duck's phase model of romantic breakdown.
   (6 marks)

3. Explain why Duck's model of relationship breakdown is called a 'phase model'. *(2 marks)*

4. This item appeared on a news website: 'Psychologists today claimed relationships do not end overnight. Breaking up is a process that takes time and goes through several phases. But the experts believe relationships can be saved at almost every stage'.

   With reference to the issues in this item, discuss Duck's phase model of relationship breakdown. *(16 marks)*

Virtual relationships in social media

Spec spotlight

Virtual relationships in social media: self-disclosure in virtual relationships; effects of absence of gating on the nature of virtual relationships.

The therapist had suggested that Sally was starting to become a bit obsessive about TikTok – but she didn't care.

Apply it

Jimmy and Thomasina have never met, but they interact on social media all the time. They have both had self-esteem issues in the past, because they think themselves unattractive. So they were glad that they were able to get to know each other online before exchanging images of each other. Jimmy sometimes worries that typed words on Facebook aren't enough to express how he feels. Thomasina is anxious that she doesn't know the real Jimmy.

How can research into virtual relationships in social media explain Jimmy's and Thomasina's relationship and feelings?

Self-disclosure

Self-disclosure is different in *FtF* and *virtual relationships*.	Self-disclosure refers to revealing personal information about yourself, and it increases as a relationship develops (see page 72).
	Self-disclosure is crucial in face-to-face (FtF) relationships but what about virtual relationships? These relationships are formed and maintained, for example by email, instant messaging, social networking sites etc. (i.e. online).
Reduced cues theory. Less self-disclosure.	Reduced cues theory (Sproull and Kiesler 1986) suggests that virtual relationships are less effective due to the lack of nonverbal cues (e.g. physical appearance, emotional responses). In FtF relationships we rely on these cues.
	Lack of cues about emotional state (voice and facial expressions) leads to **de-individuation**.
	People then feel freer from the constraints of social norms (**disinhibition**) and this leads to blunt and even aggressive communication and a reluctance to self-disclose.
Hyperpersonal model. More self-disclosure.	Hyperpersonal model (Walther 1996, 2011) suggests that, since self-disclosure happens more quickly in virtual relationships, relationships also develop more quickly.
	1. Sender has control (selective self-presentation) and may be hyperhonest and/or hyperdishonest.
	2. Receiver's feedback may reinforce sender's selective self-presentation.
	Anonymity is an important factor in virtual relationships.
	'Strangers on a train' – people may disclose a lot in anonymous situations (Bargh *et al.* 2002).

Effects of absence of gating in virtual relationships

What is a 'gate'?	McKenna and Bargh (1999) argue that 'gates' (e.g. facial disfigurements or a stammer) may be obstacles to a FtF relationship.
Absence of gating has benefits and drawbacks.	Gates are absent in virtual relationships – so such relationships are more likely to 'get off the ground' than FtF relationships and self-disclosures become deeper.
	Without gates, people are free to be more like their 'true selves' in virtual relationships.
	However, they can also create untrue identities to deceive people – they can change gender or age, a shy person can become an extravert.

One limitation is lack of support for reduced cues theory.

Online cues are not absent but different from FtF, e.g. taking time to respond on social media is more intimate than an immediate reply.

Acronyms (e.g. LOL), emoticons and emojis are effective substitutes for FtF nonverbal cues such as facial expressions (Walther and Tidwell).

This is hard for reduced cues theory to explain because it suggests virtual relationships can be as personal as FtF (i.e. no differences).

Every time she drank a cup of water she was reminded of Grant – bland, tasteless and a bit of a drip.

Another limitation is a lack of research support for the hyperpersonal model.

Ruppel *et al.*'s (2017) **meta-analysis** compared the frequency, breadth and depth of self-disclosures in FtF and virtual relationships.

In self-report studies, self-disclosure was greater in FtF relationships on all three measures. In **experimental** studies there were no significant differences.

This challenges the model's view that greater intimacy in virtual relationships should lead to greater self-disclosure than FtF.

Counterpoint

Whitty and Joinson (2009) found that conversations in virtual relationships are direct and hyperhonest. Self-presentation online can also be hyperdishonest, e.g. inventing qualities for dating profiles.

This support's the model's claims about hyperhonest and hyperdishonest self-disclosures and shows there are differences between FtF and virtual relationships.

Revision BOOSTER

This topic should be right up your street. What an opportunity to use real-world examples to improve your revision. How do you decide which Facebook profile picture to use? Could it be anything to do with an image you want to present to others? Not even a little bit perhaps? But remember that anecdotal material is not likely to be creditworthy in an exam answer.

One strength is support for absence of gating in virtual relationships.

McKenna and Bargh (2000) studied online communication by shy and socially anxious people.

In this group, 71% of the romantic relationships initially formed online survived more than two years, compared to 49% formed offline (Kirkpatrick and Davis 1994).

This suggests that shy people do benefit online presumably because the gating that obstructs FtF relationships is absent online.

Knowledge Check

1. Outline research into virtual relationships in social media.
   (6 marks)
2. Outline research into self-disclosure in virtual relationships.
   (6 marks)
3. Briefly evaluate research into the effects of absence of gating on the nature of virtual relationships.
   (6 marks)
4. This article appeared in a magazine: 'Psychologists express concern over online anonymity. People are closing their Facebook accounts because they would rather not have to read abusive posts on their timelines.'

   Discuss virtual relationships in social media. Refer in your answer to the issues raised in the magazine article. *(16 marks)*

Evaluation extra: Online versus multimodal.

The hyperpersonal model and absence of gating suggest that forming relationships online may be easier, especially for some people.

But Walther (2011) argues all relationships are multimodal, conducted both online and offline so both modes influence each other.

This suggests we cannot ignore theories of virtual relationships but it is wrong to focus on one mode rather than both.

Parasocial relationships

Spec spotlight

Parasocial relationships: levels of parasocial relationships, the absorption addiction model and the attachment theory explanation.

It wasn't the first time Maxwell had been mistaken for a celebrity – but the fact they thought he was Justin Bieber came as a bit of a surprise.

Apply it

To begin with, Conor enjoyed watching Game of Thrones. He followed each series and liked to discuss the episodes with his colleagues at work.

Eventually, Conor spent more and more time telling his colleagues all about Game of Thrones. He felt strongly that he and Cersei Lannister had a lot in common and fantasised about being her.

Recently, Conor has described himself as Game of Thrones' biggest fan. He thinks about Cersei all the time. He has spent a lot of money on merchandise and is in debt. He is planning to go to work dressed as Cersei.

1. Identify the levels of parasocial relationship that Conor displays.

2. Outline how **two** theories explain how Conor's parasocial relationship begins and progresses.

Levels of parasocial relationships

CAS assesses celebrity attraction.	The *Celebrity attitude scale* (CAS) was used by Maltby *et al.* (2006) to identify three levels of parasocial relationship.
Three levels.	First level is *entertainment-social*. This is the least intense level where celebrities are viewed as sources of entertainment and fuel for social interaction.
	Second level is *intense-personal*, an intermediate level where someone becomes more personally involved with a celebrity and this may include obsessive thoughts.
	Third level is *borderline-pathological*, the strongest level of celebrity worship where fantasies are uncontrollable and behaviour is more extreme.

The absorption addiction model

Explains parasocial relationships in terms of *life deficiencies*.	McCutcheon (2002) suggests that parasocial relationships can make up for personal deficiencies (e.g. lack of fulfilment).
	Parasocial relationships also provide an escape from mundane lives.
	People may be pushed towards the intense-personal level by stressful life events such as a bereavement.
Model has two components.	Absorption – seeking fulfilment in celebrity worship motivates an individual to focus their attention on the celebrity, to become absorbed in the celebrity's existence and identify with them.
	Addiction – like a physiological addiction, an individual needs to increase their 'dose' of involvement to gain satisfaction. This may lead to more extreme behaviours and delusional thinking.

Attachment theory explanation of parasocial relationships

Links early attachment problems to parasocial relationships.	Bowlby's attachment theory suggests that early difficulties in attachment may lead to difficulties in forming successful relationships later in life.
	Such difficulties may lead to a preference for parasocial relationships to replace those within one's own social circle as parasocial relationships do not require the same social skills.
Insecure attachment types are linked to parasocial relationships.	Ainsworth (1979) identified two attachment types associated with unhealthy emotional development:
	• Insecure–resistant types are most likely to form parasocial relationships because they want to have their unfulfilled needs met in a relationship where there is no real threat of rejection.
	• Insecure–avoidant types prefer to avoid the pain and rejection of any type of relationship, either social or parasocial.

One strength of levels approach is research support.

McCutcheon *et al.* (2016) found that people in borderline-pathological and intense-personal categories had a high degree of anxiety in intimate relationships.

People at the entertainment-social level generally did not (although even this level was associated with other relationship problems).

This suggests that 'celebrity-worshippers' can usefully be classified into three categories and that these are predictive of actual behaviour.

Another strength is support for the absorption addiction model.

Maltby *et al.* (2005) studied teenagers who had an intense-personal relationship with a female celebrity whose body shape they admired.

They found that the female adolescents had a poor body image and suggested absorption-addiction may contribute to development of an eating disorder.

This finding shows that there is a **correlation** between level of parasocial relationship and poor psychological functioning.

Fans of Harry Styles are likely to run in only 'one direction' – towards him!

A further strength of attachment theory is it applies universally.

Dinkha *et al.* (2015) compared attachment and parasocial relationships in contrasting cultures – **collectivist** (Kuwait) and **individualist** (US).

In both cultures people with insecure attachments were the most likely to form intense parasocial relationships with TV characters.

This supports the view that attachment type may be a universal explanation for the need to form parasocial relationships.

Counterpoint

However, McCutcheon *et al.* (2006) found that participants with insecure attachments were no more likely to form parasocial relationships than participants with secure attachments.

Therefore parasocial relationships are not ways of compensating for unfulfilled emotional needs due to childhood attachment problems.

Evaluation extra: Causation and correlation.

Studies like McCutcheon *et al.*'s (2016) use correlational analysis, so do not show causal relationships – could be opposite direction or an unmeasured third variable.

However, correlations (or **natural experiments**) can suggest links (but not causes), and may be the only option we have.

Therefore although correlational data should be treated with caution, it can be valuable for its insights into parasocial relationships' links with other variables.

Knowledge Check

1. Explain what is meant by 'levels of parasocial relationships'. *(4 marks)*

2. Outline the attachment theory explanation of parasocial relationships. *(6 marks)*

3. Evaluate the absorption addiction model of parasocial relationships. *(6 marks)*

4. Denise has just started at secondary school. Her parents are concerned because she watches Zoella's YouTube channel a lot more than she used to. Denise spends more time talking about Zoella than she does doing her homework.

   Using Denise's experience as an example, discuss research into parasocial relationships. *(16 marks)*

Sex and gender

Spec spotlight

Sex and gender. Sex-role stereotypes.

Of course people would make reference to their featureless faces and the fact that their heads were not in contact with the rest of their bodies – but Polly and Dilbert loved each other, and that was all that mattered.

Apply it

A recent report by psychologists concluded that parents (and others) still tend to treat boys and girls differently. 'The 'pinkification' of girls has progressed to the point where almost all advertising aimed at girls is for something pink. Toys and activities aimed at boys usually involve aggression and competition. Girls' and boys' playground activities are just as gender-related as they were 50 years ago. Even some teachers have different expectations of boys and girls, especially in maths and sciences.'

Use your knowledge of sex, gender and sex-role stereotyping to discuss the issues raised in the report.

Sex and gender

Sex is a biological status (innate).	Someone's sex is biologically determined by their genetic make-up, namely their sex chromosomes (XX for females and XY for males).
	Chromosomes influence hormonal and anatomical differences that distinguish males and females (e.g. reproductive organs, body shape and hair growth).
Gender is a psychosocial status (nurture).	Gender, described as masculine or feminine, reflects all the attitudes, behaviours and roles we associate with being male or female.
	Biological sex is innate and cannot be changed. But gender is 'assigned' and partly determined by nurture (fluid), e.g. being masculine or feminine depends on social context.
Gender dysphoria is where sex and gender do not correspond.	For most people their biological sex and gender identity correspond.
	However, some people experience *gender dysphoria* (explained further on page 108) when their biological sex does not reflect the way they feel inside and the gender they identify themselves as being.
	Gender reassignment surgery allows people to bring their sexual identity in line with their gender identity.

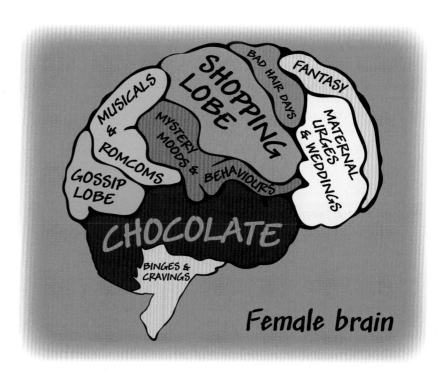

Sex-role stereotypes

Sex-role stereotypes are *social expectations*.	Sex-role stereotypes are shared by a culture or social group and consist of expectations regarding how males and females should behave.
	These expectations are transmitted through a society and reinforced by members of it (e.g. parents, peers, etc.).
Sex-role stereotypes may or may not represent something real.	Some expectations have some basis in reality.
	For example, it might be the male in a heterosexual couple who is responsible for DIY whilst the female sends the birthday cards from both of them.
	However, there is no biological reason for this to be the case.
	Many sex-role stereotypes are incorrect assumptions and can lead to sexist and damaging attitudes.
	For example, the stereotype that women are too emotional to cope with high-powered jobs.
Research confirms sex-role stereotypes in the media.	A study of TV adverts (Furnham and Farragher 2000) found men were more likely to be shown in autonomous roles in professional contexts, whereas women were seen occupying familial roles in domestic settings.
	This along with other studies demonstrates both the existence of sex-role stereotypes and the role the media has in reinforcing them.

Nurse or doctor? The irony was that Nathan was neither but since he'd passed the first aid course, he'd taken to wearing scrubs at the office.

Revision BOOSTER

This topic is likely to have just short-answer questions and likely not to involve evaluation. If you were set a discuss question then you might use research evidence such as Furnham and Farragher on the left, and Smith and Lloyd on page 105.

Knowledge Check

1. Explain the difference between sex and gender.
   (4 marks)

2. Explain what is meant by the term 'sex'. *(2 marks)*

3. Describe what research has shown about sex-role stereotypes. *(4 marks)*

4. Brian makes sure the car is working properly, puts the bins out and is responsible for the TV remote control. Shirley does most of the housework, including the cooking, and is the one who remembers everybody's birthdays.

   With reference to Brian **and** Shirley's behaviour, describe research into sex-role stereotypes. *(8 marks)*

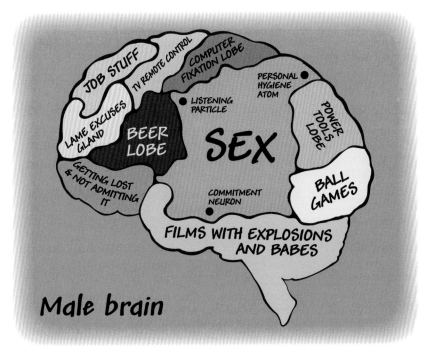

Androgyny

Spec spotlight

Androgyny and measuring androgyny including the Bem Sex Role Inventory.

Androgyny – not so much a 'look' as a state of mind.

Revision BOOSTER

'Androgyny' is a key term, named in the specification. Like other such key terms, you need to make sure you can write a brief description/explanation of it for up to 3 marks.

Apply it

Two psychology students want to conduct a study into the link between androgyny and psychological well-being. They consider using the Bem Sex Role Inventory to assess androgyny, but are aware that it has been criticised. They don't know enough about the issues to make a decision, so they turn to you for advice.

Using your knowledge of how psychologists measure androgyny, how would you advise the students?

Defining androgyny

Androgyny is a *balance* of masculine and feminine characteristics.	Everyday understanding of the term *androgyny* relates to appearance as being neither female nor male. Psychologically it refers to the presence of a balance of masculine and feminine traits, behaviours and attitudes. For example, someone who is sensitive at home but aggressive at work.
Androgyny is a positive attribute.	Bem (1974) suggested that high androgyny is associated with psychological well-being. Individuals who have a balance of masculine and feminine traits are better equipped to adapt to a range of situations. Androgyny needs to be distinguished from over-representation of opposite-sex characteristics. For example, a female who is very masculine or a male who is very feminine would not exhibit the necessary balance of male and female traits and may not be androgynous.

Measuring androgyny: The Bem Sex Role Inventory (BSRI)

Items on the BSRI are *masculine, feminine* or *neutral.*	Masculine items include dominant, competitive and athletic. Female items include gentle, affectionate and sympathetic. Neutral items are characteristics which do not apply more specifically to one sex than another, including sincere, friendly and unpredictable.
BSRI has 60 questions and a 7-point scale.	BSRI has 20 feminine, 20 masculine and 20 neutral trait items. Participants use a 7-point rating scale to rate each trait (1 is 'never true of me' and 7 is 'always true of me').
Masculine and feminine categorisation.	In total there are four categorisations that can be made: 1. A masculine categorisation results from a high score on masculine items and low score on feminine items. 2. A feminine categorisation results from a high feminine score and a low masculine score.
Androgynous and undifferentiated categorisation.	The other two categorisations are consistently high or consistently low: 1. An androgynous categorisation results from a high score on both masculine and feminine scales. 2. An undifferentiated categorisation results from a low score on both the masculine and feminine scales.

One strength is that gender identity is measured quantitatively.

Bem's numerical approach is useful when it is necessary to quantify a dependent variable but Spence (1984) suggests a qualitative approach may represent gender identity better.

One compromise is to combine different scales. For example, the Personal Attribute Questionnaire (PAQ) adds another dimension (instrumentality and expressivity) to Bem's masculinity–femininity dimension.

This suggests that quantitative together with qualitative approaches may be useful for studying different aspects of gender identity.

Expected behaviour for men and women has changed over time – as I was saying to my sister the other day when she walked off the rugby field.

Another strength is that the BSRI has been found to be both valid and reliable.

Development of the scale involved 50 males and 50 females judging 200 traits in terms of gender desirability. The top 20 in each case were used. Piloting with 1000 students showed the BSRI reflected their gender identity (**validity**).

A follow-up study involving a smaller sample of the same students produced similar scores when the students were tested a month later, suggesting high test-retest **reliability**.

Together this evidence suggests that the BSRI had a degree of both validity and reliability at the time it was developed.

Understanding yourself

The full version of the BSRI is available all over the internet. Your teacher might ask you to do this anyway, but why not fill it in for yourself? Become familiar with it and learn a few examples of masculine, feminine and neutral items for the exam.

Counterpoint

Stereotypical ideas of masculinity and femininity have changed since the BSRI was developed 40 years ago. Also, it was devised by a panel who were all from the US.

This suggests that the BSRI may lack **temporal validity** and be culturally biased and not a suitable measure of gender identity today.

One limitation is people may lack insight into their gender identity.

Gender is a social construct which may be more open to interpretation than, say, sex (which is a biological fact).

Furthermore, the questionnaire's scoring system is subjective and people's application of the 7-point scale may differ.

This suggests that the BSRI may not be a scientific way of assessing gender identity.

Revision BOOSTER

It really pays to practise writing 16-mark essays with your book shut and timing yourself – about 20 minutes for a 16-mark essay. Don't think it will magically come right on the day – test yourself.

Evaluation extra: Androgyny and well-being.

Bem emphasised that androgynous individuals are more psychologically healthy as they can deal with situations that demand a masculine, feminine or mixed (androgynous) response.

However, some argue that people with a greater proportion of masculine traits are better adjusted as these are more highly valued in Western culture (Adams and Sherer 1985).

This means that having more masculine traits may have advantages for psychological health, at least in the West, but overall a flexible approach is likely to be better.

Knowledge Check

1. Explain what is meant by 'androgyny'. *(3 marks)*

2. Outline research into androgyny. *(6 marks)*

3. Discuss **one** criticism of the Bem Sex Role Inventory. *(4 marks)*

4. Describe **and** evaluate how psychologists have measured androgyny. *(16 marks)*

The role of chromosomes and hormones

Spec spotlight

The role of chromosomes and hormones (testosterone, oestrogen and oxytocin) in sex and gender.

It's clear how the X chromosome got its name but Y?

Apply it

Erika Schinegger won the women's world downhill skiing championship in 1966. She had a medical before the 1968 Winter Olympics that showed she was chromosomally male. Erika discovered she had XY chromosomes and internal male organs but an external female appearance which was why she was presumed to be female. She underwent surgery and hormonal treatment to live as a man. As Erik, he married and fathered two children.

What does Erik's experience tell us about the roles of chromosomes and hormones in sex and gender?

Revision BOOSTER

No you have not slipped into a Biology revision book! The good news is these biological concepts are very factual. There is nothing to understand and students always do well on such topics. Be positive.

The role of chromosomes

Chromosome pair 23 determines biological sex.	Chromosomes are made from DNA – genes are short sections of DNA. Humans have 23 pairs of chromosomes – 23rd pair determines biological sex.
	Under a microscope these chromosomes are either X or Y shape. Female sex chromosomes are XX and male are XY.
	A baby's sex is determined by whether the sperm that fertilises the egg is an X or a Y chromosome.
Y chromosome has *SRY gene*.	The Y chromosome carries a gene called the sex-determining region Y (SRY). This causes androgens to be produced in a male embryo.

The role of hormones

Gender development governed by hormones.	Prenatally hormones act upon brain development and cause development of the reproductive organs.
	At puberty a burst of hormonal activity triggers secondary sexual characteristics such as pubic hair.
	Males and females produce the same hormones but in different concentrations.
Testosterone. Key role in male development and aggression.	**Testosterone** controls the development of male sex organs before birth. If a genetic male produces no testosterone, then no male sex organs appear. If a genetic female produces high levels of testosterone then male sex organs may appear.
	High levels of testosterone are linked to aggression because such behaviour is **adaptive** for males, e.g. for competing with other males to mate with a fertile female and also for hunting (while females tend children).
Oestrogen. Key role in female development and behaviour.	**Oestrogen** controls female sexual characteristics including menstruation.
	During the menstrual cycle some women experience heightened emotionality and irritability – *premenstrual tension* or *premenstrual syndrome* (a diagnosable disorder).
	In extreme cases PMS has been used (controversially) as a defence for violent behaviour in women.
Oxytocin. Implicated in lactation and bonding.	Women typically produce **oxytocin** in larger amounts than men.
	• Stimulates lactation post-birth.
	• Reduces the stress hormone cortisol.
	• Facilitates bonding.
	• May explain why females are more interested in intimacy in relationships than men – though amounts are the same in men and women when kissing and during sex.

One strength is evidence supports the role of testosterone.

Wang *et al.* (2000) gave 227 hypogonadal men (men with low levels of testosterone) testosterone therapy for 180 days.

Testosterone replacement improved sexual function, libido and mood, and significantly increased muscle strength in the sample.

This study suggests that testosterone exerts a powerful and direct influence on male sexual and physical behaviour even in adult males.

Counterpoint

In another study increasing testosterone levels in healthy young men did not significantly increase either interactional (frequency of sexual intercourse) or non-interactional (libido) components of sexual behaviour (O'Connor *et al.* 2004).

This suggests that, in 'normal' adults, additional testosterone has no effects on sexual or aggressive behaviour – though this doesn't challenge the role of testosterone in early development.

One limitation is that biological accounts ignore social factors.

Hofstede *et al.* (2010) claim that gender roles are more about social factors than biology.

Countries that value competition and independence above community (**individualist** cultures), e.g. US and UK, are more masculine, and masculine traits more valued than in **collectivist** cultures.

This challenges biological explanations of gender behaviour and suggests social factors may ultimately be more important in shaping gender behaviour and attitudes.

Another limitation is that biological explanations are reductionist.

Accounts that reduce gender to the level of chromosomes and hormones exclude alternative explanations.

Cognitive explanations include the influence of, for example, **schema** (see page 100). **Psychodynamic** explanations include the importance of childhood experiences (see page 102).

This suggests that gender is more complex than its biological influences alone.

Evaluation extra: Pathologising gender.

Premenstrual syndrome (PMS) is a medical condition caused by fluctuating hormone levels. A diagnosis means a person can access treatment on the NHS to control symptoms.

However, some see PMS as a social construction, not a biological fact, which encourages damaging stereotypes of 'irrational woman', affecting how women are treated (Rodin 1992).

This suggests that the benefits of treatment may not be justified because enhancing negative expectations about women may, for example, damage their equal rights in the workplace.

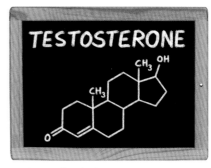

Aggression fuel.

Revision BOOSTER

Have you checked out our revision advice on pages 4 to 9?

Download suggested answers to the Knowledge Check questions from tinyurl.com/yd3ezhkb

Knowledge Check

1. Briefly explain the roles of testosterone, oestrogen **and** oxytocin in sex **and/or** gender.
   (2 marks + 2 marks + 2 marks)

2. Outline the role of chromosomes in sex. *(6 marks)*

3. Evaluate research into the role of hormones in sex **and** gender. *(6 marks)*

4. This item appeared in a newspaper: Cheat! Caster Semenya is no woman. The South African 800m runner has no ovaries, and three times the normal level of testosterone for a woman. 'She' has internal testes and in our book that makes 'her' a man. This newspaper says, 'Don't let Caster compete as a woman.'

   With reference to the issues in the above item, discuss the role(s) of chromosomes **and/or** hormones in sex **and** gender. *(16 marks)*

Atypical sex chromosome patterns

Spec spotlight

Atypical sex chromosome patterns: Klinefelter's syndrome and Turner's syndrome.

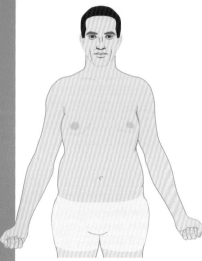

The additional breast tissue and soft body contours associated with a man who has Klinefelter's syndrome.

A woman with Turner's syndrome may have a wide 'webbed' neck, a broad 'shield' chest and narrow hips.

Klinefelter's syndrome

XXY chromosomal structure.

About 1 in 600 males have Klinefelter's syndrome.

Individuals who have this condition are biological males with male anatomy but have an additional X chromosome.

10% of cases are identified prenatally but up to 66% may not be aware of it. Diagnosis often comes about accidentally via a medical examination for some unrelated condition.

Physical characteristics

Lack of body hair, health problems.

Some physical effects of XXY chromosome structure are:
- Reduced body hair compared to a typical male.
- Some breast development at puberty (gynaecomastia).
- Underdeveloped genitals.
- More susceptible to health problems that are usually associated with females, such as breast cancer.

Psychological characteristics

Poor language skills, shy.

Klinefelter's syndrome is often linked to psychological characteristics such as:
- Poorly developed language skills and reading ability.
- Passive, shy and lacking interest in sexual activity.
- Tend not to respond well to stressful situations.
- Problems with what are called executive functions, such as problem-solving.

Turner's syndrome

XO chromosomal structure.

1 in 5000 females have Turner's syndrome.

Caused by an absence of one of the two X chromosomes leading to 45 rather than 46 chromosomes.

Physical characteristics

Sterility and immature body shape.

Individuals with Turner's syndrome have the following physical characteristics:
- No menstrual cycle as their ovaries fail to develop, leaving them sterile.
- A broad 'shield' chest and no developing of breasts at puberty.
- Characteristic low-set ears and a 'webbed' neck.
- Hips are not much bigger than the waist.

Psychological characteristics

High reading ability, social immaturity.

Psychological characteristics of Turner's syndrome include:
- Higher-than-average reading ability.
- Lower-than-average performance on spatial, visual memory and mathematical tasks.
- Tendency to be socially immature.

AO3 Evaluation

One strength of the research is its contribution to the nature–nurture debate.

Comparing both chromosome-typical and atypical individuals highlights psychological and behavioural differences. For example, Turner's syndrome is associated with higher verbal ability.

It might be logically inferred that these differences have a biological basis and are a direct result of the abnormal chromosomal structure.

This would suggest that innate 'nature' influences have a powerful effect on psychology and behaviour.

Counterpoint

However, behavioural differences may result from social influences. Social immaturity in Turner's may be because individuals are treated that way due to their immature appearance.

This shows that it could be wrong to assume that psychological and behavioural differences in people with atypical sex chromosome patterns are due to nature.

Another strength of research is its application to managing the conditions.

Continued research into atypical sex chromosome patterns leads to earlier and more accurate diagnoses and positive outcomes.

A study of 87 individuals with Klinefelter's syndrome showed that those identified when young benefitted in terms of managing their condition (Herlihy et al. 2011).

This suggests that increased awareness of these conditions has real-world application.

One limitation is there may be a sampling issue.

Generally, only those people who have the most severe symptoms are included in the Klinefelter's database, therefore the typical profile may be distorted.

The use of prospective studies show the majority of those with Klinefelter's don't have **cognitive** or psychological problems, and many are highly successful (Boada et al. 2009).

This suggests that the typical picture of Klinefelter's (and Turner's) syndrome may be exaggerated.

Not everyone agrees with this conclusion. What do you think?

Evaluation Extra: Knowing or not knowing.

Knowing you have Klinefelter's or Turner's creates a self-fulfilling prophecy. A child may try less hard if they expect, for example, to have language difficulties.

However, early knowledge of the condition means the child doesn't feel their differences are 'their fault'. They can also access medical and psychological support.

This suggests that the benefits of knowing one's condition may outweigh the potentially negative effects on one's self-concept.

Apply it

Ryan is 16 and has very little body hair. He is very uncoordinated and clumsy. He is tall with long limbs and is also developing some breast tissue.

Tamara is 18 and has never had a period. She has recently been diagnosed as infertile. Her body shape suggests she has not been through puberty.

1. These are some of the physical characteristics of people with Klinefelter's and Turner's syndromes. Outline what Ryan's and Tamara's *psychological* characteristics are likely to be.

2. How can people like Ryan and Tamara help us understand gender?

Revision BOOSTER

Here's a very common evaluative point: 'The study was correlational, so it did not establish cause and effect.' That's too easy. It's a useful way of remembering the issue for yourself. But in an exam answer, you should be doing more with it. Fully explain the point for maximum credit – what are the alternative factors involved, or the direction of causality?

Knowledge Check

1. Using an example, explain what is meant by 'atypical sex chromosome pattern'. *(2 marks)*

2. Outline **one** atypical sex chromosome pattern. *(6 marks)*

3. Evaluate research into **either** Klinefelter's syndrome **or** Turner's syndrome. *(6 marks)*

4. Describe **and** evaluate research into Klinefelter's syndrome **and/or** Turner's syndrome. *(16 marks)*

Cognitive explanations: Kohlberg's theory

Spec spotlight

Cognitive explanations of gender development, Kohlberg's theory, gender identity, gender stability and gender constancy.

Hopefully you've got my trousers in that briefcase, dear – I couldn't leave the house all day.

Apply it

Here are some comments made by children:

Claire: 'When I grow up I'm going to be a daddy.'

Ollie: 'Pop has long hair. He must be a lady.'

Justin: 'That man's wearing a dress; he looks funny.'

1. Approximately how old do you think Claire, Ollie **and** Justin are?

2. Identify the stages of gender development they are at.

3. Outline how Kohlberg's theory explains each of these examples of gender development.

Cognitive-developmental theory of gender development

Cognitive-developmental approach.	Kohlberg's (1966) theory is **cognitive** because a child's *thinking* about their gender is emphasised. Developmental because the theory is concerned with *changes* in thinking over time.
Gender development parallels intellectual development.	Piaget (see pages 110 to 113) proposed that the way a child thinks changes with age – it is a biological process based on changes in the brain. This can be applied to gender development. Kohlberg identified three stages in gender development, related to Piaget's ideas. There are gradual rather than sudden transitions between stages and consequently the ages are approximate.
Stage 1 *Gender identity*, from about 2 years old.	Children are able to correctly identify themselves as a boy or a girl. By 3 years, most children are able to identify other people as male or female, and can select the correct pictures when asked, 'Which one of these is like you?' Their understanding of gender appears limited to labelling and they have no sense of the permanence of gender. For instance, a boy at this stage may say, 'when I grow up I will be a mummy'.
Stage 2 *Gender stability*, from about 4 years old.	Children realise that they will stay the same gender over time. However, they still find it challenging to apply this logic to: • Other people (e.g the idea that a man remains a man even if he grows his hair long). • Other situations (e.g. believing that people change sex if they engage in activities which are more often associated with the opposite gender – such as a female builder or a male nurse).
Stage 3 *Gender constancy*, from about 6 years old.	Children now recognise that gender remains constant across time and situations. And can apply this to other people as well as to themselves. They may be amused by someone with the external appearance of the other sex (e.g. a man in a dress), but they understand he is still a man.
Gender constancy = the start of a search for gender-appropriate role models.	Gender constancy also marks the point when children begin to seek out gender-appropriate role models to identify with and imitate. Kohlberg suggests that once the child has a fully developed and internalised concept of gender at the constancy stage, they look for evidence which confirms it and gender stereotyping begins to occur.

Speech bubble: WELCOME HOME

One strength is that there is supporting research evidence.

Damon (1977) told children a story of George, a boy who liked to play with dolls. The children were asked to comment.

4-year-olds said it was fine. 6-year-olds thought it was wrong – they had developed rules about what they ought to do (gender stereotyping).

This would suggest that children who have achieved constancy have, as predicted, formed rigid stereotypes regarding gender-appropriate behaviour.

Counterpoint

Bussey and Bandura (1999) found that children as young as 4 years old reported 'feeling good' about playing with gender-appropriate toys and 'bad' about doing the opposite.

This contradicts Kohlberg's theory and suggests that children begin to absorb gender-appropriate information as soon as they develop gender identity.

I want to tell my parents that I'm getting rather fed up with being forced to crawl through this flimsy polythene tube but, unfortunately, my age-appropriate but underdeveloped linguistic skills prohibit me from doing so. So, the tube it is then.

One limitation is the methodology of supporting studies.

Bem (1989) suggests it is no wonder younger children are confused by changes in appearance because our culture demarcates gender through e.g. clothes and hairstyle.

Bem found 40% of children aged 3–5 demonstrated constancy if they were first shown a naked photo of the child-to-be identified.

This suggests the typical way of testing gender constancy may misrepresent what younger children actually know.

Revision BOOSTER

Approximate ages for each stage in Kohlberg's theory are included here. It's worth learning them so you can use them in the exam to give that little bit more detail that could make your answer stand out from the rest.

Another limitation is there may be different degrees of constancy.

Martin et al. (2002) suggest an initial degree of constancy may help children choose friends or seek gender information, for instance, and develops before age 6.

A second degree (which develops later) may heighten responsiveness to gender norms under conditions of conflict, such as choosing appropriate clothes or attitudes.

This suggests that the acquisition of constancy may be a more gradual process and begins earlier than Kohlberg thought.

Knowledge Check

1. In relation to cognitive explanations of gender development, explain what is meant by 'gender identity' **and** 'gender constancy'.
   (2 marks + 2 marks)

2. Outline Kohlberg's theory as a cognitive explanation of gender development. *(6 marks)*

3. Discuss **one or more** limitations of Kohlberg's theory of gender development. *(6 marks)*

4. Ryan is 5 years old. When his mum tells him that daddy has a new job as a nurse, Ryan is shocked. 'Does that mean daddy is a lady now?' he asks.

   With reference to Ryan's comment, discuss **one** cognitive explanation of gender development. *(16 marks)*

Evaluation extra: Nature or nurture?

Kohlberg's theory has cross-cultural support (e.g. Munroe et al. 1984), suggesting that the cognitive changes described may be universal, and therefore biological.

Bussey and Bandura (1999) claim that observation, imitation and identification with role models play a much more influential role in gender development than cognitive structures.

This suggests that it is likely that the development of gender-related concepts in the maturing child involves an interaction of nature and nurture.

Cognitive explanations: Gender schema theory

Spec spotlight

Cognitive explanations of gender development, gender schema theory.

Apply it

Mandy and Brad decided that they would try to raise their children with a neutral gender identity. So they called their son Skyler and gave him a mix of traditional boys' and girls' toys (e.g. dolls, trains, cooking). Skyler didn't seem quite content until he went to nursery for the first time. He came home one day and said he no longer wanted to do any sewing.

Use your knowledge of gender schema theory to explain why Skyler may have developed new preferences.

Are you in with the in-crowd? This bunch would be an ingroup for a boy but an outgroup for a girl.

Gender schema theory (GST)

GST suggests understanding changes with age.	Martin and Halverson's (1981) gender schema theory (GST), like Kohlberg's theory, is also **cognitive**-developmental, i.e. thinking changes with age.
	Like Kohlberg's theory, GST also suggests that children actively structure their own learning of gender.
	This contrasts with **social learning theory (SLT)** which suggests that children passively observe and imitate role models (SLT is discussed on page 104).
Gender schema organise our knowledge of gender.	**Schema** are mental constructs that develop via experience (with some basic, limited ones present from birth).
	They are used by us to organise our knowledge.
	Gender schema contain what we know in relation to gender and gender-appropriate behaviour.
Gender schema develop after gender identity.	GST suggests that first a child establishes gender identity (around 2–3 years).
	The child then begins to look around for further information to develop their schema.
Search for gender information.	GST suggests the search for gender-appropriate information occurs much earlier than Kohlberg suggested.
	Kohlberg proposed that children needed to first achieve gender constancy (around the age of 7 years) but GST proposes this starts after gender identity forms around age 3.
Gender stereotypes develop.	Gender-appropriate schema expand over time to include a range of behaviours and personality traits based on stereotypes (e.g. boys liking trucks and girls liking dolls).
	The schema direct the child's behaviour based on stereotypes (e.g. 'I am a boy so I play with trucks').
	By 6 years of age Martin and Halverson suggest children have acquired a rather fixed and stereotypical idea about what is appropriate for their gender.
Ingroup gender information is remembered better than *outgroup*.	Children pay more attention to, and have a better understanding of, the schema appropriate to their own gender (ingroup) than those of the opposite gender (outgroup).
	Ingroup identity bolsters the child's level of self-esteem as there is always a tendency to judge ingroups more positively.
	At around 8 years of age children develop elaborate schema for both genders.

One strength is that GST has research support.

Martin and Halverson (1983) found that children under 6 were more likely to recall gender-appropriate photographs than gender-inappropriate ones when tested a week later.

Children tended to change the gender of the person carrying out the gender-inappropriate activity in the photographs when asked to recall them.

This supports gender schema theory which predicts that children under 6 would do this (in contrast with Kohlberg who said this happens in older children).

Cannot compute! Images of females occupying a stereotypical male role would be ignored or misremembered by children.

One limitation is that gender identity probably develops earlier.

Zosuls *et al.* (2009) analysed twice-weekly reports from 82 mothers on their children's language from 9–21 months and videotapes of the children at play.

Children labelled themselves as a 'boy' or 'girl' (gender identity), on average, at 19 months – almost as soon as they began to communicate.

This suggests that Martin and Halverson may have underestimated children's ability to use gender labels for themselves.

Counterpoint

However, for Martin and Halverson the ages are *averages* rather than absolutes. It is the *sequence* of development that is more important.

This suggests that Zosuls *et al.*'s finding is not a fundamental criticism of the theory.

Another strength is that GST can account for cultural differences.

Cherry (2019) argues gender schema not only influence how people process information but also what counts as culturally-appropriate gender behaviour.

In societies where perceptions of gender have less rigid boundaries, children are more likely to acquire non-standard gender stereotypes.

This contrasts with some other explanations of gender development, such as **psychodynamic** theory (next spread), which suggests gender identity is more driven by unconscious biological urges.

Evaluation extra: Timing.

Kohlberg argues that children must achieve gender constancy (at age 6) before they begin to show gender-appropriate behaviour and look for role models to imitate.

Martin and Halverson argue that children show signs of gender-appropriate behaviour shortly after gender identity (at age 2).

This suggests that Kohlberg was wrong and gender-appropriate behaviour begins before gender constancy or, it could be, that gender constancy itself develops before age 6.

Revision BOOSTER

One kind of question in the exam is the 'mini essay' (worth 8 marks, for example). Clearly, not as much material is required for one of these compared with a full-blown 16-marker. So consider this as you revise the evaluative points on each AO3 page. Which are your 'favourites'? Which would you opt for if you only needed two? Go for the ones that you can explain and elaborate most fully. In a mini essay never try to squeeze in all of them – less is more.

Knowledge Check

1. Outline **one** cognitive explanation of gender development. *(6 marks)*
2. Outline gender schema theory as a cognitive explanation of gender development. *(6 marks)*
3. Evaluate gender schema theory as an explanation of gender development. *(10 marks)*
4. Outline **and** evaluate **two** cognitive explanations of gender development. *(16 marks)*

Other explanations of gender development: Psychodynamic

Spec spotlight

Psychodynamic explanation of gender development, Freud's psychoanalytic theory, Oedipus complex; Electra complex; identification and internalisation.

Nigel had decided it was never too early to teach his son the basic skills in life. Tomorrow – driving lessons.

Apply it

Tors is a 5-year-old boy who, up until now, wanted to spend most of his time with his mum. He resisted being with his dad and always sought out his mum when he was upset or distressed. However, recently Tors has preferred to spend time with his dad and is no longer interested in the cuddles he used to enjoy from mum. He is even copying some of his dad's behaviour.

1. How can Tors' behaviour be explained by Freud's psychoanalytic theory of gender development? Refer in your answer to the concepts of the Oedipus complex, identification and internalisation.

2. Write a brief scenario like the one above, but illustrating a girl's experience at the same age, to reflect the concept of the Electra complex.

Freud's psychoanalytic theory

Phallic stage is the key time for gender development.	Freud's (e.g. 1905) **psychodynamic** developmental theory explains five psychosexual stages: oral, anal, phallic, latent and genital. Pre-phallic stage – children have no concept of gender identity. They have no understanding of 'male' or 'female' and do not categorise themselves or others this way. Phallic stage – around 3–6 years, boys experience the Oedipus complex and girls experience the Electra complex.
Oedipus complex in boys. Desire for mother, jealous of father.	During the phallic stage boys develop incestuous feelings towards their mother. They want their mother for themselves. Thus they feel a jealous hatred for their father who has what the boy desires (the mother). Boys recognise that their father is more powerful. They fear that, on discovering their son's desire for the mother, their father will castrate the son (and experience *castration anxiety*).
Electra complex in girls. Mother is rival, and blamed for castration.	Jung used the term Electra complex to describe the conflict that girls experience. Freud called it penis envy. During the phallic stage girls feel competition with their mother for their father's love. Girls also resent their mother because they believe that she is responsible for their lack of a penis.
Resolution through *identification* with same-sex parent.	For a boy the conflict between his desires and his castration anxiety is resolved when the boy gives up his love for his mother and begins to identify with his father. Girls acknowledge that they will never have the penis that they desire. They substitute this with a desire to have their own children and through this they finally identify with their mother and her gender.
Identification leads to *internalisation*.	Boys adopt the attitudes and values of their father, and girls adopt those of their mother. Freud referred to this process as internalisation of parents' identity. This happens all at once.
Little Hans study illustrates the Oedipus complex.	Little Hans was a 5-year-old boy with a morbid fear of being bitten by a horse. His fear appeared to stem from an incident when he had seen a horse collapse and die in the street. Freud's interpretation was that Hans's fear of horses represented his actual fear of being castrated by his father because of Hans's love for his mother. Freud suggested that Hans had transferred his fear of his father onto horses via displacement (a defence mechanism).

One strength is there is some support for the Oedipus complex.

Freud's theory means that, for boys, 'normal' development depends on being raised by at least one male parent. There is some support for this idea.

Rekers and Morey (1990) rated the gender identity of 49 boys (aged 3–11). 75% of those judged 'gender disturbed' had no biological or substitute father living with them.

This suggests that being raised with no father may have a negative impact upon gender identity, in line with what Freud's theory would predict.

Lloyd was jealous of Maria for many reasons – she had a better job, a fancier computer and, of course, she had a womb.

Counterpoint

Bos and Sandfort (2010) compared 63 children with lesbian parents and 68 children from 'traditional' families. There were no differences in terms of psychosocial adjustment or gender identity.

This contradicts Freud's theory as it suggests that fathers are not necessary for healthy gender identity development.

One limitation is Freud's theory does not fully explain female development.

Freud's idea of penis envy has been criticised as merely reflecting the era he lived and worked in, where males held so much of the power.

Horney (1942) argued that in fact men's womb envy was more prominent (a reaction to women's ability to nurture and sustain life).

This challenges the idea that female gender development was founded on a desire to want to be like men (an **androcentric bias**).

Another limitation is that the theory is pseudoscientific.

Freud is criticised for the lack of rigour in his methods (**case studies**). Also many of his concepts (e.g. penis envy) are unconscious and untestable.

This makes Freud's theory *pseudoscientific* (not genuine science) as his key ideas cannot be *falsified*, i.e. proved wrong through scientific testing.

This questions the **validity** of Freud's theory as it is not based on sound scientific evidence.

Do you agree with this conclusion?

Evaluation extra: The nature of development.

Freud said children do not begin to show gender-appropriate behaviour until after age 6. Kohlberg agrees gender constancy occurs at age 6.

However, Kohlberg suggests the gender concept develops gradually in stages. Freud suggests that gender is acquired all at once.

Freud's view seems overly simplistic, it is unlikely that such a complex concept arrives all at once as Freud suggested.

Revision BOOSTER

What are your evaluations like? Why not try and make them more like ours? Start with your initial point – a strength or a limitation in most cases. Then... elaborate! Develop your evaluation point in three more steps, just as we've done on all of these AO3 pages. Have a close look at each evaluation to see what they have in common.

Knowledge Check

1. With reference to Freud's psychoanalytic theory of gender development, explain what is meant by the 'Oedipus complex' **and** the 'Electra complex'.
   (2 marks + 2 marks)

2. Explain the role of identification **and** internalisation in the psychoanalytic theory of gender development. *(6 marks)*

3. Briefly evaluate Freud's psychoanalytic theory of gender development. *(5 marks)*

4. Some psychologists believe that boys and girls go through different processes of gender development. But both sexes experience identification **and** internalisation.

   Describe **and** evaluate **one** psychodynamic explanation of gender development. Refer in your answer to the comments above. *(16 marks)*

Other explanations of gender development: Social learning

Spec spotlight

Social learning theory as applied to gender development.

Apply it

Louis, a 4-year-old boy, is very boisterous and active and sometimes quite aggressive when he plays. He enjoys the rough and tumble of wrestling with his dad and prefers toys such as soldiers, guns, etc.

Lionel is quite a feminine boy who enjoys playing with dolls and playing make-up games with his mum. He chose to dress as a 'zombie bride' at Halloween.

Explain how social learning theory would account for both Louis' and Lionel's gender development.

Modelling

Modelling can refer to when a fashion model models some clothing – or it can mean a form of learning where individuals learn a particular behaviour by observing another individual performing that behaviour.

Hang on – it's the same thing!

Yes, Gary was a male model, handsome and the envy of his friends – but it was some comfort to them that, at 22, he still couldn't put a coat on properly.

Social learning theory applied to gender development

Gender is learned through *observation* and *reinforcement* in a social context.	**Social learning theory (SLT)** acknowledges the role of social context in gender development. Gender behaviour is learned from observing others and being reinforced for the imitation of the behaviour. SLT draws attention to the influence of the environment (nurture) in shaping gender development. Influences can include peers, parents, teachers, culture and the media.
Direct reinforcement. Genders reinforced differently.	Children are reinforced for gender-appropriate behaviour. For example, boys may be praised for being active and assertive and punished for being passive or gentle. Differential reinforcement explains why boys and girls learn distinctly different gender behaviours – they are reinforced for different behaviours, which they then reproduce.
Indirect. *Vicarious reinforcement* and *punishment*.	Vicarious reinforcement – if consequences of another person's behaviour are favourable, that behaviour is more likely to be imitated by a child (e.g. if a girl sees her mother being complimented when wearing a pretty dress). Vicarious punishment – if consequences of behaviour are seen to be unfavourable (i.e. punished), behaviour is less likely to be imitated (e.g. if a little boy sees another boy teased for displaying feminine behaviour they are unlikely to copy it).
Children will identify with *role models*.	A child will identify with people around them that they perceive to be 'like me' or like someone 'I want to be'. These role models tend to be: <ul><li>Part of the child's immediate environment (parents, teachers, siblings, etc.).</li><li>In the media (pop or sports stars).</li><li>Attractive, high status.</li><li>The same sex as the child.</li></ul>
Behaviour *modelled* and then imitated.	**Modelling** in gender development occurs in two ways: 1. A mother may *model* stereotypically feminine behaviour when tidying the house or preparing dinner. 2. When a girl copies her mother setting the table, or attempts to 'feed' her doll using a toy bottle, she is *modelling* the behaviour she has observed.
Mediational processes – the cognitive factors that determine the production of an observed behaviour.	Four mediational processes in learning gender behaviour: <ul><li>Attention – for instance, a little boy might watch what his favourite footballer does.</li><li>Retention – remembering the skills of the footballer and trying to reproduce these when he plays.</li><li>Motivation – desire to be like his hero.</li><li>Motor reproduction – be physically capable of doing it.</li></ul>

One strength is supporting evidence for differential reinforcement.

Smith and Lloyd (1978) observed adults with babies aged 4–6-months who (irrespective of their actual sex) were dressed half the time in boys' clothes and half the time in girls' clothes.

Babies assumed to be boys were encouraged to be adventurous and active and given a hammer-shaped rattle. Babies assumed to be girls were reinforced for passivity, given a doll and praised for being pretty.

This suggests that gender-appropriate behaviour is stamped in at an early age through differential reinforcement and supports the SLT explanation of gender development.

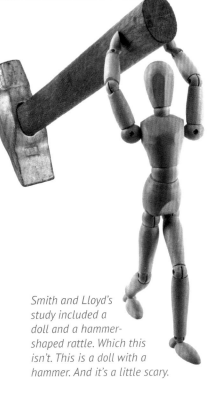

Smith and Lloyd's study included a doll and a hammer-shaped rattle. Which this isn't. This is a doll with a hammer. And it's a little scary.

Counterpoint

Differential reinforcement may not be the *cause* of gender differences. Adults may respond to innate gender differences in their own children e.g. encouraging naturally boisterous boys to be active.

This suggests that it is likely that social learning is only part of the explanation of how children acquire gender-related behaviours.

Another strength is that SLT can explain cultural changes.

There is more androgyny (less of a clear-cut distinction between stereotypically masculine and feminine behaviour) in many societies today than there was in, say, the 1950s.

This shift in social expectations and cultural norms means new forms of gender behaviour are unlikely to be punished and may be reinforced.

This shows that social learning not biology can better explain gender behaviour (**cognitive** factors could also explain cultural changes in terms of **schema**/stereotypes).

Revision BOOSTER

If you were an athlete preparing for a big race you would do lots of timed practice runs. You should do the same with your exam answers. Shut your book and try to write answers to the questions below – you have just over a minute per mark. Afterwards, criticise your own answer.

One limitation is that SLT does not explain the developmental process.

The implication of SLT is that modelling of gender-appropriate behaviour can occur at any age, i.e. from birth onwards.

It's illogical that children who are, say, 2 learn in the same way as children who are 9 (this conflicts with Kohlberg's theory, for instance).

This shows that influence of age and maturation (i.e. development) on learning gender concepts is not considered by SLT, a limitation.

Evaluation extra: Identification.

Freud, like SLT, thought identification was important in gender development. Freud claimed the key process is internalising the gender identity of the same-sex parent.

In contrast, the SLT view of identification also includes a whole host of gender-appropriate role models, e.g. siblings, peers, media.

This suggests that it is likely that key people, such as a same-sex parent, might well be a key influence but not the sole influence.

Knowledge Check

1. Outline social learning theory as applied to gender development. *(6 marks)*
2. Explain the difference between the social learning and the psychodynamic explanations of gender development. *(4 marks)*
3. Explain **one** strength of social learning theory as applied to gender development. *(4 marks)*
4. Discuss social learning theory as applied to gender development. *(16 marks)*

The influence of culture and media on gender roles

Spec spotlight

The influence of culture and media on gender roles.

In some cultures owning a tractor is a good way to advertise your wealth and resources. Just saying...

Apply it

In an online conversation on Mumsnet, many contributors voiced concerns that what their children like to watch on TV reinforces gender role stereotypes. Others were optimistic that things are changing, arguing that films such as Frozen and Brave challenge traditional stereotypes.

With reference to these **two** positions, explain how the media can influence gender roles.

Culture and gender roles

Nature versus nurture.	Nature – if a gender behaviour is consistent across cultures we consider it innate or biological.
	Nurture – if a gender behaviour is culturally-specific we consider this is due to the influence of shared norms and socialisation.
The role of *nurture.* Mead's research (cultural differences).	Mead's (1935) research on cultural groups in Samoa supported the cultural determination of gender roles. • Arapesh were gentle and responsive (similar to the stereotype of femininity in industrialised societies). • Mundugumor were aggressive and hostile (similar to the stereotype of masculinity in industrialised societies). • Tchambuli women were dominant and they organised village life, men were passive and considered to be decorative (reverse of gender behaviour in industrialised societies).
The role of *nature.* Buss's research (cultural similarities).	Buss (1995) found consistent mate preferences in 37 countries studied across all continents. In all cultures: • Women sought men offering wealth and resources. • Men looked for youth and physical attractiveness. Munroe and Munroe (1975) found that in most societies, division of labour is organised along gender lines.

Media and gender roles

Same-sex media role models preferred.	Children are most likely to imitate role models who are the same sex as they are and who are engaging in gender-appropriate behaviour. This maximises the chance of gender-appropriate behaviours being reinforced.
The media creates rigid gender stereotypes.	Bussey and Bandura (1999) found that the media provides rigid gender stereotypes, for example: • Men are independent, ambitious and advice-givers. • Women are dependent, unambitious and advice-seekers. Furnham and Farragher (2000) found that men were more likely to be shown in autonomous roles within professional contexts, whereas women were often seen occupying familial roles within domestic settings.
The media increases self-efficacy.	Seeing other people perform gender-appropriate behaviours increases a child's belief that they are capable of such behaviours (= **self-efficacy**). Mitra *et al.* (2019) found girls in India who watched a programme challenging gender stereotypes were more likely to see themselves as capable of working outside the home than non-viewers.

One strength is that the influence of culture has research support.

In industrialised cultures, changing expectations of women are a function of their increasingly active role in the workplace (Hofstede 2001).

In traditional societies women are still house-makers as a result of social, cultural and religious pressures.

This suggests that gender roles are very much determined by the cultural context.

One limitation is that Mead's research has been criticised.

Freeman (1983) studied the Samoan people after Mead's study, and claimed Mead had been misled by some of her participants.

He also claimed Mead's preconceptions of what she would find had influenced her reading of events (*observer bias* and *ethnocentrism*).

This suggests that Mead's interpretations may not have been objective and questions the conclusions that she drew.

Evaluation extra: Nature or nurture?

Evidence of similarities in gender roles across cultures (e.g. Buss), suggests that gender roles may be biologically-determined and the result of nature.

However, other research (e.g. Mead), supports gender roles as transmitted within cultures, i.e. nurture.

This suggests that gender roles are best seen as an interaction of nature and nurture influences.

One strength of media influence is that it has a theoretical basis.

The more time individuals spend 'living' in the media world, the more they believe it reflects the social reality of the 'outside' world (cultivation theory).

Bond and Drogos (2014) found a positive **correlation** between time spent watching *Jersey Shore* and permissive attitudes towards casual sex (other factors controlled).

This suggests the media 'cultivates' perception of reality and this affects gender behaviour (e.g. sexual behaviour).

One limitation is there may not be a causal relationship.

Durkin (1985) argues that even very young children are not passive recipients of media messages, family norms are a bigger influence.

If media representations confirm gender roles held by the family, norms are reinforced in a child's mind. If not, then they are likely to be rejected.

This suggests that media influences are secondary to other influences, such as family.

Evaluation extra: Counter-stereotypes.

The media can challenge gender stereotypes. Pingree (1978) found gender stereotyping was reduced among children when shown TV adverts of women in non-stereotypical roles.

However, the stereotypes of older boys in the study became stronger, they wanted to differ from the adult view.

This suggests that counter-stereotypes need to be carefully targeted and presented in a way that takes account of who the audience is.

Revision BOOSTER

The term 'imposed etic' is not on the specification, but an understanding of it is really useful here as well as elsewhere. For example, it's used in relation to cultural bias in Chapter 4 on issues and debates in psychology. It's also a criticism of Ainsworth's Strange Situation (called a 'culture-bound test'). Try to cross-reference between different topics like this – it will strengthen your understanding. Make sure you use the term in the exam if you get the chance.

As far as gender is concerned, neither route provides the best answer.

Knowledge Check

1. Outline research into the influence of culture on gender roles. *(6 marks)*

2. Explain what research on the media has shown about the influence of culture on gender roles. *(6 marks)*

3. Evaluate research into the influence of **either** culture **or** the media on gender roles. *(6 marks)*

4. Describe **and** evaluate research into the influence of culture **and/or** the media on gender roles. *(16 marks)*

Spec spotlight

Atypical gender development: gender dysphoria; biological and social explanations for gender dysphoria.

Apply it

The High Court in October 2016 heard the case of a mother who was 'absolutely convinced that her 7-year-old son perceived himself as a girl'. The boy (referred to as 'X') wore girls' clothes to school, was registered as a girl with the local doctors' surgery and showed 'feminine mannerisms'. He played with girls' toys and was said to 'disdain his penis' and wanted to have it removed.

How would biological and social explanations of gender dysphoria explain X's experience?

Twin studies

MZ twins share 100% of genes but DZ twins only 50% (on average) – so we would expect a greater likelihood of both MZ twins developing GD if it is mostly genetic.

This is because it is assumed that both MZ and DZ twins share the same environment, but MZ twins have a greater degree of genetic similarity than DZs.

Separation anxiety can be avoided by symbiotic fusion. Er... come again?

Gender dysphoria

GD occurs where sex and gender do not correspond.	Gender dysphoria (GD) – a mismatch between a person's biological sex and the gender they feel they are. **DSM**-5 specifically excludes atypical gender conditions with a biological basis (e.g. Klinefelter's syndrome).

Biological explanations

Brain sex theory. Looks at the BST.	The *bed nucleus of the stria terminalis* (BST) is involved in emotional responses and male sexual behaviour in rats. This area is larger in men than women and is female-sized in transgender females (Kruijver *et al.* 2000). People with GD have a BST which is the size of the sex they identify with, not the size of their biological sex. This fits with people who are transgender who feel, from early childhood, that they were born the wrong sex (Zhou *et al.* 1995).
Genetic basis. Indicated in twin studies.	Coolidge *et al.* (2002) studied 157 twin pairs (**MZ** and **DZ**) and suggest that 62% of these cases could be accounted for by genetic variance. Heylens *et al.* (2012) found that nine (39%) of their sample of MZ twins were concordant for GD, but none of the DZs were.

Social explanations

Social constructionist. GD explained in terms of socialisation.	Gender identity 'invented' by societies, not biological. Gender confusion (dysphoria) arises because people have to select a gender. Therefore dysphoria is not pathological (a mental disorder) but due to social factors.
	For example, McClintock (2015) studied biological males in New Guinea born with female genitals due to genetic condition. At puberty genitals change and accepted as *kwolu-aatmwol* – females-then-males. However, after contact with West *kwolu-aatmwol* are seen as abnormal instead of normal.
Psychoanalytic theory. Explains male GD in terms of separation anxiety.	Ovesey and Person (1973) suggest GD in biological males is caused by a child experiencing extreme separation anxiety before gender identity has been established. The boy fantasises about a symbiotic fusion with his mother to relieve his anxiety and remove his fear of separation. As a result the boy 'becomes' the mother and thus adopts a female gender identity. Stoller (1973) found that GD in biological males did describe overly close mother–son relationships that would lead to greater female identification and confused gender identity in the long term.

One limitation is that brain sex theory assumptions have been challenged.

Hulshoff Pol et al. (2006) scanned transgender individuals' brains during hormone treatment – size of BST changed significantly.	Kruijver et al. and Zhou et al. examined the BST post-mortem and after transgender individuals had received hormones during gender reassignment treatment.	This suggests that differences in the BST may have been an effect of hormone therapy, rather than the cause of gender dysphoria.

One strength is that there may be other brain differences.

Rametti et al. (2011) analysed brains of both male and female transgender individuals, crucially *before* they began hormone treatment as part of gender reassignment.	In most cases, the distribution of white matter corresponded more closely to the gender the individuals identified themselves as being rather than their biological sex.	This suggests that there are early differences in the brains of transgender individuals.

Evaluation extra: Socially-sensitive research.

Classifying dysphoria as a medical category removes responsibility from the person. They may be less likely to assume the way they feel is 'their fault'.	However, such a description risks stigmatising those who are subject to it, characterising them as 'ill' or 'sick' rather than merely 'different'.	This suggests that researchers and clinicians should avoid reinforcing damaging stereotypes where possible.

One strength is evidence of more than two gender roles.

Some cultures recognise more than two genders, e.g. *fa'afafine* of Samoa, challenging male versus female.	Increasing numbers of people now describe themselves as non-binary, showing cultural changes now match the lived experience of many.	This suggests that gender identity (and dysphoria) is best seen as a social construction than a biological fact.

One limitation is issues with psychoanalytic theory.

Ovesey and Person's theory does not explain GD in biological females and only applies to transgender females.	Rekers (1986) found that GD in transgender females is due to the absence of the father rather than fear of separation from the mother.	This suggests that psychoanalytic theory does not provide a comprehensive account of gender dysphoria.

Evaluation extra: Different outcomes.

Some people with GD will decide to have gender reassignment surgery.	However, GD may not continue through to adulthood – only 12% of GD girls were still GD at 24 years old (Drummond et al. 2008).	This suggests that gender reassignment surgery before the age of consent must be very carefully managed with appropriate support and safeguards.

TRANS**GENDER**

Previous versions of the DSM used the term 'gender identity disorder' to describe gender dysphoria. DSM-5 has dropped this term to discourage people from seeing gender dysphoria as a disorder.

Revision BOOSTER

Names and dates – what a pain! Students always ask: 'Do I have to learn all these names and dates?' Here's the answer: 'Don't sweat the small stuff, as our American friends would say'. Focus on key psychologists and learn some names you are likely to use in the exam (Kruijver from this section is a good example). But if you forget some names and have to write 'Researchers found that...', then it's not the end of the world. You can still get a top grade if the rest of the detail and elaboration are good.

Knowledge Check

1. In relation to atypical gender development, explain what is meant by 'gender dysphoria'.
   (3 marks)

2. Briefly outline **one** biological **and one** social explanation for gender dysphoria.
   (3 marks + 3 marks)

3. Evaluate research into atypical gender development.
   (6 marks)

4. Psychologists debate the causes of gender dysphoria. Some believe it is the outcome of biological influences, whereas others emphasise the role of social and psychological factors.

   With reference to the debate outlined above, discuss **two** explanations for gender dysphoria. *(16 marks)*

Piaget's theory of cognitive development

Spec spotlight

Piaget's theory of cognitive development: schema, assimilation, accommodation, equilibration.

Confused? Yousef was experiencing what psychologists refer to as a state of disequilibrium.

Apply it

Adelaide is 8 years old and is going shopping for clothes with her mum. She has been shopping before so she knows what's involved in choosing something she likes. For the first time ever, Adelaide is allowed to go to the checkout and pay for her shopping herself. She is unclear about what to do and appears a bit anxious in case she gets it wrong. But she asks her mum to explain, and is much happier when she has. Adelaide said afterwards, 'That was easy – I know what to do now for next time.'

Use your knowledge of Piaget's theory of cognitive development to explain Adelaide's experience.

Revision BOOSTER

It's crucial that you understand the differences between assimilation and accommodation – otherwise you won't really have a detailed understanding of Piaget's theory. Both terms are named on the specification, so be prepared to describe/explain them for up to maybe even 4 marks.

Piaget's theory of cognitive development	
Qualitative differences in children's thinking.	Piaget (1926, 1950) asserted that children do not just know less than adults, they actually think differently.
	Piaget suggested that the way children think changes through a series of stages (described on the next spread).
	He also proposed that *motivation* plays an important role in learning and drives *how* learning takes place.
	We begin with the key concept of **schema**.
Schema are units of knowledge.	Our knowledge of the world is represented in the mind and organised in schema.
	Infants are born with a few schema but construct new ones right from the start, including the 'me-schema' in which all the child's knowledge about themselves is stored.
	Cognitive development involves the construction of increasingly detailed schema for people, objects, physical actions and also for more abstract ideas like justice or morality.
Motivation to learn. Starts with *disequilibrium*.	When a child cannot make sense of their world because existing schema are insufficient, they feel a sense of disequilibrium which is uncomfortable.
	To escape this, and adapt to the new situation, the child explores and learns more. The result is a state of equilibration.
Equilbration is the preferred mental state.	Equilibration is a pleasant state of balance and occurs when experiences in the world match the state of our current schema.
Assimilation. New experiences understood within existing schema.	Any new experience creates disequilibrium because, as yet, it does not fit our existing schema.
	Assimilation takes place when the new experience does not radically change our understanding of the schema so we can incorporate the new experience into our existing schema.
	For example, when a child with dogs at home meets another dog of a different breed, the child will simply add the new dog to their dog-schema (assimilation).
Accommodation. New experiences require major schema change.	An experience that is very different from our current schema cannot be assimilated. Accommodation involves the creation of whole new schema or major changes to existing ones.
	For example, a child with a pet dog may at first think of cats as dogs (because they have four legs, fur and a tail) but then recognise the existence of a separate category called 'cats'.
	This accommodation will involve forming a new 'cat-schema'.

One strength of Piaget's theory is research support.

Howe *et al.* (1992) put 9–12-year-olds in groups to discuss how objects move down a slope. They found that the level of children's knowledge and understanding increased after the discussion.

Crucially though, the children did not reach the same conclusions or pick up the same facts about movement down a slope.

This means that the children formed their own individual mental representations of the topic – as Piaget would have predicted.

Piaget thought that children's cognitive development would be enhanced through contact with other children – though, as this picture shows, that perhaps depends on the child.

Another strength is that Piaget's ideas revolutionised teaching.

In 1960s, children sat copying text. In Piaget's activity-oriented classrooms children construct their own understanding, e.g. investigate physical properties of sand.

At A level, discovery learning may be 'flipped' lessons where students read up on content, forming their own basic mental representation of the topic prior to teaching.

This shows how Piaget-inspired approaches may facilitate the development of individual mental representations of the world.

Counterpoint

There is no firm evidence to suggest that Piaget's teaching ideas are any more effective than others – the input from teacher may be the key (Lazonder and Harmsen 2016).

This means that the value of Piaget's theory to education may have been overstated.

Revision BOOSTER

In a 16-mark essay you don't have to write everything on this spread. This spread contains more than 1000 words!! For a 16-mark essay you probably only have time to write 500 words – but don't cut down the elaboration of the AO3 points. Better to do three elaborated points rather than four briefer ones.

One limitation is that Piaget underestimated the role of other people.

Piaget recognised that other people can be important in learning, for example as sources of information.

However others (e.g. Vygotsky) argued that knowledge first exists between the learner and someone with more knowledge. Supported by evidence.

This means that Piaget's theory may be an incomplete explanation for learning because it neglects the role of other people in learning.

Knowledge Check

1. In the context of Piaget's theory of cognitive development, explain what is meant by 'schema' **and** 'equilibration'.
(2 marks + 2 marks)

2. In relation to Piaget's theory of cognitive development, explain the difference between assimilation and accommodation. *(4 marks)*

3. Outline Piaget's theory of cognitive development.
(6 marks)

4. Discuss Piaget's theory of cognitive development.
(16 marks)

Evaluation extra: The role of motivation.

Piaget believed that we are born with an innate motivation to learn in order to escape the unpleasant state of disequilibrium.

However, Piaget may have overestimated this motivation to learn, possibly because he studied an unrepresentative sample of children.

This suggests that children are born with a degree of intellectual curiosity, but perhaps less than that proposed by Piaget.

Piaget's stages of intellectual development

Spec spotlight

Piaget's theory of cognitive development: stages of intellectual development. Characteristics of these stages, including object permanence, conservation, egocentrism and class inclusion.

Until 7 years of age children are egocentric and assume that the view they have represents the view of others. Observe this kid. To the rest of us, he's stood in the middle of a field – to him, he's found the perfect hiding place.

'Operations' refers to mental rules based on some form of externally-verifiable logic. Pre-operational children are following rules but these rules don't match 'reality'.

Apply it

Calvin has two young children – Hazel aged 4 years and Hector aged 8 years. Whenever Calvin asks his children if they want some juice, Hazel insists on having it in her special cup which is tall and thin. She always refuses the alternative short and fat cup. Hector thinks this is funny – he is happy to have any cup because he can see that daddy is pouring each of them from the same-sized juice bottle.

Identify which of Piaget's stages of intellectual development Hazel and Hector are at. Explain which cognitive skill is illustrated here.

Piaget's stages of intellectual development

Four stages each with a different level of reasoning ability.	Piaget's theory (previous spread) explains how knowledge is acquired through **schema** and disequilibrium/equilibration.
	He also explained **cognitive** development as a set of stages, each characterised by a different level of reasoning ability.
	Exact ages vary but all children go through the same *sequence* of stages.
Sensorimotor stage (0–2 years). Includes *object permanence*.	A baby's focus is on physical sensations and basic co-ordination between what they see and body movement.
	Babies also develop object permanence (the understanding that objects still exist when they are out of sight):
	• Before 8 months, babies immediately switch their attention away from an object once it is out of sight.
	• After 8 months babies continue to look for it. This suggests that babies then understand that objects continue to exist when removed from view.
Pre-operational stage (2–7 years). Includes *egocentrism* and lack of *class inclusion*.	Conservation was tested e.g. by pouring water from wider glass into tall, thin one and asking children if the two glasses held the same amount of liquid.
	Pre-operational said no (because they looked different). They were not able to understand that quantity remains constant even when the appearance of objects changes.
	Egocentrism was tested in the three mountains task (Piaget and Inhelder 1956), each mountain had a different feature: a cross, a house or snow.
	Pre-operational children tended to find it difficult to select a picture that showed a view other than their own.
	Class inclusion was tested, e.g. using a picture of five dogs and two cats, 'Are there more dogs or animals?'
	Pre-operational children tend to respond that there are more dogs (Piaget and Inhelder 1964). They cannot simultaneously see a dog as a member of the dog class and the animal class.
Concrete operations stage (7–11 years). Includes *conservation*.	Children have mastered conservation and are improving on egocentrism and class inclusion.
	However they are only able to reason or operate on physical objects in their presence (concrete operations).
Formal operations stage (11+ years). Includes *syllogisms*.	Abstract reasoning develops – being able to think beyond the here and now. Children can now focus on the form of an argument and not be distracted by its content.
	For example, they can process syllogisms: 'All yellow cats have two heads. I have a yellow cat called Charlie. How many heads does Charlie have?' The answer is two but younger children are distracted by the fact that cats do not have two heads.

One limitation is that Piaget's conservation research was flawed.

Piaget's method may have led children to believe that something must have changed – or why would the researcher change the appearance and then ask them if it was the same?

McGarrigle and Donaldson (1974) used a 'naughty teddy' who accidentally rearranged the counters. 72% of children under 7 correctly said the number remained the same.

This means that children aged 4–6 could conserve, as long as they were not put off by the way they were questioned.

Another limitation is that class inclusion ability is questioned.

Siegler and Svetina (2006) found that, when 5-year-olds received feedback that pointed out subsets, they did develop an understanding of class inclusion.

This was contrary to Piaget's belief that class inclusion was not possible until a child had reached the necessary intellectual development at 7 years of age.

This again means that Piaget underestimated the cognitive abilities of young children.

A further limitation is that the assertions about egocentrism are not supported.

Hughes (1975) found that even at 3½ years a child could position a boy doll in a model building with two intersecting walls so that the doll could not be seen by a policeman doll.

They could do this 90% of the time. 4-year-olds could do this 90% of the time when there were two police officers to hide from.

This again suggests the manner of Piaget's studies and tasks led him to underestimate children's intellectual abilities.

Counterpoint

In all the studies outlined on this page the criticisms relate to the age at which a particular ability appears. The sequence of the stages is not challenged and Hughes' evidence shows that there is progression.

Therefore the core principles of Piaget's stages remain unchallenged but the methods he used meant the timing of his stages was wrong.

Evaluation extra: Domain general and domain-specific.

Piaget believed that cognitive development is a single process (domain-general). Different abilities develop in tandem, which is the basis for teaching children in age groups.

However, the existence of learning difficulties such as autism, in which some abilities develop much faster than others, suggest cognitive development is domain-specific.

Therefore it appears that development is best seen as domain-specific, which may have implications for education.

Revision BOOSTER

Students always overdo the AO1 for this topic because it is relatively easy to learn – focus on how much you actually need for the exam.

This really is a naughty teddy. He's having a wee behind the door.

Knowledge Check

1. In relation to Piaget's stages of intellectual development, explain what is meant by 'object permanence' **and** 'conservation'.
   (3 marks + 3 marks)

2. Identify **one** stage of Piaget's theory of intellectual development **and** outline the features of this stage. *(4 marks)*

3. Explain **one** method that Piaget used to investigate stages of intellectual development. *(4 marks)*

4. Describe **and** evaluate Piaget's stages of intellectual development. *(16 marks)*

Vygotsky's theory of cognitive development

Spec spotlight

Vygotsky's theory of cognitive development, including the zone of proximal development and scaffolding.

Scaffolding. Helping learners negotiate the intellectual challenges of life. I'm wasted in this job, I should have been a poet.

An expert

An expert is any person with more knowledge. This can be an adult or could be a peer.

Apply it

Jamela trains primary teachers and spends a lot of time in the classroom observing trainees. She has noticed that the best trainees spend time with individual children. They can quickly identify where the child is in their understanding and what they need to know to progress further. These trainees use various strategies to capture and keep the child's interest. They get them started on a task and encourage them to keep going with it. Good trainees also get children to do lots of work in pairs.

Use your knowledge of Vygotsky's theory of cognitive development to explain Jamela's observations.

Vygotsky's theory of cognitive development

Social processes matter.	Vygotsky (1934) agreed with Piaget that children develop reasoning skills sequentially but believed that this process was mainly dependent on social processes. Vygotsky claimed knowledge is: • First *intermental* (between someone more expert and someone less expert). • Then *intramental* (within the individual).
Cultural differences in cognitive abilities.	Reasoning abilities are acquired via contact with those around us and as a result there will be cultural differences in **cognitive** development because we all grow up and learn about the world surrounded by cultural values and beliefs. Children pick up the mental 'tools' that are most important for life from the world they live in.
ZPD is the gap between current and potential capabilities.	The *zone of proximal development* (ZPD) is the gap between: • What a child knows or can do alone, and • What the child is capable of, following interaction with someone more expert. The role of a teacher is to guide the child through this gap to as full a level of understanding as the child's developmental ability will allow.
Advanced reasoning ability.	For Vygotsky cognitive development was not just about acquiring more facts but about becoming more skilled at reasoning. The most advanced (formal) reasoning can only be achieved with the help of experts, not simply through exploration.
Experts use *scaffolding* to help learner cross the ZPD.	The process of helping a learner cross the ZPD and advance as much as they can, given their stage of development. Typically the level of help given in scaffolding declines as the learner crosses the ZPD.
Progressive scaffolding strategies.	Wood *et al.* (1976) identified progressive strategies that can be used to scaffold learning. For example, prompts might be (from most to least help): • Demonstration (e.g. mother draws an object with crayons). • Preparation for child (e.g. mother helps child hold crayon). • Indication of materials (e.g. mother points to crayons). • Specific verbal instructions (e.g. mother says, 'How about using the green crayon?'). • General prompts (e.g. mother says, 'Now draw something else.').

One strength of Vygotsky's theory is support for the ZPD.

Roazzi and Bryant (1998) asked one group of 4–5-year-olds to estimate the number of sweets in a box. Most failed to give a close estimate.

A second group of 4–5-year-olds were guided by older (expert) children and most then mastered the task.

This means that children can develop more advanced reasoning with help from a more expert individual.

Another strength is support for the idea of scaffolding.

Conner and Cross (2003) observed 45 children at age 16, 26, 44 and 54 months, finding that mothers used less direct intervention as children developed.

The mothers also increasingly offered help when it was needed rather than constantly.

This means that adult assistance with children's learning is well-described by the concept of scaffolding.

How many sweets? Er... certainly fewer than there were before he turned up.

A further strength is the real-world applications of Vygotsky's ideas.

Educational techniques such as group work, peer tutoring and individual adult assistance are all based on Vygotsky's ideas. Increasingly used in the 21st century.

Van Keer and Verhaeghe (2005) found that 7-year-olds tutored by 10-year-olds, in addition to their whole-class teaching, progressed further in reading than a **control group** who only had class teaching.

This means that Vygotsky's theory has real-world value in education.

Counterpoint

In China classes of 50 children learn effectively in lecture-style classrooms with few individual interactions with peers or tutors (Liu and Matthews 2005).

This means that Vygotsky may have overestimated the importance of scaffolding in learning.

Do you agree with this conclusion?

Evaluation extra: Vygotsky versus Piaget.

There is evidence to support Vygotsky's idea that interaction with a more experienced other can enhance learning (e.g. Conner and Cross).

However, if Vygotsky was right about interactive learning, we would expect children learning together to learn the same things. However it varies a lot.

This means that Piaget might have described learning better than Vygotsky, in spite of Vygotsky's useful emphasis on interaction.

Revision BOOSTER

In question 4 below you are required to refer to the scenario. If you don't then the maximum mark you could get is 12 because 4 of the 16 marks are for application (and 6 for AO1 and 6 for AO3). Applying your knowledge is a tricky skill and well worth practising – there are a lot of marks at stake.

Knowledge Check

1. In the context of Vygotsky's theory of cognitive development, what is meant by 'zone of proximal development' **and** 'scaffolding'? *(2 marks + 2 marks)*

2. Outline Vygotsky's theory of cognitive development. *(6 marks)*

3. Describe research into scaffolding in the context of Vygotsky's theory of cognitive development. *(6 marks)*

4. Uriah is an Ofsted inspector. Over the years he has noticed that excellent learning happens when children who can do a task help children who cannot do it yet.

   Discuss Vygotsky's theory of cognitive development. Refer to Uriah's experience in your answer. *(16 marks)*

Baillargeon's explanation of infant abilities

Spec spotlight

Baillargeon's explanation of early infant abilities, including knowledge of the physical world; violation of expectation research.

An unexpected event?

Apply it

Some babies are watching the 'mouse man'. The mouse man is magic – he can make a mouse appear out of a handkerchief and then disappear, just like that. He forms a 'mouse' from his handkerchief, which peeks out from his hand. Then it turns back into a handkerchief. The babies watch this very carefully – some of them even seem to smile at what the mouse man is doing.

*Explain why the babies might be so fascinated by the mouse man. Refer to violation of expectations **and** Baillargeon's explanation of infant abilities in your answer.*

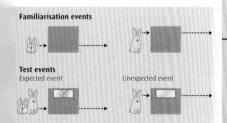

In the VOE study (right) babies were first 'familiarised' with the task (top row). They were then shown the test events to see how they would react.

Baillargeon's explanation of infant abilities

Object permanence is due to poor motor skills.	Piaget suggested that babies don't reach for a hidden object because they lack an understanding of object permanence.
	Baillargeon suggested babies have a better understanding of the physical world than Piaget proposed. Their behaviour might be better explained by poor motor skills or being easily distracted.
VOE research.	Baillargeon (2004) developed the *violation of expectation* (VOE) technique to compare babies' reactions to an expected and an unexpected event and thus was able to make inferences about the infant's **cognitive** abilities (the VOE method is described in the study below).
Innate *PRS* gives infant a basic world understanding.	Baillargeon *et al.* (2012) proposed that we are born with a *physical reasoning system* (PRS) to enable us to learn details of the physical world more easily.
	Baillargeon referred to *object persistence* (similar to Piaget's object permanence) – we know that objects do not disappear.
An example.	From birth, babies identify *event categories* (ways that objects interact), e.g. occlusion events when one object blocks another.
	Since babies know about object persistence they quickly learn that one object can block another (occlusion).

Baillargeon and Graber (1987) VOE study

PROCEDURE

24 babies, aged 5–6 months, were shown a tall or a short rabbit passing behind a screen with a window:

- Expected condition – the tall rabbit can be seen passing the window but the short one cannot.
- Unexpected condition – neither rabbit appeared at the window.

FINDINGS AND CONCLUSIONS

The babies looked for an average of 33.07 seconds (unexpected condition) compared to 25.11 seconds (expected condition).

This was interpreted as meaning that the babies were surprised at the unexpected condition.

This demonstrates an understanding of object permanence at less than 6 months of age.

Other studies tested understanding of containment and of support.

One strength is the validity of the VOE technique.

Piaget made a flawed assumption that loss of interest in an object means the baby thinks it has ceased to exist. But the baby may have just been distracted.

Baillargeon's VOE method controls for this because distraction would not affect the outcome.

This control of a **confounding variable** means the VOE method has greater **validity**.

Counterpoint

Piaget claimed that acting in accordance with a principle is not the same as understanding it. Understanding involves being able to think about it consciously.

This means that babies' responses to unexpected conditions may not represent a change in their cognitive abilities.

Ey up, here he comes again – that psychologist just won't leave me alone.

One limitation is the assumption that response to VOE = unexpectedness.

A methodological issue is that babies' response may not be to the unexpectedness of the event. All VOE shows is that babies find certain events more *interesting*.

We are inferring a link between this response and object permanence. Actually, the different levels of interest in the two different events may be for any number of reasons.

This means that the VOE method may not be a valid way to study a very young child's understanding of the physical world.

Another strength is PRS can explain why physical understanding is universal.

We all have a good understanding of the physical world regardless of culture and experience. So if we drop a key ring we all understand that it will fall to the ground.

This universal understanding suggests that a basic understanding of the physical world is innate. Otherwise we would expect cultural and individual differences.

This means that Baillargeon's PRS appears to be a good account of infant cognitive abilities.

Evaluation extra: Credibility.

There have been challenges to the PRS. It is hard to determine whether a baby is really responding to the unexpected nature of an event, and even if it is this may not indicate understanding.

However, the idea of the PRS fits with what we already know about development of other visual systems e.g. distance perception.

This means that the PRS is probably a credible idea.

Revision BOOSTER

In an exam answer, be careful how you express the criticisms made of Piaget by Baillargeon (and Vygotsky). Neither of them disagree with Piaget's theory in its entirety – they suggest how it can be developed and refined. Be clear about what these refinements are – Baillargeon's focus was on how Piaget's methodology led him to underestimate young children's abilities.

Knowledge Check

1. Explain what is meant by 'knowledge of the physical world' in relation to Baillargeon's explanation of early infant abilities. *(2 marks)*

2. Describe **one** study into violation of expectation in the context of Baillargeon's explanation of early infant abilities. In your answer, explain what the researcher(s) did **and** what was found. *(6 marks)*

3. Evaluate research into Baillargeon's explanation of early infant abilities. *(6 marks)*

4. Describe **and** evaluate Baillargeon's explanation of early infant abilities. *(16 marks)*

Spec spotlight

The development of social cognition: Selman's levels of perspective-taking.

Oh yeah, all Selman thinks about is how other people would feel if I was rescued – how would Holly feel, how would her Dad feel, how would her friend feel? Well, no one ever asks how I would feel. Maybe I like being stuck up here. Maybe I don't want to be rescued... has anyone considered that?

Guys? Guys – come back, I was only joking! Help!

Apply it

Peggy is 11 and her brother Pavel is 7. They both have a tablet, but their parents try to keep their use to a minimum. So Peggy and Pavel are not allowed to use them in bed, for instance. Pavel says, 'I want to use it in bed because I like it and it's mine.' But his sister explains to him, 'Mummy and daddy don't want us to stay up all night playing games on our tablet. They want us to go to sleep – it's for our own good.'

Use your knowledge of Selman's theory of the development of social cognition to explain Pavel's and Peggy's comments.

Levels of perspective-taking

Domain-general versus domain-specific.	Selman (1971, 1976) disagreed with Piaget's domain-general approach to development and proposed that social perspective-taking develops separately from other aspects of **cognitive** development (domain-specific).
Perspective-taking research.	Selman's assessment procedure involved asking children to take the perspective of different people in a social situation and consider how each person felt.
	One scenario featured a child called Holly who has promised her father she will no longer climb trees, but who then comes across her friend whose kitten is stuck up a tree.
	The child participant was asked to explain how each person (Holly, her friend and her father) would feel if Holly did or did not climb the tree to rescue the kitten.
Selman's stage theory.	Selman (1976) found that children of different ages responded in different ways. He used these differences to build a stage theory of how thinking about social situations changes.
	• Stage 0 (3–6 years) *Egocentric* – a child cannot distinguish between their own emotions and those of others nor explain the emotional states of others.
Children progressively see another person's perspective.	• Stage 1 (6–8 years) *Social-informational* – a child can now distinguish between their own point of view and that of others, but can only focus on one perspective at a time.
	• Stage 2 (8–10 years) *Self-reflective* – a child can explain the position of another person and appreciate their perspective but can still only consider one point of view at a time.
	• Stage 3 (10–12 years) *Mutual* – a child is now able to consider their own point of view and that of another at the same time.
The final stage focuses on social conventions.	• Stage 4 (12 years +) *Social and conventional system* – a child recognises that understanding others' viewpoints is not enough to allow people to reach agreement. Social conventions are needed to keep order.
Selman identified three key elements.	(1) *Interpersonal understanding* – this is what Selman measured in his earlier research.
	(2) *Interpersonal negotiation strategies* – having to develop other skills, e.g. learning to negotiate and manage conflict.
	(3) *Awareness of personal meaning of relationships* – being able to relate social behaviour to the particular people we are interacting with.

One strength is research support for stages in perspective-taking.

Selman (1971) tested 60 children aged 4–6 (cross-sectional study) and found positive **correlations** between age and the ability to take different perspectives.

This is supported by **longitudinal** follow-up studies (e.g. Gurucharri and Selman 1982) which confirm that perspective-taking develops with age.

This means that Selman's stages have support from different lines of research.

Bullies were actually found not to have perspective-taking deficits. They were just mean. Plain and simple.

Another strength is support for the importance of perspective-taking.

Buijzen and Valkenburg (2008) observed child–parent interactions in shops when parents refused to buy things their child wanted.

The researchers found negative correlations between both age/perspective-taking and coercive behaviour, i.e. trying to force parents to buy them things.

This suggests that there is a relationship between perspective-taking abilities and healthy social behaviour.

Counterpoint

Not all research supports the link between perspective-taking and social development. Gasser and Keller (2009) found that bullies displayed no difficulties in perspective-taking, in fact scoring higher than victims.

This suggests that perspective-taking may not be a key element in healthy social development.

One limitation of Selman's stages is they are overly cognitive.

Selman's theory looks only at cognitive factors whereas children's social development involves more than their developing cognitive abilities.

For example, internal factors (e.g. empathy) and external factors (e.g. family atmosphere) are important and it is likely social development is due to a combination of these.

This means that Selman's approach to explaining perspective-taking is too narrow.

Not everyone agrees with this conclusion. What do you think?

Evaluation extra: Nurture or nature?

Wu and Keysar (2007) compared American and matched Chinese children and found that the Chinese children were significantly more advanced. This suggests cultural influence.

However, Selman believed that his stages of perspective-taking were based primarily on cognitive maturity and so universal (Vassallo 2017).

This suggests there may be an interaction between nurture and nature, and perhaps Selman wrongly downplayed this.

Revision BOOSTER

Disagree with one of our conclusions? Great! We don't claim to be perfect but we are getting better.

Try to write your own, improved version.

ADHD (sometimes referred to as 'ADD') stands for **attention deficit hyperactivity disorder**, a condition characterised by inappropriate inattention, impulsiveness and motor hyperactivity which is inappropriate for a child's age.

Knowledge Check

1. Explain what is meant by 'social cognition'. **(4 marks)**
2. In the context of the development of social cognition, outline Selman's levels of perspective-taking. **(6 marks)**
3. In relation to the development of social cognition, describe how Selman investigated levels of perspective-taking. **(6 marks)**
4. Parents post on a website about their children's ability to understand other people's points of view. Parents with more than one child agree that it all depends on how old the child is.

   Describe **and** evaluate Selman's levels of perspective-taking as an explanation of the development of social cognition. **(16 marks)**

Social cognition: Theory of mind

Mum, where's my chocolate? I don't want to be in the psychological study anymore, I just want my chocolate!!

False belief

A false belief is a belief in something that is incorrect. For example, Maxi holds a false belief that the chocolate is in the blue cupboard. ToM enables you to understand that what is in your mind is not the same as what is in someone else's mind, i.e. you or someone else may have a false belief.

The Sally–Anne task

Sally puts the marble in her basket.

While Sally is away Anne moves the marble to her box.

When Sally returns, where will she look for her marble?

Theory of mind (ToM)

ToM is the ability to mind-read.	ToM is not a theory like 'Piaget's theory' but a personal theory or belief about what other people know, are feeling or thinking. It is tested via different methods depending on age.
Testing ToM in toddlers – *beads in a jar*.	Meltzoff (1988) allowed children to observe adults placing beads into a jar. • **Experimental condition** – adults appeared to struggle with this and dropped some of the beads outside the jar. • **Control condition** – adults successfully placed the beads in the jar. In both conditions toddlers successfully placed the beads in the jar, suggesting that they were imitating what the adult intended to do rather than what they actually did, demonstrating ToM.
Testing ToM using a *false belief task*.	Wimmer and Perner (1983) told 3–4-year-olds a story in which: • Maxi left his chocolate in a *blue* cupboard in the kitchen. • After Maxi's mother had used some of the chocolate in her cooking she placed the remainder in a *green* cupboard. The children had to say where Maxi would look for his chocolate. Most 3-year-olds incorrectly said that Maxi would look in the green cupboard whilst most 4-year-olds correctly identified the blue cupboard, demonstrating ToM.
Testing ToM using the *Sally–Anne task*.	Children were told a story involving two dolls, Sally and Anne. • Sally places a marble in her basket. • Sally leaves the room. • Anne moves the marble to her box. • Sally returns. • Where does Sally look for her marble? In order to understand that Sally does not know that Anne has moved the marble, a child needs an understanding of Sally's false belief about where it is.
Lack of ToM demonstrated in children with *ASD*.	Baron-Cohen *et al.* (1985) used the Sally–Anne task to test 20 high-functioning children diagnosed with autism spectrum disorder (ASD), and **control groups** of 27 children without a diagnosis and 14 with Down syndrome. 85% of children in the control group correctly identified where Sally would look for her marble but only 20% of the children with ASD did, suggesting that ASD involves a ToM deficit.
Testing ToM using the *Eyes Task*.	Older children with ASD can succeed on false belief tasks, despite problems with empathy, social communication, etc. This questions whether ASD can be explained by ToM deficits. Baron-Cohen *et al.* (1997) developed the Eyes Task as a more challenging test of ToM and found that adults with high functioning ASD struggled. This supports the idea that ToM deficits might be the cause of ASD.

One limitation is the reliance on false belief tasks to test the theory.

Bloom and German (2000) suggest that false belief tasks require other **cognitive** abilities (e.g. visual memory) as well as ToM, so failure may be due to a memory deficit and not ToM.

Furthermore, children who cannot perform well on false belief tasks still enjoy pretend-play, which requires a ToM.

This means that false belief tasks may not really measure ToM, meaning ToM lacks evidence.

Woman: 'I wonder what he's thinking. I wonder if he's wondering what I'm thinking. Maybe we're thinking the same thing.'

Man: 'I wonder if United are winning.'

Another limitation is it's difficult to distinguish ToM from perspective-taking.

Perspective-taking (see previous spread) and ToM are different cognitive abilities. It can be very difficult to be sure we are measuring one and not the other.

For example, in intentional reasoning tasks a child might be visualising the beads task from the adult perspective rather than expressing a conscious understanding of their intention.

This means that tasks designed to measure ToM may actually measure perspective-taking.

Apply it

Paul is 2½ years old and has left his favourite teddy carefully on his bookshelf. While he was at nursery, his mum tidied his room and placed his teddy in a box by his bed.

Using your knowledge of theory of mind, suggest where Paul would look for his teddy and explain why.

One strength of ToM research is its application to understanding ASD.

People with ASD find ToM tests difficult which shows they do have problems understanding what others think.

This in turn explains why people with ASD find social interaction difficult – because they don't pick up cues for what others are thinking and feeling.

This means that ToM research has real-world relevance.

Counterpoint

ToM does not provide a complete explanation for ASD. Not everyone with ASD experiences ToM problems, and ToM problems are not limited to people with ASD (Tager-Flusberg 2007).

This means that there must be other factors that are involved in ASD, and the association between ASD and ToM is not as strong as first believed.

Knowledge Check

1. In relation to the development of social cognition, outline the Sally–Anne study. *(6 marks)*

2. In the context of the development of social cognition, outline theory of mind as an explanation for autism. *(6 marks)*

3. Explain **one** limitation of theory of mind in relation to the development of social cognition. *(4 marks)*

4. Discuss theory of mind as an explanation of the development of social cognition. *(16 marks)*

Evaluation extra: Nature and nurture.

Perner (2002) suggests that ToM develops alongside other cognitive abilities, largely as a result of maturity. Research shows same development of ToM cross-culturally (Liu et al. 2004).

Wilde Astington (1998) suggests ToM develops from interactions with others, supported by Liu et al. who also found that ToM appeared at different ages in different cultures.

This means that the rate of development is modified by the social environment – nature and nurture.

Social cognition: The mirror neuron system

Spec spotlight

The role of the mirror neuron system in social cognition.

Makes you feel like yawning? That'll be your mirror neurons.

Apply it

Two brothers are sitting opposite each other colouring in drawings. Their mum is watching them. Slowly, Lachlan lifts his right hand, points his finger and picks his nose with it. Without any fuss at all, Lancelot does exactly the same thing. Mum has noticed this before in other ways too and she wonders what the explanation could be.

With reference to psychological research, explain how mirror neurons could be responsible for Lachlan's and Lancelot's contagious nose-picking.

The role of mirror neurons

Mirror neurons respond to motor activity of others.	Rizzolatti *et al.* (2002) noted that the same neurons in a monkey's motor cortex became activated when: • Monkeys observed a researcher reaching for his lunch. • The monkey itself reached for food.
Experiencing the *intentions* of others.	Gallese and Goldman (1998) suggested that mirror neurons respond not just to observed actions but to intentions behind behaviour. We need to understand the intentions of others in order to interact socially. Research on mirror neurons suggests we actually simulate the action of others in our own brains and thus experience their intentions through our mirror neurons.
Perspective-taking and *ToM*.	Mirror neurons give us a neural mechanism for experiencing, and hence understanding other people's perspectives and emotional states. This underlies perspective-taking and ToM.
Human social evolution.	Ramachandran (2011) suggested that mirror neurons have shaped human **evolution**, in particular how we have evolved as a social species. Mirror neurons enable us to understand intention, emotion and perspective. These are fundamental requirements for living in large groups with the complex social roles and rules, both of which characterise human culture.
Understanding of *autism* (ASD).	ASD is associated with problems related to social-**cognitive** abilities, such as difficulty with perspective-taking, understanding intention, emotion and ToM. It follows that people with ASD might have a poor mirror neuron system.
The *'broken mirror' theory* of ASD is based on mirror neurons.	Ramachandran and Oberman (2006) have proposed the 'broken mirror' theory of ASD. According to this theory ASD develops due to neurological deficits, including dysfunction in the mirror neuron system. Such dysfunction prevents a child imitating and understanding social behaviour in others. Researchers have observed that, in infancy, children who are later diagnosed with ASD typically mimic adult behaviour less than children with no diagnosis. This may demonstrate innate problems with the mirror neuron system.

One strength is research support for the role of mirror neurons.

Haker *et al.* (2012) demonstrated using brain scans that *Brodmann's Area 9* (part of the brain rich in mirror neurons) is involved in contagious yawning (a simple example of human empathy).

Mouras *et al.* (2008) found when men watched heterosexual pornography, activity in the *pars opercularis* was followed by sexual arousal. Presumably mirror neurons allowed the viewer to experience what they were watching (perspective-taking).

This means that mirror neurons may have a role in empathy and perspective-taking.

One limitation is the difficulties involved in studying the system in humans.

Studies where electrodes are inserted in animal brains are not ethical in humans and the animal findings don't **generalise** to human cognition.

Brain scanning (e.g. Haker *et al.* above) can be used but doesn't measure individual cells.

Therefore there is no gold standard for measuring mirror neuron activity in humans (Bekkali *et al.* 2019), and no direct evidence for mirror neuron activity in humans.

'Look pal, quit staring or there's gonna be trouble.' Dermot was not quite old enough to understand how mirrors work.

Another strength is the application to explaining ASD.

Hadjikhani (2007) reported that the *pars opercularis* (linked to perspective-taking) had a smaller-than-average thickness in people with ASD.

Scanning has also shown lower activity levels in regions of the brain believed to be associated with high concentrations of mirror neurons compared to neurotypical brains.

This suggests that a cause of ASD may be related to the mirror neuron system.

Counterpoint

These findings are not reliable – according to a review of 25 studies by Hamilton (2013) evidence in this area is highly inconsistent.

This means there may not be a link between ASD and mirror neuron activity after all.

Evaluation extra: Mirror neurons and perspective-taking.

Maranesi *et al.* (2017) found specific mirror neurons in monkeys' motor cortex fired according to the position and angle from which experimenters gestured – shows physical perspective is encoded by mirror neurons.

However, Soukayna Bekkali *et al.* (2019) concluded that there is only weak evidence linking mirror neurons to social cognition in humans.

This means that the idea that mirror neurons underlie human perspective-taking in social situations remains unproven.

Revision BOOSTER

You could get this question in the exam: Explain what is meant by a 'mirror neuron'. (2 marks). Nice! But let's face it, you're more likely to get: Explain the role of the mirror neuron system in social cognition. (6 marks). So consider very carefully what that word 'role' means (in understanding intentions, enabling perspective-taking, allowing social evolution).

Knowledge Check

1. In the context of social cognition, explain what is meant by the 'mirror neuron system'. *(2 marks)*

2. Outline research (theories and/or studies) into the mirror neuron system in social cognition. (6 marks)

3. Briefly evaluate the role of the mirror neuron system in social cognition. *(4 marks)*

4. Discuss the role of the mirror neuron system in social cognition. *(16 marks)*

Introduction to schizophrenia

Spec spotlight

Classification of schizophrenia. Positive symptoms of schizophrenia, including hallucinations and delusions. Negative symptoms of schizophrenia, including speech poverty and avolition.

Reliability and validity in diagnosis and classification of schizophrenia, including reference to co-morbidity, culture and gender bias and symptom overlap.

Auditory hallucinations.

Revision BOOSTER

You have just over a minute to spend writing for each mark – but make sure you give that time to the short-answer questions. It's probably easier to boost your mark on these rather than on essay questions.

Apply it

Aiden is an 18-year-old student. He has said to his friends that a voice has told him he has been singled out for great things. Aiden's conversations have recently changed – he rarely gets to the end of a sentence, he seems distracted all the time and often repeats himself.

Explain why Aiden might be diagnosed with schizophrenia. Refer to positive and negative symptoms.

Diagnosis and classification of schizophrenia

Prevalence.	Serious mental disorder affecting 1% of population.
	More common in males, city-dwellers and lower socio-economic groups.
Diagnosis.	Diagnosis and classification are interlinked. To diagnose a specific disorder, we need to be able to distinguish one disorder from another.
	Classification – identify symptoms that go together = a disorder.
	Diagnosis – identify symptoms and use classification system to identify the disorder (e.g. depression, OCD, schizophrenia etc.).
DSM-5 and *ICD-10* differ.	There are two main classification systems in use:
	DSM-5 – one positive symptom must be present (delusions, hallucinations or speech disorganisation).
	ICD-10 (V11 published but not used for diagnosis until 2022) – two or more negative symptoms are sufficient for diagnosis (e.g. avolition and speech poverty).

Symptoms of schizophrenia

Positive symptoms = additional experiences beyond those of ordinary existence.

1: *Hallucinations.*	Unusual sensory experiences that have no basis in reality or distorted perceptions of real things. Experienced in relation to any sense.
	For example, hearing voices or seeing people who aren't there.
2: *Delusions.*	Beliefs that have no basis in reality – make a person with schizophrenia behave in ways that make sense to them but are bizarre to others.
	For example, beliefs about being a very important person or the victim of a conspiracy.

Negative symptoms = loss of usual abilities and experiences.

1: *Speech poverty.*	A reduction in the amount and quality of speech. May include a delay in verbal responses during conversation.
	DSM emphasises speech disorganisation and incoherence as a positive symptom.
2: *Avolition.*	Severe loss of motivation to carry out everyday tasks (e.g. work, hobbies, personal care).
	Results in lowered activity levels and unwillingness to carry out goal-directed behaviours.

One strength of diagnosis of schizophrenia is good reliability.

A reliable diagnosis is consistent between clinicians (inter-rater) and between occasions (test-retest).

Osório *et al.* (2019) report excellent reliability for schizophrenia diagnosis (DSM-5) – inter-rater agreement of +.97 and test-retest reliability of +.92.

This means that the diagnosis of schizophrenia is consistently applied.

One limitation of diagnosis of schizophrenia is low validity.

Criterion validity involves seeing whether different procedures used to assess the same individuals arrive at the same diagnosis.

Cheniaux *et al.* (2009) had two psychiatrists independently assess the same 100 clients. 68 were diagnosed with schizophrenia with ICD and 39 with DSM.

This means that schizophrenia is either over- or under-diagnosed, suggesting that criterion validity is low.

Schizophrenia is often 'co-morbid' with depression.

Counterpoint

In the Osório study (above) there was excellent agreement between clinicians using different procedures both derived from the DSM system.

This means that the criterion validity for schizophrenia is good provided it takes place within a single diagnostic system.

Another limitation is co-morbidity with other conditions.

If conditions often co-occur then they might be a single condition. Schizophrenia is commonly diagnosed with other conditions.

For example Buckley *et al.* (2009) concluded that schizophrenia is co-morbid with depression (50% of cases), substance abuse (47%) or OCD (23%).

This suggests that schizophrenia may not exist as a distinct condition.

A further limitation is gender bias.

Men are diagnosed with schizophrenia more often than women, in a ratio of 1.4:1 (Fischer and Buchanan 2017).

This could be because men are more genetically vulnerable, or women have better social support, masking symptoms.

This means that some women with schizophrenia are not diagnosed so miss out on helpful treatment.

A further limitation is culture bias.

Some symptoms e.g. hearing voices, are accepted in some cultures, e.g. Afro-Caribbean societies 'hear voices' from ancestors.

Afro-Caribbean British men are up to ten times more likely to receive a diagnosis as white British men, probably due to overinterpretation of symptoms by UK psychiatrists.

This means that Afro-Caribbean men living in the UK appear to be discriminated against by a culturally-biased diagnostic system.

A final limitation is symptom overlap.

There is overlap between the symptoms of schizophrenia and other conditions e.g. both schizophrenia and bipolar disorder involve delusions and avolition.

Schizophrenia and bipolar disorder may be the same condition (a classification issue). Schizophrenia is hard to distinguish from bipolar disorder (a diagnosis issue).

This means that schizophrenia may not exist as a condition and, if it does, it is hard to diagnose.

Revision BOOSTER

The specification lists a number of issues in the diagnosis and classification of schizophrenia (see top left of facing page). In essence these are evaluation points. When using these issues as evaluation, be careful to actually apply the concepts to schizophrenia rather than just, for example, explaining why co-morbidity is a problem in the diagnosis and classification of schizophrenia.

Knowledge Check

1. Briefly describe **two** symptoms of schizophrenia.
   (2 marks + 2 marks)

2. Explain the difference between positive and negative symptoms of schizophrenia. *(4 marks)*

3. In relation to diagnosis **and/or** classification of schizophrenia, explain what is meant by 'co-morbidity' **and** 'symptom overlap'.
   (2 marks + 2 marks)

4. Discuss reliability **and** validity in the diagnosis **and/or** classification of schizophrenia. *(16 marks)*

Biological explanations for schizophrenia

Spec spotlight

Biological explanations for schizophrenia: genetics and neural correlates, including the dopamine hypothesis.

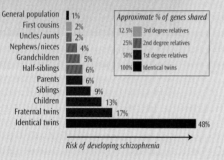

As genetic similarity increases so does the probability of sharing schizophrenia. Source: Gottesman (1991)

Findings from Gottesman's study.

The genetic basis of schizophrenia

Family studies.	Strong relationship between the degree of genetic similarity and shared risk of schizophrenia.
	Gottesman's (1991) large-scale study found (for example) someone with an aunt with schizophrenia has a 2% chance of developing it, 9% for a sibling and 48% for an identical twin.
	Family members also share environment but still indicates support for genetic view.
Candidate genes.	Early research looked unsuccessfully for a single genetic variation to explain schizophrenia.
	Schizophrenia is polygenic – requires several genes.
	It is also aetiologically heterogeneous, i.e. risk is affected by different combinations.
	Ripke *et al.* (2014) combined all previous data from genome-wide studies. Found 108 separate genes associated with slightly increased risk of schizophrenia.
Mutation.	Schizophrenia can also have a genetic origin in the absence of a family history because of mutation in parental DNA.
	Evidence comes from the **correlation** between paternal age (associated with increased risk of sperm mutation) and risk of schizophrenia (Brown *et al.* 2002).

Twin studies

MZ twins share 100% of genes but **DZ twins** only 50% (on average) – so we would expect a greater likelihood of both MZ twins developing schizophrenia if it is mostly genetic.

This is because both MZ and DZ twins are raised together in the same environment, but MZ twins have a greater degree of genetic similarity than DZs.

Neural correlates of schizophrenia

Role of *dopamine*.	**Dopamine** (DA) is widely believed to be involved in schizophrenia because it is featured in the functioning of brain systems related to the symptoms of schizophrenia.
Original DA hypothesis. *Hyperdopaminergia* linked to subcortex.	High dopamine activity in subcortex (central areas of the brain) associated with hallucinations and poverty of speech (e.g. excess of DA receptors in pathways linking from subcortex to Broca's area).
	May explain specific symptoms e.g poverty of speech and auditory hallucinations.
Updated version. *Hypodopaminergia* linked to prefrontal cortex.	Updated hypothesis has added low levels of DA in the prefrontal cortex (responsible for thinking), could explain negative symptoms.
	Explains origins of abnormal DA – genetic variations (see above) and early experiences of stress make some people more sensitive to cortical *hypo*dopaminergia and hence subcortical *hyper*dopaminergia (Howes *et al.*).

Revision BOOSTER

Many students oversimplify the dopamine hypothesis: 'High dopamine levels cause schizophrenia'. But it's not as simple as that, as hopefully you can see from this spread.

Chapter 8: Schizophrenia

One strength is the strong evidence base.

Family studies (e.g. Gottesman, facing page) show risk increases with genetic similarity. Twin study found 33% concordance for MZ and 7% for DZ twins (Hilker *et al.* 2018).

Adoption studies (e.g. Tienari *et al.* 2004) show that biological children of parents with schizophrenia are at greater risk even if they grow up in an adoptive family.

This shows that some people are more vulnerable to schizophrenia because of their genes.

One limitation is evidence for environmental risk factors.

Biological risk factors include birth complications (Morgan *et al.* 2017) and smoking THC-rich cannabis in teenage years (Di Forti *et al.* 2015).

Psychological risk factors include childhood trauma e.g. 67% with schizophrenia (38% matched controls) reported at least one childhood trauma (Mørkved *et al.* 2017).

This means genes alone cannot provide a complete explanation for schizophrenia.

Evaluation extra: Genetic counselling.

If potential parents have a relative with schizophrenia, they can be advised of risk of having a child with the condition.

However the risk estimate is just an average figure based on genetic similarity to relatives, doesn't take account of the future child's environment.

This means that genetic counselling only provides a crude idea of vulnerability and is of limited use.

One strength is support for dopamine in the symptoms of schizophrenia.

Amphetamines (increase DA) mimic symptoms (Curran *et al.* 2004). Antipsychotic drugs (reduce DA) reduce intensity of symptoms (Tauscher *et al.* 2014).

Candidate genes act on the production of DA or DA receptors.

This strongly suggests that dopamine is involved in the symptoms of schizophrenia.

One limitation is evidence for a central role for glutamate.

Post-mortem and scanning studies found raised glutamate in people with schizophrenia (McCutcheon *et al.* 2020).

Also, several candidate genes for schizophrenia are believed to be involved in glutamate production or processing.

This means that a strong case can be made for a role for other neurotransmitters in schizophrenia.

Evaluation extra: Amphetamine psychosis.

Tenn *et al.* (2003) induced schizophenia-like symptoms in rats using amphetamines (raise DA), then relieved symptoms using drugs that reduce DA.

However, apomorphine also increases DA but no symptoms (Dépatie and Lal 2001), and amphetamine psychosis not same as schizophrenia (Garson 2017).

This means that amphetamine psychosis is probably not strong enough evidence for a link between DA and schizophrenia.

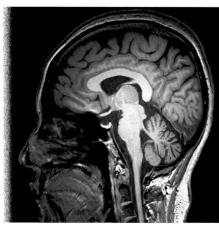

Is schizophrenia a problem in the brain?

Apply it

Scarlett does not know that the man she has called 'dad' all her life is not her biological father. Her mum is now concerned because Scarlett is planning to start a family, and they never got round to telling her the truth. Scarlett's biological father had schizophrenia and her mum thinks this might be passed on to her grandchildren.

Use your knowledge of schizophrenia to explain why Scarlett's mum is both right and wrong to be concerned.

Knowledge Check

1. In relation to biological explanations for schizophrenia, explain what is meant by 'neural correlates'. *(2 marks)*

2. Outline the dopamine hypothesis as a biological explanation for schizophrenia. *(6 marks)*

3. Evaluate genetics **or** neural correlates as a biological explanation for schizophrenia. *(6 marks)*

4. Describe **and** evaluate **one or more** biological explanations for schizophrenia. *(16 marks)*

Psychological explanations for schizophrenia

Spec spotlight

Psychological explanations for schizophrenia: family dysfunction and cognitive explanations, including dysfunctional thought processing.

Schizophrenia may be caused by communication problems.

Apply it

Connor is being interviewed by a psychiatrist because he is experiencing disturbing symptoms. He believes that aliens from Mars are beaming ideas into his head. The interview is difficult because Connor finds it hard to concentrate and his conversation is very disorganised. He mixes up words so his speech doesn't make sense.

How could the psychiatrist explain Connor's behaviour in terms of cognitive factors?

Delicious dates

'Do we have to remember all these dates?' Every teacher is asked this about 83 times a year. The answer is, 'No. Although the examiner will be impressed if you can remember the main ones…'. We provide the dates in this guide just to give you a sense of psychology's timeline.

Family dysfunction

Schizophrenogenic mothers. Rejecting and controlling.	Fromm-Reichmann's (1948) **psychodynamic** explanation of patients' early experiences of 'schizophrenogenic mothers' (mothers who cause schizophrenia). These mothers are cold, rejecting and controlling, and create a family climate of tension and secrecy. This leads to distrust and paranoid delusions and schizophrenia.
Double-bind theory. Conflicting family communication.	Bateson *et al.* (1972) described how a child may be regularly trapped in situations where they fear doing the wrong thing, but receive conflicting messages about what counts as wrong. They cannot express their feelings about the unfairness of the situation. When they 'get it wrong' (often) the child is punished by withdrawal of love – they learn the world is confusing and dangerous, leading to disorganised thinking and delusions.
Expressed emotion. Criticism and hostility lead to relapse.	Expressed emotion (EE) is the level of emotion (mainly negative) expressed including: • Verbal criticism of the person with schizophrenia. • Hostility towards them. • Emotional over-involvement in their life. High levels of EE cause stress in the person, may trigger onset of schizophrenia or relapse.

Cognitive explanations

Dysfunctional thought processing.	Lower levels of information processing in some areas of the brain suggest cognition is impaired. For example, reduced processing in the ventral striatum is associated with negative symptoms.
Metarepresentation leads to hallucinations.	Metarepresentation is the **cognitive** ability to reflect on thoughts and behaviour (Frith *et al.* 1992). This dysfunction disrupts our ability to recognise our thoughts as our own – could lead to the sensation of hearing voices (hallucination) and experience of having thoughts placed in the mind by others (thought insertion, a delusion).
Central control dysfunction leads to speech poverty.	Frith *et al.* (1992) also identified dysfunction of central control as a way to explain speech poverty – central control being the cognitive ability to suppress automatic responses while performing deliberate actions. People with schizophrenia experience derailment of thoughts because each word triggers automatic associations that they cannot suppress.

One strength is evidence linking family dysfunction to schizophrenia.

A review by Read *et al.* (2005) reported that adults with schizophrenia are disproportionately likely to have insecure attachment (Type C or D).

Also, 69% of women and 59% of men with schizophrenia have a history of physical and/or sexual abuse.

This strongly suggests that family dysfunction does make people more vulnerable to schizophrenia.

Family evidence for schizophrenia may be flawed.

One limitation is the poor evidence base for any of the explanations.

There is almost no evidence to support the importance of traditional family-based theories e.g. schizophrenogenic mother and double bind.

Both theories are based on clinical observation of patients and informal assessment of the personality of the mothers of patients.

This means that family explanations have not been able to explain the link between childhood trauma and schizophrenia.

Evaluation extra: Parent-blaming.

Research in this area may be useful, e.g. showing that insecure attachment and childhood trauma affect vulnerability to schizophrenia.

However, research is socially sensitive because it can lead to parent-blaming. This creates additional stress for parents already seeing their child experience schizophrenia and taking responsibility for their care.

This means that research into family dysfunction and schizophrenia will always be very controversial but worth it for potential benefits.

One strength is evidence for dysfunctional thought processing.

Stirling *et al.* (2006) compared performance on a range of cognitive tasks (e.g. Stroop task) in people with and without schizophrenia.

As predicted by central control theory, people with schizophrenia took over twice as long on average to name the font-colours.

This supports the view that the cognitive processes of people with schizophrenia are impaired.

One limitation is only proximal origins of symptoms explained.

Cognitive explanations for schizophrenia are proximal explanations – they explain what is happening *now* to produce symptoms.

Cognitive explanations are weaker as distal explanations (i.e. what causes cognitive problems), possible distal explanations are genetic and family dysfunction.

This means that cognitive theories alone only provide partial explanations.

Evaluation extra: Psychological or biological?

The cognitive approach provides an excellent explanation for the symptoms of schizophrenia, suggesting it is a psychological condition.

However, abnormal cognition is probably partly genetic in origin and the result of abnormal brain development (Toulopoulou *et al.* 2019).

This means that although it has psychological symptoms, schizophrenia is perhaps best seen as a biological condition.

Revision BOOSTER

Only family dysfunction and dysfunctional thought processing are named on the specification as psychological explanations for schizophrenia. There are plenty of others, but don't feel you have to learn additional material. LESS IS MORE! It is much better to have a really clear understanding of two explanations than to know a little bit about lots of them.

Knowledge Check

1. In relation to psychological explanations for schizophrenia, explain what is meant by 'dysfunctional thought processing'. *(3 marks)*

2. Briefly outline **two** psychological explanations for schizophrenia. *(3 marks + 3 marks)*

3. Explain **one** strength of cognitive explanations for schizophrenia. *(4 marks)*

4. Outline **and** evaluate family dysfunction as a psychological explanation for schizophrenia. In your answer refer to another explanation for schizophrenia. *(16 marks)*

Biological therapy for schizophrenia

Spec spotlight

Drug therapy: typical and atypical antipsychotics.

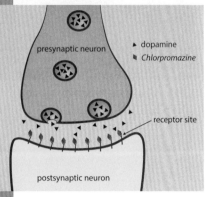

presynaptic neuron
▶ dopamine
▪ *Chlorpromazine*

receptor site

postsynaptic neuron

Chlorpromazine *acts as a dopamine antagonist, i.e. it acts against dopamine, in this case by blocking dopamine receptors at the postsynaptic neuron.*

Revision BOOSTER

Typical and atypical antipsychotics are named on the specification. This means you could be asked to outline one or the other or both. For the full 6 AO1 marks, it's very unlikely you would have to describe just one of them. So your best strategy is to revise 3 marks' worth of AO1 material for each.

Apply it

Coral is a 19-year-old university student recently diagnosed with schizophrenia. Her parents are concerned because Coral's psychiatrist has prescribed antipsychotic drugs. The psychiatrist explains that the drugs are atypical antipsychotics. Coral's parents want to know the difference between these and other antipsychotics. They also want reassurance that the drugs Coral is getting are effective without many side effects.

Use your knowledge of drug therapy to outline what the psychiatrist could tell Coral's parents.

Typical antipsychotics

Dopamine *antagonists*.	Typical antipsychotic drugs (e.g. *chlorpromazine*) have been around since the 1950s.
	They work by acting as antagonists in the **dopamine** system and aim to reduce the action of dopamine – they are strongly associated with the dopamine hypothesis.
Block dopamine receptors in the synapses.	Dopamine antagonists work by blocking dopamine receptors in the synapses in the brain, reducing the action of dopamine.
	Initially, dopamine levels build up after taking *chlorpromazine*, but then production is reduced.
	This normalises neurotransmission in key areas of the brain, which in turn reduces symptoms like hallucinations.
Chlorpromazine also has sedation effect.	*Chlorpromazine* also has an effect on histamine receptors which appears to lead to a sedation effect.
	It is also used generally to calm anxious patients when they are first admitted to hospital.

Atypical antipsychotics

Newer drugs.	The aim of developing newer antipsychotics was to maintain or improve upon the effectiveness of drugs in suppressing the symptoms of psychosis and also to minimise the side effects of the drugs used.
Clozapine acts on dopamine, glutamate and serotonin to improve mood.	*Clozapine* binds to dopamine receptors as *chlorpromazine* does but also acts on **serotonin** and glutamate receptors.
	This drug was more effective than typical antipsychotics – *clozapine* reduces depression and anxiety as well as improving **cognitive** functioning.
	It also improves mood, which is important as up to 50% of people with schizophrenia attempt suicide.
Risperidone is as effective as clozapine but safer.	*Risperidone* was developed in the 1990s because *clozapine* was involved in the deaths of some people from a blood condition called agranulocytosis.
	Risperidone like *clozapine* binds to dopamine and serotonin receptors.
	But *risperidone* binds more strongly to dopamine receptors and is therefore more effective in smaller doses than most antipsychotics and has fewer side effects.

One strength of antipsychotics is evidence of their effectiveness.

Thornley *et al.* (2003) reviewed data from 13 trials (1121 participants) and found that *chlorpromazine* was associated with better functioning and reduced symptom severity compared with **placebo**.

There is also support for the benefits of atypical antipsychotics. Meltzer (2012) concluded that *clozapine* is more effective than typical antipsychotics, and that it is effective in 30–50% of treatment-resistant cases.

This means that, as far as we can tell, antipsychotics work.

Counterpoint

Most studies are of short-term effects only and some data sets have been published several times, exaggerating the size of the evidence base (Healy 2012). Also benefits may be due to calming effects of drugs rather than real effects on symptoms.

This means the evidence of effectiveness is less impressive than it seems.

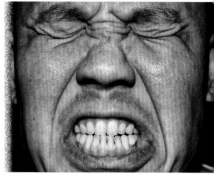

Antipsychotics may have serious side effects, such as grimacing (tardive dyskinesia).

One limitation of antipsychotic drugs is the likelihood of side effects.

Typical antipsychotics are associated with dizziness, agitation, sleepiness, weight gain, etc. Long-term use can lead to lip-smacking and grimacing due to dopamine super-sensitivity (= *tardive dyskinesia*).

The most serious side effect is *neuroleptic malignant syndrome* (NMS) caused by blocking dopamine action in the hypothalamus (can be fatal due to disrupted regulation of several body systems).

This means that antipsychotics can do harm as well as good and individuals may avoid them (reducing effectiveness).

Another limitation of antipsychotics is that we do not know why they work.

The use of most of these drugs is strongly tied up with the dopamine hypothesis and the idea that there are higher-than-usual levels of dopamine in the subcortex of people with schizophrenia.

But there is evidence that this may not be correct and that dopamine levels in other parts of the brain are too low rather than too high. If so, most antipsychotics shouldn't work.

This means that antipsychotics may not be the best treatment to opt for – perhaps some other factor is involved in their apparent success.

Do you agree with this conclusion?

Evaluation extra: The chemical cosh.

It is believed that antipsychotics are used in hospital situations to calm people with schizophrenia and make them easier for staff to work with.

However, calming people distressed by hallucinations and delusions probably makes them feel better, and allows them to engage with other treatments (e.g. **CBT**) and services.

On balance then there are clear benefits to using antipsychotics to calm people with schizophrenia and in the absence of a better alternative they should probably be prescribed.

Knowledge Check

1. Explain the difference between typical and atypical antipsychotics as drug therapies for schizophrenia.
   (4 marks)
2. Outline typical antipsychotics as a drug therapy for schizophrenia.   *(4 marks)*
3. Briefly evaluate atypical antipsychotics as a drug therapy for schizophrenia.
   (4 marks)
4. Discuss drug therapy for schizophrenia. Refer to **both** typical **and** atypical antipsychotics in your answer.
   (16 marks)

Psychological therapy for schizophrenia

Spec spotlight

Cognitive behaviour therapy and family therapy as used in the treatment of schizophrenia.

CBT is a form of talking therapy.

Apply it

Zara has returned home after a spell on a hospital psychiatric ward. She has been diagnosed with schizophrenia and now lives with her mother, two brothers and sister. The family has always been very close and emotions often run high. Although Zara's symptoms are now under control, her community psychiatric nurse is concerned that she might have a relapse. The nurse discusses the possibility of family therapy with Zara's relatives.

Explain how family therapy could help Zara. Use research evidence to support your explanation.

Revision BOOSTER

Because CBT and family therapy are both named on the specification, you need to revise both of these psychological therapies – you could be asked questions specifically on either of them.

If a 16-mark essay was asked on just one of these there is about 120 words for each explanation on this page, which is enough for the 6 AO1 marks in an essay.

Chapter 8: Schizophrenia

Cognitive behaviour therapy (CBT)

Identify and change *irrational thoughts*.	The aims of **CBT** in general are to help clients identify irrational thoughts (e.g. delusions and hallucinations) and try to change them. 5–20 sessions, individually or in a group.
CBT helps clients to understand their symptoms.	Clients are helped to make sense of how their delusions and hallucinations impact on their feelings and behaviour. For example, a client may hear voices and believe they are demons so they will be very afraid. *Normalisation* involves explaining to the client that hearing voices is an ordinary experience.
Case example.	Turkington *et al.* (2004) treated a paranoid client who believed the Mafia were plotting to kill him. The therapist acknowledged the client's anxiety, and explained that there were other, less frightening possibilities and gently challenged the client's evidence for his belief in the Mafia explanation.

Family therapy

Reduce *negative emotions*.	Family therapy aims to reduce levels of *expressed emotion* (EE), especially negative emotions such as anger and guilt which create stress. Reducing stress is important to reduce the likelihood of relapse.
Improve family ability to help.	The therapist encourages family members to form a therapeutic alliance whereby they all agree on the aims of therapy. The therapist also tries to improve families' beliefs about and behaviour towards schizophrenia. A further aim is to ensure that family members achieve a balance between caring for the individual with schizophrenia and maintaining their own lives.
A model of practice.	Burbach's (2018) model: • Phases 1 and 2 – share information and identify resources family can offer. • Phases 3 and 4 – learn mutual understanding, and look at unhelpful patterns of interaction. • Phases 5, 6 and 7 – skills training (e.g. stress management techniques), relapse prevention and maintenance.

One strength of CBT is evidence for its effectiveness.

Jauhar et al. (2014) reviewed 34 studies of CBT for schizophrenia, and concluded that there is evidence for significant effects on symptoms.

Pontillo et al. (2016) found reductions in auditory hallucinations. Clinical advice from NICE (2019) recommends CBT for people with schizophrenia.

This means both research and clinical experience support CBT for schizophrenia.

One limitation is the quality of the evidence.

Thomas (2015) points out that different studies have focused on different CBT techniques and people with different symptoms.

Overall modest benefits of CBT for schizophrenia may conceal a range of effects of different techniques on different symptoms.

This means that it is hard to say how effective CBT will be for treating a particular person with schizophrenia.

Evaluation extra: Does CBT cure?

CBT may improve quality of life but not 'cure'. As schizophrenia is a biological condition CBT should only improve ability to live with schizophrenia.

But studies report significant reductions in positive and negative symptoms. This suggests CBT does more than enhance coping.

On balance then it may well be that CBT may be a partial cure for schizophrenia.

One strength of family therapy is evidence of its effectiveness.

McFarlane (2016) concluded family therapy is effective for schizophrenia. Relapse rates were reduced by 50–60%.

Particularly promising during time when mental health initially starts to decline. NICE recommends family therapy.

This means that family therapy is good for people with both early and 'full-blown' schizophrenia.

Another strength is the benefits for the whole family.

Therapy is not just for benefit of identified patient but also for the families that provide bulk of care for people with schizophrenia (Lobban and Barrowclough).

Family therapy lessens the negative impact of schizophrenia on the family and strengthens ability of the family to give support.

This means family therapy has wider benefits beyond the obvious positive impact on the identified patient.

Evaluation extra: Which matters most?

Family therapy reduces relapse rates and makes families better able to provide the bulk of care so it has economic benefits.

However family therapy also has therapeutic benefits for people with schizophrenia and their families.

This suggests that everyone wins, ultimately therapy should be for the benefit of the person and then their family, and any economic gain is a bonus.

Several generations of a family can benefit from family therapy.

Revision BOOSTER

Question 2 below includes the word 'how'. This means you must focus on what a therapist would actually do when delivering treatment.

CBT may not cure schizophrenia but it may contribute to better self-care.

Knowledge Check

1. Explain what is meant by 'family therapy'. Use an example in your answer.
   (4 marks)

2. Explain how cognitive behaviour therapy is used as a treatment of schizophrenia.
   (6 marks)

3. Evaluate family therapy as a treatment of schizophrenia.
   (6 marks)

4. CBT and family therapy are used in the treatment of schizophrenia.

   Describe **and** evaluate these treatments of schizophrenia.
   (16 marks)

Management of schizophrenia

Spec spotlight

Token economies as used in the management of schizophrenia.

Patients may swap their tokens for a reward – though a film or some food is more likely than a gold star.

Apply it

Jenna was a nocturnal IT systems administrator and singer in a Goth Band before becoming quite disorientated and experiencing hallucinations – she was eventually diagnosed with schizophrenia. She is an introvert but has always liked to take care of her appearance. Jenna's passions are music and film. She has been hospitalised for a year now and is showing signs of institutionalisation.

Explain how you might design a token economy system to help Jenna. Think carefully about target behaviours **and** the kinds of reward you would like to build in.

Revision BOOSTER

Both token economy and management of schizophrenia are named on the specification, an exam question could ask for either. The content is the same however.

Token economies for schizophrenia

Development of *token economies*.	Ayllon and Azrin (1968) used a token economy in a schizophrenia ward. A gift token was given for every tidying act. Tokens were later swapped for privileges e.g. films.
	Token economies were extensively used in the 1960s and 70s. Decline in the UK due to a shift towards care in the community rather than hospitals and because of ethical concerns.
	Token economies still remain a standard approach to managing schizophrenia in many parts of the world.
Rationale for token economies.	Institutionalisation occurs in long-term hospital treatment.
	Matson *et al.* (2016) identified three categories of institutional behaviour that can be tackled using token economies: personal care, condition-related behaviours (e.g. apathy) and social behaviour.
	Modifying these behaviours does not cure schizophrenia but has two major benefits.
1. Quality of life.	Token economies improve the quality of life within the hospital setting, e.g. putting on make-up or becoming more sociable with other residents.
2. 'Normalises' behaviour.	Encourages return to more 'normal' behaviour, making it easier to adapt back into the community e.g. getting dressed or making your bed.
What is involved in a token economy?	Tokens (e.g. coloured discs) given immediately after a desirable behaviour. Target behaviours are decided individually based on knowledge of the person (Cooper *et al.* 2007).
	Tokens have no value themselves but are swapped for rewards e.g. sweets or magazines, or activities like a film or a walk outside.
	Tokens are given immediately following target behaviours because delayed rewards are less effective.
The theory behind token economies – *operant conditioning*.	Token economies are an example of behaviour modification, based on **operant conditioning**.
	Tokens are secondary reinforcers – exchanged for rewards (primary reinforcers which are directly rewarding e.g. food).
	Tokens that can be exchanged for a range of different primary reinforcers are called *generalised reinforcers*. These have a more powerful effect.

One strength is evidence of effectiveness.

Glowacki *et al.* (2016) identified seven high quality studies published between 1999 and 2013 on the effectiveness of token economies in a hospital setting.

All the studies showed a reduction in negative symptoms and a decline in frequency of unwanted behaviours.

This supports the value of token economies.

Counterpoint

Seven studies is quite a small evidence base. One issue with such a small number of studies is the file drawer problem – a bias towards publishing positive findings.

This means that there is a serious question over the effectiveness of token economies.

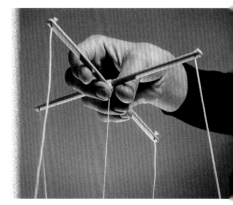

Patients may feel as though they are being controlled by medical professionals.

One limitation is the ethical issues raised.

Professionals have the power to control people's behaviour and this means imposing one person's norms on to others (e.g. a patient may like to look scruffy).

Also restricting the availability of pleasures to people who don't behave as desired means that very ill people, already experiencing distressing symptoms, have an even worse time.

This means that benefits of token economies may be outweighed by the impact on freedom and short-term reduction in quality of life.

Revision BOOSTER

The secret to revision notes is keeping them VERY short – just note key words to-be-remembered. And then practise how you would put them together to write a well-expressed AO1 or AO3 point. If you can't remember the full explanation, then have a look again at what we have written here, and see if you can remember it better next time.

Another limitation is the existence of more pleasant and ethical alternatives.

Other approaches do not raise ethical issues, e.g. art therapy is a high-gain low-risk approach to managing schizophrenia (Chiang *et al.* 2019).

Even if the benefits of art therapy are modest, this is true for all approaches to treatment and management of schizophrenia and art therapy is a pleasant experience.

This means that art therapy might be a good alternative to token economies – no side effects or ethical abuses.

Download suggested answers to the Knowledge Check questions from tinyurl.com/yd3ezhkb

Not everyone agrees with this conclusion. What do you think?

Evaluation extra: Benefits.

A problem with token economies is that they are hard to continue outside a hospital setting. Target behaviours cannot be monitored closely and tokens cannot be given immediately.

On the other hand, some people may only get the chance to live outside a hospital if their personal care and social interaction improves.

This suggests that it is worth it, despite the issues around using them in hospital to give people a chance outside the hospital.

Knowledge Check

1. In relation to the management of schizophrenia, explain what is meant by 'token economy'.
   (2 marks)

2. Explain how a token economy might be used in the management of schizophrenia.
   (4 marks)

3. Explain **one** limitation of using a token economy in the management of schizophrenia.
   (3 marks)

4. Discuss the use of token economies in the management of schizophrenia. *(16 marks)*

The interactionist approach to schizophrenia

Spec spotlight

The importance of an interactionist approach in explaining and treating schizophrenia; the diathesis-stress model.

Can a genetic vulnerability be 'triggered' by cannabis use to lead to schizophrenia?

Apply it

Lorenzo was sexually abused as a child. At 14 years old, he started smoking very powerful cannabis.

Amaya and Cecilia are identical twins. Their father was recently diagnosed with schizophrenia. Amaya is at university facing very important final exams.

Explain how an interactionist approach can help us understand the risk of Lorenzo, Amaya and Cecilia developing schizophrenia.

Revision BOOSTER

In a 16-mark essay you don't have to write everything on this spread. What is here is actually about 800 words. For a 16-mark essay you probably only have time to write 500 words – but don't cut down the elaboration of the AO3 points. Better to do three elaborated points rather than four briefer ones.

The diathesis-stress model

Diathesis-stress model. Vulnerability + trigger = schizophrenia.	*Diathesis* means vulnerability. *Stress* in this context refers to negative experiences that trigger the vulnerability. The **diathesis-stress model** says both a vulnerability and a trigger are needed to develop schizophrenia. Individually may not create schizophrenia – it is the interaction that is key.
Meehl's model. Diathesis is genetic.	In the original diathesis-stress model, diathesis was entirely the result of a single 'schizogene'. Meehl (1962) argued that someone without this gene should never develop schizophrenia, no matter how much stress they were exposed to. But a person who does have the gene is vulnerable to the effects of chronic stress (especially a *schizophrenogenic mother*). The schizogene is necessary but not sufficient for the development of schizophrenia.
Modern understanding of diathesis.	It is now believed that diathesis is not due to a single 'schizogene'. Instead it is thought that many genes increase vulnerability. Also, diathesis doesn't have to be genetic. It could be early psychological trauma affecting brain development. For example, child abuse affects the *hypothalamic-pituitary-adrenal* (HPA) system, making a child vulnerable to stress.
Modern understanding of stress.	A modern definition of stress (in relation to diathesis-stress) includes anything that risks triggering schizophrenia. Can be psychological (e.g. parenting) or biological (e.g. cannabis use). Cannabis use can increase the risk of schizophrenia up to seven times depending on dose – probably because it interferes with the **dopamine** system.

Treatment according to the interactionist model

Antipsychotic medication and CBT.	Antipsychotic drugs taken in combination with **CBT**. But this requires adopting an interactionist model – it is not possible to adopt a purely **biological** approach, tell patients that their condition is purely biological (no psychological significance to their symptoms) and then treat them with CBT (Turkington *et al.* 2006).
UK adopts more interactionist approach compared to US.	In Britain it is increasingly standard practice to treat patients with a combination of drugs and CBT. In the US there is more of a conflict between psychological and biological models of schizophrenia and this may have led to slower adoption of the interactionist approach.

One strength is support for the dual role of vulnerability and stress.

Tienari et al. (2004) studied children adopted away from mothers diagnosed with schizophrenia. The adoptive parents' parenting styles were assessed and compared with a **control group** of adoptees with no genetic risk.

A child-rearing style with high levels of criticism and conflict and low levels of empathy was implicated in the development of schizophrenia but only for children with a high genetic risk.

This shows that a combination of genetic vulnerability and family stress leads to increased risk of schizophrenia.

Parenting style could contribute to the onset of schizophrenia.

One limitation of the original diathesis-stress model is it is oversimplistic.

Multiple genes increase vulnerability, each with a small effect on its own – there is no schizogene. Stress comes in many forms, including dysfunctional parenting.

Researchers now believe stress can also include biological factors. For example, Houston et al. (2008) found childhood sexual trauma was a diathesis and cannabis use a trigger.

This means that there are multiple factors, biological and psychological, affecting both diathesis and stress.

Another strength is real-world application of interaction.

Tarrier et al. (2004) **randomly allocated** 315 participants to (1) medication + CBT group, or (2) medication + supportive counselling group, or (3) control group (medication only).

Participants in the two combination groups showed lower symptom levels than those in the control group – but no difference in hospital readmission.

This means that there is a clear practical advantage to adopting an interactionist approach in the form of superior treatment outcomes.

Counterpoint

Jarvis and Okami (2019) suggest this argument is the same as claiming that because alcohol reduces shyness, shyness is caused by a lack of alcohol, the *treatment-causation fallacy*.

Therefore we cannot automatically assume that the success of combined therapies means interactionist explanations are correct.

Evaluation extra: Urbanisation.

Schizophrenia is more commonly diagnosed in urban than rural areas, may support the interactionist position (urban living is a stressor).

However, schizophrenia may simply be more likely to be noticed in cities, or people with a diathesis for schizophrenia may migrate to cities.

On balance the greater chances of diagnosis in cities is not strong support for the interactionist position.

Knowledge Check

1. Outline the interactionist approach in explaining **and** treating schizophrenia. *(6 marks)*
2. Describe the importance of the diathesis-stress model in explaining **and** treating schizophrenia. *(6 marks)*
3. Discuss **one** limitation of the interactionist approach in explaining schizophrenia. *(4 marks)*
4. Thea has been diagnosed with schizophrenia. Her father had also been diagnosed with schizophrenia and she had a traumatic and unpredictable childhood. She is now taking antipsychotics each day and attending CBT sessions.

   Referring to Thea's experience, discuss the diathesis-stress model in the context of explaining **and** treating schizophrenia. *(16 marks)*

Spec spotlight

Explanations for food preferences: the evolutionary explanation, including reference to neophobia and taste aversion.

It had been a long day.

Evolutionary explanations

The evolutionary argument is that any common food preferences we see today must exist because they provided an adaptive advantage. Those distant ancestors who had such preferences would have been more likely to survive and reproduce and thus we have inherited such preferences.

Apply it

Kassidy is just a year old and seems to have some firm food preferences. He likes crisps and definitely does not like vegetables. He pulls a 'yuk' face whenever his parents try to get him to eat broccoli. His older sister Gianna went through a similar phase but soon started eating different things. But now she is at primary school she is refusing to try anything new.

How would evolutionary explanations for food preference explain Kassidy's and Gianna's behaviour?

Food preferences

Sweetness. Reliable signal of high-energy food.	Steiner (1977) found sugar on tongues of newborn babies produced positive facial expressions (upturned mouth corners).
	Fructose is especially sweet and babies consume large amounts if allowed – this makes **evolutionary** sense because fructose is a 'fast-acting' sugar in fruit, providing energy quickly.
Salt. Used in many cell functions.	Salt taste preference appears in humans at about 4 months.
	Harris *et al.* (1990) found breastfed babies at 16–25 weeks preferred salted cereal – breast milk is low in salt, so this suggests salt preference is innate and not learned.
Fat. High in calories and makes foods palatable.	High-calorie foods were usually unavailable to ancestors so learning a preference for fat was an advantage for survival.
	Fat has twice the calories of equivalent carbohydrate/protein – a preference for fat is an efficient route to ensuring high energy food consumption.
	Fat also makes food taste pleasant (palatability).

Neophobia

Innate unwillingness to try unfamiliar foods that could cause harm.	Food neophobia most pronounced from 2 to 6 years of age.
	Birch (1999) claims neophobia appears when children start to explore and encounter foods independently of parents. Untried foods are potentially dangerous, neophobia is **adaptive** because the child is less likely to eat something causing illness or death.
	Neophobia reduces when we learn specific foods won't poison us – then it is replaced by a different evolutionary mechanism encouraging a varied diet of important nutrients.

Taste aversion

Innate ability to quickly learn to dislike foods that may cause harm.	Seligman's (1971) *biological preparedness* concept says we acquire some aversions quicker than others – to objects/situations of greatest threat to our distant ancestors' survival.
	Garcia and Koelling (1966) found rats acquired taste aversion to sweetened water when paired with poison (**classical conditioning**) but not when paired with electric shocks.
	This is an adaptive response aiding survival.
Bitterness. Example of an adaptive taste aversion.	Bitter tastes are usually a reliable warning sign of toxins in food – it benefits survival to detect these quickly.
	Steiner (1977) found negative facial expressions in babies in response to bitter taste before any learning of preference, strongly suggesting an innate mechanism.

One strength of the evolutionary explanation is research supports it.

Torres *et al.*'s (2008) review of studies concluded humans have a tendency to prefer high-fat foods in periods of stress.

Stress triggers the fight or flight response which creates high energy demands.

Therefore an increased fat preference during times of stress supports the view that such a preference is important for survival.

What? Seriously, what? Do I have something on my face?

One limitation is that neophobia may no longer be adaptive.

Most food we consume is sold by retailers and subject to strict laws, so is very safe with little threat to our survival.

Caution about trying new foods in childhood (neophobia) protected us from sickness and death but now it prevents us from eating safe foods from an early age.

Therefore neophobia restricts a child's diet and limits access to a wider variety of safe foods that provide nutritional benefits.

Revision BOOSTER

You will never need more than 6 marks' worth of material to describe the evolutionary explanation (or any explanation). So let's do the maths. This is about 150–200 words. If you know six basic points and can write 25 words (on average) for each, then you'll be fine. That's why the AO1 pages of this guide are divided into six points.

Another limitation of the explanation is individual differences in taste aversion.

If food preferences are adaptive we would expect that everyone has the same preferences e.g. a dislike of the bitter-tasting chemical PROP.

Drewnowski *et al.* (2001) found that not everyone can detect the taste of PROP and it is likely to be an inherited trait.

Therefore it seems that some adaptive preferences are not selected in the way we would expect according to evolutionary theory.

Delicious dates

'Do we have to remember all these dates?' Every teacher is asked this about 83 times a year. The answer is, 'No. Although the examiner will be impressed if you can remember the main ones…' We provide the dates in this guide just to give you a sense of psychology's timeline.

Counterpoint

Some bitter compounds may be protective against cancer, so people insensitive to PROP would eat foods that contained them.

This suggests that a preference for bitter foods in our evolutionary history could be an adaptive trait after all.

Not everyone agrees with this conclusion. What do you think?

Knowledge Check

1. In relation to the evolutionary explanation for food preferences, explain what is meant by 'neophobia' **and** 'taste aversion'.
   (3 marks + 3 marks)

2. Outline the evolutionary explanation for food preferences. Refer in your answer to neophobia **and** taste aversion. *(6 marks)*

3. Briefly evaluate the evolutionary explanation for food preferences. *(4 marks)*

4. Discuss the evolutionary explanation for food preferences. *(16 marks)*

Evaluation extra: Cultural and evolutionary influences.

Cashdan (1998) argues that culture plays a major role in food preferences (e.g. someone brought up in a Jewish Kosher household would not eat a prawn cocktail).

However, evolutionary factors may be at work – different cultures share similar food preferences, and food preferences are difficult to change.

Therefore, evolutionary influences seem to be more important in food preferences because they underlie even cultural differences.

Explanations for food preferences: The role of learning

Spec spotlight

Explanations for food preferences: the role of learning in food preference, including social and cultural influences.

Classical conditioning

UCS   unconditioned stimulus
UCR   unconditioned response
NS   neutral stimulus
CS   conditioned stimulus
CR   conditioned response

Before conditioning:
UCS produces UCR

During conditioning:
NS associated with UCS and becomes CS

After conditioning:
CS produces CR

They loved watching the telly. Imagine how much more they'd enjoy it if they actually turned it on.

Apply it

Madison has just started at primary school and at lunchtime carefully watches what her friends have to eat. Two friends always have vegetables and love eating them but Madison has never liked them. In class the children all enjoy playing a game on their tablets where they get points for collecting healthy food. Within a few months Madison starts eating all her vegetables, whereas she never did before.

1. What role does learning play in food preferences?

2. Explain Madison's behaviour in terms of this theory.

The process of learning in food preference

Classical conditioning. Through *flavour–flavour learning*.	We develop preference for new food by associating it with flavours we already like. We innately prefer sweetness so we learn to prefer new foods by sweetening them. This association eventually leads to liking new food on its own.
Operant conditioning. Children's preferences *reinforced* by parents.	Parents provide rewards (e.g. praise) or punishments for eating certain foods – but it is still hard to establish preference (e.g. to green vegetables) in children using rewards. Therefore classical conditioning is probably a more powerful form of food preference learning than operant conditioning.

Social influences

Social learning theory explains social influences such as family.	**Social learning theory (SLT)**: children acquire food preferences of role models they observe eating certain foods, especially if the model is rewarded and the child identifies with them. *Family influences* – these are the most obvious social influence on preference learning because parents are 'gatekeepers' of children's eating.
Other social influences include peers and media.	*Peer influences* – Birch (1980) found children changed vegetable preferences in response to observing other children. *Media influences* – non-family models become important as children get older and more independent of parents' food choices, e.g. TV adverts for 'unhealthy' foods (containing salt, sugar, fat), promoted by characters children identify with.

Cultural influences

Cultural influences on food preferences exerted through *cultural norms*.	Cultural influences are the most significant indicator of food preferences. Cultural norms establish preferences (e.g. attitudes towards what constitutes a 'proper meal'). For example: • 'Meat and two veg' – Sunday roast dinner was a common cultural ideal in British households. • In France the cultural tradition is to eat every part of an animal (offal – kidneys, liver, etc.), less so in UK and the US where the preference is steaks/burgers.
Cultural influences involve *classical conditioning* and *vicarious reinforcement*.	Classical conditioning – we associate many foods we eat as adults with happiness growing up (enjoyable times with friends and family, culturally-specific feasts). Vicarious reinforcement – culture influences which foods are presented to children, children see their cultural group enjoying these foods (rewarding).

One limitation is a lack of support for classical conditioning.

Baeyens *et al.*'s (1996) student participants tasted previously untried flavours paired with a sweet taste.

Compared with a **control group** (new flavours paired with tasteless substance), the students were no more likely to prefer the new flavours after pairing.

Therefore classical conditioning (in the form of flavour–flavour learning) is at best an incomplete explanation of food preferences.

Counterpoint

However, Baeyens *et al.* also showed that participants acquired an aversion to new flavours when paired with Tween (soapy, bitter flavour).

Therefore classical conditioning does play a role in eating behaviour, but in food aversion rather than preference.

Christmas. A time for family, culturally-determined food values and horrific jumpers apparently.

One strength is research supports the role of SLT in preferences.

Jansen and Tenney (2001) found that children preferred the taste of a yoghurt drink that they saw a teacher drinking, praising and enjoying.

The children identified with the teacher so modelled their preference on the teacher and imitated the teacher's behaviour.

This supports SLT in terms of **modelling** and vicarious reinforcement as preference was influenced by the teacher's praise and enjoyment.

Another strength is that cultural factors are shown to influence preferences.

Cultural changes in industrialised societies have increased availability of food outside the home, e.g. fast food restaurants.

This has led to a preference for foods from fast food restaurants, i.e. foods that can be consumed quickly and also high in fat, salt and sugar.

This shows that wider cultural changes strongly influence the kinds of things that people eat.

Evaluation extra: Short- and long-term.

Short-term effects are powerful, e.g. Hare-Bruun *et al.* (2011) found that Danish children who watched the most television also had the most unhealthy food preferences.

However, this effect was much weaker in a six-year follow-up study of the same children – other factors (e.g. friends) influenced preferences more strongly.

Taken together this suggests that the combined effects of all social learning influences are long-term.

Revision BOOSTER

There may be 'mini-essays' on the exam, perhaps worth 8 marks. At A level the split will reflect the 16-mark essay split (so 6 + 10 for a 16-mark question becomes 3 + 5 for an 8-mark question). If you do get a mini-essay then you don't need all the material here. What is presented here is more than enough for a 16-mark essay. So think about what you would *select* for your mini-essay version.

Knowledge Check

1. Explain **one** social influence on the learning of food preference. *(3 marks)*
2. Outline social **and/or** cultural influences on the learning of food preference. *(6 marks)*
3. Evaluate the role of learning in food preference. *(6 marks)*
4. Maricel is explaining to Jade what he and his family from the Philippines eat. They like sapin-sapin, a rice and coconut dessert. Jade explains that she and her family love fish and chips.

   Outline **and** evaluate the roles of social **and** cultural influences on food preferences. Refer to Maricel's and Jade's conversation in your answer. *(16 marks)*

Neural and hormonal mechanisms in eating behaviour

Spec spotlight

Neural and hormonal mechanisms involved in the control of eating behaviour, including the role of the hypothalamus, ghrelin and leptin.

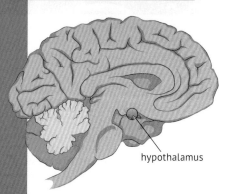

The hypothalamus. A little structure with a big appetite.

hypothalamus

Abbreviate!

VMH. LH. NPY. CCK. There are many common abbreviations that are acceptable – so don't feel you have to memorise all those big words. You can just use the abbreviations.

Apply it

Olga is obese and is continuing to gain weight. She feels hungry most of the time even though she eats a lot of snacks between meals. But it's never long before she wants to eat again. She eats more than everyone else when she goes out for a meal with her friends. Olga finds her eating behaviour difficult to explain, and wonders if there is something physically wrong with her.

Using your knowledge of neural **and** hormonal mechanisms involved in the control of eating behaviour, suggest why Olga may have gained weight.

Neural mechanisms

Hypothalamus controls neural and hormonal mechanisms (and maintains homeostasis).	Hypothalamus regulates level of glucose (energy source) in blood. Glucose strongly influences eating behaviour.
	Neural – glucose-sensing neurons in hypothalamus detect fluctuations in blood glucose concentration.
	Link to hormones – hypothalamus regulates glucose via insulin and anti-insulin hormones (e.g. glucagon) in the pancreas.
	Homeostasis – hypothalamus plays key role in maintaining blood glucose homeostasis within narrow range of values.
Dual-centre model of eating.	Two structures of hypothalamus provide homeostatic control: • 'On switch' – lateral hypothalamus (LH). • 'Off switch' – ventromedial hypothalamus (VMH).
Lateral hypothalamus (LH). On switch.	LH contains cells to detect glucose in the liver. LH is activated when glucose falls below a certain level ('set point') so the person becomes hungry, triggering a motivation to eat.
	Neuropeptide Y (NPY) also secreted. NPY injected into rats' hypothalamus causes them to eat excessively, becoming obese.
Ventromedial hypothalamus (VMH). Off switch.	Eating leads to a rise in levels of glucose in the bloodstream and liver (glycogen) – detected by cells in VMH.
	VMH is triggered once levels increase past a set point – LH activity is inhibited at the same time, so a person becomes satiated (feels full and stops eating).
	Damage to VMH – Reeves and Plum (1969) studied a woman whose weight doubled in two years. She had a tumour on her VMH causing the normal 'stop eating' function to fail.

Hormonal mechanisms

Ghrelin. Appetite stimulant (secreted by stomach).	The longer we go without food (more empty stomach) the more ghrelin is released – the level is detected by receptors in the *arcuate nucleus* of the hypothalamus.
	When levels rise above a set point the arcuate nucleus signals LH to secrete NPY.
	Wren *et al.* (2001) found intravenous ghrelin caused a short-term increase in amount of food eaten.
Leptin. Appetite suppressant (secreted by adipose cells).	Leptin blood level increases with fat level and is detected by VMH – part of VMH satiety mechanism.
	Level of leptin increases beyond a set point – person feels full and stops eating.
	Licinio *et al.* (2004) studied a rare genetic condition – inability to produce leptin associated with severe obesity. Individuals treated with leptin replacement therapy saw 40% average weight loss and 49% reduction in food intake over 18 months.

Neural and hormonal mechanisms in eating behaviour

One strength of the dual-centre model is research support.

Hetherington and Ranson (1942) showed that lesioning the VMH of rats caused them to become *hyperphagic* (overeat), leading to severe obesity.

Anand and Brobeck (1951) lesioned the LH of rats and found *aphagia* (cessation of eating/starvation).

This confirms the homeostatic mechanism – two brain centres with opposing functions as predicted by dual-centre model.

Counterpoint

Gold (1973) claims Hetherington and Ranson's operation also damaged the rats' paraventricular nucleus (PVN). If lesions are limited to the VMH hyperphagia doesn't occur.

This suggests that physiological control of eating behaviour may involve more than two brain centres.

One limitation is that the models are oversimplified.

Valassi *et al.* (2008) highlight the contribution of the hormone *cholecystokinin* (CCK) to the 'stop eating' mechanism – a more powerful appetite suppressant than leptin.

Other biochemicals are also involved (e.g. **serotonin** and **dopamine**), interacting to enhance or inhibit each other's activities.

This shows that the true nature of neural and hormonal control of eating behaviour is extremely complex.

I'm not overweight, just big-boned.

Another limitation is that social/cultural factors are underplayed.

Woods (2004) points out that the LH feeding centre detects falling blood glucose and stimulates hunger only in severe energy deprivation.

Neurochemistry plays a lesser role in everyday eating onset, which is more controlled by social/cultural factors (e.g. times of day for meals).

This suggests a **biological** approach ignores potentially important nonbiological factors that may contribute more to controlling eating behaviour.

Evaluation extra: Animal research.

Neural and hormonal mechanisms in eating behaviour are similar in non-human animals and humans (hypothalamus, leptin, ghrelin), so animal research useful.

However, human eating behaviour is more complex because it is influenced by social, cultural and psychological factors not considered in animal research.

Therefore animal studies help us understand the neurochemistry of eating behaviour but we should take account of the equally important contributions of non-biological factors in humans.

Revision BOOSTER

'Neural' refers to how the nervous system/brain controls eating behaviour. 'Hormonal' is about how the endocrine system controls eating behaviour. The wording of the specification means you might have to write about one or the other or both. So getting them mixed up would be bad news for your marks.

Knowledge Check

1. Briefly outline the roles of the hypothalamus, ghrelin **and** leptin in the control of eating behaviour.
   (2 marks + 2 marks + 2 marks)
2. Describe the neural **and** hormonal mechanisms involved in the control of eating behaviour. *(6 marks)*
3. Briefly evaluate the roles of ghrelin **and** leptin in the control of eating behaviour.
   (4 marks)
4. Discuss neural **and/or** hormonal mechanisms involved in the control of eating behaviour. *(16 marks)*

Biological explanations for anorexia nervosa

Spec spotlight

Biological explanations for anorexia nervosa, including genetic and neural explanations.

Is there a genetic basis to eating disorders such as anorexia?

AN = anorexia nervosa
MZ = monozygotic twin
DZ = dizygotic twin

Twin studies

MZ twins share 100% of genes but DZ twins only 50% (on average) – so we would expect a greater likelihood of both MZ twins developing anorexia nervosa if it is mostly genetic.

This is because both MZ and DZ twins are raised together in the same environment, but MZ twins have a greater degree of genetic similarity than DZs.

Apply it

A counselling psychologist runs a therapy group for young women with AN. As she has been doing this for several years, she has noticed that many of her clients are not the only ones in their families to have this disorder. Most of them have a female relative, often a mother or grandmother, who also had AN. Some have relatives with other disorders, especially depression.

Use your knowledge of neural **and** genetic explanations for anorexia to explain the psychologist's experience.

Genetic explanation

Runs in families. Inherited links demonstrated in twin studies.	Holland *et al.* (1988) found **MZ concordance rate** of 56% but only 5% for **DZs**. Other studies have found smaller differences but still strong evidence for the role of genes.
Candidate genes. Such as *Ephx2*.	*Candidate-gene association study* (CGAS) by Scott-Van Zeeland *et al.* (2014) sequenced 152 candidate genes possibly linked with features of AN and found only one gene significantly associated with AN – *Ephx2* (epoxide hydrolase 2). This codes for an enzyme involved in cholesterol metabolism. Many people in acute phase of AN (when symptoms are severe) have abnormally high levels of cholesterol.
Genome-wide association studies (GWAS). Look at the whole collection of human genes.	In contrast with CGAS, GWAS make no assumptions about which genes might be involved in anorexia. Boraska *et al.* (2014) identified 72 separate genetic variations but none were significantly related to AN – possibly because the study was not sensitive enough to detect genetic influences.

Neural explanation

Effects of serotonin and dopamine studied through *metabolites*.	Neurotransmitter levels in nervous system not studied directly – researchers measure levels of metabolites (chemical byproducts) instead. The main metabolite of **serotonin** is *5-HIAA* (5-hydroxyindoleacetic acid). Main metabolite of **dopamine** is *HVA* (homovanillic acid).
Serotonin. Involved in many AN-related behaviours (e.g. obsessiveness).	Bailer and Kaye (2011) found low levels of 5-HIAA in people with AN return to normal after short-term weight recovery – levels actually increase beyond normal in long-term. Attia *et al.* (2014) found participants with AN who did not return to pre-illness weight responded less well to serotonin agonists (drugs) than AN participants restored to a healthy weight. The pattern of results clearly indicates underactivity of the serotonin system in AN.
Dopamine. Dysfunction associated with AN.	Kaye *et al.* (1991) found HVA lower in recovered AN participants compared with controls. Bailer *et al.* (2012) gave amphetamine to participants to increase dopamine release – healthy participants experienced pleasure but participants with AN experienced anxiety. Eating increases dopamine release so perhaps participants with AN restrict food intake to reduce their anxiety levels.

One limitation is that twin studies may lack validity.

We assume MZ twins share their environment to the same extent that DZ twins share theirs (the *equal environments assumption*).

However, MZ pairs are treated more similarly than DZ pairs by parents, friends, etc., so the assumption may be wrong.

Therefore concordance rates for AN are inflated and genetic influences are not as great as twin studies suggest.

One strength is that gene studies illustrate the polygenic nature of AN.

Gene studies have been unsuccessful in identifying any single gene for AN, many candidate genes have been discarded.

No single gene can be responsible for the wide variety of physical and psychological symptoms of AN (e.g. appetite loss, body image distortions).

Therefore gene studies have shown that AN is polygenic – many genes make important but modest contributions to the disorder.

Evaluation extra: Diathesis-stress.

Genes lay the foundation for AN e.g. candidate genes. This creates a *diathesis* (a predisposition) that makes an individual more likely to develop AN.

The diathesis only expresses itself when the individual experiences an environmental *stressor* (e.g. trying to lose weight).

Therefore, it is an interaction between genetic and non-genetic factors – though we can do something about non-genetic ones.

Studies of MZ and DZ twins may be complicated by their dissimilar environments.

One strength of the dopamine explanation is supporting evidence.

Many studies measure HVA in cerebrospinal fluid – HVA is a chemical byproduct of dopamine metabolism.

Kaye *et al.* (1999) found 30% lower HVA in participants with AN (severely underweight) compared with non-AN control participants.

These findings strongly suggest that a disturbance of dopamine metabolism may contribute to the symptoms of AN.

One limitation of neural explanations is that they can be simplistic.

Nunn *et al.* (2012) argue serotonin alone does not distinguish between people with and without AN.

A better explanation involves interaction with noradrenaline, and other neurotransmitters (e.g. **GABA**) are also involved.

This is an important reminder that neurotransmitter systems do not operate in isolation, but in complex interactions.

Evaluation extra: Drug treatments.

Drugs increasing serotonin and dopamine may help treat AN symptoms (e.g. SSRIs for depression) – current drugs help avoid relapse (Kaye *et al.* 2001).

However, no drug treatment for AN has been consistently successful – perhaps AN is caused by *high* levels of serotonin and dopamine rather than low.

Therefore, despite inconsistent outcomes, it is probably worth continuing to find better treatments even with a poor success rate.

Revision BOOSTER

You should understand the background behind twin studies (i.e. what MZ and DZ concordance rates mean). But don't spend exam time explaining it, otherwise what you write will be too generic. Focus instead on what the difference between MZ and DZ twins tells us about the genetics of AN.

Knowledge Check

1. In relation to anorexia nervosa, explain what is meant by 'neural explanations'. *(2 marks)*
2. Explain the difference between genetic and neural explanations for anorexia nervosa. *(4 marks)*
3. Evaluate the neural explanation for anorexia nervosa. *(6 marks)*
4. Many psychologists believe that anorexia nervosa runs in families. Others argue that most cases are due to chemical imbalances in the brain.

   Describe **and** evaluate **one or more** biological explanations for anorexia nervosa. *(16 marks)*

Spec spotlight

Psychological explanations for anorexia nervosa: family systems theory, including enmeshment, autonomy and control.

Some researchers think anorexia may be an expression of a need for independence.

Apply it

Prudence is a teenager who is eating less and less and losing weight. She is fed up because her mum is always getting at her about everything. She feels very strongly that she is not a child anymore, but is always treated like one. No one ever lets her do anything. Prudence's mum is very irritated with Prudence because she seems ungrateful for all the nice things her parents give her. Prudence wants to talk about this with her parents, but they always change the subject.

Use family systems theory to explain why Prudence is losing weight and is vulnerable to developing AN.

Revision BOOSTER

In a 16-mark essay you don't have to write everything on this spread. What is here is actually more than 1000 words!! For a 16-mark essay you probably only have time to write 500 words – but don't cut down the elaboration of the AO3 points. Better to do less AO1 and focus on AO3.

Family systems theory (FST)

FST focuses on *family interactions*.	FST is a **psychodynamic** approach, looking at the interactions centred on one member's symptoms which distract from family conflicts.
	Minuchin *et al.* (1978) focused on the relationship between mother and daughter and identified four main features of a typical anorexic family, as listed below.
(1) *Enmeshment.* Members of anorexic families are too involved with each other.	In anorexic families the boundaries are 'fuzzy' – poorly defined roles and lack of leadership. Family members spend lots of time together and assume they know what the others think. Self-identities of each member are tied up with one another.
	An adolescent daughter in an anorexic family tries to differentiate her identity and assert her independence by refusing to eat.
(2) *Overprotective.* Obsessive nurturing leaves no room for independence.	Palazzoli (1974) described an enmeshed family in which the mother of a daughter with AN felt that all her decisions were for her daughter's benefit and not her own. It is then much easier to blame the daughter with AN when things go wrong.
(3) *Rigidity.* Interactions within anorexic family are inflexible.	Family members deny the need for change and try to keep things as they are. Problems arise when situations change due to pressure – the family is too rigid to adapt so is thrown into crisis.
	For example, an adolescent daughter seeks independence but the rest of the family quash her attempt at self-differentiation. The outcome is sometimes AN.
(4) *Conflict avoidance.* Family prevents or suppresses conflict.	Family members avoid or suppress conflict (e.g. no discussion of issues where difference of opinion might arise). So problems are not resolved and continue to fester until crisis develops.
	Anorexic daughter continues to refuse to eat, starves herself, and her family refuses to accept there is anything to discuss.
Bruch added *need for autonomy* and *control* as a family issue.	Bruch (1978) suggested AN is caused by an adolescent daughter's struggle to achieve autonomy and control. The mother, domineering and intrusive, does not accept the daughter's need for independence.
	The confused daughter expresses this in major symptoms of AN – distorted body image, inability to identify hunger and overwhelming feeling of loss of control. She controls her destiny by controlling her body – the thinner she gets, the greater the degree of control.

One strength is support for FST from research studies.

Strauss and Ryan (1987) found that females diagnosed with AN showed greater disturbances of autonomy than healthy controls.

Those with AN also had a more rigid style of regulating their own behaviour, were more enmeshed in their families and perceived poorer communication between members.

These findings show that desire for autonomy, rigidity and enmeshment may all be risk factors for AN in females.

Counterpoint

Aragona et al. (2011) found families of females with AN no more enmeshed/rigid than other families – contradictory findings may be due to vague concepts defined differently in studies.

This means that it is difficult to find conclusive support for FST theory, and ultimately it is not a scientific theory because the concepts cannot be tested.

The obvious implication of FST is that therapy should be family-focused as is the case with BFST.

Another strength is FST-based therapy for AN has shown some success.

Behavioural family systems therapy (BFST) tries to disentangle family relationships and reduce parental control over eating.

Robin et al. (1995) found that six out of 11 females with AN recovered after 16 months, and another three had recovered by the one-year follow-up.

This suggests that FST concepts may have some practical value.

*FST was originally developed to explain the effects of family dysfunction on many psychological disorders in terms of different family relationships. But because AN overwhelmingly affects adolescent females, FST has focused on the mother–daughter relationship almost to the exclusion of all others. You might want to consider this from the point of view of **gender bias**.*

One limitation is that family influences on AN depend on other factors.

Davis et al. (2004) studied such *mediating factors* and found that family interactions affected eating disorders only in adolescents with high anxiety.

Young et al. (2004) found that family factors had no effect on eating disorders in cases where there is no depression and no peer influences.

These mediating factors are mostly independent of family factors which shows that family factors alone cannot explain AN.

Evaluation extra: Validity of FST.

FST explains two features of AN other theories struggle with: its tendency to appear in adolescence (link with autonomy) and its much greater incidence in females.

However, it follows that FST has trouble explaining AN in non-adolescent females and in males, and it also ignores the role of fathers in family dysfunction.

Therefore FST may be a useful and valid theory of AN in most cases, but it is worth bearing in mind that the theory is limited in scope.

Knowledge Check

1. In relation to the family systems theory of anorexia nervosa, explain what is meant by 'enmeshment' **and** 'autonomy'. *(2 marks + 2 marks)*

2. Explain the difference between autonomy and control in the context of family systems theory of anorexia nervosa. *(4 marks)*

3. Describe **one** psychological explanation for anorexia nervosa. *(6 marks)*

4. Outline **and** evaluate family systems theory as a psychological explanation for anorexia nervosa. *(16 marks)*

Psychological explanations for anorexia nervosa: SLT

Spec spotlight

Psychological explanations for anorexia nervosa: social learning theory, including modelling, reinforcement and media.

The term 'model' does not refer to a model such as Cara Delevingne – it is a generic term referring to someone on whom we model our behaviour. It might of course be the case that you model yourself on someone who is a model.

Apply it

A researcher has interviewed several young women who have AN. They give many reasons for why they have lost weight, but one is very common. Most say they would love to be like the very thin models and celebrities they see on TV and read about in magazines. Young women envy the glamorous lifestyles, wealth and attention.

Explain the researcher's finding using your knowledge of social learning theory.

Social learning theory (SLT)

Direct and *indirect* learning.	Direct learning of anorexia nervosa (AN) involves **classical** and **operant conditioning** of an individual's behaviour.
	Social learning theory (SLT) (indirect learning) involves observation of other people – behaviour is modelled/imitated if it is vicariously reinforced.

AN acquired indirectly through *modelling* an observed model.	Four main features of a model in AN:
	1. Provides 'template' to imitate (**modelling**).
	2. Can exist in real life (e.g. family member) or be symbolic (e.g. cartoon character).
	3. Modifies social norms by establishing acceptable or usual behaviour (e.g. child observes older sibling restricting food intake and learns this is 'normal').
	4. Especially influential if child identifies with model (e.g. respects model or perceives them as glamorous and associates their thinness with desirable characteristics).

Vicarious reinforcement increases chance that eating behaviour will be imitated.	Observer sees model rewarded (praised) and learns behaviour (losing weight) has positive consequences – observer is then more likely to imitate behaviour.
	Family members are major sources of vicarious reinforcement because their behaviour is repeatedly observed.

The *media* is a powerful transmitter of cultural ideals of body shape/size.	The ideal body shape for women (and men) has become thinner over time (e.g. Size Zero).
	Women may identify with glamour of celebrities who conform to 'thin ideal' – motivated to lose weight and achieve thinness (dieting, exercise).
	Behaviour vicariously reinforced by fame and success observed in female role models.

Dittmar *et al.* (2006) SLT and AN

PROCEDURE	162 British girls aged 5–8 years were shown images of either Barbie dolls, Emme dolls or control objects (flowers, etc.).
	If Barbie was scaled up to adult human size, her waist would be 39% smaller than most women with AN. Emme dolls have a bigger more realistic body shape.

FINDINGS AND CONCLUSIONS	Girls who saw Barbie images were more dissatisfied with own body shape and had lower body esteem.
	Young girls identify with Barbie because of glamour associated with body shape – makes them vulnerable to developing AN.

One strength is support from a natural experiment in Fiji.

Becker et al. (2002) used EAT-26 to measure adolescent females' attitudes towards eating in 1995 (when TV broadcasts began) and 1998.

13% in 1995 gained a high score (eating disorder risk) and 29% in 1998 – influenced by body shape ideals transmitted in media.

This shows that eating disorders can be the outcome of social learning processes.

Counterpoint

However, this study used two different samples in 1995 and 1998, with the 1998 girls not measured for eating attitudes before TV was introduced.

This serious methodological limitation undermines the researchers' claim that media influences were involved in AN-related changes.

Is our preoccupation with thinness a result of media and cultural icons (like Barbie)?

Another strength is that SLT explains cultural changes in AN.

Chisuwa and O'Dea (2010) highlight the increased incidence of AN in Japan over 40 years as traditional 'healthy plumpness' is displaced by thinness ideal from **individualistic** cultures.

This change is probably related to media representations – more AN symptoms were seen in young Japanese women who read magazines promoting thinness.

This shows that AN may be driven by processes such as modelling media representations of the ideal female body shape.

One limitation is that SLT has not led to an effective therapy.

SLT may be useful alongside different therapies (e.g. showing healthy body shapes), but is not enough on its own.

This contrasts with usefulness of other explanations e.g. neural explanations led to drug therapies, **cognitive** theories (next spread) led to **CBT**.

Therefore the practical value of SLT in helping people with AN is very limited.

Evaluation extra: Validity.

SLT explains AN in terms of media influences especially in young women, who use social media and experience the highest incidence of AN.

However, if social learning factors are responsible we would expect to see many more women with AN, so another factor must be involved (diathesis).

Therefore, an explanation of AN based on SLT processes alone is not sufficient, it is probably best to include both biological and nonbiological factors.

Knowledge Check

1. In relation to the social learning theory of anorexia nervosa, explain what is meant by 'modelling' **and** 'reinforcement'.
(3 marks + 3 marks)

2. Outline the social learning theory of anorexia nervosa.
(6 marks)

3. Explain the role of the media as an explanation for anorexia nervosa. *(4 marks)*

4. Lillia is 14 and her mum has had depression and eating disorders since Lillia was small. Lillia and her mum often shop together for food and eat together, although her mum rarely finishes a meal. Her dad often talks about how beautiful Lillia's mum is and comments on how similar Lillia and her mum are.

   Discuss **one** biological **and one** psychological explanation for anorexia nervosa. Refer to Lillia **and** her mum in your answer.
(16 marks)

Psychological explanations for anorexia nervosa: Cognitive

Spec spotlight

Psychological explanations for anorexia nervosa: cognitive theory, including distortions and irrational beliefs.

A distorted perception of body image may be at the root of anorexia.

Apply it

A college counsellor sees many young women who have issues with their body shape and size. Some of them perceive themselves as fat when any observer would consider them slim. Many are very high-achieving students, but they all report spending hours and hours on their work, often stressing over the smallest things. They tend to make very harsh judgements of their own abilities, including their ability to lose weight.

Using your knowledge of psychological theories of AN, explain the cognitive processes that these young women are experiencing.

Cognitive distortions

Cognitive distortions are a cause of anorexia nervosa (AN).	**Cognitive** distortions of body image are central to the diagnosis of AN in **DSM**-5 – so it makes sense that cognitive distortions may be a cause of AN.
	People with AN filter experiences of life through the three factors identified below.
Factor 1 *Disturbed perceptions* about body shape and weight.	Murphy *et al.* (2010) argue that the main clinical features of AN stem from disturbed perceptions.
	These cause preoccupations with thoughts of food, eating, body shape.
	Leads to behaviours such as food restriction and checking (e.g. constantly looking in mirror). People with AN misinterpret emotional states as 'feeling fat', even as they get thinner.
Overestimation of body size and weight.	Williamson *et al.* (1993) asked people with AN and a non-AN **control group** to estimate current and ideal body sizes.
	Found that AN participants' estimates were significantly less accurate, with a marked tendency to overestimate size.
	Their ideal body size was significantly thinner than for controls.
Factor 2 *Irrational beliefs* defy logic.	Irrational beliefs are views and attitudes about AN that do not make sense.
	Such thoughts give rise to *automatic negative thoughts* (Beck), for example:
	• 'If I don't control my weight, I'm worthless' (all-or-nothing thinking).
	• 'I ate half a biscuit, I've got no willpower' (catastrophising).
Perfectionism is a key irrational belief in AN.	A person who exhibits perfectionism:
	• Feels they must meet demanding standards in all areas of life but especially eating, body shape, weight loss.
	• Uses intensive record-keeping to ensure they are achieving their goals.
	• Raises standards even higher once targets are reached – forever pursuing unrealistic goals in a vicious cycle of irrational perfectionism and starvation.
Factor 3 *Cognitive inflexibility* (e.g. difficulty in set-shifting).	People with AN have problems switching fluently between tasks requiring a different set of cognitive skills (set-shifting). They apply the same skills in a changed situation where they are no longer useful.
	Treasure and Schmidt (2013) proposed the *cognitive interpersonal maintenance model* of AN – when vulnerable person begins weight loss process, they rigidly persist and continue to perceive themselves as needing to lose weight. They cannot switch to a more **adaptive** way of thinking about body size. Weight loss is a solution to a problem that no longer exists, but they can't perceive this accurately.

One strength of the explanation is research support for disturbed perceptions.

Sachdev *et al.* (2008) found no differences in brain activity between people with AN and non-AN controls when they viewed images of other people's bodies.

However, when viewing images of their own bodies, AN participants showed less activity (than non-AN) in parts of brain involved in attention.

This shows that disturbed perceptions exist in AN in terms of how people with AN attend to their own body.

People with AN only show brain activity differences in attention when viewing their own body.

Another strength is that there is research support for perfectionism.

Halmi *et al.* (2012) studied women diagnosed with AN, who completed the SIAB to assess current symptoms and the EATATE Interview to retrospectively measure childhood perfectionism.

They found that childhood perfectionism (e.g. schoolwork perfectionism) was associated with current AN symptoms.

This suggests perfectionism precedes onset of AN, so is a potential risk factor for development of the disorder.

Counterpoint

However, Halmi *et al.* used retrospective recall to assess perfectionism (recalling perfectionism in childhood). It is likely that such recall was distorted, especially in those with AN.

This suggests that link between childhood perfectionism and development of AN may be artificially inflated.

One limitation is that there is some contradictory research.

Cornelissen *et al.* (2013) used a morphing task – women adjusted a computerised image of themselves until it matched their estimate of body size.

There was no significant difference between women with and without AN in the **correlation** between estimated and actual body mass index (BMI).

This suggests that women with AN do not have a distorted body perception, challenging a key element of the cognitive theory of AN.

Evaluation extra: Issues of causation.

Research covered on this spread shows that several cognitive factors are key features of AN. Cognitive theory goes further and argues that these are causal in the development of AN. This is a very strong claim, especially given other alternative causal theories (e.g. genes).

However, it is just as likely that cognitive factors are consequences (effects) of AN rather than causes. The research we have studied supports this view. For example, Murphy *et al.* (facing page) studied preoccupations with body shape which may be an effect of AN.

Therefore, cognitive factors are more likely to be consequences of AN, but they can also be a cause as they affect the course of the disorder over time.

Revision BOOSTER

Students are often disappointed to find they haven't got as many marks for evaluation in an essay answer as they expected. This is usually because they aren't evaluating – they're describing. For example, you could evaluate the cognitive theory of AN by addressing the evidence for cognitive distortions. But if all you do is say what the evidence is ('Sachdev did some brain scans and what he found was...'), then that's not evaluation.

Knowledge Check

1. In relation to the cognitive theory of anorexia nervosa, explain what is meant by 'distortions' **and** 'irrational beliefs'. *(3 marks + 3 marks)*

2. Briefly outline research into distortions **and** irrational beliefs in relation to the cognitive theory of anorexia nervosa. *(6 marks)*

3. Briefly evaluate **two** psychological explanations for anorexia nervosa. *(6 marks)*

4. Describe **and** evaluate the cognitive theory of anorexia nervosa. *(16 marks)*

Biological explanations for obesity

Spec spotlight

Biological explanations for obesity, including genetic and neural explanations.

Obesity rates run in the family.

Apply it

Ptolemy is a 12-year-old boy who is clinically obese. His dad is also seriously overweight and has Type 2 diabetes. But his mum is within the normal weight range.

Tate and Lyle are teenage twins who are both very overweight. There are several obese people in their family.

Nazir has been under a lot of stress for several months, in her work and at home. She copes with this by eating and therefore is now obese. She gets no pleasure from eating anymore but it distracts her from the stress.

Use these cases to describe how genetic and neural factors explain obesity.

Revision BOOSTER

Write a very brief essay plan for each possible essay and then practise writing the essay in full from the plan. Time yourself – 20 minutes for a 16-mark essay.

Genetic explanation

Obesity runs in families.	There are family-related patterns of body mass index (BMI), i.e. it is a characteristic shared by genetically-related people.
Examples of family-related patterns come from *family and twin studies.*	Family studies – BMI **concordance rates** for obesity in first-degree relatives are 20–50% (Chaput *et al.* 2014). Twin studies – **MZ** concordance rates for obesity are 61–80%, shows a substantial genetic component (Nan *et al.* 2012).
Genetic inheritance of obesity is *polygenic.*	No single genetic cause of obesity – many genes involved with small effects interacting to produce overall outcome. Locke *et al.* (2015) found 97 genes associated with variations in BMI but accounted for only 2.7% of BMI variation – up to 400 genes may be involved in heritability of obesity. Plus there are other ways of measuring obesity (e.g. waist-to-hip ratio), so different genes may influence different aspects of obesity.

Neural explanation

Neurotransmitters such as serotonin and dopamine.	**Serotonin** – regulates eating behaviour by influencing activity of the hypothalamus (especially the VMH). **Dopamine** – crucial role in brain's reward and motivation system involving hypothalamus, hippocampus and amygdala.
Low *serotonin* levels.	Serotonin normally signals satiety to hypothalamus. Dysfunctions of serotonin system from co-morbid disorders (e.g. depression), may be genetically inherited. Results in abnormally low levels of serotonin and therefore inaccurate satiety signals sent to hypothalamus. The result is that eating behaviour is **disinhibited** (i.e. not controlled), leading to carbohydrate cravings (i.e. desire for energy-dense foods including sugars) causing weight gain through excess calories.
Low *dopamine* levels.	Dopamine activity associated with pleasure from eating and associated cues (e.g. smell of food). Wang *et al.* (2001) found obese people have fewer dopamine D2 receptors in the *striatum* than normal-weight controls. Low dopamine means it cannot perform usual pleasurable reward function in response to eating. Overeating is an attempt to increase dopamine and activate reward centres in the brain, providing pleasure. Obesity is the outcome of food addiction operating neurochemically like other addictions.

One strength is a plausible mechanism to explain how genes work.

Genes may influence responses to the environment (O'Rahilly and Farooqi 2008).	For example, sensitivity to food-related cues and influence on neurotransmitter systems linked with obesity (see below).	This ability to explain how genes operate in obesity increases the **validity** of the genetic explanation.

One limitation is evidence doesn't support most obvious genes.

Paracchini *et al.* (2005) conducted a meta-analysis of 25 studies investigating genes regulating leptin.	There was no link between obesity and these genes – surprising because the activity of leptin is central to weight regulation.	This raises doubts about the validity of the genetic explanation because we would expect these genes to be involved in obesity.

Evaluation extra: Diathesis-stress.

Genes make a significant contribution to obesity, but they do not determine it – they create a diathesis.	However, environmental stressors (e.g. eating as a coping mechanism for life events) may 'trigger' the diathesis – these can be controlled or changed.	Therefore environmental factors may be more important because we can influence them to reduce the likelihood of obesity.

One strength of the neural explanation is evidence for the role of serotonin.

Ohia *et al.* (2013) highlight the importance in obesity of one serotonin receptor – the 2C receptor.	Studies of 'knockout' mice (specific genes are removed) with no functioning 2C receptors show they develop late-onset obesity.	This research suggests there is a link between obesity and a dysfunctional serotonin system, at least in mice.

Another strength is that there is also evidence for the role of dopamine.

Spitz *et al.* (2000) found one version of *DRD2* gene (B1 allele) was twice as common in obese (than non-obese) participants.	Possibly people with low dopamine (fewer D2 receptors) get less dopamine-activated reward from eating, and overeat to gain satisfaction.	This finding supports both neural and genetic explanations – there may be a genetic basis to dysfunctions of the dopamine reward system in obesity.

Evaluation extra: Drug treatments.

Neural explanations led to drug treatments for obesity that increase serotonin and dopamine. Greater knowledge of neural activity leads to better drugs.	However, obesity is a chronic (long-term) disorder but drugs are for short-term use because of side effects (so make lifestyle changes instead).	Therefore, as many obese people do not make lifestyle changes, it is probably worth continuing to find better drug treatments with fewer side effects.

A serotonin molecule – low levels are implicated in obesity.

Revision BOOSTER

Getting your head around the specialist terms like monozygotic, ventromedial hypothalamus and 5-hydroxyindoleacetic acid can be a struggle. By all means use recognised initialisms (don't make up your own) such as MZ, VMH and *5-HIAA*. It's understanding what the terms mean that really matters.

Knowledge Check

1. Explain the difference between genetic and neural explanations of obesity. *(4 marks)*

2. Briefly outline **one or more** genetic explanation(s) for obesity. *(4 marks)*

3. Briefly evaluate **one** biological explanation for obesity. *(8 marks)*

4. This item appeared on a news website: 'Obesity crisis is all in the genes. Psychologists said yesterday that obesity runs in families. But others have pointed out that this does not mean that obesity is definitely genetic'.

   With reference to the issues raised in this item, outline **and** evaluate **two** biological explanations for obesity. *(16 marks)*

Psychological explanations for obesity

Spec spotlight

Psychological explanations for obesity, including restraint theory, disinhibition and the boundary model.

The restrained eater has to think about food much of the time.

Revision BOOSTER

An exam question may require you to write about just one of these explanations – or it may require psychological explanations. In the case of the latter don't make the mistake of describing all three as you will have far too much AO1.

Hunger boundary		Satiety boundary
Aversion hunger	Zone of biological indifference (ZBI)	Aversion satiety

Increasing food intake ⟶
Normal eater

Hunger boundary	Diet boundary		Satiety boundary
Aversion hunger	Zone of biological indifference (ZBI)		Aversion satiety

Increasing food intake ⟶
Restrained eater

Herman and Polivy's boundary model suggests that restrained eaters do not eat according to their biological needs, as normal eaters do.

Restraint theory

Restricting food intake.	Herman and Polivy (1975) suggest that dieters restrain eating (deliberately restrict food/calorie intake) which is self-defeating.
Restrained eaters exert *cognitive control*.	Restrained eater has to think (**cognitive**) about eating much of the time. They categorise foods into 'good' and 'bad' and create rules about which foods are allowed and which are forbidden.
The outcome of restrained eating is *paradoxical*.	Restrained eater becomes more preoccupied with food not less. No longer eats when hungry and stops when full. Eating behaviour becomes **disinhibited** (not controlled) and they eat more and gain weight – opposite outcome to goal.

Disinhibition

Restraints loosened.	Period of restrained eating often followed by disinhibited eating in which individual eats as much as they want.
Disinhibitors lead to loss of control.	A disinhibitor is a food-related cue, either internal (e.g. mood, feeling depressed) or external (e.g. media images). Restrained eaters are sensitive to these cues and vulnerable to loss of control leading to unrestrained eating (a binge).
Disinhibition controlled by cognitive factors.	For example, distorted thinking maintains disinhibited eating for remainder of binge. For example, all-or-nothing thinking – no point stopping, 'I blew it, I might as well eat all of this.'

Boundary model

Biological process. Both hunger and satiety are aversive.	Herman and Polivy (1984) aim to explain the impact of restrained eating and disinhibition (see diagram left). Hunger – when energy levels dip below 'set point' we feel aversive state of hunger and are motivated to eat. Satiety – eating to fullness creates aversive state of discomfort so we are motivated to stop eating.
Psychological process. ZBI.	Zone of biological indifference (ZBI) – when we feel neither hungry nor full (i.e. the area between hunger and satiety boundaries). In this zone psychological factors (cognitive and social) have more influence than biological ones on food intake.
ZBI wider for restrained eaters.	People who restrict food intake have lower hunger boundary and higher satiety boundary. So more of their eating behaviour is under cognitive rather than biological control – making them vulnerable to disinhibition.

One strength is research supporting the roles of restraint and disinhibition.

Wardle and Beales (1988) **randomly allocated** 27 obese women to a diet (restrained eating), exercise or control (no treatment) group.

Restrained eaters consumed significantly more calories – they generally ate less but experienced occasional disinhibition when they would eat beyond feeling full.

This shows that restraint leading to disinhibition is a causal factor in overeating which inevitably leads to weight gain and obesity.

Counterpoint

In a prospective study, Savage *et al.* (2009) found that increases in restrained eating were linked to decreases in weight in 163 women over a six-year period.

Therefore restrained eating leads to weight loss rather than weight gain in the long term, the opposite outcome to that predicted by restraint theory.

Disinhibition is a causal explanation of binge eating.

Another strength is support for food-related cues in disinhibition.

Boyce and Kuijer (2014) showed images of thinness to restrained (dieters) and unrestrained eaters, then measured food intake in a ten-minute 'taste test' (unlimited snacks).

Restrained eaters ate significantly more than unrestrained eaters after seeing the images (food-related cues), with no difference for neutral images, e.g. furniture.

This shows that food-related cues act as disinhibitors which may trigger overeating and obesity in restrained eaters.

Apply it

Charity is on a diet but her weight is going in the wrong direction. She thinks about food more than she used to and notices the smells of food all the time. Her friends mean well but are always asking her how the diet is going. When Charity has a bad day at work, she thinks about how she is going to treat herself to a piece of chocolate – but ends up eating the lot.

Explain Charity's behaviour in terms of restraint, disinhibition and the boundary model. Use some research evidence in your answer.

One limitation is that restraint is complex.

There are two forms of restraint: rigid (all-or-nothing approach to limiting food intake) and flexible (allows limited amounts of 'forbidden' foods without triggering disinhibition).

Only rigid restraint is likely to lead to obesity – could explain why some research has found that restrained eating produces weight loss.

Therefore the boundary model is a limited explanation of obesity because it fails to consider the true complexity of restraint.

Knowledge Check

1. Explain the difference between restraint theory and disinhibition as psychological explanations for obesity.
   (4 marks)

2. Briefly outline the boundary model as an explanation for obesity. *(4 marks)*

3. Briefly evaluate disinhibition as an explanation for obesity. *(4 marks)*

4. Describe **and** evaluate **two or more** psychological explanations for obesity.
   (16 marks)

Evaluation extra: Research methods.

Lab **experiments** of the boundary model control **confounding variables**, and therefore can establish that restrained eating is a *cause* of overeating and obesity.

However, they are also highly controlled, and therefore unlike real-world food environments. They also feature **demand characteristics**.

Therefore, even though lab experiments are useful for establishing psychological causes of obesity, they may not tell us much about real-world obesity problems.

Explanations for the success and failure of dieting

Spec spotlight

Explanations for the success and failure of dieting.

Revision BOOSTER

Exam questions will always use the wording of the specification. So, in this case, you will only be asked about 'the success and failure of dieting'. Use one or more of the explanations on this page to discuss this. One may be enough. Less is always more.

Bear in mind. Just stop thinking about me. Can't do it, can you?

Apply it

A friend of yours is a dietician. He advises obese people about diets that will lead to weight loss and reduce the risk of Type 2 diabetes. However, he has noticed that the more he helps some people, the more likely they are to put weight on rather than lose it. He works out that there must be quite a lot of psychology involved – weight loss is not just a physical thing.

1. **What advice would you give your friend that he can pass on to his clients?**

2. **Outline some reasons why diets fail and how they can be successful. Base your advice on psychological evidence.**

The spiral model

Diet failure leads to sense of personal deficiency.	Heatherton and Polivy (1992) suggested that food-restricted dieting often begins in adolescence when body dissatisfaction leads to low self-esteem and desire to lose weight.
	There is initial success but then weight is often regained leading to a sense of personal deficiency (e.g. 'I didn't try hard enough').
Downward spiral created.	Failed dieters make a bigger effort and experience more emotional distress making them vulnerable to **disinhibited** eating.
	Metabolic changes make weight loss physically harder (e.g. ghrelin levels increase, leptin levels decrease).
	Result is more failure followed by more attempts to 'diet harder', lowering of self-esteem, increase in depression.

Ironic processes theory

Being on a diet increases preoccupation with food.	Wegner *et al.* (1987) suggested that asking people not to think about a white bear almost guarantees they do. Paradoxical outcome of trying to suppress a thought is to make it more likely.
	Certain foods become more salient (stand out) because a dieter labels them 'forbidden'. Leads to increased thinking about food and disinhibition of eating, loss of control, excessive food intake, dieting failure.
Trying to distract yourself doesn't work.	Distraction (e.g. reading a book) requires mental activity – so dieter has less **cognitive** capacity to suppress thoughts of food.
	Central irony of restrained-eating diet – to be successful at preventing thoughts of food, dieter has to spend their time, energy and undivided attention trying not to think about food.

Disinhibition and dieting

Restraint leads to spiralling and ironic processes.	Most diets limit food intake but this means dieters are vulnerable to internal and external food-related cues (images, smells, etc.).
	Spiral model – continuous restraint leads to emotional frustration and distress, dieter tries to combat by eating.
	Ironic processes – dieter reminded of foods they cannot eat, so think about food more than usual.
These processes lead to *disinhibition*.	Dieter loses control and overeats, losing no more weight than someone who was not dieting and maybe even gaining some.

Chapter 9: Eating behaviour

One strength of the model is it shows how dieting can be successful.

Heatherton and Polivy suggest that people who diet to lose weight often have low self-esteem.

But those who restrain their eating to avoid gaining weight have higher self-esteem (Lowe and Kleifield 1988).

Therefore dietary success may be achieved by ending attempts to lose weight and accepting oneself as one is, thereby promoting self-esteem.

People who think about avoiding putting on weight are more likely to make a success of dieting.

Another strength is evidence for the role of ironic processes.

Adriaanse *et al.*'s (2011) participants were shown diet intentions in negative form (e.g. 'When I am sad, I will not eat chocolate').

They kept snack diaries the following week which showed they ate more unhealthy snacks and calories than a **control group** – ironic rebound effect.

This finding shows how just thinking of oneself as dieting can lead to the failure of the diet.

Counterpoint

But Adriaanse *et al.*'s study may not explain success/failure of dieting. Wegner admitted that the effects of ironic processes are short-term whereas dieting takes much longer.

Therefore other factors (e.g. self-esteem) are probably more important in determining diet success.

Revision BOOSTER

Lots of people have opinions about dieting (and obesity, and anorexia nervosa). Anecdotal evidence is useful and personal opinions are important. But they are no substitute for objective scientific evidence. Fill your answers with clear psychological content rather than opinion. That's yet another reason why research studies are so useful.

One limitation is that these theories do not account for individual differences.

Ogden (2010) argues that these theories do not explain why people lose weight even when they are preoccupied with food (e.g. people with anorexia nervosa).

One explanation is locus of control – 'internals' believe weight loss depends on their own efforts but 'externals' believe they do not have control.

Therefore, the explanations on this spread cannot offer a general prediction of who is likely to fail or succeed in losing weight.

Do you agree with this conclusion?

Evaluation extra: Is dieting pointless?

Diets do work if self-esteem is improved (spiral model) or avoid seeing some foods as forbidden (ironic processes).

However, dieting is pointless because evolved response to situations where food is scarce is to overeat, backfires when food is plentiful (we overeat).

Therefore, dieting often fails but it is not entirely pointless because there are ways of improving the chances of success.

Knowledge Check

1. Outline **one** explanation for the success **and** failure of dieting. *(6 marks)*

2. Outline what research has shown about the success and/or failure of dieting. *(6 marks)*

3. Briefly evaluate **one** explanation for the success and failure of dieting. *(4 marks)*

4. Leander and Uday are arguing about diets. Leander says none of them work, you just need to eat less. Uday believes they do work if you do it slowly and have other things to focus on.

   Discuss **one or more** explanation(s) for the success and failure of dieting. Refer to Leander's **and** Uday's positions in your answer.

   (16 marks)

The physiology of stress

Spec spotlight

The physiology of stress, including general adaptation syndrome, the hypothalamic-pituitary-adrenal system, the sympathomedullary pathway and the role of cortisol.

Stressors come in many forms.

Apply it

When Luther thinks about his upcoming exams, he sweats and shakes, his heart beats faster and he feels sick. The same thing happened when his girlfriend told him they were splitting up. And when he sang and played guitar in the college concert. He responded to these very different situations in basically the same way.

1. Use your knowledge of the physiology of stress to explain what is happening to Luther when he experiences these symptoms.

2. Apply what you know about the general adaptation syndrome to explain why Luther's responses in different situations are so similar.

General adaptation syndrome (GAS)

First stage: *Alarm reaction.*	Selye (1936) suggested that the stress response is initially **adaptive** (beneficial) – the **sympathetic branch** of the **autonomic nervous system (ANS)** activated by hypothalamus.
	Stimulates adrenal medulla to release adrenaline and noradrenaline to prepare body for fight or flight.
Second stage: *Resistance.*	Body continues to adapt by resisting stressor.
	Body's resources consumed at harmful rate (e.g. stress hormones become depleted).
	Parasympathetic branch activated to conserve energy.
Third stage: *Exhaustion.*	Adaptation to chronic stressor fails because resources needed to resist are drained.
	Symptoms of sympathetic arousal (e.g. raised heart rate). Adrenal glands damaged, immune system suppressed.
	Stress-related illnesses now likely (e.g. raised blood pressure, coronary heart disease and depression).

Physiological stress response

Acute (short-term) stress response. *Sympathomedullary pathway* (SAM), also called fight or flight response.	Immediate response to stressor – hypothalamus activates sympathetic branch of ANS.
	Stimulates adrenal medulla to release adrenaline and noradrenaline into bloodstream (heart beats faster, muscles tense, liver converts stored glycogen into glucose to provide energy to fuel fight or flight response).
	Once stressor stops – **parasympathetic nervous system** activated and physiological arousal decreases – priority now is energy conservation, rest and digest response.
Chronic (long-term) stress response. *Hypothalamic-pituitary-adrenal* system (HPA).	If stressor continues – HPA now activated.
	Hypothalamus produces corticotropin releasing factor (CRF).
	Detected by anterior lobe of pituitary gland and causes release of adrenocorticotropic hormone (ACTH).
	ACTH detected by adrenal cortex which secretes cortisol.
Cortisol is the major stress hormone.	Cortisol affects glucose metabolism and restores energy.
	Has other effects (e.g. suppresses immune system).
	HPA is self-regulating via negative feedback loop – cortisol in bloodstream monitored at pituitary and hypothalamus.
	High levels of cortisol trigger reduction in both CRF and ACTH, resulting in corresponding reduction in cortisol.

One strength of the GAS is Selye's own research supports it.

Selye (1936) subjected rats to stressors (e.g. extreme cold, surgical injury). Found the same collection of responses ('syndrome') regardless of stressor.

The syndrome appeared after 6–48 hours, not unique to a specific stressor. He tracked the responses through resistance and exhaustion.

This demonstrates the same general response regardless of the particular stressor.

One limitation of the GAS is that it may not actually be a general response.

Mason (1971) **replicated** Selye's procedures using monkeys.

Effects varied depending on stressor (extreme cold increased urinary cortisol, extreme heat reduced it, exercise had no effect).

These findings challenge the **validity** of the GAS by showing that specific stressors produce specific responses.

Evaluation extra: Animal research.

Stress research depends on using non-human mammals to study for ethical reasons and because the physiological systems in the stress response are almost identical.

However, stress is more complex in humans because it is affected by psychological factors e.g. **cognitive** appraisal (see below).

Therefore, animal studies may help us to understand the basic physiology of stress but their applicability to humans is limited.

De-stressors come in many forms.

One strength is that knowledge of physiology has real-world value.

People with Addison's disease (disorder of adrenal glands) cannot produce cortisol, so in stress situations do not mobilise energy to deal with stressor.

This triggers an Addisonian crisis (mental confusion, low blood pressure, etc.). Individuals self-administer cortisol replacement therapy and must be aware of dangers of stress.

Therefore a better understanding of stress physiology has improved the lives of some people.

One limitation is that physiological explanations ignore psychological factors.

Cognitive appraisal was demonstrated in one study where students watched a gruesome medical procedure (Speisman *et al.* 1964).

Heart rates increased in those who perceived procedure as traumatic, but decreased in those told the procedure was voluntary initiation rite.

This finding cannot be explained by a purely physiological theory.

Evaluation extra: Gender bias.

Fight or flight is a universal physiological response to an acute stressor – based on male animals (avoiding females because of hormone fluctuations).

However, Taylor *et al.* (2000) argue that females 'tend and befriend' instead (tend offspring, befriend other females for co-operation). **Oxytocin** inhibits fight or flight response in females.

This suggests that there is no single baseline stress response – it varies depending on gender and circumstances.

Revision BOOSTER

The maximum you will have to write to describe the general adaptation syndrome is about 150–200 words. This is the amount appropriate for a 6-mark answer. That's about 40 words for each of the three stages of the GAS plus some general background.

Knowledge Check

1. In relation to the physiology of stress, describe the general adaptation syndrome.   *(6 marks)*

2. Outline the role of cortisol in the physiology of stress.
   (6 marks)

3. In relation to the physiology of stress, outline the hypothalamic-pituitary-adrenal system **and** the sympathomedullary pathway.
   (6 marks)

4. Describe **and** evaluate research into the physiology of stress.   *(16 marks)*

The immune system

The immune system protects bodies from invading germs and other foreign bodies (*antigens*) by deploying several defensive cells, for example *T cells* and *natural killer (NK) cells*.

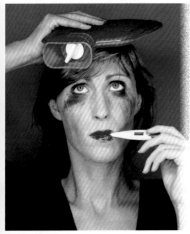

Scientific proof that stress can affect your mascara.

Immunosuppression

Immune system suppressed.	Directly – *cortisol* produced by the *hypothalamic-pituitary-adrenal system* (HPA) inhibits production of immune cells.
	Indirectly – stress influences lifestyle behaviours (smoking, drinking) that have a negative effect on immune functioning.
Chronic stress of exams → *decrease* in NK and killer T cells.	Kiecolt-Glaser *et al.* (1984) tested 75 medical students before the exam period (low-stress) and on the day of the first exam (high-stress). Students also completed questionnaires measuring sources of stress and psychological symptoms.
	The activity of natural killer (NK) and killer T cells decreased between first and second samples – evidence of an immune response suppressed by a chronic stressor.
	Decline was greatest in students who reported feeling lonely and experiencing other sources of stress (e.g. life events).
Chronic stress of caring for ill relative → *increase* in immune antibodies.	Kiecolt-Glaser *et al.* (1991) compared caregivers (looking after a relative with Alzheimer's) with a matched group of non-caregivers.
	Over 13 months caregivers had weaker cell-based immune response compared with control participants.
	Caregivers also had more infectious illnesses and higher levels of depression (32% of caregivers; 6% of **control group**).

Cardiovascular disorders (CVDs)

Stress associated with CVDs (CHDs and stroke).	CVDs are disorders of heart and blood vessels – including coronary heart disease (CHD) and stroke (blocked blood vessels in the brain).
	Acute stress leads to high levels of adrenaline with direct and continuing effects on heart muscles (e.g. increased heart rate).
Acute stress caused by watching football match → CVDs.	Wilbert-Lampen *et al.* (2008) looked at incidences of heart attacks during football matches (sudden emotional arousal – an acute stressor) played in Germany during the 1996 World Cup.
	On days Germany played, cardiac emergencies increased by 2.66 times compared with a **control** period – acute emotional stress of watching favourite football team more than doubled participants' risk of a cardiovascular event.
Chronic stressors e.g. workplace stressors → heart attack.	Yusuf *et al.*'s (2004) INTERHEART study compared 15,000 people who'd had a heart attack (myocardial infarction, MI) with a similar number of people who had not.
	Several chronic stressors had a strong link to MI including stressful life events (page 162) and workplace stress (page 166) – role of stress greater than obesity and third behind smoking and cholesterol.

One limitation is that some research shows stress can be protective.

Stress can have *immunoenhancing* effects, e.g. Dharbhar (2008) exposed rats to mild acute stressors which stimulated a major immune response.

Immune cells (e.g. lymphocytes) flooded into bloodstream and body tissues to protect against acute stress – chronic stress may be more damaging.

This suggests that the relationship between stress, the immune system and illnesses is complex and not yet fully understood.

One strength is research into stress and illness may have real-world application.

Dharbhar's research could lead to patients getting low doses of stress hormones before surgery to improve recovery.

Students who took a relaxation programme seriously had better immune functioning during exams (Kiecolt-Glaser and Glaser 1992).

These applications benefit real people and confirm the relevance of stress to the immune system.

Evaluation extra: Research methods.

Lab **experiments** measure the effects of acute stressors while controlling **confounding variables** – can establish causation.

However, lab experiments are unlike real-world stressful situations and also feature **demand characteristics**.

Therefore, lab experiments are useful for establishing the apparent causes of immunosuppression, but they may not actually be causes in the real world.

One limitation is the effects of stress on CVDs are mostly indirect.

The evidence for stress as an indirect factor in CVDs is much stronger than evidence that it directly causes CVDs.

Orth-Gomer *et al.* (2000) found that marital stress tripled the risk of heart attack in women who already had CVD – different from causing CVD.

This suggests that stress increases vulnerability to CVDs, mainly through indirect effects (e.g. lifestyle).

One strength is research to support the link between stress and CVDs.

Song *et al.* (2019) compared people diagnosed with stress-related disorders to their unaffected siblings and members of the general population (controls).

People with stress disorders had a 64% greater risk of a CVD in the first year after diagnosis.

This shows that exposure to chronic psychological stress can significantly increase CVD risk.

Evaluation extra: What's the real cause?

The cause of CVDs could be physiological – stress triggers a physiological response that damages the cardiovascular system (e.g. heart muscle).

However, the cause could be psychological, e.g. personality – some people perceive stressors negatively and have a strong physiological reaction.

This suggests that while physiology may be the immediate direct cause of CVDs, the real cause is psychological.

Graham brought a new meaning to the phrase 'getting stuck into a book'.

Revision BOOSTER

There are three topics from these pages mentioned on the specification – the role of stress in illness, immunosuppression and CVDs. You could get a question on any of these. 'The role of stress in illness' means you can write about either or both of the other two (remember: less is more). But a question specifically on immunosuppression or CVDs is a different matter.

Knowledge Check

1. In relation to the role of stress in illness, explain what is meant by 'immunosuppression' **and** 'cardiovascular disorders'.
   (3 marks + 3 marks)

2. Explain what research (theories and/or studies) has shown about the effects of stress on cardiovascular disorders. *(4 marks)*

3. Briefly evaluate the role of stress in illness. *(4 marks)*

4. Fabrizio is experiencing increasingly ill health, from niggly sniffles to aches and pains and an irregular heartbeat. His girlfriend thinks it is because of stress, as Fabrizio lost his job recently.

   Discuss the role of stress in illness. Refer to Fabrizio's experience in your answer.
   (16 marks)

Sources of stress: Life changes

Spec spotlight

Sources of stress: life changes.

They'd found the perfect dress – now all they needed were the shoes...

Life changes as a source of stress

Sources of stress are often the big events in our lives.	Major sources of stress are the really important but infrequent things that happen to us.
	For example, getting married/divorced, close relative dies, financial state changes (better or worse), new child is born.
Life changes require significant adjustment, so are stressful.	Life changes are stressful because you make major psychological adjustment to adapt to changed circumstances – the bigger the change, the greater the adjustment and associated stress.
	Life changes are cumulative – they add together to create more stress because they require even more change to adapt.
	Applies as much to positive life changes as to negative ones.
Life changes measured using *SRRS*, calculating LCUs.	Holmes and Rahe's (1967) *Social readjustment rating scale* (SRRS) gives number of *life change units* (LCUs).
	The higher the LCU value, the more adjustment the life change needs, making it more stressful (e.g. divorce is 73 LCUs, marriage is 50).
	Participants tick all the life changes they recall over previous months (usually 12).
Life changes linked to illness if *LCUs* more than 300.	Rahe (1972) claimed that under 150 LCUs means you are likely to experience reasonable health in following year.
	Between 150 and 300 LCUs means you have 50% chance of experiencing illness the next year.
	Over 300 LCUs means an 80% chance.

Apply it

Two psychology students conduct a survey of their fellow sixth-formers. They want to identify the experiences that are most stressful for students. Some have sadly lost family members. For others, their parents have divorced. Some have moved to the college from a different part of the country, others have celebrated the arrival of a baby in their family. All of them have been through important exams. The psychology students find that the people who have experienced the most events tend to be the ones who report being depressed, anxious and physically ill.

Use your knowledge of life changes to explain the psychology students' findings. Support your explanation with some evidence.

Rahe *et al.* (1970) Life changes and illness

PROCEDURE	US Navy personnel assigned to three ships completed a version of the SRRS called *Schedule of recent experiences*.
	Total LCU score was calculated for each participant for a six-month period before tour of duty, and every illness on board ship was reported to the medical unit.
	At the end an independent researcher reviewed the medical records and calculated an illness score for each participant.
	Neither participants nor on-board medical staff aware of the purpose of study or what data was being used for.
FINDINGS AND CONCLUSIONS	Researchers found a significant positive **correlation** (of +.118) between LCU scores and illness scores aboard ship.
	Those who experienced most stressful life changes in the final six months before leaving had most illnesses on ship.
	Researchers concluded life changes were a reasonably robust predictor of later illness.

One strength of the life changes concept is supportive research evidence.

Lietzén et al. (2011) followed 16,000 asthma-free adults from the HeSSup study in Finland – prospective study like Rahe et al. (1970).

They found that a high level of life change stress reliably predicted asthma onset (not explained by other factors e.g. being a smoker).

This study suggests that stressful life changes can contribute to the onset of a chronic illness.

Counterpoint

48% of participants experienced just one or no life changes in the above study. Lazarus et al. (1980) argue that daily hassles are more important sources of stress than life changes.

Therefore daily hassles may have been better predictors of asthma than life changes for most participants in Lietzén et al.'s study.

One limitation of life changes research is it ignores individual differences.

Stress perceived differently by different individuals, e.g. moving house is more stressful when due to a lack of money than as a result of being better off.

Byrne and Whyte (1980) were able to predict heart attacks using SRRS scores, but only if subjective interpretations of life changes were taken into account.

Therefore the life changes approach lacks **validity** because it does not consider individual differences in how life changes are perceived.

Another limitation is that the SRRS includes positive and negative life changes.

The life changes approach assumes all change is stressful but Turner and Wheaton (1995) found (when asking participants) that negative SRRS items caused most stress.

They argued this is because there are frustrations associated with negative changes that are not associated with positive ones.

This challenges the validity of the life changes approach, because positive and negative life changes have different effects.

Do you agree with this conclusion?

Evaluation extra: Issues of causation.

The approach on this spread claims life changes directly *cause* stress – change requires psychological adjustment with direct effects on health.

However, the relationship may not be causal as most research is correlational – a third factor could cause both life changes and illness (e.g. anxiety).

Therefore, the evidence that life changes are related to stress and illness is reasonably strong, but this relationship is probably not directly causal.

'Yellow and green should never be seen.' Sid had heard it all before – but it was Christmas and he was determined to make a point.

Revision BOOSTER

It really pays to practise writing 16-mark essays with your book shut and timing yourself – about 20 minutes for a 16-mark essay.

Knowledge Check

1. In relation to sources of stress, explain what is meant by 'life changes'. *(4 marks)*

2. Explain what research has shown about life changes as a source of stress. *(4 marks)*

3. Evaluate research into **one** source of stress. *(6 marks)*

4. Tad and Tadita have both had a stressful year. Tad split up with his wife and had to move house and start a new job. Tadita got married and had a baby.

   Outline **and** evaluate life changes as a source of stress. Refer to Tad's and Tadita's experiences in your answer.
   (16 marks)

Spec spotlight

Sources of stress: daily hassles.

Mental note: buy more post-its!

Apply it

Hadrian has noticed the following about daily life. The laptop always takes longer to boot up when you need it most. The weather can be beautiful until you go on holiday, when it pours. What you are looking for is always in the last place you check. A pound coin dropped on the floor always rolls miles away. Hadrian believes that these experiences are frustrating and irritating and gang up on us to cause us harm.

1. Use research on daily hassles to explain Hadrian's experiences.

2. What is the evidence that he is right?

3. Is there another explanation?

Revision BOOSTER

In a 16-mark essay you don't have to write everything on this spread. What is here is actually more than 1000 words!! For a 16-mark essay you probably only have time to write 500 words – but don't cut down the evaluation. That's worth 10 marks so it is always better to do more evaluation.

Daily hassles as a source of stress

Daily hassles are frequent and everyday irritations and frustrations.	According to Lazarus *et al.* (1980) daily hassles range from: • Minor inconveniences (e.g. can't find keys). • Greater pressures and difficulties (e.g. not enough time). Each hassle on its own does not have the impact of a significant life change – but their added effects leave us feeling stressed.
Psychological appraisal = primary + secondary appraisal.	Primary appraisal – at the start we work out subjectively how threatening an experience is to psychological health. Secondary appraisal – if we deem that the hassle is threatening we subjectively consider how well equipped we are to cope with the hassle.
Daily hassles measured with *HSUP*.	*Hassles and uplifts scale* (HSUP) is a self-report measure of: • Hassles – how many experienced and how severe they are (e.g. losing things, not having enough time). • Uplifts – small, daily pleasant and enjoyable things that offset stress of hassles (e.g. getting on well with friends).
Effects of *life changes and* daily hassles are *different.*	Life changes have indirect effects – they are *distal* sources of stress. Daily hassles have direct and immediate effects on our everyday lives – they are *proximal* sources of stress.

Kanner *et al.* (1981) Hassles and psychological symptoms

PROCEDURE	100 participants completed several scales: • *Hassles scale* every month for nine consecutive months. • *Life changes scale* one month before study started (thinking back over 2½ years) and again at end of study. • *Hopkins symptom checklist* to measure psychological symptoms of anxiety and depression.
FINDINGS AND CONCLUSIONS	Researchers found significant positive **correlations** between hassle frequency and psychological symptoms at start and end of study. The more hassles a participant experienced the more severe were the psychological symptoms of depression and anxiety. Hassles were a stronger predictor of psychological symptoms than life changes.

One strength is research support for the effects of daily hassles.

Ivancevich (1986) used the HSUP and found that daily hassles were strong predictors of poor health, poor job performance and work absenteeism.

In terms of work-related stress it seems that minor day-in day-out stressors can accumulate and have significant effects.

This suggests that daily hassles is a valid explanation of stress experienced by many people.

Counterpoint

Ivancevich's study depends on retrospective recall of daily hassles and life changes over previous month – hassles are more minor and more easy to forget than life changes.

This means the **validity** of hassles research may be doubtful.

Bad hair day? We've all had one.

Another strength is that the hassles approach explains individual differences.

People differ in their understanding of hassles – the stress of a hassle depends on how someone interprets it (Lazarus *et al.*).

One person perceives losing keys as a disaster, another does not (primary appraisal). One person believes they can cope, another does not (secondary appraisal).

Therefore the daily hassles approach can explain individual differences in how stress affects our health and behaviour.

Revision BOOSTER

A lot of research has addressed the issue of which is the best predictor of illness – life changes or daily hassles? You could tackle evaluation bearing this in mind. You could compare and contrast the two sources of stress. But keep your focus on the topic of the exam question.

One limitation is that hassles research is mostly correlational.

Even the strongest correlation does not show causation, so we can't necessarily conclude that hassles cause stress.

Another (unmeasured) factor may be causal, e.g. depression may cause someone to experience hassles more intensely and at the same time cause them to feel stressed.

This suggests the link between hassles and stress may be indirect and depends on other factors.

Knowledge Check

1. Using examples, explain the difference between life changes and daily hassles. *(4 marks)*

2. Describe what research (theories and/or studies) has shown about daily hassles as a source of stress. *(6 marks)*

3. Briefly evaluate research into daily hassles as a source of stress. *(4 marks)*

4. Discuss daily hassles as a source of stress. *(16 marks)*

Evaluation extra: Hassles versus life changes.

Daily hassles are stressful because they happen a lot and their effects are cumulative – they make life changes seem worse.

However, life changes may be more stressful because they are major events with powerful effects – going through one creates more daily hassles.

Therefore, in the end it is the life changes that contribute most to stress because they have the biggest impact and lead to the daily hassles.

Sources of stress: Workplace stress

Spec spotlight

Sources of stress: workplace stress, including the effects of workload and control.

No one can be that happy to do housework. Their secret? The bottles are filled with vodka.

Revision BOOSTER

In an exam everyone feels some measure of anxiety – use your understanding of stress to help cope with exam anxiety.

Apply it

Harmony is an A level student who is struggling under a big workload. She has six essays to do in ten days. She feels she is working harder than she did at GCSE. But because there is so much to do, she feels she has no control over her work. There's no time for planning and now she has another piece of work – she is part of a group preparing a presentation on workplace stress.

Using your knowledge of sources of stress, identify the features of Harmony's situation that make it particularly stressful. Explain how she might feel and why. Refer to some research in your explanation.

Research into workplace stress

Workload and *control.*	Workload = the amount of time/effort required in a job. Can refer to underload but is usually overload.
	Control = extent a worker feels able to make own decisions, work independently, have more flexibility to set own pace (e.g. scheduling tasks themselves).
Job demands-control model control acts as a buffer.	Karasek's (1979) job demands-control model states stressful demands of a job (e.g. workload) can lead to poor health, dissatisfaction and absenteeism – but this relationship is modified by amount of control the employee has over work.
	When two people have equally demanding workloads, only the one who lacks control over work becomes ill.

Bosma *et al.* (1997) Civil servants and stress

PROCEDURE

This was a series of prospective studies of over 10,000 civil servants (who work in Whitehall, London) in a wide range of job grades.

A questionnaire measured workload and job control.

Participants were also examined for symptoms of CHD and followed up after five years.

FINDINGS AND CONCLUSIONS

No **correlation** between workload and illness – so job demands were not a significant workplace stressor.

But employees who reported low job control at the start of the study more likely to have CHD five years later – even when other risk factors (e.g. lifestyle, diet) statistically accounted for.

Finding existed across all job grades – status and support given to higher grade civil servants did not offset risk of developing CHD if job lacked control.

Johansson *et al.* (1978) Swedish sawmill

PROCEDURE

Natural experiment in Swedish sawmill compared group of wood 'finishers' and group of cleaners.

Measured employee illness, absenteeism, and levels of the stress hormones adrenaline and noradrenaline.

Finishers had little control over work because it was set by the machine – but job demands were high because it was complex, skilled and carried a lot of responsibility.

FINDINGS AND CONCLUSIONS

Researchers found higher level of stress hormones in finishers overall – higher even before they got to work and increased over the day (but cleaners' levels decreased).

More stress-related illness and absenteeism among finishers.

One strength is that workload is a culturally generalisable concept.

Liu *et al.* (2007) asked workers in China (**collectivist**) and the US (**individualist**) to describe stressful work events in the previous month (qualitative method).

Chinese and US workers differed in views on several work-related stressors but not perceptions of workload – both groups rated it as the third most stressful workplace stressor.

This suggests that workload is understood as stressful in very different cultures and can therefore be **generalised**.

Counterpoint

However, Gyŏrkŏs *et al.* (2012) found job control was perceived as more stressful in individualist cultures – control may be hard to generalise to collectivist cultures.

This and the previous point show that 'workplace stress' has many aspects, not all of them generalisable across cultures.

If I look stressed enough maybe I can sneak in a little kip and no one will notice...

One limitation is the job demands-control model is simplistic.

Lack of control and workload are stressors for many workers (in some cultures) but not the only ones – stress depends on interaction of other factors.

These include the kind of work they do and how well they use coping mechanisms, also important is the *perception* of control/ workload.

The job demands-control model lacks **validity** because of its simplistic focus on just two major workplace stressors.

Another limitation is evidence that having job control is more stressful.

Depends on **self-efficacy** (a person's belief in their ability to perform tasks) – employees with low self-efficacy feel stressed in jobs giving them control (Meier *et al.*).

Control means taking decisions, but people with low self-efficacy find this difficult so control is another workplace stressor for them.

This shows that job control is not stressful in itself but depends on individual differences such as self-efficacy.

Evaluation extra: Validity.

Workplace stress research is often in real workplaces not labs (Johansson *et al.*), these tend to have high **external validity** because people are going about their usual jobs.

However, these studies are usually natural experiments – job roles are already assigned so employees could differ in ways affecting the outcome, reducing **internal validity**.

This suggests that the findings of real-world studies ultimately lack validity.

Knowledge Check

1. Explain what is meant by 'workload' **and** 'control' in relation to workplace stress.
   (2 marks + 2 marks)

2. Describe what research has shown about the effects of workload **and** control in relation to workplace stress.
   (6 marks)

3. Evaluate research into the effects of control on workplace stress. *(6 marks)*

4. The following item appeared in a newspaper: 'Work kills, say psychologists. Experts yesterday told us what we all know already. If you have too much work to do, and you can't control it, then you will get ill.'

   Referring to the issues raised in this item, outline **and** evaluate research into the workplace as a source of stress. *(16 marks)*

Spec spotlight

Measuring stress: self-report scales (Social readjustment rating scale and Hassles and uplifts scale) and physiological measures, including skin conductance response.

Apply it

An organisational psychologist has been asked by an NHS trust to measure levels of stress amongst its staff. Because he feels that just one measure is not enough to understand stress fully, he chooses two methods – one to measure people's feelings about the stress they experience, and the other to measure the physical effects of stress. He expects he will find a correlation between the two measures. His report will have to include a brief assessment of the strengths and limitations of both measures.

1. Describe **two** specific measures that would meet the psychologist's needs.

2. Briefly outline his assessment of them – what strengths **and** limitations could he include in his report?

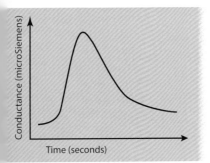

A typical skin conductance response (SCR): a slope at the start indicating the onset of the response, which takes time to rise, reaches a peak and then decays in a long 'tail' on the trace, all within four or five seconds.

Self-report measures of stress

SRRS 43 life events linked to change.	*Social readjustment rating scale* (SRRS) created by Holmes and Rahe (1967) using medical records to identify events in patients' lives that happened before they became ill. 43 life events, major positive and negative life changes.
LCU scores provide measure of stress.	Life change unit (LCU) calculated for each life event by asking a group of people to estimate readjustment required for each, using marriage (500 units) as a baseline. Participants indicate which life events they have experienced in the past 12 months – LCUs for these are added to give an overall (global) stress score.
Hassles scale 117 items.	Kanner *et al.* (1981) created *Hassles and uplifts scale* (HSUP) to measure daily hassles and uplifts as indicators of stress. Hassles scale has 117 items selected from categories such as 'work', 'health' and 'environment' (e.g. 'troublesome neighbours', 'too much responsibility'). Measures severity of each hassle on a three-point scale: somewhat, moderately or extremely severe.
Uplifts scale 135 items.	135 Uplifts scale items were produced from the same categories as the Hassles scale – uplifts include getting enough sleep, liking fellow workers. Individual identifies all the uplifts that apply and indicates their frequency over a specific time period (e.g. that day).

Physiological measures of stress

Skin conductance response (SCR) ANS produces sweat.	Stress creates arousal in **autonomic nervous system (ANS)** and we sweat more. Human skin is a good conductor of electricity and sweat enhances that. To measure conductance:
	• Electrodes are attached to index and middle fingers.
	• Tiny current is applied to electrodes.
	• Conductance measured (in microSiemens) – the signal is amplified and displayed on a screen.
	Tonic conductance is when we are not experiencing a stimulus (used as baseline). *Phasic conductance* occurs when something happens (e.g. asked a question) – produces SCR (see left).
Other physiological measures.	Increased adrenaline (sign of acute stress), increased cortisol (chronic stress). Measured in urine and blood (also saliva for cortisol). Baseline measures taken for comparison because levels vary naturally during the day.

One strength of self-report is that it is a valid way to measure stress.

Stress is personal so the best way to understand it is to ask people about their experiences.

Asking questions about experiences 'makes sense' to people as a way to measure stress, so people are more honest.

Therefore the findings of studies based on self-report measures are true reflections of the stress participants feel.

Counterpoint

However, Dohrenwend *et al.* (1990) found that the most stressed people made the most negative interpretations of scale items (e.g. 'Serious illness').

This means there is an inbuilt bias that inflates stress scores and reduces the **validity** of self-report measures.

One limitation is that self-report scales mix causes and effects of stress.

SRRS and HSUP items (causes of stress) overlap with symptoms (effects of stress), e.g. 'Personal injury or illness' (SRRS).

Like saying, 'You have a stress-related illness because you are experiencing a personal illness' – scales *reflect* illness, not *predict* it.

This is why self-report measures should be abandoned and replaced by direct observations of behaviour.

Evaluation extra: Subjective versus objective.

Self-report measures are subjective, so they are prone to biases (**social desirability**) but stress is a deeply subjective experience.

Physiological measures are objective – they are not affected by personal biases but similar physiological responses are linked to different experiences.

Therefore, in terms of validity, the subjective approach is probably best as it informs us of the stress experience.

Well I fixed that leaky tap. That gushing sound? Yeah, sorry about that. I think you might need a plumber... and perhaps the fire service.

One limitation is that people differ systematically in their SCRs.

SCR measurement takes a baseline because people have individual patterns. But people can be divided into two groups based on their SCRs.

Stabiles have SCRs that vary little at rest and are not much affected by thoughts or events. But labiles produce many SCRs even at rest.

Therefore SCR measurement is not a straightforward matter of comparing baseline (tonic) SCRs against stimulated (phasic) SCRs.

Validity revisited

Validity can be a confusing topic, but here it's happily straightforward. It's all about these questions: 'Does the method really measure stress? Or something else? How do we know it really measures stress?'

One strength is that physiological measures are scientific.

Physiological indicators are reliably associated with stress, but researchers must take into account that they all have a baseline varying between people.

These measures are free of biases that affect self-reports, e.g. cortisol levels are not affected by social desirability.

This means that physiological measures are considered more scientific measures of the body's physiological stress response.

Knowledge Check

1. Explain the difference between self-report scales and physiological measures in measuring stress. *(4 marks)*

2. Briefly outline the skin conductance response as a way of measuring stress. *(4 marks)*

3. Evaluate self-report scales as ways of measuring stress. *(6 marks)*

4. Discuss **two** ways of measuring stress. *(16 marks)*

Spec spotlight

Individual differences in stress: personality types A, B and C and associated behaviours.

For the twenty-seventh time today... I have not been involved in an accident!

CVD? CHD?

What's the difference? CVD stands for cardiovascular disorder and refers to disorders of the heart (coronary) and blood vessels (vascular). So this includes heart attacks and strokes (lack of blood supply to the brain).

CVD also includes CHD, i.e. coronary heart disease. So CHD is a specific type of CVD.

It doesn't really matter if you get them mixed up but we thought we would make the difference clear!

Ah this is the life... Eh? What water? And where did my front room go??

Type A and B personality

Type A Competitive, time-urgent and hostile.	Friedman and Rosenman (1959) observed that patients with coronary heart disease (CHD) shared a pattern of behaviour, which they called Type A personality: • Competitive – achievement-motivated, ambitious, aware of status. • Time-urgent – fast-talking, impatient, proactive, multitaskers. • Hostile – aggressive, intolerant and quick to anger.
Type B Laid back.	Friedman and Rosenman also identified the characteristics of Type B personality – relaxed, tolerant, reflective, 'laid back' and less competitive than Type As.
Western collaborative group study (WCGS).	3000 males in California were medically assessed as free of CHD at the start of the study (Friedman and Rosenman 1959). Assessed for personality type by answering 25 questions in a structured interview. Interviews were conducted to incite Type A-related behaviour (e.g. interviewer would be aggressive and frequently interrupt).
Link to *CHD*.	Eight-and-a-half years later (Friedman and Rosenman 1974), 257 men had developed CHD – 70% of these had been assessed at the start of the study as Type A. Type As had higher levels of adrenaline and noradrenaline and higher blood pressure/cholesterol. Suggests Type A personality makes people vulnerable to stressors because impatience and hostility cause raised physiological stress response.

Type C personality

Type C Pathological niceness, repress emotions.	Type C people demonstrate 'pathological niceness', are 'people pleasers', compliant, passive and self-sacrificing. They avoid conflict by repressing emotions, especially anger (particularly relevant to cancer-proneness).
Link to *cancer*.	Temoshok (1987) proposed Type C is linked with cancer. Dattore *et al.* (1980) studied 200 veterans of the Vietnam War – 75 cancer patients and others with non-cancer diagnoses. Cancer patients reported significantly greater emotional repression and fewer depression symptoms (unlikely to acknowledge depression because repressing emotions). This is evidence of a link between Type C and cancer-proneness.

One strength is that Type A/B research has real-world application.

Ragland and Brand (1988) followed up heart attack survivors from the WCGS – years later, death rate for Type Bs was higher than for Type As.

One explanation is that Type A survivors of a heart attack were more likely than Type Bs to change their behaviour – healthier, less stress.

Therefore data from research can be useful in convincing Type A individuals to change their behaviour and thus live longer.

Counterpoint

However, WCGS and follow-up participants were men – knowledge based on how men respond to stress, not tested with women and may be less relevant to women (beta bias).

Therefore, research into Type A/B may be **gender-biased** as some of our knowledge is based on male participants only.

One limitation is that the Type A concept is much too broad.

Researchers have focused on the hostility component (selfish, mistrusting, contemptuous) to explain the link between stress and CHD.

Carmelli *et al.* (1991) found very high CHD-related deaths after 27 years in a subgroup of WCGS men with high hostility scores.

Therefore, it looks like it is not the broad Type A personality that is linked to illness but the narrower hostility component.

Another limitation is evidence challenging the role of Type C in cancer.

Greer and Morris (1975) found a link between breast cancer and emotional suppression of Type C – as predicted by the theory.

But the link only existed in women under the age of 50. Research generally has inconsistent findings.

This suggests that the role of personality in cancer is not straightforward and is moderated by age and probably other biological factors.

Evaluation extra: Type A and Type B.

Evidence suggests two distinct personality types (A and B) that respond to stress differently. Type As are more likely to deal with stress in a way that harms their health.

However, other evidence shows this link is weak and **correlational** – inconsistent and contradictory findings suggest the Type A/B distinction is blurred.

Therefore Type A is no longer a particularly useful concept because it cannot be used to predict who will become ill in response to stress.

Apply it

Harold has a very responsible job with a major charity. He wants to lead the charity one day so he is always trying to do three things at once, impatiently rushing around. Harold is very demanding of everyone around him so he often snaps at them.

Henrika is a volunteer with a support group for children with autism. She is very laid back and relaxed with the children and their parents. She has an unhurried and calm approach to her work and life.

Hester's aim in life is to make sure everyone around her is happy. Because she wants to please everyone, she often 'bites her lip' and keeps her thoughts to herself. She often finds herself agreeing with the last person she spoke to.

1. Identify the **three** personality types described here.

2. Use your knowledge of individual differences in stress to explain your choices.

Knowledge Check

1. In relation to individual differences in stress, explain what is meant by 'Type B' **and** 'Type C' personality.
   (3 marks + 3 marks)

2. Outline research into personality types in relation to individual differences in stress. *(6 marks)*

3. Describe how research (theories and/or studies) has investigated the effect of personality types on stress.
   (6 marks)

4. Discuss **one or more** individual differences in stress. *(16 marks)*

Individual differences in stress: Hardiness

Spec spotlight

Individual differences in stress: hardiness, including commitment, challenge and control.

Still trying, son (see our Year 2 Student Book).

Apply it

Kalil works for an organisation that helps young people cope with life's problems. He runs courses and activity weekends where teenagers learn the value of being able to stand up to stress and beat it. Kalil himself used to be addicted to heroin, but now he is determined to overcome all the setbacks that life throws at him. He tells the young people they can do the same by developing their 'Three Cs'.

1. Use your knowledge of individual differences in stress to explain what Kalil means by the 'Three Cs'.

2. How could the 'Three Cs' help the young people to overcome stress? Refer to **one** piece of research in your answer.

Revision BOOSTER

Write a very brief essay plan for each possible essay and then practise writing the essay for the stress topic in full from this. Time yourself – 20 minutes for a 16-mark essay.

Hardiness

Hardiness *protects against stress, 'existential courage'.*	Kobasa (1979) proposed hardiness is a set of personality characteristics that protect us against stress. Maddi (1986) argues hardiness gives us 'existential courage' – the determination to keep going despite setbacks life throws at us and uncertainties about the future.
Three dimensions to hardiness: *commitment, challenge, control.*	Commitment – hardy people deeply involved in relationships and activities. They throw themselves wholeheartedly into life, optimistic they will learn something valuable. Challenge – hardy people are resilient and welcome change as an opportunity rather than a threat. They recognise life is unpredictable, but this is exciting. Control – hardy people have a strong belief that they are in charge of events. They actively strive to influence environments rather than being passive.

Kobasa (1979) Hardiness and stress

PROCEDURE

Kobasa measured life changes of 670 male American middle and senior managers aged 40–49 years.

Used *Schedule of recent experiences* (forerunner of SRRS) to identify who experienced high stress over previous three years.

Also analysed absenteeism records and levels of illness.

FINDINGS AND CONCLUSIONS

Managers responded to same stress very differently.

Some were more resilient – they coped with their highly stressful jobs without becoming ill or taking time off work.

These resilient managers scored highly on the Three Cs, confirming the role of hardiness.

Maddi (1987) Hardiness at work

PROCEDURE

Maddi studied 400 managers and supervisors at the Bell Telephone company in the US over several years.

The Bell Telephone company underwent one of the biggest reorganisations in American corporate history when thousands of people lost their jobs – also extremely stressful experience for those who stayed.

FINDINGS AND CONCLUSIONS

Significant declines in performance and health in about two-thirds of participants (e.g. heart attacks, strokes, depression and drug abuse).

One-third of managers scored highly on measures of the Three Cs and flourished – their health did not deteriorate, they felt happier and more fulfilled at work and were rejuvenated by the whole stressful experience.

One strength is that hardiness has application in the real world.

Bartone et al. (2008) measured hardiness in candidates for US Army Special Forces, a highly stressful job with a tough selection course.

Those who passed the course were significantly hardier than those who failed – elite US military units now routinely select hardy people.

Therefore knowledge of hardiness might be useful in certain jobs to predict who can resist stress and who cannot.

Cut out that negativity!

Another strength of hardiness is that there is evidence to support it.

Contrada (1989) looked at cardiovascular responses to a stressful lab task – participants who scored highest on hardiness had lower resting blood pressure.

The lowest blood pressure was found in participants who were hardy and had a Type B personality (interaction between personality characteristics).

This shows that hardiness affects the physiological stress response and may protect from some stress-related illnesses.

Counterpoint

Contrada's study used five measures of hardiness, indicating that it is a poorly-defined concept – only the challenge component was linked to blood pressure.

This suggests that much research into hardiness, stress and illness is based on measures that lack **validity**.

One limitation is that the concept of hardiness may be too broad.

Hull et al. (1987) argued that research should focus on control, as research shows it is so important to well-being. And to a lesser extent, commitment.

However, Contrada (1989) claims that challenge is the most important component of hardiness.

This suggests the concept of hardiness is so broad it has very little validity and may not exist at all.

Evaluation extra: Direct or indirect?

Hardiness may have direct beneficial effects on health (e.g. Maddi 1987) – hardy people under stress have a reduced level of physiological arousal.

However, the effects of hardiness could be indirect e.g. hardy people may be more motivated to behave in healthy ways.

This means it does not matter whether the effects are direct or indirect because hardiness is beneficial either way and should be developed through training.

Revision BOOSTER

Personality type (previous topic) and hardiness are named on the specification so you could get questions specifically on these. Or the question could be on 'individual differences'. If this is the case then it is good news, because you can choose – one or the other or both. But be careful not to spend too long on AO1.

Knowledge Check

1. Define 'commitment', 'challenge' **and** 'control' in relation to hardiness.
   (2 marks + 2 marks + 2 marks)
2. Outline research into hardiness. *(6 marks)*
3. Evaluate research into hardiness in relation to individual differences in stress. *(6 marks)*
4. Padraig works in a big college which is undergoing major changes. Some of his colleagues are showing signs of stress, but he does not feel stressed at all. He explains that this is a chance for him to develop, learn new things, and work hard to come through hard times.

   Describe **and** evaluate research into hardiness in relation to individual differences in stress. Refer to Padraig's experience in your answer. *(16 marks)*

Managing and coping with stress: Drug therapy

Spec spotlight

Managing and coping with stress: drug therapy (benzodiazepines, beta blockers).

Er, I think I might need a glass of water.

Apply it

Olympia is a teacher of children with learning support needs. After a few years in this very stressful job she found the demands overwhelming because her workload increased and she had less say in how she did things. One day she felt very light-headed and dizzy. She went to her doctor who measured her blood pressure and found it was very high. He immediately gave Olympia a tablet to take and a prescription for more of the drug. But Olympia would like to consider her options.

1. Explain how drug therapy could benefit Olympia.

2. Why is she right to consider alternatives?

Benzodiazepines (BZs)

BZs act on *CNS*.	BZs (e.g. *diazepam*) reduce the anxiety associated with stress by reducing central nervous system (CNS) arousal.
	They enhance one way the body naturally combats anxiety.
Mode of action. *GABA* activity.	Gamma-aminobutyric acid (**GABA**) is a neurotransmitter that inhibits activity of neurons in most brain areas.
	GABA achieves this during normal synaptic transmission by combining with receptors on the postsynaptic neuron.
	This makes it less likely the postsynaptic neuron will fire, so signals are less likely to be passed on from one neuron to the next. The net effect is reduced activity in the CNS.
BZ drug molecules combine with GABA receptors.	BZs enhance this natural inhibition. Like GABA, BZ drug molecules combine with postsynaptic receptors, making the receptors more responsive to GABA.
	Neural activity is therefore inhibited throughout the CNS, neurons cannot be stimulated by other neurotransmitters for a period and the individual feels less anxious.

Beta blockers (BBs)

BBs act on *sympathetic nervous system*.	Beta-adrenergic blockers (beta blockers) reduce anxiety by reducing arousal of the **sympathetic nervous system**.
	BBs (e.g. *atenolol*) are usually prescribed to reduce blood pressure and treat heart problems but are also useful for stress.
Mode of action. Involves *adrenaline and noradrenaline*.	Stress hormones adrenaline and noradrenaline are produced as part of the sympathomedullary (SAM) pathway.
	These hormones combine with beta-adrenergic receptors in the cardiovascular system (mainly in heart and blood vessels).
	This is why heart rate and blood pressure increase during stress.
BBs block *beta-adrenergic receptors*.	BBs block beta-adrenergic receptors so these receptors are not stimulated by adrenaline and noradrenaline. So heart rate, blood pressure, etc. do not increase, heart does not need more oxygen.
	BBs reduce stress-related anxiety without altering alertness because they don't affect the brain. Ideal for people who want to eliminate physical symptoms of stress but remain alert (e.g. stage performers, surgeons).

One strength of BZs is high-quality research shows they are effective.

In a double-blind placebo-controlled trial, half the participants take a **placebo** (inactive version of the drug), but neither they nor the researcher knows who is taking it.

Baldwin et al.'s (2013) review of these high-quality studies concluded that BZs are significantly better than placebo in reducing acute anxiety.

This is strong evidence that BZs are a good choice of drug treatment for people wishing to reduce anxiety, at least in the short term.

Another strength is that research shows BBs are also effective.

Kelly (1980) concluded that BBs reduced anxieties associated with exams, public speaking and civil disturbances of living in Northern Ireland in 1970s.

Studies consistently demonstrate BBs may be even more effective when used with other drugs such as BZs (Hayes and Schulz 1987).

Therefore, drug combination therapy with BBs and BZs may be the best way to treat the physiological symptoms of stress for most people.

Counterpoint

However, drugs do not remove causes of anxiety (usually long-term) so symptoms return when person stops taking the drug, may mask deeper problems.

Therefore drug therapy is not a long-term solution to stress-related anxiety.

One limitation of drug therapy is side effects.

BZs can cause breathing problems and paradoxical reactions (opposite effects) e.g. impulsive behaviours and uncontrollable emotions (Gaind and Jacoby 1978).

BBs may reduce heart rate and blood pressure too much in some people, not suitable for people with diabetes or severe depression.

Therefore side effects are problematic because, as a consequence, a person may stop taking the drug making them ineffective.

Evaluation extra: Costs and benefits.

Drugs have costs because of side effects. They do not offer a cure for anxiety/stress. Dependency is an issue because BZs are addictive with long-term use.

However, there are benefits because they give short-term relief, which means psychological therapies can be used. They are also cost-effective and non-disruptive.

Therefore the benefits outweigh the costs as long as anti-anxiety drugs are only used to relieve short-term stress.

Feeling better? Great. Now any chance I could have the glass back? It's my favourite.

Revision BOOSTER

Note the phrase 'mode of action'. It's not on the specification, but it's crucial to your description of drug therapies. Explain *how* BZs and BBs work in the nervous system – be familiar with the physiological details.

Knowledge Check

1. In relation to managing **and** coping with stress, explain what is meant by 'drug therapy'. *(4 marks)*
2. Outline drug therapy as a way of managing stress. Refer to benzodiazepines **and** beta blockers in your answer. *(6 marks)*
3. Evaluate drug therapy as a way of managing **and** coping with stress. *(10 marks)*
4. In relation to managing **and** coping with stress, discuss drug therapy. *(16 marks)*

Managing and coping with stress: SIT

Spec spotlight

Managing and coping with stress: stress inoculation therapy.

Of course I'm not stressed anymore, I'm euphoric!

Apply it

Our learning support teacher Olympia is now taking beta blockers to reduce her blood pressure. But she is investigating her other options for coping with stress. She speaks to a friend who tried stress inoculation therapy (SIT) and found it helped her a lot. So Olympia gets a referral to a clinical psychologist, who starts by telling her that there will be three stages to the therapy.

1. Outline the **three** stages of SIT. For each, give **one** practical way in which Olympia can be helped by SIT in her specific situation.

2. Use your knowledge of SIT to explain how effective the therapy could be for Olympia.

Stress inoculation therapy (SIT)

SIT focuses on how we *think* about stress.	SIT is a **cognitive behaviour therapy**. Meichenbaum and Cameron (1973) identified phases of SIT – each focuses on practical steps to help the client. Phases are not distinct or in order – they overlap with some going backwards before moving on.
Focus is on *cognitive appraisal*.	**Cognitive** appraisal – client learns to think differently, to see stressors as challenges to overcome. The client also learns to focus on aspects of a stressful situation that can be changed rather than aspects that can't.
Phase 1 *Conceptualisation.* To understand stressors.	Client and therapist work together to identify and understand stressors the client faces. Client learns about the nature of stress and its effects. There should be a warm and collaborative rapport between therapist and client. Client retains responsibility for their progress and learns to attribute success to their own skills (internal locus of control).
Phase 2 *Skills acquisition and rehearsal.* Coping self-statements.	Client learns skills to cope with stress (e.g. relaxation, social skills, communication, cognitive restructuring). Major element of skills acquisition is learning to monitor and use self-talk – client uses coping self-statements ('You can do this!') to replace anxious internal dialogue. Client plans in advance how to cope when stress occurs – how they can overcome it through skills they learn.
Phase 3 *Real-life application and follow-through.* Role play, homework tasks.	Therapist creates opportunities for client to try out skills in a safe environment. Various techniques increase realism (e.g. role playing, visualisation, virtual reality, mobile apps). Learned skills are gradually transferred to the real world through homework tasks for client to seek out moderately stressful situations and use their coping skills in everyday life ('personal experiments'). Relapse prevention is important, e.g. client learns to cognitively restructure setbacks as temporary learning opportunities and not permanent catastrophic failures.
Duration of therapy.	This varies from client to client. Typically nine to 12 sessions, one hour each week or over longer period, also follow-ups.

Chapter 10: Stress

One strength of SIT is research supporting its effectiveness.

Saunders *et al.*'s (1996) **meta-analysis** found SIT reduced anxiety in performance situations (e.g. public speaking) and enhanced performance under stress (e.g. doing better in exams).

They also found that SIT was just as effective for people experiencing extreme anxiety as for those with moderate or normal levels of anxiety.

This suggests that SIT works for a wide range of people with anxiety and can help change behaviour in a positive direction.

Being in control may be what matters.

One limitation of SIT is that it is a very demanding therapy.

Clients must make big commitments of time and effort and be highly motivated. Training involves self-reflection and learning new skills.

It is challenging to apply SIT techniques to everyday life, e.g. some people are less able to use coping self-statements when experiencing anxiety in a stressful situation.

Therefore the demands placed on clients and their experiences of failure mean that many do not continue the treatment.

Counterpoint

SIT is very flexible with a variety of stress management techniques tailored to specific needs (e.g. people with learning difficulties) to encourage commitment/motivation.

This flexibility means SIT can help clients manage almost any form of stress.

Another limitation is that SIT is overcomplicated.

SIT uses a lot of techniques but perhaps personal control is the one key feature that accounts for its success.

Hensel-Dittman *et al.* (2011) found that SIT did not work with asylum seekers who could not exert control (they could have been deported at any time).

This suggests that control may be the vital element of SIT because the therapy does not work with people who have no opportunity to exert control.

Evaluation extra: Quick fix versus slow fix.

SIT may be better to manage stress because it is a 'slow fix' – 'future oriented', longer-term benefits, clients learn techniques so they can cope when same stressful situations arise.

However, drugs may be preferable because they are a 'quick fix' for anxiety, no effort is required (taking a pill) and gives a 'window' to learn to cope.

Therefore drugs may be better because they help stressed clients reach a point where other stress management methods (e.g. SIT) could benefit them more.

Revision BOOSTER

When asked to describe SIT, focus on the practical details of how the therapy proceeds. What actually happens? What does the therapist do? And the client? There's a lot of material to choose from, and only 6 marks' maximum – not too difficult to give a detailed description of SIT, but dangerous if you do too much in an essay because you reduce the time for the AO3 writing.

Knowledge Check

1. Explain the difference between stress inoculation therapy **and one other** way of managing stress. *(4 marks)*

2. Outline stress inoculation therapy as a way of managing **and** coping with stress. *(6 marks)*

3. Briefly evaluate stress inoculation therapy in relation to managing stress. *(4 marks)*

4. Describe **and** evaluate **two** ways of managing **and** coping with stress. *(16 marks)*

Spec spotlight

Managing and coping with stress: biofeedback.

Of course Helen knew it was important to relax, but she still had to check her emails!

Apply it

Dr. Mair is preparing a presentation to a group of health workers about ways of coping with stress. Unfortunately, she knows little about biofeedback so she does some research. She speaks to several people who have experienced biofeedback. Some found it helped them, others didn't. But they were all able to help Dr. Mair understand how the procedure works.

Pretend you are Dr. Mair and prepare a short talk on biofeedback based on her research and what others are likely to have reported to her. Include details of the underlying concepts, the procedure involved and its effectiveness. Use some research evidence in your explanation.

Biofeedback

Aims of biofeedback training.	Biofeedback trains people to control *involuntary* physiological processes (e.g. heart rate, muscle tension).
	This can be done by turning physiological signals into something the client can see or hear.
	Budzynski (1973) identified three phases, outlined below.
Phase 1 *Awareness* of own physiological response.	Client is connected to a machine which converts physiological activity into visual and/or auditory signal.
	• Muscular tension measured using electromyogram (EMG) – muscle activity converted into audible tone.
	• Electroencephalogram (**EEG**) measures brain activity – shown on a screen.
	• Skin conductance responses (SCRs) indicate sweating activity and can similarly be displayed.
	Feedback from machines is meaningful representation of physiological process being monitored.
Phase 2 *Learn to control* the physiological response.	Client applies learned stress management techniques.
	Client monitors the effect of changes – e.g. sees that reduced breathing changes a visual display in the desired direction (e.g. altering the line of the graph).
	Biofeedback with children uses game-based interface – client adjusts physiological response to complete on-screen maze.
	Altering signal is rewarding and reinforces client's behaviour, making further success more likely (i.e. **operant conditioning**).
Phase 3 *Transfer* to everyday life.	Client practises stress management techniques in stressful situations rather than in the therapy room.
	No machine is necessary.

Davis (1986) Biofeedback and cancer

PROCEDURE	Biofeedback training with 25 women treated for breast cancer, 13 sessions lasting 45 minutes, over 8 weeks.
	Clients learned deep-breathing and relaxation techniques.
FINDINGS AND CONCLUSIONS	At eight-month follow-up, urinary cortisol and reported anxiety were significantly lower than at the start.
	Cortisol levels increased in control participants who had no form of therapy.
	This was evidence of significant stabilisation of the *hypothalamic-pituitary-adrenal* (HPA) system by biofeedback.

One strength of biofeedback is research support.

Lemaire *et al.* (2011) trained medical doctors to use biofeedback three times a day for 28 days. They also completed a stress questionnaire.

Mean stress scores fell significantly over the study – scores also fell for a **control group** but by a much smaller amount.

This suggests that biofeedback can help to improve the psychological state of someone experiencing stress.

Counterpoint

However, Lemaire *et al.* also took physiological measures (e.g. blood pressure) and found that biofeedback had no effect (no more than **placebo**).

Therefore the effectiveness of biofeedback depends on the outcome measure, what it is you actually aim to 'treat'.

'So look,' said Lee excitedly. 'I can have exactly the same thing on my phone and my watch – at the same time!'

Who said technology is pointless?

Another strength of biofeedback is its relative convenience.

Biofeedback is easy and inexpensive because of developments in technology, e.g. smaller size of devices (about the same as a mobile phone).

Colourful displays make the task enjoyable and such devices can be used in everyday situations and also require no supervision.

This means that people are likely to continue biofeedback treatment to the point where it is successful.

Revision BOOSTER

What are your evaluations like? Why not try and make them more like ours? Start with your initial point – a strength or a limitation in most cases. Then... elaborate! Develop your evaluation point in three more steps, just as we've done on all of these AO3 pages. Have a close look at each one to see what they have in common.

One limitation is biofeedback is challenging.

Biofeedback does not suit everyone – need to understand link between physiology and signals, and be motivated to alter the signals.

Gaming element improves motivation but also need to practise skills in the real world outside the safety of the clinic.

This means that many people drop out of biofeedback so it is hard to assess just how successful it really is.

Not everyone agrees with this conclusion. What do you think?

Knowledge Check

1. Explain the difference between biofeedback and stress inoculation therapy as ways of managing stress. *(4 marks)*
2. Outline biofeedback as a way of managing **and** coping with stress. *(6 marks)*
3. Evaluate biofeedback as a way of managing stress. *(6 marks)*
4. Two psychology teachers are discussing ways of coping with stress. Parveneh argues that drugs are the best option for most people. But Percy reckons that biofeedback is best because it worked for him.

   Discuss **two or more** ways of managing **and** coping with stress. Refer to the two psychology teachers in your answer. *(16 marks)*

Evaluation extra: Just relax?

Benefits of biofeedback come from operant conditioning – a client's heart rate eventually reduces 'automatically' without him or her consciously thinking about it.

However, it may be relaxation that reduces heart rate. Learning this skill gives a client tools to reduce stress response and greater sense of control.

Therefore it is likely that relaxation is enough to manage stress and so the training and technology associated with biofeedback are not necessary.

Spec spotlight

Managing and coping with stress: gender differences in coping with stress.

Clive reflected that perhaps his new bedroom wallpaper was, well... a bit random.

Revision BOOSTER

Always think 'less is more' – writing about fewer things gives you the opportunity to demonstrate your detailed understanding. But, in a 16-mark essay, try to include something on each of the six points identified here.

Apply it

In times of stress, Rodrigo tries to tough it out with a 'stiff upper lip', tackling the issue just like he would any other problem. He was brought up to rely on himself and not to bother other people with his feelings. Gabriella has a different approach. She has lots of friends, so she gets help from as many of them as she can, especially her closest female friends. This helps to calm her and make her feel better about the situation.

Use your knowledge of gender differences in coping with stress to explain Rodrigo's and Gabriella's behaviour.

Gender differences

Men tend to use *problem-focused* methods.	Lazarus and Folkman (1984) suggest problem-focused methods reduce stress by tackling root causes in a direct, practical and rational way.
	For example, taking control to remove or escape from stress, learning new skills such as time management or relaxation techniques.
Women tend to use *emotion-focused* methods.	Lazarus and Folkman suggest emotion-focused methods reduce stress indirectly by tackling the anxiety associated with a stressor.
	For example, various forms of avoidance such as keeping busy and using **cognitive** appraisal to think about the stressor more positively.
Research.	Peterson *et al.* (2006) assessed coping strategies of men and women diagnosed as infertile.
	Men were more likely to use planful problem-solving – a problem-focused approach.
	Women were more likely to accept blame and use various avoidance tactics – an emotion-focused approach.
Tend and befriend response in women.	Taylor *et al.* (2000) argue from an **evolutionary** perspective that fight or flight is disadvantageous for females because confronting or fleeing from a predator makes it hard to protect one's offspring.
	Different response has evolved in females:
	• Tending is protecting, calming and nurturing offspring, blending in with environment.
	• Befriending involves seeking support from social networks at times of stress in order to cope.
Research.	Women very strongly favour befriending in stressful situations – review of 26 studies (Luckow *et al.* 1998).
	But it is used selectively – tends to be with other women. Lewis and Linder (2000) found most female participants preferred to wait for female support during a stressful experience rather than seek it from a man – might have evolved as a mechanism for protecting females and offspring against threatening males.
Oxytocin drives tend and befriend response.	**Oxytocin** is mainly a female hormone. It promotes feelings of goodwill and affiliation with others, and helps the body recover more quickly from physiological effects of stressors.
	Taylor *et al.* (2002) found higher levels of oxytocin linked with lower cortisol levels only in female participants.
	Female sex hormone **oestrogen** increases effects of oxytocin, but male hormones (e.g. **testosterone**) reduce them – so oxytocin effects are stronger in women, creating reduced stress response.

One limitation is the distinction between emotion- and problem-focused.

Peterson et al. (2006) found that men and women used coping methods that could not be easily categorised as emotion-focused or problem-focused.

E.g. social support can be both and women and men used it extensively to seek information (problem) and to feel better (emotion).

This suggests that the distinction is unworkable and that it is not valid to conclude that women mostly use one and men the other.

We're laughing manically because we've had too much coffee!

One strength is support for tend and befriend in females.

Tamres et al. (2002) carried out a meta-analysis of 26 studies of coping – women were more likely than men to seek social support (tend and befriend).

Women create and use social networks to promote caring for offspring, a side effect is support in stressful times.

This suggests that there are gender differences in social support/tend and befriend, with this response being more prevalent in females.

Counterpoint

Females can be aggressive ('fight') to protect offspring and men's coping response can be tend and befriend in some cases (Taylor et al. 2000).

This suggests that the distinction between men and women in the use of social support/tend and befriend is in fact blurred and complex.

Another limitation is that studies of emotion-focus involve retrospective recall.

De Ridder (2000) found the expected gender difference in coping when participants recalled retrospectively (women used emotion-focus more than men).

However, there was no gender difference when a concurrent method (*ecological momentary assessment*) was used and participants reported coping as it happened.

Therefore the gender difference in coping focus may depend very much upon what participants can remember.

Evaluation extra: Gender or stressor?

Men and women differ in coping because of biological differences (e.g. hormones testosterone, oestrogen and oxytocin) – men respond with fight or flight, women tend and befriend.

However, perhaps men and women may use different methods because they face different stressors – e.g. more relationship-related for women, so emotion-focused coping is more suitable.

This suggests that differences in coping strategies may not depend on gender-related biological differences but on the nature of the stressful situation.

Revision BOOSTER

There are a few research studies here – you don't have to include all of them in your answer. But it is important to provide some specific evidence. If you just say that 'lots of studies support gender differences', then that's quite a weak evaluation point. You need to make it clear that you have knowledge and understanding of specific studies which support your arguments.

If studies are used as AO3 then focus on the conclusions not the procedures.

Download suggested answers to the Knowledge Check questions from tinyurl.com/yd3ezhkb

Knowledge Check

1. Explain **one** gender difference in coping with stress. *(4 marks)*
2. Outline research into gender differences in coping with stress. *(6 marks)*
3. Briefly evaluate research into gender differences in coping with stress. *(6 marks)*
4. Discuss gender differences in coping with stress. *(16 marks)*

Spec spotlight

Managing and coping with stress: the role of social support in coping with stress; types of social support including instrumental, emotional and esteem support.

Awkward high-five alert!

The role of social support

Instrumental support. Practical and tangible.	Schaefer *et al.* (1981) suggest instrumental support involves: • Physically doing something (e.g. giving someone a lift to the hospital). • Providing information (e.g. telling someone what you know about stress).
Emotional support. Concern and affection.	Emotional support is given when we say 'I really feel for you', or 'I'm sorry you're going through a tough time' – it expresses warmth, concern, affection and sympathy. Emotional support isn't intended to offer practical help, but to make the stressed person feel better, to lift their mood.
Esteem support. Reinforce a person's faith in themselves.	'Esteem' refers to how we regard someone else. Esteem support reinforces someone's faith in themselves and their ability to tackle a stressful situation. Increasing confidence reduces feelings of stress.
All three are interrelated.	There is overlap between these types of support, e.g. being a 'shoulder to cry on' involves all three types. Even practical instrumental support can help emotionally because of what it means to the individual who receives it, a sign of caring. All three can be provided without physical presence – emotional and esteem support are given every day over online social networks (e.g. Facebook), or just by listening to someone on the TV.

Apply it

Nadim helped Naomi with the shopping, cooking and cleaning after Naomi came out of hospital.

Raisa has had a very difficult year. But she is encouraged by the posts she reads on Facebook and Twitter from her friends and even people she doesn't know.

Wilmot got a letter through the post the other day. It was from a friend who knew he was depressed. The friend told Wilmot that she believed in him and was sure he'd pull through.

1. Identify the types of social support described for each person.

2. Do any of the cases describe more than one type of support? Explain your answer.

3. Use your knowledge of coping with stress to explain what benefits social support brings.

Cohen et al. (2015) Hugs as social support

PROCEDURE	404 healthy adult participants were telephoned every evening for 14 days to report how many hugs they'd received that day. Also completed questionnaire on perceived social support. Researchers placed participants in quarantine, exposed them to a common cold virus and monitored them for illness (stress acts as immunosuppressant so we expect people who are more stressed to become ill).
FINDINGS AND CONCLUSIONS	Participants who experienced most stress (interpersonal conflicts such as arguments) were most likely to become ill. Those who perceived they had greater social support had a significantly reduced risk of illness – hugs accounted for up to one-third of the protective effect of social support. Participants who had the most frequent hugs were less likely to become infected (or symptoms were less severe). Suggests that perceived social support is a buffer against stress.

One strength is research confirming social support is useful.

Fawzy et al.'s (1993) participants with skin cancer had emotional and instrumental support in a group, one session a week for six weeks.

Six years later, these participants had better NK cell function and were more likely to be alive and cancer-free than control participants.

This shows that there are substantial benefits to social support that last long after it is given.

Counterpoint

However, after ten years there was no benefit of support in terms of cancer recurrence, much weaker benefit for survival compared with earlier study.

This suggests that social support can be beneficial, but such benefit gradually disappears over time.

'Don't worry Chip, it'll soon be varnish day again.'

One limitation is social support does not benefit men and women equally.

Research shows women and men benefit from social support but in different ways. It depends on the type of social support.

Luckow et al.'s (1998) review of studies showed that women used emotional support much more than men, but men did use instrumental support more.

This suggests that men may only benefit from the support of others in certain circumstances.

Another limitation is that support can have negative effects.

Emotional support from friends/relatives/online is usually welcomed, but instrumental support from these sources can be unreliable.

Even emotional support from a friend/relative can be unhelpful, e.g. they go with us to a hospital appointment and we feel more anxious.

This suggests that social support is not universally beneficial but depends on many factors.

Evaluation extra: Support versus hardiness.

Social support helps us cope with stress, e.g. Cohen et al. (facing page) showed direct benefits on immunity. It can also benefit both women and men.

However, support may be less beneficial than hardiness, Kobasa (1979) argued being hardy reduces stress. Also does not have negative effects like support can.

Therefore social support has an important role to play in coping with stress but its value may have been exaggerated.

Revision BOOSTER

What's the Number One route to evaluating an explanation or concept? The answer is – THINK LINK. You've probably noticed that the evaluation sections of this Revision Guide are chock-full of research studies. You need to make sure you use them effectively. THINK LINK – how does the study relate to the concept? What does Taylor's study tell us about gender differences in social support? Don't get sidetracked into describing the evidence at length. Instead, THINK LINK – explain how it supports the therapy. That's effective evaluation.

Knowledge Check

1. Briefly explain **three** types of social support in coping with stress.
   (2 marks + 2 marks + 2 marks)

2. Outline what research (theories and/or studies) has shown about the role of social support in coping with stress. *(6 marks)*

3. Evaluate the role of social support in coping with stress. *(8 marks)*

4. Outline **and** evaluate research into the role of social support in coping with stress. Refer to **at least two** types of social support in your answer. *(16 marks)*

Neural and hormonal mechanisms in aggression

Spec spotlight

Neural and hormonal mechanisms in aggression, including the roles of the limbic system, serotonin and testosterone.

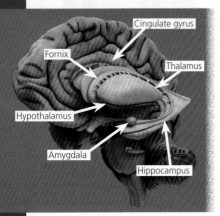

The limbic system is made up of several subcortical structures, of which the amygdala is most closely associated with aggression.

Apply it

Boris has frequently bullied other children at his primary school. His bullying is often physical and this time one of the teachers caught him slapping another child. Although he has been warned many times before, Boris continues to behave in this way – it's almost as if he can't help himself and behaves like this on the spur of the moment.

Use psychological evidence relating to both neural **and** hormonal mechanisms in aggression to explain Boris's behaviour.

Revision BOOSTER

It really pays to practise writing 16-mark essays with your book shut and timing yourself – about 20 minutes for a 16-mark essay. Don't think it will magically come right on the day – test yourself.

Neural mechanisms in aggression

Limbic system.	Papez (1937) and Maclean (1952) linked the limbic system to emotions e.g. aggression. The system includes the hypothalamus, amygdala and parts of the hippocampus.
Amygdala.	The more reactive the amygdala is to environmental threats the more likely that aggression will be shown.
	Gospic *et al.* (2011) used brain scans (**fMRI**) with participants in a lab-based game that provoked aggression.
	Aggressive reactions were associated with a fast and heightened response by the amygdala.
	Benzodiazepine (reduces arousal of the **autonomic nervous system**) taken before the game decreased amygdala activity and decreased aggression.
Orbitofrontal cortex and *serotonin.*	Normal levels of **serotonin** in the *orbitofrontal cortex* inhibit neurons (reduced firing) and are linked to greater behavioural self-control.
Low levels, increased aggression.	Decreased serotonin disturbs this mechanism, reduces self-control and increases impulsive behaviours, including aggression (Denson *et al.* 2012).
	Virkkunen *et al.* (1994) found lower levels of serotonin metabolite 5-HIAA in violent impulsive offenders compared with non-impulsive offenders.

Hormonal mechanisms in aggression

Testosterone. Higher in men and linked to aggression.	**Testosterone** helps regulate social behaviour via influence on brain areas involved in aggression.
	Males are more aggressive towards other males at 20+ years, when testosterone levels peak (Daly and Wilson 1998).
	Dolan *et al.* (2001) found a positive **correlation** between testosterone and aggression in male offenders with histories of impulsively violent behaviour.
Animal studies show aggression linked to testosterone.	Removing testes (castration) reduces aggression in many species, injecting testosterone restores aggressive behaviour (Giammanco *et al.* 2005).
Progesterone. Low levels inked to aggression in women.	Progesterone levels vary in menstrual cycle (lowest during and just after menstruation).
	Negative correlation between progesterone levels and self-reported aggression (Ziomkiewicz *et al.* 2012).

One limitation is that non-limbic brain structures are also involved.

Limbic structures function jointly with the non-limbic orbitofrontal cortex (OFC). This is involved in impulse-regulation and inhibition of aggression.

Coccaro *et al.* (2007) claim OFC activity is reduced in psychiatric disorders featuring aggression – this disrupts the OFC's impulse-control function, increasing aggression.

This shows that the neural regulation of aggression is more complex than theories focusing on the amygdala suggest.

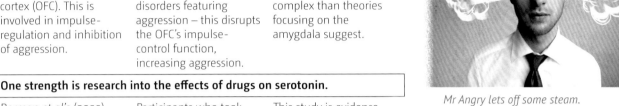

Mr Angry lets off some steam.

One strength is research into the effects of drugs on serotonin.

Berman *et al.*'s (2009) participants took part in a lab-based game, giving and receiving electric shocks in response to provocation.

Participants who took *paroxetine* (enhances serotonin) consistently gave fewer and less intense shocks than a **placebo** group.

This study is evidence of a *causal* link between serotonin and aggression.

Evaluation extra: Direct or indirect?

Neural factors may be directly linked to aggression, e.g. Gospic *et al.* (facing page). Serotonin also reduces aggression by inhibiting neuronal activity.

However, neural factors may be indirect. Denson *et al.* (facing page) found a link between serotonin and aggression but other factors may influence this link.

This suggests that the evidence that neural mechanisms are related to aggression is reasonably strong, but this relationship is probably not direct.

One strength is support from research with non-human animals.

Giammanco *et al.*'s (2005) review confirms the role of testosterone, e.g. increase in testosterone and aggression in male rhesus macaque monkeys during mating season.

In rats, castration of males reduces testosterone and mouse-killing. Injecting female rats with testosterone increases both.

These findings show that testosterone plays a key role in aggression in a range of animal species.

One limitation is that evidence linking testosterone and aggression is mixed.

Carré and Mehta's (2011) dual-hormone hypothesis suggests high levels of testosterone lead to aggression but only when cortisol levels are low.

High cortisol blocks testosterone's influence on aggression. Cortisol is a hormone that is key to the body's chronic stress response (see page 158).

Therefore the combined activity of testosterone and cortisol may be a better predictor of aggression than either hormone alone.

Evaluation extra: Animal research.

Hormonal mechanisms in human and mammalian aggression are likely to be similar. Research on this spread shows that most knowledge about hormones comes from non-human studies.

However, aggression in humans is more complex than in other mammals. Carré and Mehta's findings about cortisol apply only to humans and **cognitive** factors are involved.

Therefore, animal studies can help us understand hormonal influences on aggression but findings must be treated cautiously because human aggression is more complex.

Revision BOOSTER

Evaluation points about methodology are only relevant to the studies themselves. For this topic you have to evaluate the explanation rather than the study. If you criticise the methodology of a study you need to link this to the explanation/theory – how does this limitation affect our understanding of the neural/hormonal mechanisms involved in aggression?

Knowledge Check

1. Outline neural mechanisms in aggression. Refer to the roles of the limbic system **and** serotonin in your answer.
   (6 marks)

2. Outline the role of testosterone as a hormonal mechanism in aggression.
   (6 marks)

3. Briefly evaluate **either** neural **or** hormonal mechanisms in aggression. *(4 marks)*

4. Petra already has a criminal record for violence at the age of 20. She feels angry most of the time and then just lashes out when she 'boils over'. She feels she has no control over her behaviour. Petra also frequently feels depressed and may even have a sleep disorder.

   Describe **and** evaluate the role of neural **and** hormonal mechanisms in aggression. Refer to Petra's experience in your answer. *(16 marks)*

Genetic factors in aggression

Spec spotlight

Genetic factors in aggression, including the MAOA gene.

Twin studies

MZ twins share 100% of genes but DZ twins only 50% (on average) – so we expect greater similarities in aggressive behaviour between MZ twins if aggression is mostly genetic.

This is because both MZ and DZ twins are raised together in the same environment, but MZ twins have a greater degree of genetic similarity than DZs.

Lily and Millie tended not to settle their disputes over a cup of tea and a tête-à-tête.

Apply it

Pete has four older brothers who have all been in trouble with the law for violent offending. His mother and father were also very aggressive towards them all when they were growing up. Social services and the police were involved with the family several times. All of the boys were known as bullies at school, and now Pete appears to be bullying other children at his primary school.

Use your knowledge of genetic factors in aggression to explain why Pete is behaving like this.

Genetic factors in aggression

Twin studies. 50% of variance in aggressive behaviour.	Coccaro *et al.* (1997) studied adult male monozygotic (**MZ**) and dizygotic (**DZ**) twins. For direct physical aggression, the researchers found **concordance rates** of 50% for MZ twins and 19% for DZs. For verbal aggression the figures were 28% for MZ twins and 7% for DZ twins.
Adoption studies. 41% of variance in aggressive behaviour is genetic.	Similarities in aggressive behaviour between an adopted child and biological parents suggest genetic influences are operating; but similarities with adoptive parents suggest environmental factors. Rhee and Waldman's (2002) **meta-analysis** of adoption studies found genetic influences accounted for 41% of the variance in aggression.
MAOA gene is linked to low serotonin.	The MAOA gene controls production of the enzyme *monoamine oxidase A* (MAO-A) which regulates **serotonin** (a monoamine). On the previous spread we saw that serotonin is thought to play a role in impulsive aggression. Genes come in different variants. Low-activity variant of MAOA (MAOA-L) is linked to increased aggression.
MAOA-L variant is nicknamed the 'warrior gene'.	MAOA-L variant possessed by 56% of New Zealand Maori males (34% Caucasians). Maori warriors historically ferocious, hence nicknamed the 'warrior gene' (Lea and Chambers 2007).
MAOA-L linked with extreme violence in a Dutch family.	Brunner *et al.* (1993) studied 28 male family members repeatedly involved in impulsively violent criminal behaviours (e.g. rape, attempted murder, assault). These men had both abnormally low levels of the enzyme MAO-A in their brains and the MAOA-L variant (the 'Brunner syndrome').
Gene–environment (G×E) interactions.	Frazzetto *et al.* (2007) found an association between antisocial aggression and the MAOA-L gene in adult males but only in those who experienced significant trauma (e.g. physical abuse) during the first 15 years of life. Those with no trauma were not especially aggressive as adults even if they possessed the MAOA-L gene variant. This is strong evidence of a gene–environment interaction (sometimes called **diathesis-stress**).

One strength is support for the role of the MAOA gene.

Research on the facing page shows the low-activity variant is associated with high aggression. Mertins *et al.* (2011) found the converse is also true.

Male participants with the high-activity MAOA gene variant were more co-operative and less aggressive in a money-distributing game.

This finding supports the relationship between MAOA gene activity and aggression, increasing the **validity** of this genetic theory of aggression.

Counterpoint

However, Mertins *et al.* also found that even participants with low-activity MAOA variant behaved co-operatively when they knew others were also being co-operative.

Therefore genes do not operate in a vacuum but are influenced by environmental factors that are at least as important in aggression.

One limitation is that the mechanism linking MAOA and serotonin is unclear.

Research on the previous spread shows aggression is linked with low serotonin, but we expect people with MAOA-L to have high serotonin.

This is because low-activity enzyme means serotonin not deactivated (the normal outcome), so should leave more serotonin – better viewed as disrupted activity (not high or low).

This shows that the relationship between the MAOA gene, serotonin and aggression is not yet fully understood.

Gus tended to take paintballing a little too seriously...

Another limitation is that twin studies may lack validity.

Both individuals in a twin pair share the same environment (raised together). But DZ twins may not share environments to the same extent that MZs share theirs.

The *equal environments assumption* is wrong because MZs are treated very similarly (e.g. parents praise them equally for aggression), but DZs are treated less similarly.

This means that concordance rates are inflated and genetic influences on aggression may not be as great as twin studies suggest.

Do you agree with this conclusion?

Evaluation extra: Nature and nurture.

Evidence shows that genes are direct causes of aggression. This includes twin and adoption studies, research on the MAOA gene and animal studies.

On the other hand, environmental factors are also important. This is supported by criticisms of twin studies and research into early trauma. Environment affects whether genes are expressed.

Therefore, ultimately, it could be argued that environmental factors are more important because, though we may have predispositions, these are only expressed in certain conditions.

Revision BOOSTER

Don't cut down the elaboration of the AO3 points, better to do two elaborated points rather than four briefer ones.

Knowledge Check

1. Outline research into genetic factors in aggression. *(6 marks)*
2. Describe research into the MAOA gene in relation to genetic factors in aggression. *(6 marks)*
3. Evaluate research into genetic factors in aggression. *(6 marks)*
4. Estelle has been in trouble many times for fighting at school. She says the other kids provoke her, but she is aggressive towards just about everyone. Because Estelle's dad is in prison for serious assault, her mum says it's not surprising that Estelle is following in his footsteps.

   Discuss the role of genetic factors in aggression. Refer to Estelle and her family in your answer. *(16 marks)*

The ethological explanation of aggression

Spec spotlight

The ethological explanation of aggression, including reference to innate releasing mechanisms and fixed action patterns.

Apply it

Burak has just bought a new cat, Walker, and is worried that it might fight with the neighbour's cat. One day he saw Walker rearing up on his hind legs, meowing loudly, with his fur standing on end. He then noticed his neighbour's cat reacting in a similar way, whilst inching closer to Walker. Later he saw that Walker had no scratches or other injuries.

Using your knowledge of the ethological explanation of aggression, explain Walker's behaviour.

Aggression within a species (intra-species aggression) may end with an appeasement display. Doesn't look that playful does it?

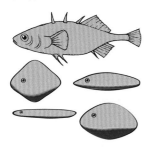

Tinbergen's stickleback models. A realistically shaped model (top) did not provoke aggressive behaviour because it lacked a red underbelly. All the other models did provoke aggression, despite their unstickleback-like shapes.

The ethological explanation of aggression

Adaptive. To (1) reduce competition and (2) establish dominance.	Aggression is beneficial to survival because it: 1. Reduces competition as a defeated animal is rarely killed but forced into territory elsewhere, reducing competition pressure. 2. Establishes dominance hierarchies. A male chimpanzee's dominance gives him special status (e.g. mating rights). Pettit *et al.* (1988) observed how aggression in children at play led to dominance hierarchies – this is **adaptive** (therefore naturally selected) because dominance over others brings benefits.
Ritualistic. A series of behaviours carried out in a set order.	Lorenz (1966) observed most intra-species aggression consisted of ritualistic signalling (e.g. displaying teeth) and rarely caused physical damage. Intra-species aggression usually ends with an appeasement display – indicates acceptance of defeat and inhibits aggression in the winner, preventing injury to the loser. This is adaptive because every aggressive encounter ending with the death of an individual could threaten existence of species.
IRM. Triggered by an environmental stimulus.	An innate releasing mechanism (IRM) is an inbuilt physiological process or structure (e.g. a network of neurons in the brain). An environmental stimulus (e.g. facial expression) activates the IRM. It triggers or 'releases' a fixed action pattern (FAP).
FAP. Universal and ballistic.	A fixed action pattern (FAP) is a pattern of behaviours triggered by an IRM. Lea (1984) argues that a FAP is a relatively unchanging behavioural sequence (ritualistic) found in every individual of a species (universal) and follows an inevitable course which cannot be altered before it is completed (ballistic).

Tinbergen (1951) Male stickleback and aggression

PROCEDURE	Another male entering a stickleback's territory in the mating season initiates a sequence of aggressive behaviours (a FAP) – red on the competing male's underbelly is the stimulus that triggers the IRM that in turn leads to the aggressive FAP. Tinbergen (1951) presented male sticklebacks with a series of wooden models of different shapes.
FINDINGS AND CONCLUSIONS	If the model had a red underside the stickleback would aggressively display and attack it – but no red meant no aggression. Tinbergen also found the aggressive FAP did not change from one encounter to another – once triggered it always ran its course to completion without any further stimulus.

One strength is support from research related to genetics and evolution.

Genetic evidence is strong (see previous spread) e.g. Brunner *et al.* (1993) showed a link between MAOA-L gene and aggression, twin and adoption studies also suggest a genetic component.

On the next spread we look at the case for seeing aggression as an adaptive behaviour (e.g. Wilson and Daly 1996) and therefore genetically-based.

This suggests the ethological approach is correct in claiming that aggression is genetically determined, heritable and adaptive.

Counterpoint

Nisbett (1993) found homicides based on reactive aggression (responding to threat) were more common in the southern US than in the north – 'culture of honour' less prevalent in the north.

Therefore culture can override innate influences, which is hard for ethological theory to explain.

One limitation is that same-species aggression is not always just ritualistic.

Goodall (2010) observed male chimps killing members of another community – the aggression was systematic.

The killing continued even when victims were offering appeasement signals, which did not inhibit aggressive behaviour as would be predicted by ethological theory.

This challenges the ethological view that same-species aggression has evolved into a self-limiting and relatively harmless ritual.

Another limitation is that Lorenz's view of FAPs is outdated.

Hunt (1973) argued that FAPs are influenced by environment and learning. The sequence of behaviours in an aggressive FAP varies between individuals and situations.

FAPs are not fixed but modifiable by experience, so ethologists prefer the term 'modal behaviour pattern' to reflect this flexibility.

Therefore patterns of aggressive behaviour are much more flexible than Lorenz thought, especially in humans.

Evaluation extra: Born to be aggressive?

Ethologists argue aggression is an innate instinct, which implies that humans are inevitably aggressive and will fight each other (e.g. wars), FAPs show this.

However, other approaches (e.g. **cognitive**) suggest aggression is not inevitable, is under rational control and more affected by learning and social norms.

Therefore aggression may have instinctive elements but in humans it is more strongly influenced by cognitive and social factors.

Keith was beginning to regret uttering the immortal words, 'What's a half-nelson?'

Proactive and reactive aggression

There are huge problems in defining aggressive behaviour, but many psychologists accept the distinction between proactive and reactive aggression. Proactive aggression is cold, planned and unprovoked. Reactive aggression is angry and impulsive retaliation in the heat of the moment. Some of the research on this spread only applies to reactive aggression rather than all aggressive behaviour.

Knowledge Check

1. In relation to the ethological explanation of aggression, explain the difference between innate releasing mechanisms and fixed action patterns. *(3 marks)*

2. Describe innate releasing mechanisms **and/or** fixed action patterns as explanations of aggression. *(6 marks)*

3. Evaluate the ethological explanation of aggression. *(6 marks)*

4. Discuss the ethological explanation of aggression. *(16 marks)*

Evolutionary explanations of human aggression

Spec spotlight

Evolutionary explanations of human aggression.

Barry wasn't the first man to lose his girlfriend to Pinterest – and he wouldn't be the last.

Apply it

Mayra is a counselling psychologist who runs a therapy group for survivors of domestic abuse. Over the years, she has noticed that her clients have had similar experiences of abusive partners. For example, most abusers keep a close eye on what their partners are doing. Abusers ask a lot of questions about where their partners have been and who they've been with. Abusers also make threats of violence and, of course, often eventually become physically aggressive.

Using your knowledge of evolutionary explanations of human aggression, explain Mayra's clients' experiences.

Evolutionary explanations of human aggression

Anti-cuckoldy behaviours naturally selected.	Cuckoldry (having to raise another man's offspring) is a waste of a male's resources because it contributes to survival of a rival's genes and leaves the 'father' with fewer resources to invest in his own future offspring.
	Men in our **evolutionary** past who could avoid cuckoldry were more reproductively successful – so psychological mechanisms evolved to increase anti-cuckoldry behaviours in men (e.g. sexual jealousy is stronger in men).
	This drives aggressive mate retention strategies men use to prevent partners from 'straying' – these were **adaptive** in our evolutionary history.
Mate retention strategies include direct guarding and negative inducements.	Wilson and Daly (1996) identify two major mate retention strategies involving aggression: • Direct guarding – a man's vigilance over a partner's behaviour, e.g. checking who they've been seeing. • Negative inducements – e.g. threats of consequences for infidelity – 'I'll kill myself if you leave me'.
Mate retention strategies linked to physical violence.	Wilson *et al.* (1995) found women who reported mate retention strategies in partners were twice as likely to experience physical violence at their hands – 73% of these women required medical attention and 53% said they feared for their lives.
Bullying may be an adaptive form of aggression.	Bullying is a power imbalance in which a stronger individual uses aggression repeatedly against a weaker person. Researchers have viewed bullying as a maladaptive behaviour (e.g. poor social skills or childhood abuse) – but evolutionary ancestors may have used it to increase chances of survival by creating reproduction opportunities.
In men, bullying ensures access to females and reduces threats from males.	In men bullying suggests dominance, acquisition of resources, strength – and also wards off potential rivals (Volk *et al.* 2012). These characteristics deliver the ideal combination of access to more females and minimal threat from competing males – so aggressive bullying was naturally selected because these males would have reproductive success. Also benefits the bully's health because other children avoid them so they experience less aggression and stress (Sapolsky 2004).
In women, bullying helps secure partner's fidelity.	Female bullying more often takes place within rather than outside a relationship, and is a method of controlling a partner. The partner continues to provide resources for future offspring – again, such behaviour would be naturally selected because it enhanced the woman's reproductive success (Campbell 1999).

One strength is explaining gender differences in uses of aggression.

Gender differences could be due to socialisation but some are due to adaptive strategies e.g. Campbell (1999) argues physical aggression is not adaptive for a female with offspring.

This would put a mother's own and her offspring's survival at risk, so a more adaptive strategy is to use verbal aggression to retain a resource-providing partner.

Therefore such arguments can provide support for the evolutionary approach to explaining aggression.

The Lynx effect.

One limitation is cultural differences in aggressive behaviour.

Aggression is not universal, e.g. the !Kung San people of Africa have very negative attitudes towards the use of aggression.

It is discouraged from childhood in boys and girls and is rare because it is linked with loss of status within the community (Thomas 1958).

Therefore, since some cultures do not show aggressiveness, such behaviour may not necessarily be adaptive.

Counterpoint

However, Lee (1979) questions this 'peaceable' view (e.g. high homicide rate in !Kung San). Such contradictions may be explained by observer bias and also using different samples of people.

These methodological issues mean that observations by 'outsiders' may not be useful (lacks **validity**).

Another strength is real-world applications to bullying.

Anti-bullying strategies usually address a bully's deficiencies, but bullying is still prevalent so perhaps a better approach is to view bullying as adaptive.

Bullies gain advantages from bullying, so the 'meaningful roles' approach increases the costs of bullying and the rewards of prosocial alternatives (Ellis *et al.* 2016).

Therefore viewing bullying as an adaptive behaviour may lead to more effective anti-bullying interventions.

Evaluation extra: Determinism versus free will.

The evolutionary argument is biologically **determinist**. Aggression is the result of adaptations that are beyond our control, so it is inevitable and not our 'fault'.

However, **humanistic** psychologists see aggression as subject to **free will. Cognitive** factors allow us to think about behaviour and there are also cultural differences.

Therefore a balanced position is **soft determinism**. We may be predisposed to aggression by evolutionary influences but actual aggressive acts depend on other factors.

Revision BOOSTER

This topic is about evolution, so the examiner wants to see some detail about the evolutionary reasons why humans are aggressive. So make sure you include specific evolutionary-related words in your answer such as 'adaptive', 'survival', 'innate' and 'resources'.

Knowledge Check

1. In terms of human aggression, explain what is meant by 'evolutionary explanations'. *(2 marks)*

2. Describe **one or more** evolutionary explanations of aggression. (6 marks)

3. Briefly evaluate the evolutionary explanations of human aggression. *(4 marks)*

4. This item appeared on a news website: 'Men are more jealous than women, say psychologists. Men abuse their partners to prevent them straying because they are jealous. Bullying could also be a way of attracting and keeping a partner. "You get this sort of behaviour in lots of different parts of the world," added the experts.'

   With reference to the issues raised in this item, outline **and** evaluate evolutionary explanations of human aggression. *(16 marks)*

Social psychological explanations: Frustration-aggression

Spec spotlight

Social psychological explanations of human aggression, including the frustration-aggression hypothesis.

A frustrating morning for Malcolm, he just couldn't get his wig to 'sit right'.

Frustration-aggression (F-A) hypothesis

Frustration always leads to aggression, and aggression is always the result of frustration.	Dollard *et al.*'s (1939) hypothesis states aggression is a psychological drive similar to biological drives (e.g. hunger). We experience frustration if our attempt to achieve a goal is blocked by an external factor.
	Frustration creates an aggressive drive leading to aggressive thoughts/behaviour (violent fantasy, verbal outburst, physical violence).
Aggressive behaviour is *cathartic*.	Expressing the aggressive drive removes the negative emotion i.e. it is cathartic (**psychodynamic** concept) because it reduces the drive and makes further aggression less likely.
Aggression may be displaced.	The cause of frustration may be: • Abstract (e.g. the government). • Too powerful and we risk punishment (e.g. a teacher who gave you a low grade). • Unavailable (e.g. the teacher left). So our aggression is displaced (deflected) onto an alternative – not abstract, weaker and available (object, pet, younger sibling, etc.).
The *weapon effect* shows that cues make aggression more likely.	Berkowitz and LePage (1967) found once students became frustrated in a lab task, they were more likely to give (fake) electric shocks when they could see a weapon next to them.
	Weapon effect shows that frustration only creates a readiness for aggression. Cues increase likelihood of actual aggression.

Apply it

Edith went to see her favourite rugby league club in both the play-off final and the Challenge Cup final. They lost both. Each time, she was convinced her team would win, and was really excited and happy to be watching them. But after long journeys back home with late trains and missed buses, Edith arrived back feeling angry and depressed. She immediately started an argument with her brother, and there is now a small dent in the wall where she kicked it.

Use your knowledge of the frustration-aggression hypothesis to explain Edith's behaviour.

Geen (1968) Frustration and aggression

PROCEDURE

Male university students completed a jigsaw puzzle, frustration was manipulated in one of three ways.

• For some participants the puzzle was impossible to solve.
• Others ran out of time because another student (a **confederate**) kept interfering.
• Others were insulted by the confederate.

The participants later had the chance to give (fake) electric shocks to the confederate.

FINDINGS AND CONCLUSIONS

Insulted participants gave the strongest shocks on average, then the interfered group, then the impossible-task group.

All three groups selected more intense shocks than a (non-frustrated) **control group**.

Chapter 11: Aggression

One strength is support for the key concept of displaced aggression.

Marcus-Newhall *et al.* (2000) conducted a **meta-analysis** of studies where aggression was directed at a human target other than the one that caused frustration.

Provoked participants who could not retaliate against the original source were more likely to aggress against an innocent target than participants who were not provoked.

This shows that frustration can lead to aggression against a weaker or more available target.

The most frustrating thing as far as Isla was concerned was that she'd just ripped her nice new shorts.

One limitation is that aggression may not be cathartic.

Bushman (2002) found that people who vented anger by repeatedly hitting a punchbag became more aggressive rather than less (doing nothing reduced aggression more).

Using venting to reduce anger is like using petrol to put out a fire. 'The better people feel after venting, the more aggressive they are' (Bushman).

This shows that a central assumption of the frustration-aggression hypothesis may not be valid.

Another limitation is the link between frustration and aggression is complex.

Frustration does not always lead to aggression and aggression can occur without frustration – the link is not 'automatic'.

Someone who feels frustrated may behave in a range of different ways (e.g. helpless). Someone behaving aggressively may have many reasons for doing so.

This suggests that the frustration-aggression hypothesis is inadequate because it only explains how aggression arises in some situations but not in others.

Counterpoint

Berkowitz (1989) reformulated his theory as *negative affect theory* – frustration is one of many aversive stimuli (e.g. pain) that cause aggression and frustration (and other aversive stimuli) have various effects.

Therefore frustration (negative feelings) can form part of a wider explanation of what causes aggression.

Not everyone agrees with this conclusion. What do you think?

Evaluation extra: Gun control.

'The finger pulls the trigger' (Berkowitz 1989), so 'open carry' does not cause violence, individuals are responsible for weapon use even when frustrated.

However, 'the trigger may be pulling the finger', i.e. gun violence depends on cues such as open presence of a gun (Berkowitz and LePage 1967).

Therefore guns need to be controlled because their widespread availability at the very least makes aggression more likely.

Revision BOOSTER

Research studies can be used in different ways. On the facing page we have described two studies, such descriptions can receive AO1 credit – but if you want to use a research study as AO3 then you must focus only on the findings and what these findings tell us about the explanation.

Knowledge Check

1. Outline the frustration-aggression hypothesis. *(4 marks)*

2. Explain what research has shown about the frustration-aggression hypothesis. *(4 marks)*

3. Evaluate **one** social psychological explanation of aggression. *(6 marks)*

4. Two students worked very hard on their essays. Unfortunately, they both got a grade E. Camilla became very angry and headbutted a wall. Ricardo went very quiet and decided to have another go at the essay.

   Outline **and** evaluate **one** social psychological explanation of aggression. Refer to Camilla **and** Ricardo in your answer. *(16 marks)*

Spec spotlight

Social psychological explanations of human aggression, including social learning theory as applied to human aggression.

Social learning theory

A theory that explains behaviour in terms of direct reinforcement but also indirect reinforcement – learning from observing others and imitating their behaviour.

Apply it

Gabriel watches a DVD of his favourite film (not Frozen, sadly). The film features lots of shooting and fighting and a bit of swearing as well. It's clear that the main character is a hero, despite behaving very aggressively. The next day in school, Gabriel swears at a teacher, runs around firing imaginary weapons and attacks some other boys.

How can social learning theory help us to explain Gabriel's behaviour?

Perhaps Gabriel should have watched Frozen *instead?*

Revision BOOSTER

On these AO1 pages, there are nearly always six key points for each topic. This easily covers the descriptive content you would need for any essay – because description is worth 6 marks. Don't be tempted to over-describe.

Social learning theory (SLT) applied to aggression

Direct learning. *Positive* and *negative* reinforcement.	Bandura's **social learning theory (SLT)** acknowledged that aggression can be learned directly through **operant conditioning** (positive and negative reinforcement and punishment). For example, a child who angrily snatches a toy learns aggression brings rewards – direct positive reinforcement.
Indirect learning. *Observation* and *vicarious reinforcement.*	Observational learning explains most aggression: • A child observes models (e.g. parents) being aggressive. • Children also observe the consequences of a model's aggressive behaviour – if it is rewarded the child learns aggression can be effective in getting what they want. This is vicarious reinforcement – it makes it more likely that the child will imitate the model's aggressive behaviour.
Social learning requires attention, retention, reproduction and motivation.	**Cognitive** conditions needed for observational learning: • Attention – observer notices model's aggressive actions. • Retention – observer remembers model's aggressive behaviour. • Reproduction – observer repeats behaviour based on memory. • Motivation – observer imitates behaviours if they have an expectation that behaving aggressively will be rewarding.
Self-efficacy increases each time aggression brings rewards.	**Self-efficacy** is the extent to which we believe our actions will achieve a desired goal. A child's confidence in their ability to be aggressive grows as they learn that aggression can bring rewards (e.g. child who regularly hits others to get a toy learns they have the motor skills to do so and this ability comes easily to them).

Bandura *et al.* (1961) Social learning of aggression

PROCEDURE	Young children individually observed a male or female adult model playing with toys, including an inflatable plastic toy called a 'Bobo doll'. Some children observed the model behaving aggressively towards the doll (e.g. throwing, kicking, plus verbal outbursts). Children were then taken to another room where there was a Bobo doll and other toys including ones the model had used.
FINDINGS AND CONCLUSIONS	Children in the 'aggressive model' condition imitated the behaviour they observed – the closeness of imitation was often a direct copy including using specific objects and verbal phrases. Boys were more likely than girls to imitate same-sex model. Children in the 'non-aggressive model' condition showed almost no aggression later.

One strength of SLT is research support for its explanation of aggression.

Poulin and Boivin (2000) found that aggressive boys formed friendships with other aggressive boys. The friendships mutually reinforced aggression through **modelling**.

The boys observed each other successfully using proactive aggression, so they were frequently exposed to models of aggression and its positive consequences.

These social learning processes made imitation of aggressive behaviour by the boys much more likely, supporting the predictions of SLT.

Counterpoint

However, the study found no similarity between friends for reactive aggression. This was not imitated, perhaps because consequences are unpredictable.

Therefore SLT is limited because it is a relatively weak explanation of reactive aggression.

Parents should take care that their own aggressive behaviour doesn't 'rub off' on their children.

Another strength is that SLT can help reduce aggression.

Children readily imitate models when they observe them being rewarded for any behaviour (including aggression), especially if they identify with them.

The same learning processes can reduce aggression. e.g. children form friendships with children rewarded for being non-aggressive (or can be shown media characters).

Therefore SLT offers practical steps to reduce the development of aggressive behaviour in children.

Revision BOOSTER

Don't write in general terms about SLT (e.g. a non-specific outline of modelling or vicarious reinforcement). You have to *shape* what you know to explain aggression. The general rule is this: if you don't mention aggression throughout your answer, then it's unlikely to gain much credit.

One limitation is SLT underestimates influence of biological factors.

Bandura recognised the role of biology (aggressive urge is instinctive) but the form aggression takes is learned and the outcome of 'nurture'.

However, there are powerful established genetic, **evolutionary**, neural and hormonal influences on aggression that SLT barely acknowledges.

Therefore, SLT is an incomplete explanation of aggression because it underplays the role of biological factors.

Evaluation extra: Research methods.

Many SLT studies are highly controlled (e.g. Bandura *et al.* 1961). Researchers can control **confounding variables** and show that social learning processes may *cause* aggressive behaviour.

However, such studies are unlike real-world situations, creating 'ideal' conditions (e.g. Bobo dolls can't retaliate). They also feature **demand characteristics** (Bobo is designed to be hit).

Therefore controlled studies are useful for identifying potential causes of aggression but need to be validated against real-world observations.

Knowledge Check

1. Briefly outline **two** social psychological explanations of aggression. *(3 marks + 3 marks)*

2. Explain what research related to social learning theory can tell us about human aggression. *(4 marks)*

3. Evaluate social learning theory as applied to human aggression. *(6 marks)*

4. Tabitha hangs out with a group of girls who have a reputation for bullying. She finds them interesting and exciting and she watches what they do very carefully. Tabitha is beginning to develop the confidence to bully other kids herself.

   With reference to Tabitha, describe **and** evaluate social learning theory as applied to human aggression. *(16 marks)*

Social psychological explanations: De-individuation

Spec spotlight

Social psychological explanations of human aggression, including de-individuation.

DON'T MOVE THIS IS A ROBBERY

Hugh's ill-judged disguise didn't really conceal his identity. And robbing the bank where he worked was probably not the brightest idea either.

Apply it

Toby is recounting his days back in the 1970s of travelling around Britain and Europe being a football hooligan. He and his mates would cover their faces and cause trouble, provoking the opposition. There would always be a big crowd of them, and sometimes they would rip up the terraces and start hurling concrete at rival supporters. And there would usually be a good old-fashioned shirtless pitch invasion.

Using your knowledge of de-individuation, explain Toby's behaviour.

Revision BOOSTER

The title of this spread is de-individuation – when answering an exam question make sure you don't just explain de-individuation, your answer must be *using de-individuation to explain aggression*.

De-individuation applied to aggression

De-individuation explains crowd behaviour and aggression.	Le Bon (1895) argued when we join a crowd we lose restraint, self-identity and responsibility (this is **de-individuation**). So we experience less personal guilt at being aggressive, and therefore act more aggressively.
De-individuation refers to reduced sense of personal responsibility.	Zimbardo (1969) argued our behaviour is usually individuated (rational, conforms to norms). But when de-individuated (e.g. part of a crowd) we lose self-awareness, stop monitoring our behaviour, ignore social norms. De-individuated behaviour is irrational, impulsive, **disinhibited**, anti-normative.
Anonymity is a major condition of de-individuation.	Several conditions of de-individuation promote aggression (e.g. darkness, uniforms) – a major one is anonymity. We have less fear of retribution because we are unidentifiable in a crowd – the bigger the crowd, the greater the anonymity. Anonymity provides fewer opportunities for others to judge us negatively.
Self-awareness is reduced.	Prentice-Dunn and Rogers (1982) argue that anonymity reduces two types of self-awareness: • *Private self-awareness* – attention to our own feelings is reduced because it is focused outwards on events around us. • *Public self-awareness* – reduced because we realise we are anonymous and our behaviour is less likely to be judged by others. So we become less accountable for our aggressive actions.

Dodd (1985) Student de-individuation

PROCEDURE	Dodd asked 229 psychology students: 'If you could do anything humanly possible with complete assurance that you would not be detected or held responsible, what would you do?'. Students knew their answers were anonymous. Three independent raters who did not know the hypothesis decided which categories of prosocial or antisocial behaviour the responses belonged to.
FINDINGS AND CONCLUSIONS	36% of responses involved a form of antisocial behaviour and 26% actual criminal acts (most common was 'rob a bank'). Only 9% of responses were prosocial behaviours (e.g. helping people). In terms of how people *imagine* they would behave, this study demonstrates a link between anonymity, de-individuation and aggressive behaviour.

One strength is research support for de-individuation.

Douglas and McGarty (2001) found that the most aggressive messages posted on social media were from people who hid their real identities.

This is a common behaviour of online 'trolls' and has been implicated in high-profile cases of self-harm and even suicide.

This supports a link between aggressive behaviour and anonymity, a key element of de-individuation.

Counterpoint

Gergen *et al.* (1973) told participants in a darkened room they could do what they liked and would never meet again. They soon started touching and kissing. In a second study they were told they would meet and there was much less touching/kissing.

Therefore de-individuation may not always lead to aggression.

'Anonymity shapes crowd behaviour' (Dixon and Mahendran 2012).

Another strength is de-individuation can explain 'baiting crowds'.

Mann (1981) identified 21 newspaper reports of baiting crowds encouraging suicidal people to jump from buildings.

These events all were in darkness, the crowds were large and distant from the 'jumper' – all conditions predicted to lead to de-individuation and aggressive behaviour.

Therefore there is some **validity** to the idea that a large group can become aggressive in a de-individuated 'faceless' crowd.

One limitation is de-individuation is normative rather than anti-normative.

De-individuation theory argues we behave against social norms when we are less aware of our private identity. But Spears and Lea's (1992) SIDE model disagrees.

Instead, they argue that de-individuation leads to *conformity* to group norms (could be prosocial or antisocial norms). Anonymity shifts individual's attention from private identity to social identity as a group member.

This suggests that people who are in a de-individuated state remain sensitive to norms rather than ignoring them.

Original footage from the Gergen et al. (1973) study. Pretty racy stuff, eh?

Evaluation extra: Nurture and nature.

De-individuation highlights nurture factors in aggression (whatever reduces private and public awareness). People who are not usually aggressive become so in a crowd (e.g. online).

However, nature plays an important role in causing aggression (genetic, ethological, **evolutionary**). People are aggressive in crowds perhaps because the situation makes you feel stressed.

Therefore it could be argued that de-individuation is a less powerful influence on aggressive behaviour than factors related to nature, even in crowds.

Knowledge Check

1. Explain the difference between de-individuation **and one other** social psychological explanation of aggression. *(3 marks)*

2. Describe de-individuation as a social psychological explanation of aggression. *(6 marks)*

3. Evaluate de-individuation as a social psychological explanation of aggression. *(10 marks)*

4. Outline **and** evaluate **two or more** social psychological explanations of aggression. *(16 marks)*

Institutional aggression in the context of prisons

Spec spotlight

Institutional aggression in the context of prisons: dispositional and situational explanations.

The Premier Lodge's 'panoramic sea view' wasn't quite what was described on the website.

Revision BOOSTER

You might be asked about dispositional or situational explanations separately. There is plenty here for each of them – about 150 words of each which is enough for 6 marks of description. For evaluation you could include comparisons with the alternative model.

Apply it

A psychologist has been asked to prepare a report on a prison which has experienced an outbreak of violence amongst the inmates. She has visited the prison several times and her report notes that many inmates were involved in violent criminal gangs before they came to the prison. The prison itself has a harsh regime, where the rules do not seem to be applied consistently. Several of the prisoners are in solitary confinement and there is a high proportion of female staff. The budget for food has been cut several times.

Referring to issues raised in the psychologist's report, explain aggressive behaviour in prison.

Dispositional explanation – importation model

Institutional aggression results from *characteristics of prisoners*.	Irwin and Cressey (1962) argued that inmates bring with them (import) into prisons a subculture typical of criminality – including beliefs, norms, attitudes, learning experiences and personal characteristics (e.g. gender and ethnicity).
	Inmates import these characteristics which then influence their use of aggression to establish power, status and access to resources.
	Aggression is the result of individual characteristics of inmates and not of the prison environment.
Prisoner characteristics include anger and traumatic experiences.	DeLisi *et al.* (2011) studied juvenile delinquents in Californian institutions who imported many different negative backgrounds.
	For example, childhood trauma, anger, histories of substance abuse and violent behaviour.
Outcomes include self-harm and prisoner violence.	The DeLisi *et al.* study compared two groups of inmates – one group with negative characteristics they were importing into the prison (see above) and a **control group** without such characteristics.
	The 'negative' inmates were more likely to engage in suicidal activity, sexual misconduct and acts of physical aggression.

Situational explanation – deprivation model

Institutional aggression due to *stress created by prison environment* itself.	Clemmer (1958) argued that harsh prison conditions cause stress for inmates who cope by behaving aggressively.
	Aggression results from being deprived of freedom, material goods, etc. It is made worse by an unpredictable prison regime that regularly uses 'lock-ups' to control behaviour. This reduces access to goods (e.g. TV) even further.
	Aggression becomes an **adaptive** solution to deprivation.
Harsh conditions include psychological and physical factors.	Psychological factors (e.g. deprived of freedom, independence and heterosexual intimacy).
	Physical factors (e.g. deprivation of material goods increases aggressive competition amongst inmates).
Prison-level factors are independent of prisoners' dispositions.	Steiner (2009) investigated factors predicting aggression in 512 US prisons – inmate-on-inmate violence was more common in prisons where there was a higher proportion of female staff, overcrowding and more inmates in protective custody.
	These are prison-level factors because they are independent of individual characteristics of prisoners – they reliably predicted aggressive behaviour in line with the deprivation model.

One strength of the importation model is research support.

Camp and Gaes (2005) found no significant difference in aggression over two years between inmates randomly placed in low- (33%) and high-security prisons (36%).

The researchers concluded that features of the prison environment are less important predictors of aggressive behaviour than characteristics of inmates.

This is strong evidence for importation because there was **random allocation** of inmates.

One limitation of the importation model is it ignores key factors.

Dilulio (1991) claims the model ignores other factors that influence prisoners' behaviour, such as the prison officers and the way the prison is run.

Dilulio's *administrative control model* (ACM) suggests poorly managed prisons have the worst violence – weak leadership, distant staff and few educational opportunities.

Therefore, importation is an inadequate explanation because institutional factors are probably more important than inmate characteristics.

Evaluation extra: Determinism and free will.

The importation model may be **determinist**. Prisoners aggress because of 'negative' dispositions they can't control, implying prison aggression is inevitable.

However, perhaps prison aggression results from prisoners exercising their **free will**. **Cognitive** factors also play a role, so aggression is not inevitable.

Therefore, on balance, the model is **soft determinism**. Prisoners may be predisposed to aggression but aggressive behaviour ultimately depends on other factors.

'That's the last time I agree to tidy up the loft,' thought Waneta.

One strength of the deprivation model is research support.

Cunningham *et al.* (2010) found that inmate homicides in Texas prisons were linked to deprivations identified in Clemmer's model.

Many homicides followed arguments between cell-sharing inmates where 'boundaries' were crossed (e.g. arguments over drugs, sexual activity, personal possessions).

These are the factors identified by the deprivation model, so the findings support the model's **validity**.

One limitation is research contradicting the deprivation model.

The deprivation model predicts lack of heterosexual contact should lead to aggression in prisons.

Hensley *et al.* (2002) studied two US prisons, and found no reduced aggression in prisoners who had conjugal visits (i.e. for sex).

This suggests that situational factors do not substantially affect prison violence.

Evaluation extra: Importation versus deprivation.

The importation model is supported by well-controlled experimental evidence, e.g. DeLisi *et al.* (**natural experiment** with control group), Camp and Gaes (random allocation).

However, the deprivation model is supported by evidence that has other strengths, e.g. Steiner (wide range of 512 prisons) and Cunningham *et al.* (all Texas prisons).

Therefore the dispositional explanation is more valid because it is supported by causal evidence that is methodologically superior (e.g. control groups and random allocation).

Knowledge Check

1. With reference to institutional aggression, explain what is meant by 'dispositional' **and** 'situational' explanations.
   (2 marks + 2 marks)

2. Outline dispositional explanations of institutional aggression. *(6 marks)*

3. Evaluate situational explanations of institutional aggression. *(6 marks)*

4. Two psychology students are discussing aggression in prisons. One says, 'It's not surprising there's aggression in prisons when you look at the people in them.' The other disagrees, 'Well, I think it's more to do with the way prisons are run.'

   With reference to these arguments, discuss **two** explanations of institutional aggression in the context of prisons. *(16 marks)*

Media influences on aggression

Spec spotlight

Media influences on aggression, including the effects of computer games.

'Who called me a muppet?'

Apply it

Two psychology students would like to investigate the effects of computer game violence on aggressive behaviour. But their teacher tells them they cannot show their participants any violent or aggressive material for ethical reasons. The students are concerned that this will have serious implications for their conclusions. They have to think very carefully about how they can carry out their study. So, knowing you are a top psychologist, they ask for your help.

Outline to the students the types of study they could conduct. Explain the pros and cons of each one.

Revision BOOSTER

Always think 'less is more' – writing about fewer things gives you the opportunity to demonstrate your detailed understanding. For 6 marks AO1 you may not want to include all six of the points here to give yourself time for detail.

Effects of TV and computer games

'Excessive' TV viewing linked to aggression.	Hours watching TV in childhood associated with adult convictions for aggressive and violent crimes (Robertson *et al.* 2013 – followed 1000 New Zealanders).
	Additionally the study found watching TV was also associated with reduced social interaction and poorer educational achievement.
	Therefore link to aggression may be indirect (e.g. due to reduced social interaction).
Violent film content is the most direct media influence.	Bandura *et al.* (1963) **replicated** their earlier Bobo doll study (see page 194) but this time children watched a film of an adult model beating the doll.
	Children again imitated the model's behaviour closely, demonstrating that social learning can operate through media as well as face-to-face.
TV/film effects on aggression not strong.	A **meta-analysis** of about 200 studies found a significant positive **correlation** between viewing TV/film violence and antisocial behaviour (Paik and Comstock 1994).
	However TV/film violence accounted for only 1–10% of variance in children's aggressive behaviour, suggesting a minor effect on aggression for TV and film compared with other sources.
Computer games may have a powerful effect.	Evidence that computer games have a more powerful effect than traditional screen-based media because:
	• Game player is active (viewers are passive).
	• Game-playing is directly rewarding (**operant conditioning**).
Computer games – lab experiments.	For ethical reasons participants are not exposed to violence. Therefore studies use *Taylor competitive reaction time task* (TCRTT), giving blasts of white noise at chosen volumes to (non-existent) opponent.
	Bartholow and Anderson (2002) found that students playing violent game (Mortal Kombat) for ten minutes gave higher volumes of white noise than students who played non-violent golfing game.
Computer games – correlational studies.	Several measures of aggression are positively correlated with time spent playing violent games (e.g. in juvenile offenders, DeLisi *et al.* 2013).
	The link is so well-established that (in DeLisi *et al.*'s view) aggression should be considered a public health issue and computer game violence a risk factor.

One limitation is that aggression is defined in various ways.

Operationalised as violent behaviour (DeLisi *et al.* facing page), volume of white noise (Bartholow and Anderson), criminal convictions (Robertson *et al.*).

But although all violence is aggression, not all aggression is violence and not all aggression or violence is necessarily criminal – effects depend on definitions.

This variation in definitions means that the findings of studies are hard to compare.

Counterpoint

Meta-analyses help overcome this, e.g. Anderson *et al.* (2010) included 136 studies using different definitions and found increases in aggression linked to violent computer games.

Therefore, meta-analyses that include various definitions of aggression are a valid method for uncovering the effects of media on aggression.

Boy in blue: 'Yes, Mum's come home with a couple of encyclopedias from the bookshop!'

Boy in orange: 'Oh thank goodness. At last we can expand our minds rather than playing endless hours of FIFA.'

(True story)

Another limitation is the many unsupported conclusions.

Many studies are methodologically weak (e.g. **confounding variables**), and meta-analyses sometimes include poor-quality studies.

Many studies are correlational (no cause and effect), and experimental studies lack **external validity** (unrealistic measures of aggression so cannot be **generalised**).

Therefore some researchers may be guilty of drawing premature conclusions based on findings that lacks **validity**.

Revision BOOSTER

You don't have to memorise the exact content of the critical points given here. The explanations are meant to show you how to fully elaborate your point – explain/ example/elaborate/link. Trying to memorise all the details may just mean you have too much in your head – but do try to remember some of the detailed information to give your evaluative point critical power.

One strength is that SLT is a convincing theoretical framework.

Anderson *et al.* (2017) note that we accept that exposure to aggression at home is harmful, so logically media are important sources of social learning.

Children are more likely to imitate aggressive behaviours when they see them rewarded (vicarious reinforcement), especially when children identify with on-screen characters.

This is a key feature of science – having a unifying explanation to account for findings.

Evaluation extra: Research methods.

Research studies have limitations due to methodologies (e.g. lab studies, correlational studies), hard to claim violent media causes aggression.

However, the research includes the full range of methodologies, so strengths of one compensate for limitations of another (e.g. internal and external validity).

Therefore, taken together, the fact that a range of different methodologies come to similar conclusions suggests exposure to violent media may have a causal influence on aggressiveness.

Knowledge Check

1. Explain how computer games may lead to aggressive behaviour. *(4 marks)*
2. Explain what research has shown about the effect of computer games on aggression. *(6 marks)*
3. Briefly evaluate research into media influences on aggression. *(4 marks)*
4. Describe **and** evaluate research into the effects of computer games on aggression. *(16 marks)*

Desensitisation, disinhibition and cognitive priming

Spec spotlight

Media influences on aggression. The role of desensitisation, disinhibition and cognitive priming.

This is awful – there's no plot, no characterisation. The central protagonist is terribly one-dimensional.

Apply it

Three friends all regularly watch violent films. Paige has been doing this for so long she no longer finds them exciting or interesting. Ichabod's friends have noticed that he seems more argumentative these days. Lacey used to be quite calm, but now it's like she's on a 'hair trigger' all the time. Things other people find funny she thinks are annoying.

Use your knowledge of desensitisation, disinhibition and cognitive priming to explain these behaviours.

Role of desensitisation

Desensitisation = reduced *physiological* response (SNS arousal).	Normally when we witness aggression we experience arousal associated with the **sympathetic nervous system** (increased heart rate, blood pressure, sweat activity, etc.). But when children repeatedly view aggression on TV or play violent computer games the physiological effects are reduced (desensitisation) – i.e. a stimulus that is usually aversive has a lesser impact.
Desensitisation = reduced *psychological* response (e.g. less empathy for victim).	Repeated exposure to violent media promotes a belief that aggression to resolve conflict is socially acceptable. So negative attitudes towards violence weaken, less empathy is felt for victims, etc. (Funk *et al.* 2004). Weisz and Earls (1995) showed participants the film *Straw Dogs* (contains graphic rape scene). Males showed greater acceptance of rape myths after watching mock rape trial (compared with male viewers of a non-violent film). They also showed less sympathy to victim and were less likely to find defendant guilty (no similar effect for female participants).

Role of disinhibition

Disinhibition = exposure to violent media changes usual restraints.	Most people believe violence and aggression are antisocial – so there are strong social and psychological restraints against using aggression to resolve conflicts. Violent media gives aggressive behaviour social approval, especially where effects on victims are minimised. The usual restraints on individuals are loosened (**disinhibited**) after exposure to violent media.
Disinhibition enhanced if aggression is rewarded.	Computer games often show violence being rewarded at the same time as its consequences are minimised or justified. Such rewards strengthen new social norms in the viewer.

Role of cognitive priming

Cognitive priming = a 'script' learned about how to behave to aggressive cues.	Repeated experience of aggressive media can provide us with a 'script' about how violent situations may 'play out'. Huesmann (1998) argues that this script is stored in memory so we become 'ready' (primed) to be aggressive. This is an automatic process because a script can direct our behaviour without us being aware of it. The script is triggered when we encounter cues in a situation that we perceive as aggressive.
Songs with aggressive lyrics may trigger violent behaviour.	Fischer and Greitemeyer's (2006) male participants heard songs featuring aggressively derogatory lyrics about women. Compared with when they listened to neutral lyrics, participants later recalled more negative qualities about women and behaved more aggressively towards a female **confederate**. Similar results with female participants and 'men-hating' lyrics.

One strength of desensitisation is research support.

Krahé *et al.* (2011) showed violent and non-violent films while measuring physiological arousal (skin conductance, see page 168).

Habitual viewers of violent media showed lower arousal and gave louder bursts of white noise to a confederate without being provoked (proactive aggression).

This lower arousal in violent media users reflects desensitisation to the effects of violence, and it was also linked to greater willingness to be aggressive.

One limitation is desensitisation cannot explain some aggression.

Krahé *et al.*'s study did not link media viewing and arousal with provoked (reactive) aggression.

Catharsis may explain this – viewing violent media is a safety valve, releasing aggressive impulses without violence.

Therefore, not all aggression is the result of desensitisation and alternative explanations may be more valid.

*The three faces of Steve.**
**Psychology in-joke – ask your teacher.*

One strength of disinhibition is research support.

Berkowitz and Alioto (1973) found people who saw a film showing aggression as vengeance gave more shocks to a confederate.

Media violence may disinhibit aggression if presented as justified/ socially acceptable (as in the case of vengeance).

This demonstrates the link between removal of social constraints and subsequent aggressive behaviour.

Another strength is disinhibition can explain cartoon violence.

Children do not learn specific aggressive behaviours from cartoon models (e.g. head spinning round).

They learn that aggression is acceptable (socially normative), especially if it goes unpunished.

Therefore disinhibition explains how cartoon aggression can lead to aggression in those who observe it.

One strength of cognitive priming is real-world application.

Real-world violent situations depend on interpretation of environmental cues, which depends on **cognitive** scripts stored in memory.

Bushman and Anderson (2002) claim someone who watches violent media stores aggressive scripts more readily, so they interpret cues as aggressive.

This suggests that interventions could potentially reduce aggressive behaviour by challenging hostile cognitive biases.

One limitation of cognitive priming is confounding variables.

Violent video games tend to be more complex in gameplay than non-violent games, so complexity is a **confounding variable** (complexity not violence causes priming effect).

Zendle *et al.* (2018) found that when complexity was controlled, the priming effects of violent video games disappeared.

Therefore, the supportive findings of studies into priming may be partly due to confounding variables.

Revision BOOSTER

Evaluation points like these aren't just for long essay-style questions. You might be asked for a single strength or limitation as part of a short-answer question. Also, some questions ask for a 'brief discussion' for 6 marks. For such questions, two of these points would do the job nicely.

Knowledge Check

1. Explain what is meant by 'desensitisation' **and** 'disinhibition' in relation to aggression. *(2 marks + 2 marks)*

2. Outline the role of cognitive priming in aggression. *(4 marks)*

3. Briefly evaluate the role of disinhibition in aggression. *(4 marks)*

4. Discuss how desensitisation, disinhibition **and/or** cognitive priming might influence aggressive behaviour. *(16 marks)*

Offender profiling: The top-down approach

Spec spotlight

Offender profiling: the top-down approach, including organised and disorganised types of offender.

Fido claimed it was a case of 'mistaken identity' but he fitted the profile perfectly: small, four legs, black around the eye, furry. The game was up.

Revision BOOSTER

An application (AO2) question might ask you to explain how a given description of an offender matches the organised or disorganised profile. A good response would be to use some of the features described here – link them to the stimulus material in the question.

The top-down approach

Offender profiling. Aims to narrow the list of suspects.	The main aim of offender profiling is to narrow the list of likely suspects.
	Professional profilers are employed to work alongside the police especially in high-profile murder cases.
	The scene and other evidence are analysed to generate hypotheses about the probable characteristics of the offender (e.g. age, background, occupation, etc.).
Top-down approach. FBI data.	The FBI interviewed 36 sexually-motivated murderers and used this data, together with characteristics of their crimes, to create two categories (organised and disorganised).
	If the data from a crime scene matched some of the characteristics of one category we could then predict other characteristics that would be likely.
Offender types based on 'ways of working'.	The organised and disorganised distinction is based on the idea that offenders have certain signature 'ways of working'.
	These generally correlate with a particular set of social and psychological characteristics that relate to the individual.
Organised. Targets victim, controlled, higher IQ.	Organised offenders are characterised by: • Evidence of planning the crime – victim is deliberately targeted and the killer/rapist may have a 'type' of victim. • High degree of control during the crime and little evidence left behind at the scene. • Above-average IQ – in a skilled/professional job. • Usually married and may even have children.
Disorganised. Impulsive, lower IQ.	Disorganised offenders are characterised by: • Little evidence of planning, suggesting the offence may have been spontaneous. • The crime scene reflects the impulsive nature of the act, e.g. body still at the scene and the crime shows little control on the part of the offender. • Below-average IQ – may be in unskilled work or unemployed. • A history of failed relationships and living alone, possible history of sexual dysfunction.
FBI profile construction. Data, classification, reconstruction, profile generation.	There are four main stages in the construction of an FBI profile: 1. Data assimilation – review of the evidence (photographs, pathology reports, etc.). 2. Crime scene classification – organised or disorganised. 3. Crime reconstruction – generation of hypotheses about the behaviour and events. 4. Profile generation – generation of hypotheses about the offender (e.g. background, physical characteristics, etc.).

Chapter 12: Forensic psychology

One strength is research support for an organised category.

Canter *et al.* (2004) looked at 100 US serial killings. *Smallest space analysis* was used to assess the co-occurrence of 39 aspects of the serial killings.

This analysis revealed a subset of behaviours of many serial killings which match the FBI's typology for organised offenders.

This suggests that a key component of the FBI typology approach has some **validity**.

Bernard regretted painting his garden fence red before attempting to nick his neighbour's curtains.

Counterpoint

Godwin (2002) argues that, in reality, most killers have multiple contrasting characteristics and don't fit into one 'type'.

This suggests that the organised–disorganised typology is probably more of a continuum.

Another strength is that it can be adapted to other types of crime e.g. burglary.

Meketa (2017) reports that top-down profiling has recently been applied to burglary, leading to an 85% rise in solved cases in three US states.

The detection method adds two new categories – *interpersonal* (offender knows their victim, steals something of significance) and *opportunistic* (inexperienced young offender).

This suggests that top-down profiling has wider application than was originally assumed.

Apply it

A profiler becomes national news when a serial killer is caught. The police used the profile he composed to make an arrest. The profiler is interviewed on BBC News and is asked to explain the secret of his success. He says he uses the top-down approach. The interviewer doesn't understand, so asks him to explain what that means and why it was successful.

Outline what the profiler might say in response to the interviewer.

One limitation is evidence for top-down profiling was flawed.

Canter *et al.* (2004) argues that the FBI agents did not select a random or even large sample, nor did it include different kinds of offender.

There was no standard set of questions so each interview was different and therefore not really comparable.

This suggests that top-down profiling does not have a sound, scientific basis.

Do you agree with this conclusion?

Knowledge Check

1. In relation to offender profiling, explain the difference between organised and disorganised types of offender. *(4 marks)*

2. Outline the top-down approach to offender profiling. *(6 marks)*

3. Briefly evaluate **one** approach to offender profiling. *(4 marks)*

4. Octavia is an offender profiler investigating the scene of a murder. There is very little physical evidence, but she notices there are indications that the murderer was organised and controlling. She believes she can use this information to construct a profile.

   Discuss the top-down approach to offender profiling. Refer in your answer to Octavia's experience. *(16 marks)*

Evaluation extra: Personality.

The top-down approach is based on behavioural consistency – that serial offenders have characteristic ways of working (their *modus operandi*) so crime scene characteristics help identification.

Mischel (1968) argued that people's behaviour is much more driven by the situation they are in than by a thing called 'personality'.

This suggests that a profiling method based on behavioural consistency may not always lead to successful identification of an offender.

Offender profiling: The bottom-up approach

Spec spotlight

Offender profiling: the bottom-up approach, including investigative psychology; geographical profiling.

Heston liked to dress up and pretend to be a forensic psychologist whilst doing his gardening late at night.

Apply it

A profiler who specialises in the bottom-up approach has been asked by the police to construct a profile of an offender believed to be responsible for a series of rapes and sexual assaults. The profiler notices that the crimes were committed in an area with a radius of about three miles. Two women have also been killed just outside this area, but the police do not know if this is the same offender. The profiler notices that all of the crimes show signs of a very controlling attacker.

1. Explain how the profiler might use the bottom-up approach to construct her profile.

2. What might the profiler include in the profile?

Bottom-up or top-down?

Both are based on crime-scene data. The difference is that the top-down approach uses the data to generate the profile and, from then on, the investigator fits the profile to the crime scene. In the bottom-up version the investigator always starts again at the bottom and generates a profile.

Investigative psychology

Bottom-up approach. Offender profile emerges based on the data.	Unlike the US top-down approach, the British bottom-up model does not begin with fixed typologies. Instead, the profile is 'data-driven' and emerges as the investigator rigorously scrutinises the details of a particular offence. The aim is to generate a picture of the offenders' characteristics, routines and background through analysis of the evidence.
Statistical analysis of crime-scene evidence.	Statistical procedures detect patterns of behaviour that are likely to occur (or coexist) across crime scenes. This is done to develop a statistical 'database' which then acts as a baseline for comparison. Features of an offence can be matched against this database to suggest potentially important details about the offender, their personal history, family background, etc.
Analysis based on psychological concepts, e.g. *interpersonal coherence*.	A central concept is interpersonal coherence – the way an offender behaves at the scene (including how they 'interact' with the victim) may reflect their behaviour in everyday situations (e.g. controlling, apologetic, etc.), i.e. their behaviour 'hangs together' (has coherence). This might tell the police something about how the offender relates to women (for example) more generally.

Geographical profiling

Inferences about the offender *based on location*.	The locations of crime scenes are used to infer the likely home or operational base of an offender – known as *crime mapping*. Serial offenders restrict their 'work' to areas they are familiar with (spatial consistency). Location can also be used alongside psychological theory to create hypotheses about the offender and their *modus operandi* (habitual way of working).
Marauder and *commuter* types of offender.	Canter and Larkin (1993) proposed two models of offender behaviour: 1. The *marauder* – operates close to their home base. 2. The *commuter* – likely to have travelled a distance away from their usual residence when committing a crime.
Circle theory uses offending locations.	Canter and Larkin also suggest that the pattern of offending locations is likely to form a circle around the offender's usual residence, and this becomes more apparent the more offences there are. The offender's spatial decision-making can provide insight into the nature of the offence (planned or opportunistic, mode of transport, employment status, etc.).

One strength is that evidence supports investigative psychology.

Canter and Heritage (1990) conducted an analysis of 66 sexual assault cases using *smallest space analysis*. Several behaviours were identified in most cases (e.g. using impersonal language).

Each individual displayed a pattern of such behaviours, helps establish whether two or more offences were committed by the same person ('case linkage').

This supports one of the basic principles of investigative psychology (and the bottom-up approach) that people are consistent in their behaviour.

Counterpoint

However, the database is made up of only *solved* crimes which are likely to be those that were straightforward to link together – a circular argument.

This suggests that investigative psychology may tell us little about crimes that have few links between them and therefore remain unsolved.

The burglar's mistake was to leave gigantic red inflatable symbols in the gardens of each of the houses he robbed. An elementary error.

Another strength is that evidence also supports geographical profiling.

Lundrigan and Canter (2001) collated information from 120 murder cases in the US. *Smallest space analysis* revealed spatial consistency – a centre of gravity.

Offenders leave home base in different directions when dumping a body but created a circular effect, especially in the case of marauders.

This supports the view that geographical information can be used to identify an offender.

Revision BOOSTER

You can help the clarity of your evaluation hugely by doing what we've done here – provide introductory 'signposts' at the start of an evaluative paragraph. It keeps you on the path of evaluation and it tells the examiner what you are doing – it's a way of saying 'I'm *using* this evidence, not just describing it.'

One limitation is that geographical profiling may not be sufficient on its own.

Recording of crime is not always accurate, can vary between police forces and an estimated 75% of crimes are not even reported to police.

Even if crime data is correct, other factors matter e.g. timing of the offence and age and experience of the offender (Ainsworth 2001).

This suggests that geographical information alone may not always lead to the successful capture of an offender.

Evaluation extra: Mixed results.

Copson (1995) surveyed 48 police departments and found that advice provided by a profiler was 'useful' in 83% of cases, which suggests the approach is valid.

The same study revealed that only 3% of cases led to accurate identification! Kocsis *et al.* (2002) found chemistry students produced more accurate profiles than detectives.

This suggests that offender profiling may actually have little practical value when it comes to solving cases.

Knowledge Check

1. In relation to offender profiling, explain what is meant by the 'top-down' **and** the 'bottom-up' approaches.
   (2 marks + 2 marks)

2. Outline research into geographical profiling. *(6 marks)*

3. Briefly evaluate investigative psychology in relation to offender profiling. *(4 marks)*

4. Outline **and** evaluate the bottom-up approach to offender profiling. In your answer, refer to investigative psychology **and** geographical profiling. *(16 marks)*

Biological explanations: An historical approach

Spec spotlight

Biological explanations of offending behaviour: an historical approach (atavistic form).

Lombroso argued that primitive offenders cannot adjust to civilised society – although this lad's doing his best.

Funny word, atavistic

Here's a dictionary definition of the term atavistic: 'Relating to or characterised by reversion to something ancient or ancestral.' That's where the idea of 'criminal features' being an evolutionary throwback comes from.

Apply it

Cordelia and Regan are discussing the forensic topics they've been doing in psychology. Cordelia says, 'The offenders in those mugshots you see on telly always look well dodgy.' Regan replies, 'I know quite a few people who have gone to prison and none of them look like that.'

1. What features might Cordelia be referring to when she uses the term 'well dodgy'?

2. Explain why Regan makes a valid point about these features.

Atavistic form

Lombroso's *historical approach* laid foundations of profiling.	Lombroso (1876), an Italian physician, proposed that criminals were 'genetic throwbacks' – a primitive subspecies who were biologically different from non-criminals. This is the 'atavistic form'.
Biological approach – offenders lack evolutionary development.	Offenders were seen by Lombroso as lacking **evolutionary** development. Their savage and untamed nature meant that they would find it impossible to adjust to civilised society and would inevitably turn to crime. Therefore Lombroso saw offending behaviour as an innate tendency and thus was proposing a new perspective (for his time) that the offender was not at fault. In this way his ideas were revolutionary.
Atavistic form biologically determined.	Lombroso argued the offender subtype could be identified by their physiological 'markers'. These 'atavistic' characteristics are **biologically determined**.
Cranial and other physical and emotional features.	Characteristics of the skull (cranium) included: • A narrow, sloping brow. • A strong prominent jaw. • High cheekbones. • Facial asymmetry. Other physical features included dark skin and existence of extra toes, nipple or fingers. Other aspects included insensitivity to pain, use of slang, tattoos and unemployment.
Different types of offenders have different physical characteristics.	Lombroso also suggested that particular physiological 'markers' were linked to particular types of crime. For example, murderers were described as having bloodshot eyes, curly hair and long ears. Sexual deviants were described as having glinting eyes with swollen and fleshy lips.
Lombroso's research showed convicts had atavistic characteristics.	Lombroso meticulously examined the facial and cranial features of 383 dead convicts and 3839 living ones. He concluded that 40% of criminal acts could be accounted for by people with atavistic characteristics.

One strength of Lombroso's theory is it changed criminology.

Lombroso (the 'father of modern criminology', Hollin 1989) shifted the emphasis in crime research away from moralistic to scientific.

Also, in describing how particular types of people are likely to commit particular types of crime, the theory heralded offender profiling.

This suggests that Lombroso made a major contribution to the science of criminology.

Counterpoint

However, many of the features that Lombroso identified as atavistic (curly hair, dark skin) are most likely to be found among people of African descent, a view that fitted 19th-century eugenic attitudes (to prevent some groups from breeding).

This suggests that his theory might be more subjective than objective, influenced by racist prejudices.

One limitation is evidence contradicts the link between atavism and crime.

Goring (1913) compared 3000 offenders and 3000 non-offenders and found no evidence that offenders are a distinct group with unusual facial and cranial characteristics.

He did suggest though that many people who commit crime have lower-than-average intelligence (offering limited support for atavistic theory).

This challenges the idea that offenders can be physically distinguished from the rest of the population, therefore they are unlikely to be a subspecies.

Another limitation is Lombroso's methods were poorly controlled.

Lombroso didn't compare his offender sample with a **control group**, and therefore failed to control **confounding variables**.

For example, modern research shows that social conditions (e.g. poverty) are associated with offending behaviour, which would explain some of Lombroso's links (Hay and Forrest 2009).

This suggests that Lombroso's research does not meet modern scientific standards.

Evaluation extra: Nature or nurture?

The atavistic form suggests that crime has a biological cause, it is genetically determined.

However, facial and cranial differences may be influenced by other factors, such as poverty or poor diet, rather than inherited.

This suggests that the idea of an innate atavistic form as a predisposing factor for criminality is meaningless.

Lombroso, known to researchers in the field as the 'father of modern criminology', and known to his mum as 'our Ces'.

Revision BOOSTER

Write a very brief essay plan for each possible essay for this topic and then practise writing the essay in full from this. Time yourself – 20 minutes for a 16-mark essay.

Knowledge Check

1. In relation to biological explanations of offending behaviour, explain what is meant by 'atavistic form'.
   (2 marks)

2. Outline atavistic form as a biological explanation of offending behaviour. *(6 marks)*

3. Evaluate an historical approach to explaining offending behaviour. *(6 marks)*

4. Modern explanations of offending behaviour grew out of an historical approach which focused on cranial and other characteristics. But this approach seems very primitive by today's standards.

   With reference to the above statement, discuss **one** biological explanation of offending behaviour. *(16 marks)*

Biological explanations: Genetic and neural

Spec spotlight

Biological explanations of offending behaviour: genetics and neural explanations.

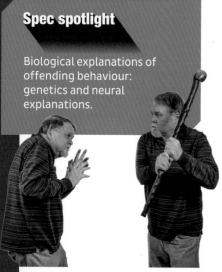

'I'm warning you Warren, stop copying my outfits or I'll chase you with this massive pipe.' It was just another typical day in the staffroom.

Twin and adoption studies

Both of these are quasi-experiments where the independent variable is genetic or environmental similarity (for example, an adoptive parent shares environment with a child and the biological parent shares genetics). The dependent variable is similarity in offending behaviour.

Apply it

Hermione and Yakira are discussing their friend Ziv who has been caught by the police for several driving offences. He also resisted arrest and hit a police officer. Hermione comments that she always knew Ziv would get into trouble because, well you only have to look at his dad. And he's got a twin brother who's just the same. Yakira agrees and adds, 'Yes, and Ziv was always doing things impulsively. I wondered if he had something wrong with his brain.'

Explain the issues raised in this conversation using your knowledge of neural **and** genetic explanations for offending behaviour.

Genetic explanations

Twin and *adoption studies* suggest genes predispose offenders to crime.	Christiansen (1977) studied over 3500 twin pairs in Denmark, finding a **concordance** for offender behaviour of 35% for **MZ** males and 13% for **DZ** males (slightly lower rates for females). This supports a genetic component in offending. Crowe (1972) found that adopted children who had a biological mother with a criminal record had a 50% risk of having a criminal record age 18. Whereas adopted children whose mother didn't have a criminal record only had a 5% risk.
Candidate genes. MAOA and CDH13.	A genetic analysis of about 800 offenders by Tiihonen *et al.* (2015) suggested two genes that may be associated with violent crime: • MAOA gene regulates **serotonin** and linked to aggressive behaviour (see page 186). • CDH13 gene linked to substance abuse and ADHD. The study found that 5–10% of all severe violent crime in Finland is attributable to the MAOA and CDH13 genotypes.
Diathesis-stress model.	If genes have an influence on offending, this influence is likely to be at least partly moderated by environmental factors. The **diathesis-stress model** suggests that a tendency to offending behaviour is due to a combination of: • Genetic predisposition (diathesis). • A biological or psychological stressor or 'trigger' (e.g. criminal role models or dysfunctional upbringing).

Neural explanations

Antisocial personality disorder (APD).	There may be neural differences in the brains of offenders and non-offenders. For example, **antisocial personality disorder** (**APD**) is associated with a lack of empathy and reduced emotional responses. Many convicted offenders have a diagnosis of APD.
Less activity in *prefrontal cortex* = less emotional regulation.	Raine *et al.* (2000) found reduced activity and an 11% reduction in the volume of grey matter in the prefrontal cortex of people with APD compared to controls. This is the part of the brain that regulates emotional behaviour.
Mirror neurons (empathy) may not always be turned on.	Keysers (2011) found that only when offenders were *asked* to empathise did they show an empathy reaction (controlled by mirror neurons in the brain). This suggests APD individuals do experience empathy, but may have a neural 'switch' that turns on and off. In a normally-functioning brain the empathy switch is permanently on.

One limitation of twin studies is assuming equal environments.

Often assumed that environmental factors are the same for MZ and DZ twins because they experience similar environments.

However, because MZ twins look identical, people (especially parents) tend to treat them more similarly which, in turn, affects their behaviour.

Therefore higher **concordance rates** for MZs may be because they are treated more similarly than DZs, suggesting conclusions lack **validity**.

One strength is the support for a diathesis-stress model of offending.

Mednick *et al.* (1984) studied 13,000 Danish adoptees having at least one court conviction.

Conviction rates 13.5% (biological or adoptive parents had no convictions), 20% (one biological parent), 24.5% (both adoptive and biological parents).

This data suggests that both genetic inheritance and environment influence criminality – supporting the diathesis-stress model of crime.

Evaluation extra: Nature and nurture.

Adoption studies separate nature and nurture – similarities due to biological parents can only be genetic.

However, many adoptions occur when children are older and many adoptees maintain contact with biological family, so still environmental influences.

This suggests that adoption studies cannot fully separate nature and nurture.

Offending behaviour runs in families.

Revision BOOSTER

The concordance rate for identical twins is not 100% – so what? Students often jump on this figure as proof that a behaviour is not completely genetically inherited. This is true, but not very interesting. A much more sophisticated evaluation recognises offending behaviour is not completely genetic, but it is partly – so the important question is: 'To what *extent* is it genetic?'

One strength is support for the link between crime and the frontal lobe.

Kandel and Freed (1989) researched people with frontal lobe damage, including the prefrontal cortex.

They found evidence of impulsive behaviour, emotional instability and inability to learn from mistakes.

This supports the idea that structural abnormalities in the brain are a causal factor in offending behaviour.

One limitation is the link between neural differences and APD is complex.

Farrington *et al.* (1981) studied adult males with high APD scores. They were raised by a convicted parent and physically neglected.

These early experiences may have caused APD *and* associated neural differences, e.g. reduced activity in the frontal lobe due to trauma.

This suggests that the relationship between neural differences, APD and offending is complex and there may be intervening variables.

Evaluation extra: Biological determinism.

The **biological** approach suggests offending behaviour is determined by factors which cannot be controlled so no responsibility.

However, justice system is based on individual responsibility. The identification of possible biological precursors to crime complicates this principle.

This suggests we should 'excuse' some people but, ultimately, this is not possible because then many could claim no responsibility.

Knowledge Check

1. Outline research into the genetic explanation of offending behaviour. *(6 marks)*
2. Briefly outline **two** biological explanations of offending behaviour. *(6 marks)*
3. Evaluate the neural explanation of offending behaviour. *(6 marks)*
4. Discuss genetic **and/or** neural explanations of offending behaviour. *(16 marks)*

Psychological explanations: Eysenck's theory

*Who says air guitar doesn't make
you look cool? Er, most of this guy's
audience actually.*

Personality

People differ in the way they think,
feel and act. The sum total of
such individual differences is
their personality.

Apply it

*Joss is a prison psychologist who
frequently runs therapy groups as
part of his job. He has noticed that
some of the more violent prisoners
have quite a lot in common. They
are reckless, unpredictable and often
cruel. They don't seem to understand
how others feel. But they are also
different in some ways. Some are
quiet and shy, others outgoing and
impulsive. Some seem quite stable
but others are insecure and anxious.*

Use Eysenck's theory of the criminal
personality to explain why the
prisoners are similar in some ways,
but different in others.

Theory of the criminal personality

Three personality dimensions.	Eysenck (1947) proposed that personality could be represented along three dimensions: • Introversion–extraversion (E). • Neuroticism–stability (N). • Psychoticism–sociability (P). The dimensions combine to form a variety of personality characteristics or types.
Innate, biological basis for personality types.	Eysenck suggested personality types are innate and based on the nervous system we inherit. • Extraverts have an underactive nervous system which means they seek excitement and engage in risk-taking. • Neurotic individuals have a high level of reactivity in the **sympathetic nervous system** – they respond quickly to situations of threat (fight or flight). This means they tend to be nervous, jumpy and overanxious so their behaviour is difficult to predict. • Psychotic individuals are suggested to have higher levels of **testosterone** – they are cold, unemotional and prone to aggression.
Criminal personality = neurotic extravert + high psychoticism.	The criminal personality type is a combination: • Neurotics are unstable and therefore prone to overreact to situations of threat. • Extraverts seek more arousal and thus engage in dangerous activities. • Psychotics are aggressive and lacking empathy.
Offending behaviour is concerned with immediate gratification.	Eysenck saw offending behaviour as developmentally immature in that it is selfish and concerned with immediate gratification. Offenders are impatient and cannot wait for things.
High E and high N scorers lack ability to learn (be *conditioned*).	During the process of socialisation children are taught to become more able to delay gratification and more socially orientated. Eysenck believed that people with high E and N scores had nervous systems that made it difficult for them to learn (be conditioned). As a result, they are less likely to learn anxiety responses to antisocial impulses and thus more likely to act antisocially.
Personality can be measured using the *EPQ*.	The notion that personality can be measured is central to Eysenck's theory and useful in research. He developed the *Eysenck Personality Questionnaire* (EPQ), a psychological test that locates respondents along the E, N and P dimensions to determine their personality type.

One strength is the evidence supporting Eysenck's theory.

Eysenck and Eysenck (1977) compared 2070 male prisoners' scores on the EPQ with 2422 male **controls**.

On measures of E, N and P (across all the age groups that were sampled) prisoners recorded higher average scores than controls.

This agrees with the predictions of the theory that offenders rate higher than average across the three dimensions Eysenck identified.

Counterpoint

However, Farrington *et al.* (1981) conducted a **meta-analysis** and reported that offenders tended to score high on measures of P, but not for E and N. Also inconsistent evidence of different cortical arousal in extraverts and introverts (Küssner 2017).

This means some of the central assumptions of the criminal personality have been challenged.

Eysenck – as in Eysenck Personality Questionnaire. How much of a coincidence is that?!

One limitation is the view that all offending is explained by personality.

Moffitt (1993) distinguished between offending behaviour that only occurs in adolescence (adolescence-limited) and that which continues into adulthood (life-course-persistent).

She considers persistence in offending behaviour to be a reciprocal process between individual personality traits and environmental reactions to those traits.

This is a more complex picture than Eysenck suggested, that offending behaviour is determined by an interaction between personality and the environment.

Revision BOOSTER

In a 16-mark essay you don't have to write everything on this spread. What is here is actually more than 1000 words!! For a 16-mark essay you probably only have time to write 500 words – but don't cut down the elaboration of the AO3 points. Better to do three elaborated points rather than four briefer ones.

Another limitation is cultural factors are not taken into account.

Bartol and Holanchock (1979) studied Hispanic and African-American offenders in a New York maximum security prison, dividing them into six groups based on offending history and offences.

All six groups were less extravert than a non-offender **control group**. Bartol and Holanchock suggested this was because the sample was a different cultural group from that investigated by Eysenck.

This questions the **generalisability** of the criminal personality – it may be a culturally relative concept.

Knowledge Check

1. Outline Eysenck's theory of the criminal personality.
(6 marks)

2. Describe what research (theories and/or studies) has shown about Eysenck's theory of the criminal personality.
(6 marks)

3. Evaluate **one** psychological explanation of offending behaviour. *(6 marks)*

4. Cruz is outwardly charming, friendly and outgoing. But he is also unfeeling, selfish, anxious and tense. He is currently in prison for serious assault.

Outline **and** evaluate Eysenck's theory of the criminal personality. Refer to Cruz in your answer. *(16 marks)*

Evaluation extra: Measuring personality.

The usefulness of the EPQ is that we can see how the criminal personality differs from the rest of the population across different dimensions.

However, personality type may not be reducible to a 'score' in this way. The criminal personality is too complex and dynamic to be quantified.

This may undermine any claims Eysenck made about being able to identify 'natural' offenders using the EPQ as personality may not be static.

Psychological explanations: Cognitive

Spec spotlight

Psychological explanations of offending behaviour: cognitive explanations; level of moral reasoning and cognitive distortions, including hostile attribution bias and minimalisation.

Kohlberg's levels of moral reasoning

Level I Pre-conventional
- Punishment orientation
- Instrumental/personal gain

Level II Conventional
- Good boy/girl orientation
- Maintenance of social order

Level III Post-conventional
- Individual rights
- Morality of conscience

One of Kohlberg's moral dilemmas – should Heinz steal the drug to save his wife? 57 varieties of possible response.

Apply it

Winona is interviewing offenders as part of her doctorate thesis. She is interested in the language offenders use to describe their crimes. She notices that many of them talk about even serious crimes like anyone else would talk about their jobs. The offenders often refuse to accept that they have caused their victims any harm. Winona has also shown the offenders several images of everyday situations involving people. The images are all neutral, but most of the offenders interpret them as hostile or aggressive.

Use your knowledge of cognitive explanations of offending behaviour to explain Winona's findings.

Level of moral reasoning

Moral development.	Kohlberg proposed that as children get older their decisions and judgements about right and wrong become more sophisticated (see left). A person's level of reasoning (thinking) affects their behaviour.
Offenders at *lower level*.	Kohlberg *et al.* (1973) used a moral dilemma technique (e.g. Heinz dilemma) and found offenders tend to be at the pre-conventional level, whereas non-offenders progress higher. Pre-conventional level is characterised by: • A need to avoid punishment and gain rewards. • Less mature, childlike reasoning. Offenders may commit crime if they can get away with it or gain rewards (e.g. money, respect).
Offenders *more egocentric* and show *less empathy*.	Research shows that offenders are often self-centred (egocentric) and display poorer social perspective-taking skills (Chandler 1973). Individuals who reason at a higher level tend to empathise more and exhibit behaviours such as honesty, generosity and non-violence.

Cognitive distortions

Faulty and biased thinking helps offenders justify behaviour.	**Cognitive** distortions are errors or biases in information processing characterised by faulty thinking. We all occasionally exhibit faulty thinking, but research shows this is a much more typical way for offenders to interpret their behaviour and justify their actions.
Hostile attribution bias. Ambiguous situations judged as threatening.	Schönenberg and Jusyte (2014) found violent offenders were more likely than non-offenders to perceive ambiguous facial expressions as angry and hostile. Offenders misread non-aggressive cues (e.g. being 'looked at') and this can trigger a disproportionate and violent response.
Minimalisation. Downplaying the significance of the crime.	Minimalisation reduces a person's sense of guilt. For example, burglars may use euphemisms, e.g. 'doing a job' or 'supporting my family' as a way of minimising the seriousness of their actions and their sense of guilt. This is particularly likely in sex offenders – Barbaree (1991) found 54% rapists denied they had committed an offence at all and a further 40% minimised the harm they had caused to the victim.

One strength is the evidence supports the role of moral reasoning.

Palmer and Hollin (1998) compared moral reasoning of offenders and non-offenders on a SRM-SF scale (11 moral dilemmas).	Offenders showed less mature moral reasoning than the non-offenders group (e.g. not taking things that belong to someone else).	This is consistent with Kohlberg's theory, and suggests his theory of criminality has **validity**.

One limitation is that moral reasoning may depend on the type of offence.

Thornton and Reid (1982) found that people whose crimes were for financial gain (e.g. robbery) were more likely to show pre-conventional level than if impulsive crime (e.g. assault).	Pre-conventional moral reasoning tends to be associated with crimes in which offenders believe they have a good chance of evading punishment.	This suggests that Kohlberg's theory may not apply to all forms of crime.

Evaluation extra: Thinking versus behaviour.

Kohlberg's theory provides insight into the criminal mind – offenders may be more childlike and egocentric when making moral judgements.	However, moral thinking is not the same as moral *behaviour*. Moral reasoning may be used to explain behaviour but only afterwards.	This suggests that understanding moral behaviour may be more useful as not everyone who has criminal thoughts will act on them.

Offenders show less mature reasoning than non-offenders. That's certainly the case with 'Billy the Hood' (pictured above), the scourge of the local nursery.

One strength of cognitive distortions is its application to therapy.

In **cognitive behaviour therapy**, offenders are helped to 'face up' to what they have done and have a less distorted view of their actions.	Studies (e.g. Harkins *et al.* 2010) suggest that reduced denial and minimalisation in therapy is associated with less reoffending.	This suggests that the theory of cognitive distortions has practical value.

One limitation is cognitive distortions depend on the type of offence.

Howitt and Sheldon (2007) found that non-contact sex offenders (accessed sexual images on the internet) used more cognitive distortions than contact sex offenders (physically abused children).	Those who had a previous history of offending were also more likely to use distortions as a justification for their behaviour.	This suggests that cognitive distortions are not used in the same way by all offenders.

Evaluation extra: Descriptive or explanatory?

Cognitive theories of offending are good at describing the criminal mind and cognitive concepts (e.g. minimalisation) may be useful for therapy.	However, cognitive theories do not explain or help in predicting future offender behaviour – just because someone has distorted thinking doesn't mean they will offend.	This suggests that the cognitive explanations are probably not explanatory because they don't predict future behaviour.

Knowledge Check

1. In relation to cognitive explanations of offending behaviour, explain what is meant by 'hostile attribution bias' **and** 'minimalisation'.
   (3 marks + 3 marks)

2. Outline level of moral reasoning as a cognitive explanation of offending behaviour. *(6 marks)*

3. Briefly evaluate cognitive distortions as an explanation of offending behaviour.
   (4 marks)

4. Discuss **one or more** cognitive explanations of offending behaviour. *(16 marks)*

Pro-crime versus anti-crime. Whoever comes out on top will tip the scales towards offending or non-offending.

Apply it

Dylan is 10 and often watches crime dramas on TV with his dad, who always criticises the police and praises the criminals.

Carli was a star pupil at school until she was 15, when she started hanging out with a group of friends who were into shoplifting.

Gilbert has spent five years in prison for robbery. This is his second time in prison and, just like before, when he leaves prison he'll be going back to his old mates in the place where he grew up.

Explain what the differential association theory tells us about how Dylan, Carli and Gilbert might behave.

Revision BOOSTER

Write a very brief essay plan for each possible essay in this chapter and then practise writing the essay in full from these. Time yourself – 20 minutes for a 16-mark essay.

Differential association theory

A set of *scientific* principles to explain offending.	Sutherland (1924) developed a set of scientific principles that could explain all types of offending. Individuals learn the values, attitudes, techniques and motives for offending behaviour through interaction with others – these 'others' are different from one person to the next (hence, *differential* association). His theory ignores the effects of class or ethnic background, what matters is who you associate with.
Offending is learned through *interactions* with significant others.	Behaviour is acquired through the process of learning. Learning occurs through interactions with significant others who the child values most and spends most time with, such as family and peer group. Offending arises from two factors: • Learned attitudes towards offending. • Learning of specific offending acts.
Learning attitudes.	When a person is socialised into a group they will be exposed to certain values and attitudes. This includes values and attitudes toward the law – some of these will be pro-crime, some will be anti-crime. Sutherland argues that if the number of pro-crime attitudes the person comes to acquire outweighs the number of anti-crime attitudes, they will go on to offend.
Learning techniques.	In addition to being exposed to pro-crime attitudes, the would-be offender may also learn particular techniques for committing offences. For example, how to break into someone's house through a locked window or how to disable a car stereo before stealing it.
Mathematical prediction about committing offences.	It should be possible to mathematically predict how likely it is that an individual will commit offences. The prediction is based on our knowledge of the frequency, intensity and duration of an individual's exposure to deviant and non-deviant norms and values.
Reoffending may be due to socialisation in prison.	Sutherland's theory can account for why so many prisoners released from prison go on to reoffend. It is reasonable to assume that whilst inside prison inmates will be exposed to pro-crime attitudes and also learn specific techniques of offending from more experienced offenders which they can put into practice upon their release.

One strength of differential association theory is the shift of focus.

Sutherland moved emphasis away from early biological explanations (e.g. Lombroso) and from theories of offending as the product of individual weakness or immorality.

Differential association theory draws attention to deviant social circumstances and environments as being more to blame for offending than deviant people.

This approach offers a more realistic solution to offending instead of eugenics (the biological solution) or punishment (the morality solution).

Counterpoint

The theory risks stereotyping people from impoverished, crime-ridden backgrounds.

This ignores that people may choose not to offend despite such influences, as not everyone who is exposed to pro-crime attitudes goes on to offend.

Just use the front door like everyone else. What? Oh you're a burglar – ah, makes sense. Anyway carry on, sorry to disturb.

Another strength is that the theory has wide reach.

Whilst some crimes (e.g burglary) are clustered in inner-city working-class communities, other crimes are clustered in more affluent groups.

Sutherland was particularly interested in so-called 'white-collar' or corporate offences and how this may be a feature of middle-class groups who share deviant norms.

This shows that it is not just the 'lower' classes who commit offences and that differential association can be used to explain all offences.

Revision BOOSTER

Have you checked out our revision advice on pages 4 to 9?

One limitation is difficulty testing the theory's predictions.

Sutherland promised a scientific and mathematical framework for predicting offending behaviour, but the concepts can't be **operationalised**.

It is unclear how we can measure the numbers of pro- or anti-crime attitudes a person is exposed to – so how can we know at what point offending would be triggered?

This means the theory does not have scientific credibility.

Knowledge Check

1. Outline differential association theory as an explanation of offending behaviour. *(6 marks)*

2. Explain the difference between **one** psychological explanation and **one** biological explanation of offending behaviour. *(4 marks)*

3. Briefly evaluate differential association theory. *(6 marks)*

4. A politician is explaining how offenders all come from a social underclass living in working-class and inner-city areas. A psychologist points out that most frauds and many driving offences are committed by middle-class people.

   Outline **and** evaluate **two or more** psychological explanations of offending behaviour. Refer to the politician's and psychologist's remarks in your answer. *(16 marks)*

Evaluation extra: Nurture or nature?

If the family supports offending activity, making it seem legitimate and reasonable, then this becomes a major influence on the child's value system.

However, the fact that offending behaviour often seems to 'run in families' could also be interpreted as supporting biological explanations, such as genetics.

The solution may be that some offences (e.g. drug offences) are related to nurture whereas others (e.g. violent offences) are more due to 'nature'.

Psychological explanations: Psychodynamic

Spec spotlight

Psychological explanations of offending behaviour: psychodynamic explanations.

Hopefully Saturn's dad is a huge baseball fan. Hopefully.

Revision BOOSTER

Maternal deprivation is not a named term in this part of the specification. But it could help you to add detail to your answer on the psychodynamic explanation. On the other hand, you might already have enough detail for 6 marks after writing about inadequate Superegos. LESS IS MORE – writing about fewer things gives you the opportunity to demonstrate your detailed understanding.

Apply it

Tyler saw his father very rarely when he was growing up. This is because his dad was in and out of prison. When he was at home, Tyler's dad was what his mum called a 'bad influence', telling Tyler all about his criminal exploits and making it sound fun. When he eventually went back into prison, Tyler always felt guilty, as if it was his fault.

1. Use your knowledge of **one** psychodynamic explanation of offending behaviour to explain whether or not Tyler is likely to become an offender himself.

2. Based on an alternative psychodynamic explanation, construct a different scenario (like the one above) involving Tyler.

Psychodynamic explanations of offending

Inadequate Superego can lead to immoral behaviour.	Freud's **psychodynamic** approach suggests that the Superego is guided by the *morality principle* leading to feelings of guilt for wrongdoing. Blackburn (1993) argued that if the Superego is inadequate (weak, deviant or over-harsh) then the Id (governed by the *pleasure principle*) is given 'free rein' – an uncontrolled Id means that offending behaviour is inevitable.
1. *Weak Superego.* Absence of same-sex parent.	During the *phallic stage* the Superego is formed through the resolution of the *Oedipus complex* (or *Electra complex*), see page 20. If the same-sex parent is absent during this stage a child cannot internalise a fully-formed Superego as there is no opportunity for identification. This would make offending behaviour more likely.
2. *Deviant Superego.* Child internalises deviant values.	A child internalises the same-sex parent's moral attitudes to form their Superego. If these internalised moral attitudes are deviant this would lead to a deviant Superego and to offending behaviour.
3. *Over-harsh Superego.* Committing crimes satisfies need for punishment.	An excessively punitive or overly harsh parent creates a child who has an over-harsh Superego and the child is crippled by guilt and anxiety. This may (unconsciously) drive the individual to perform criminal acts in order to satisfy the Superego's overwhelming need for punishment.
The role of emotion.	The psychodynamic approach deals with the emotional life of the individual and its role in offending, unlike other theories of crime. Emotions (e.g. anxiety) guide moral behaviour.
Maternal deprivation and affectionless psychopathy.	Bowlby (1944) argued that a warm, continuous relationship with a mother-figure was crucial to future relationships, well-being and development. A loss of attachment in infancy (maternal deprivation) could lead to affectionless psychopathy (lack of empathy and guilt) and increased likelihood of delinquency.
44 juvenile thieves study supports Bowlby's maternal deprivation hypothesis.	Bowlby (1944) found that 14 of the 44 thieves showed signs of affectionless psychopathy – 12 of these had prolonged separation from their mothers in infancy. In a **control group**, only two 'thieves' had experienced prolonged separation (maternal deprivation).

One strength is research support for the link to the Superego.

Goreta (1991) conducted a Freudian-style analysis of ten offenders referred for psychiatric treatment. In all those assessed, disturbances in Superego formation were diagnosed.

Each offender experienced the need for punishment manifesting itself as a desire to commit acts of wrongdoing and offend (possibly due to an over-harsh Superego).

This evidence seems to support the role of psychic conflicts and an over-harsh Superego as a basis for offending.

Counterpoint

If this theory were correct we would expect harsh, punitive parents to raise children who often experience guilt. Evidence suggests that the opposite is true – such children rarely express guilt (Kochanska et al. 2001).

This calls into question the relationship between a strong, punitive internal parent and excessive feelings of guilt within the child.

One limitation of Freudian theory is that it is gender-biased.

Psychodynamic theory assumes girls develop a weaker Superego than boys – they do not experience castration anxiety, so have less need to identify with their mothers.

However there are 20 times more men than women in prison and Hoffman (1975) found no gender differences in children's moral behaviour.

This suggests there is alpha bias at the heart of Freud's theory and means it may not be appropriate as an explanation of offending behaviour.

Freud suggested that little boys develop a stronger Superego (because the Oedipus conflict has a more powerful resolution than the Electra complex) and are therefore more moral than little girls. I have to say, I have my doubts...

Another limitation is that Bowlby's theory is based on an association.

Lewis (1954) analysed 500 interviews with young people, maternal deprivation was a poor predictor of future offending and the ability to form close relationships in adolescence.

Even if there is a link there are countless other reasons for it, for example maternal deprivation may be due to growing up in poverty.

This suggests that maternal deprivation may be one of the reasons for later offending behaviour, but not the only reason.

Not everyone agrees with this conclusion. What do you think?

Evaluation extra: Contribution.

Psychodynamic explanations were first to link moral behaviour/offending to early childhood and emotional factors.

However, unconscious concepts are not open to empirical testing. Arguments such as the inadequate Superego can only be judged on their face value.

This suggests that although psychodynamic explanations have made a useful contribution to the debate, the lack of a credible scientific basis is an issue.

Knowledge Check

1. Outline psychodynamic explanations of offending behaviour. *(6 marks)*

2. Briefly outline the psychodynamic explanation **and one other** psychological explanation of offending behaviour. *(3 marks + 3 marks)*

3. Briefly evaluate **two** psychological explanations of offending behaviour. *(6 marks)*

4. Ashton is at secondary school and has always had a reputation for being distant and unfriendly. He can be very cruel to others but never seems to feel any guilt. He never expresses warmth or positive emotion towards others. Everyone knows Ashton is a frequent shoplifter.

   Discuss **one or more** psychodynamic explanation(s) of offending behaviour. Refer to Ashton's behaviour in your answer. *(16 marks)*

Dealing with offending behaviour: Custodial sentencing

Spec spotlight

Dealing with offending behaviour: the aims of custodial sentencing and the psychological effects of custodial sentencing. Recidivism.

Tim kept bringing the family back to Butlin's every year. He had to, he was the reigning 'knobbly knees' champion.

Apply it

A newspaper website runs an article on the use of prisons as punishment for crime. Two researchers present their arguments for and against. One claims that the problem of recidivism shows that prisons do not work. The other researcher points out that prison acts as a deterrent, putting others off committing crimes. Both researchers make other arguments as well as these.

1. Briefly develop the **two** main arguments presented here.

2. Outline some of the other arguments the two researchers might present.

Aims of custodial sentencing

1. *Deterrence.* Putting people off committing crime.	Custodial sentencing involves a convicted offender spending time in prison, hospital or young offender's institute. Deterrence is based on conditioning principles (punishment and vicarious punishment): • Individual deterrence – the unpleasant experience of prison is designed to put an individual off repeating the same crime again. • General deterrence – send a message to members of society that crime will not be tolerated.
2. *Incapacitation.* Protect the public by removing offenders.	Ensures that the offender is taken out of society which protects the public from further offending. The need for incapacitation depends on the severity of the crime (e.g. society needs more protection from serial murderers compared to people who do not pay council tax).
3. *Retribution.* Revenge against the offender.	Society enacting revenge by making the offender suffer. Level of suffering should be proportionate to the severity of the crime.
4. *Rehabilitation.* Reform the offender.	Reform of the offender (i.e. he or she learns new attitudes and values and stops being an offender). Prison should provide an opportunity to, for example, develop skills, access treatments (e.g. for addiction or anger) and reflect on crime.

Psychological effects of custodial sentencing

Stress, depression, institutionalisation and prisonisation.	Several psychological effects are associated with spending time in prison: 1. Stress and depression – suicide rates and self-harm are higher in prison than in the general population. 2. Institutionalisation – inability to function outside of prison having adapted to the norms and routines of prison life. 3. Prisonisation – behaviours unacceptable outside prison are encouraged via socialisation into an 'inmate code'.

Recidivism

About 45% of UK offenders reoffend within a year.	Recidivism refers to reoffending. Recidivism rates in ex-prisoners tell us to what extent prison acts as an effective deterrent. Rates vary with age, crime committed and country. The US, Australia and Denmark record rates over 60%. In Norway rates may be as low as 20% (Yukhnenko *et al.* 2019). This last figure is significant because in Norway there is less emphasis on incarceration and greater emphasis on rehabilitation and skills development.

One limitation is the negative effects of custodial sentencing.

Bartol (1995) said prison is 'brutal, demeaning and generally devastating'. Suicide rates in prisons (England and Wales) 9 times higher than general population.	The Prison Reform Trust (2014) found that 25% of women and 15% of men in prison reported symptoms of psychosis (e.g. schizophrenia).	This supports the view that oppressive prison regimes may be detrimental to psychological health which could impact on rehabilitation.

Counterpoint

Many offenders may have had pre-existing psychological difficulties before prison (*importation model*, see page 198), this may explain their offending behaviour in the first place.

This suggests there may be **confounding variables** that influence the link between prison and its psychological effects.

He who opens a school door, closes a prison

Victor Hugo. Wise words, Victor.

One strength is that prison provides training and treatment.

The Vera Institute of Justice (Shirley 2019) claims that offenders who take part in college education programmes are 43% less likely to reoffend following release.	This will improve employment opportunities on release, which reduces likelihood of reoffending.	This suggests prison may be a worthwhile experience assuming offenders are able to access these programmes.

Revision BOOSTER

Consider the three things relevant to this topic that you could specifically be asked to write about – the aims of custodial sentencing, its psychological effects and recidivism (or a combination of these). When terms are named in the specification you can't afford to pick and choose in your revision.

Another limitation is that prison may be a school for crime.

Incarceration with long-term offenders may give younger inmates in particular the opportunity to learn the 'tricks of the trade' from more experienced prisoners.	Offenders may also acquire criminal contacts whilst in prison that they may follow up when they are released.	This form of 'education' may undermine attempts to rehabilitate prisoners and consequently may make reoffending more likely.

Knowledge Check

1. Briefly outline **one** way of dealing with offending behaviour. *(4 marks)*
2. Outline research into recidivism. *(6 marks)*
3. Evaluate research into the aims **and** psychological effects of custodial sentencing. *(6 marks)*
4. Since Dagny arrived in prison four months ago, she has self-harmed several times and attempted suicide once. She is no longer shocked by what goes on in the prison and has forgotten how to do things for herself.

   Discuss some of the psychological effects of custodial sentencing. Refer to Dagny's experience in your answer. *(16 marks)*

Evaluation extra: The purpose of prison.

In Onepoll (2015) survey, 47% of respondents saw the primary purpose of prison as being to punish the offender for their wrongdoing.	However, a similar number (40%) held the view that prison's main emphasis should be on rehabilitation, so offenders can be effectively reintegrated back into society.	This suggests custodial sentencing should be sufficiently tough to deter offenders but also offer a 'second chance' through training and treatment.

Spec spotlight

Dealing with offending behaviour: behaviour modification in custody.

Dennis's long-term escape plan was finally coming to fruition. He'd saved up 50,000 tokens during his 25-year stretch and could now exchange them for the light aircraft he'd set his heart on. In a matter of hours he'd be flying out of the prison grounds forever.

Apply it

A campaigning British newspaper is outraged to discover that offenders are being rewarded inside prisons. The article describes how offenders are given tokens which in themselves are not worth anything. But the newspaper is furious that offenders (some of them inside for terrible crimes) can swap the tokens for real things. Some offenders get free cigarettes, others have extra visits from their family. How long, the paper asks, before they are getting the finest steak with all the trimmings, and other unspecified benefits?

Reading the article, you quickly realise it is nonsense. Write a reply dealing with the points raised above, using psychological evidence.

Behaviour modification in custody

Behaviourist principles. Undesirable behaviours can be unlearned.	The **behaviourist** approach proposes that all behaviour is learned – and therefore it should be possible to unlearn behaviour using the same principles. Behaviour modification programmes reinforce obedient behaviour whilst punishing disobedience.
Token economy. Reinforce or punish.	Based on **operant conditioning** – desirable inmate behaviours are rewarded (reinforced) with tokens. Desirable behaviours might include avoiding confrontation, being quiet in the cell, following rules. Tokens may also be removed = punishment.
Tokens are *secondary reinforcers.*	Tokens are not rewarding in themselves but rewarding because they can be exchanged for something desirable (primary reinforcer). Primary reinforcers = a phone call to a loved one, time in the gym, extra cigarettes or food.
Operationalise target behaviours.	Target behaviours are **operationalised** by breaking them down into components parts e.g. 'interaction with other prisoners' may be broken down into 'speaking politely to others', 'not touching others', etc. Each 'unit' of behaviour should be objective and measurable and agreed with staff and prisoners in advance.
Scoring system.	Staff and prisoners should be made aware of how much each behaviour is worth in terms of tokens. Behaviours are hierarchical, some are more demanding than others. Tokens may be awarded directly or points may be awarded and converted to tokens. Reinforcements should outnumber punishments by a ratio of 4:1 (Gendreau *et al.* 2011).
Train staff.	Prison staff receive full training. Aim is to **standardise** procedures – so all prison staff reward the same behaviours. Keep record of what tokens awarded so progress of individual prisoners can be assessed.

One strength of behaviour modification is research support.

Hobbs and Holt (1976) studied young offenders, those taking part in a token economy programme showed more positive behaviours.

Field *et al.* (2004) found some young offenders didn't respond but did if rewards were more immediate, frequent and positive.

This suggests that token economy systems do work.

Counterpoint

Bassett and Blanchard (1977) found any benefits were lost if staff applied the techniques inconsistently due to lack of training or because of high staff turnover (an issue in many UK prisons).

This suggests that behaviour modification schemes may not be as straightforward to implement as they first appear.

Behaviour modification has been accused of being dehumanising and manipulative. Tell you what, we'll call it quits if you give me that chocolate.

Another strength of behaviour modification is that it is easy to implement.

Behaviour modification does not need a specialist professional involved, whereas this is true for other forms of treatment (e.g. anger management, next spread).

Token economy systems can be designed and implemented by virtually anyone. They are cost-effective and easy to follow once methods have been established.

This suggests that behaviour modification techniques can be established in most prisons and accessed by most prisoners.

Revision BOOSTER

There are some technical terms here (e.g. 'secondary reinforcer' and 'operationalise'). Also look out for such technical terms – using them correctly shows you have a good grasp of the topic. It also shows that you understand the psychological principles on which it is based – this is the stuff excellent answers are made of.

One limitation is that there is little rehabilitative value.

Some treatments (e.g. anger management) are longer lasting because they involve understanding causes of, and taking responsibility for, own behaviour.

In contrast, offenders can play along with a token economy system to access rewards, but this produces little change in their overall character.

This may explain why, once the token economy is discontinued, an offender may quickly regress back to their former behaviour.

Download suggested answers to the Knowledge Check questions from tinyurl.com/yd3ezhkb

Evaluation extra: Ethical issues.

Behaviour modification has been associated with decreased conflict, more successful management of prisoners and reduced stress for prison staff in a potentially hostile environment.

However, critics describe behaviour modification as manipulative and dehumanising (Moya and Achtenberg 1974). Human rights campaigners argue that withdrawal of 'privileges' is unethical.

This suggests that the question of whether behaviour modification is successful may depend on whose perspective – prison staff or prisoners.

Knowledge Check

1. In relation to dealing with offending behaviour, explain what is meant by 'behaviour modification in custody'.
   (2 marks)

2. Describe how behaviour modification can be used to deal with offending behaviour. *(6 marks)*

3. Evaluate behaviour modification in custody as a way of dealing with offending behaviour. *(6 marks)*

4. Describe **and** evaluate **two** ways of dealing with offending behaviour. *(16 marks)*

Spec spotlight

Dealing with offending behaviour: anger management.

Someone else bitterly regretting their rash choice of 'alternative' wallpaper (see page 180).

Apply it

A school decides that a good way to tackle bullying is to run an anger management programme. Clarissa is one of the first to benefit. She explains how frustrated she feels most of the time. She can feel anger welling up inside whenever she believes people are not respecting her. She sees people being disrespectful all the time, and thinks of it as a challenge that she should confront. This is when she lashes out – because she feels threatened. Being aggressive makes her believe she is doing something about the situation.

Describe the stages Clarissa will go through in the anger management programme and how each one would address her problems.

Anger management with offenders

Cognitive factors trigger arousal (aggression).	Novaco (1975) suggests that **cognitive** factors trigger the emotional arousal that comes before aggressive acts.
	In some people, anger is quick to surface in situations they perceive to be threatening or anxiety-inducing.
	Becoming angry is then reinforced by the individual's feeling of control in that situation.
CBT. Recognise triggers, learn skills.	Anger management programmes are a form of **cognitive behaviour therapy (CBT)**.
	An individual is taught to:
	• Recognise the *cognitive* factors that trigger their anger and loss of control.
	• Develop *behavioural* techniques that bring about conflict resolution without the need for violence.
Stage 1: *Cognitive preparation.* Reflect on the past.	This stage requires the offender to reflect on past experience – they learn to identify triggers to anger and the ways their interpretation of events may be irrational.
	For instance, the offender may interpret someone looking at them as confrontation. In redefining the situation as non-threatening, the therapist is attempting to break what may be an automatic response for the offender.
Stage 2: *Skills acquisition.* Techniques to deal with anger.	Offenders are introduced to a range of techniques and skills to help them deal with anger-provoking situations.
	Techniques may be:
	• Cognitive – positive self-talk to promote calmness.
	• Behavioural – assertiveness training to communicate more effectively (becomes automatic if practised).
	• Physiological – methods of relaxation and/or meditation.
Stage 3: *Application practice.* Role play.	Offenders are given the opportunity to practise their skills in a carefully monitored environment.
	For example, role play between the offender and therapist may involve re-enacting scenarios that led to anger and violence in the past.
	If the offender deals successfully with the role play this is given positive reinforcement by the therapist.
Positive outcomes with young offenders.	Keen *et al.* (2000) studied the progress of young offenders between 17 and 21 who took part in an anger management programme – eight two-hour sessions.
	Initially there were difficulties with the offenders forgetting their diaries and not taking it seriously.
	By the end offenders generally reported increased awareness of their anger and capacity for self-control.

One strength is that benefits outlast behaviour modification.

Unlike behaviour modification, anger management tackles the causes of offending, i.e. the cognitive processes that trigger anger, and ultimately, offending behaviour.

This may give offenders new insight into the cause of their criminality, allowing them to self-discover ways of managing themselves outside of prison.

This suggests that anger management is more likely than behaviour modification to lead to permanent behavioural change.

Counterpoint

However, whilst anger management may have an effect on offenders in the short term, it may not help cope with triggers in real-world situations (Blackburn 1993).

This suggests that, in the end, anger management may not reduce reoffending.

Jamie had every right to be angry, someone had just stolen his Subway sandwich.

One limitation is that success depends on individual factors.

Howells *et al.* (2005) found that participation in an anger management programme had little overall impact when compared to a **control group** who received no treatment.

However, progress was made with offenders who showed intense levels of anger before the programme and offenders who were motivated to change ('treatment readiness').

This suggests that anger management may only benefit offenders who fit a certain profile.

Another limitation is that anger management is expensive.

Anger management programmes require highly-trained specialists who are used to dealing with violent offenders. Many prisons may not have the resources.

In addition, change takes time and commitment, and this is ultimately likely to add to the expense of delivering effective programmes.

This suggests that effective anger management programmes are probably not going to work in most prisons.

Evaluation extra: Anger and offending.

The anger management approach assumes that anger is an important antecedent to offending in that it produces the emotional state necessary to commit crime.

However, Loza and Loza-Fanous (1999) found no differences in levels of anger between offenders classed as violent and those classed as non-violent.

This suggests that, if anger is not a feature of many crimes, such programmes may be unnecessary and unhelpful when it comes to tackling crime.

Revision BOOSTER

You can use a mnemonic to help you remember the three stages of anger management: **C**alm **P**eople **S**hould **A**void **A**ngry **P**eople (**C**ognitive **P**reparation, **S**kills **A**cquisition, **A**pplication **P**ractice).

It's a really good idea to get into the habit of building mnemonics into your revision.

Knowledge Check

1. Explain the difference between anger management and behaviour modification in custody as ways of dealing with offending behaviour. *(4 marks)*

2. Outline **two** ways of dealing with offending behaviour. *(6 marks)*

3. Briefly evaluate anger management as a way of dealing with offending behaviour. *(4 marks)*

4. Discuss anger management as a way of dealing with offending behaviour. *(16 marks)*

Dealing with offending behaviour: Restorative justice

Spec spotlight

Dealing with offending behaviour: restorative justice programmes.

RJ approaches prefer to use the term 'survivor' rather than 'victim'.

Mrs Forbes had marked some short essays in her time but this one took the biscuit!

Apply it

Drew was robbed in the street and suffered some injuries that had to be treated in hospital. The police eventually caught the offender, who was tried and convicted and is serving a prison sentence. Drew has been asked to participate in a restorative justice programme with his attacker. Drew doesn't know what this means or what would be involved.

What would you tell Drew about the process of restorative justice and what he might experience?

Restorative justice programmes

Individual versus state.	Historically, a person convicted of a criminal offence would have been regarded as committing a crime against the state.
	In contrast restorative justice (RJ) programmes switch the emphasis from the need of the state (to enforce the law) to the needs of the survivor (to feel compensated in some way and come to terms with the crime).
A healing process.	RJ is less about 'retribution' – that is, punishing the offender.
	More about 'reparation' – repairing the harm caused.
	RJ seeks to focus on two things:
	• The survivor (victim) of the crime and their recovery.
	• The offender and their recovery/rehabilitation process.
Key features of RJ.	RJ programmes can be quite diverse but most share key features:
	• Trained mediator supervises the meeting.
	• Non-courtroom setting where offender voluntarily meets with survivor(s).
	• Face-to-face meeting or remotely via video link.
	• Survivor explains how the incident affected them, so offender can understand effects.
	• Active rather than passive involvement of all parties.
	• Focus on positive outcomes for both survivors and offenders.
	• Other relevant community members may be involved and explain consequences (e.g. neighbours, friends, family members).
Sentencing.	RJ may occur pre-trial and may affect sentencing.
	It may be given as an alternative to prison (especially if the offender is young).
	RJ could occur while in prison as an incentive to reduce the length of a sentence.
Restitution.	Restitution is a monetary payment by the offender to the survivor for harm from the offence.
	• Financial – offender pays.
	• Practical – offender does repair themselves.
	• Emotional – support healing process by helping to rebuild the survivor's confidence.
The RJC.	Restorative Justice Council (RJC) sets and monitors standards, and supports survivors and specialists in the field.
	The RJC promotes the use of RJ principles as a general way to prevent and manage conflict e.g. in schools, workplaces and communities.

One strength of RJ is that it supports needs of survivors.

The Restorative Justice Council (Shapland *et al.* 2008) reported the results of a 7-year project. 85% of survivors said they were satisfied with the process.

78% would recommend it, about 60% said the process made them feel better about the incident, 2% said it made them feel worse.

This suggests that restorative justice is a worthwhile experience and helps survivors of crime cope with the aftermath of the incident.

Counterpoint

RJ programmes are not always as survivor-focused as reported in satisfaction surveys. Survivors of crime may be used to help rehabilitate offenders, not the other way round (Wood and Suzuki 2016).

This suggests that the needs of the survivor may be seen as secondary to the need to rehabilitate offenders.

STOP DOMESTIC VIOLENCE

In all seriousness.

Another strength is that RJ leads to a decrease in offending.

In a **meta-analysis** Strang *et al.* (2013) found offenders who experienced RJ were less likely to reoffend – though reduction was larger in cases of violent crime than property crime.

Bain (2012) found lowered recidivism with adult offenders who had one-to-one contact with their survivor (rather than community contact).

This suggests that RJ has a positive impact on reoffending, maybe more so for some types of offence than others and some approaches.

Revision BOOSTER

When you write critical points you should explain them thoroughly, like we've done here. Start with a statement of your point (P). Give some further explanation (E) using examples and/or evidence (E). If you can, end your criticism with a link (L) back to the point you were making or a conclusion (=PEEL). Such elaborated critical points should be about 50–60 words.

One limitation is that offenders may abuse the system.

The success of RJ hinges on an offender genuinely feeling regret for their actions.

Van Gijseghem (2003) suggests that offenders may use restorative justice to avoid punishment, play down their faults or even take pride in their relationship with the survivor.

This would explain why not all offenders ultimately benefit from restorative justice and go on to reoffend.

Knowledge Check

1. Explain the difference between restorative justice and anger management as ways of dealing with offending behaviour. *(4 marks)*

2. Describe how restorative justice can be used as a way of dealing with offending behaviour. *(6 marks)*

3. Evaluate restorative justice as a way of dealing with offending behaviour. *(10 marks)*

4. Discuss restorative justice **and one other** way of dealing with offending behaviour. *(16 marks)*

Evaluation extra: Domestic violence.

In domestic violence cases, the power imbalance between abuser and abused puts pressure on survivors to go along with their partner's suggestions during mediation.

However, RJ in domestic violence cases has produced positive results for survivors, e.g. where a couple wishes to stay together to address the harm caused (Sen *et al.* 2018).

This suggests that for some types of crime the offender may manipulate the situation so great care is needed.

Describing addiction

Spec spotlight

Describing addiction: physical and psychological dependence, tolerance and withdrawal syndrome.

Go on, you know you want one... Saying no to a cigarette (or three) is not easy when you are addicted.

Apply it

Jess plays online poker on most days. She enjoys the excitement and it distracts her from her day-to-day troubles. But over the past few weeks Jess has been playing more often and she doesn't get the same thrill out if it that she used to. She also gets very anxious and angry when she can't get online or something else stops her from playing.

Explain Jess's behaviour in terms of the concepts on these pages.

Knowledge Check

1. Explain what is meant by 'addiction'. Use an example in your answer. *(3 marks)*
2. In terms of addiction, explain the difference between physical and psychological dependence. *(4 marks)*
3. In relation to addiction, explain what is meant by 'tolerance' **and** 'withdrawal syndrome'. *(2 marks + 2 marks)*

Chapter 13: Addiction

Physical and psychological dependence

Physical dependence. Results in withdrawal syndrome.	Physical dependence occurs when a withdrawal syndrome is produced by stopping.
	It's only possible to establish that someone is physically dependent on a substance (e.g. a drug) when:
	• They abstain from it (or reduce intake).
	• Withdrawal symptoms are apparent.
Psychological dependence. Compulsion to continue.	Psychological dependence refers to the compulsion to experience the effects of a substance for:
	• An increase in pleasure, or
	• A reduction of discomfort.
	Psychological dependence leads to the substance/behaviour becoming a habit, despite the harmful consequences.

Tolerance

Greater doses needed for same effect.	Tolerance occurs when an individual's response to a substance is reduced.
	This means they need greater doses to produce the same effect on behaviour.
	Tolerance is caused by repeated exposure to a substance.
Behavioural tolerance and *cross-tolerance.*	Behavioural tolerance – individual learns through experience to adjust their behaviour to compensate for the effects of a substance, e.g. a person addicted to alcohol walks more slowly when they are drunk to avoid falling over.
	Cross-tolerance – developing tolerance to one substance can reduce sensitivity to another type, e.g. people who have developed a tolerance to the sleep-inducing effects of alcohol need higher doses of anaesthetic in surgery.

Withdrawal syndrome

Symptoms associated with abstaining or reducing use.	Symptoms are usually the opposite of ones created by the substance (e.g. withdrawal of nicotine leads to irritability, anxiety).
	Withdrawal indicates a physical dependence on the substance has developed, symptoms are experienced whenever the substance is not available.
	Motivation for taking the substance is partly to avoid these symptoms.
Withdrawal has two phases.	1. *Acute withdrawal phase* within hours and features intense cravings reflecting dependence.
	2. *Prolonged withdrawal phase* over months/years, high sensitivity to cues associated with substance (e.g. locations).

AO1
Description

AO3
Evaluation

Introducing risk factors

229

Introduction to risk factors

1. Genetic vulnerability.	People inherit a predisposition ('vulnerability') to dependence. Genes may determine neurotransmitter activity (e.g. **dopamine**), which affects behaviours (e.g. impulsivity).
2. Stress.	Includes present and past events (e.g. trauma in childhood). People under stress may use substances to self-medicate (i.e. experience pleasure or avoid pain).
3. Personality.	Individual traits (e.g. hostility and neuroticism) may increase risk of addiction. But there is probably no such thing as an 'addictive personality'.
4. Family influences.	Increased risk of addiction from living in a family who use addictive substances and/or have positive attitudes about addictions.
5. Peers.	As children get older, peer relationships become a more important risk factor than family. Peers' attitudes towards substance abuse are influential even when they have not used such substances themselves.

Spec spotlight

Risk factors in the development of addiction, including genetic vulnerability, stress, personality, family influences and peers.

Risk factor

Anything that increases chances that someone will take an addictive substance (or engage in addictive behaviour), or increase their use.

On the next spread we look at each of these five risk factors in more detail.

Surely the other Scrabble players would realise that Hector had given himself two extra tiles.

Proximate means now. Ultimate means the real reason.

Evaluation

One limitation of individual factors is this ignores the effect of interactions.

No single risk factor is causal, combinations matter more. Mayes and Suchman (2006) argue different combinations partly determine nature and severity of addiction.

Also, 'risk' factors can be protective. Personality traits, genetic characteristics, family/peer influences can reduce addiction risk (e.g. parental monitoring, lower impulsivity).

Therefore a more realistic view of risk is to think in terms of multiple 'pathways' to addiction which include different combinations interacting and some having a positive effect.

One strength of understanding risk factors is the link to genetic influence.

Most factors are *proximate* (immediate influence), e.g. high stress and novelty-seeking directly increase risk. But these (and other) factors are partly genetic.

To fully understand risk factors we have to look further back in the chain of influences to the *ultimate* risk factor, which is often genetic.

Therefore, genetic vulnerability may be the most significant risk factor because it has the ultimate influence on the others.

Knowledge Check

1. Explain what is meant by 'risk factors' in relation to the development of addiction. *(2 marks)*
2. Briefly explain how **one** risk factor may be involved in the development of addiction. *(2 marks)*
3. Outline **and** evaluate genetic vulnerability as a risk factor in the development of addiction. (You will need to draw on some information from the next spread to answer this question.) *(8 marks)*

Risk factors in the development of addiction

Spec spotlight

Risk factors in the development of addiction, including genetic vulnerability, stress, personality, family influences and peers.

Apply it

Damien experienced considerable trauma during his upbringing. His parents gave him a lot of independence to set his own rules about his behaviour. Damien's family moved to a different part of the country and he joined a college where he met a group of people who seemed interesting and exciting. They appeared to be able to get hold of alcohol whenever they wanted and drank a lot.

Use your knowledge of risk factors in the development of addiction to explain Damien's vulnerability to developing an addiction.

Impulsivity – a key component of APD.

Revision BOOSTER

Genetic vulnerability, stress, personality, family influences and peers are all named key words on the specification for this topic. You can be asked short-answer questions on any one of them but it's very unlikely you'll get an essay question on one of these alone. Answering a general question on 'risk factors' means you can describe any of the factors here – but for 6 marks just two or three of them is probably enough. Remember – less is more!

Risk factors in the development of addiction

Genetic vulnerability. Low D2 receptors CYP2A6 enzyme	Two mechanisms can explain genetic vulnerability as a risk factor: • **Dopamine** activity – low numbers of D2 receptors inherited, people compensate by engaging in addictive behaviour. • Nicotine metabolised by CYP2A6 enzyme – people are *less* likely to smoke if enzyme is *not* fully functioning because nicotine levels are higher.
Stress. Adverse childhood experiences (ACEs).	Early experiences of severe stress (ACEs) damage the young brain in a sensitive period of development, creates vulnerability to later stress. Stress in adolescence triggers this vulnerability, may lead to self-medication with certain substances (Andersen and Teicher 2008).
Personality. Strong link to APD.	There is no generally addictive personality but most people with **antisocial personality disorder** (**APD**) are also addicted substance abusers. APD is a causal risk factor because having APD means that a person breaks social norms, is impulsive, may behave criminally and seeks to satisfy their own desires, so it is almost inevitable that someone with APD will try addictive substances (Robins 1998).
Family influences. Exposure and perceived parental monitoring.	Adolescents start using alcohol in families where it is an everyday feature. Livingston *et al.* (2010) found children allowed to drink alcohol at home in their final school year were more likely to drink excessively at college the next year. Adolescents drink excessively when they *believe* their parents have no interest in monitoring their behaviour.
Peers. Attitudes, opportunities and overestimation.	O'Connell *et al.* (2009) suggest there are three major elements to peer influence for alcohol addiction: • Attitudes about drinking are influenced by associating with peers who use alcohol. • Peers provide more opportunities to use alcohol. • Individuals overestimate how much their peers are drinking and attempt to keep up with the perceived norm.

One strength is that there is research support for genetic vulnerability.

Kendler *et al.* (2012) looked at adults who had been adopted-away as children. At least one biological parent had an addiction.

These children later, when adults, had a significantly greater risk of developing an addiction compared to adopted-away adults with no addicted biological parent.

This supports the role of genetic vulnerability as an important risk factor, and it is supported by other research (e.g. twin studies).

One limitation of stress as a risk factor is the issue of causation.

There is a strong positive **correlation** between stress and addiction, but this does not mean stress is the risk factor – it depends which develops first.

Some people become addicted without previous life stressors, but then addiction creates stress due to negative effects of the lifestyle.

Therefore we cannot conclude stress is a significant risk factor based on correlational studies alone.

Stress is correlated with, but not necessarily the cause of, addiction.

Another strength is support for the APD/addiction link.

APD and alcohol dependence are co-morbid (often occur together), but the nature of the link has been questioned – does APD cause addiction?

Bahlmann *et al.* (2002) found that in 18 alcohol-dependent people with diagnosed APD, the APD developed on average four years before the addiction.

This finding suggests that APD is indeed a personality-related risk factor for alcohol addiction.

Revision BOOSTER

It really pays to practise writing 16-mark essays with your book shut and timing yourself – about 20 minutes for a 16-mark essay. Don't think it will magically come right on the day – test yourself.

A further strength is research support for family influences.

Madras *et al.* (2019) found a strong positive correlation between parents' use of cannabis and their adolescent children's use of cannabis and other addictive substances.

Perhaps adolescents observe their parents' use and model their behaviour. They may also infer parents approve of substance abuse generally, so use other substances.

This supports the view that parental substance abuse is a potential risk factor for wider addiction in adolescent offspring.

Knowledge Check

1. Explain how both family influences **and** peers can be risk factors in the development of addiction.
   (6 marks)

2. With reference to addiction, explain what is meant by 'genetic vulnerability'. *(3 marks)*

3. Briefly evaluate genetic vulnerability **and** stress as risk factors in the development of addiction. *(6 marks)*

4. Tim comes from a family of alcohol addicts. Kim believes she is the 'sort of person' who gambles. Jim smokes because he is having a tough time.

   With reference to these experiences, discuss risk factors in the development of addiction. *(16 marks)*

A final strength is real-world application of peer evidence.

Social norms marketing advertising aims to change mistaken beliefs about how much peers drink, using mass media to give messages and statistics.

E.g. beer mats and posters in a Student Union bar with messages such as 'Students overestimate what others drink by 44%', gives accurate picture.

This means that identification of risk factors can suggest ways to reduce the influence of such factors.

Explanations for nicotine addiction: Brain neurochemistry

Spec spotlight

Explanations for nicotine addiction: brain neurochemistry, including the role of dopamine.

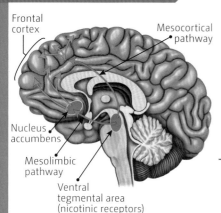

Frontal cortex
Mesocortical pathway
Nucleus accumbens
Mesolimbic pathway
Ventral tegmental area (nicotinic receptors)

The desensitisation hypothesis

Nicotine stimulates nicotinic receptors primarily located in the ventral tegmental area (VTA) of the brain. This causes dopamine to be transmitted along the mesolimbic and mesocortical pathways to the nucleus accumbens and the frontal cortex (green arrows). Dopamine is then released into the frontal cortex (blue arrows) creating rewarding effects.

Addiction is then explained by the nicotine regulation model.

Apply it

Karen runs a 'quit smoking' group. She has found that most people are well aware of the health risks of smoking, but they carry on as if they cannot help it. Almost all of her clients particularly enjoy the first cigarette of the day each morning. They also report needing to smoke more and more to get the same effects.

Using your knowledge of brain neurochemistry, explain Karen's clients' experiences of nicotine addiction.

The role of dopamine

Key role of *dopamine.*	Dani and Heinemann (1996) focused on **dopamine** in their *desensitisation hypothesis* of nicotine addiction.
nAChRs and dopamine.	Acetylcholine (ACh) is a key neurotransmitter in the CNS so there are ACh receptors on the surfaces of many neurons.
Desensitised and downregulated.	One special subtype is the *nicotinic acetylcholine receptor* (nAChR), activated by ACh or nicotine. When activated by nicotine: • nAChRs are stimulated and transmit dopamine. • They then immediately shut down and temporarily cannot respond to neurotransmitters (nAChRs are *desensitised*, also *downregulated* because fewer active nAChRs are available).
Operant conditioning. Creating a pleasurable effect.	nAChRs are concentrated in the *ventral tegmental area* (VTA). When stimulated by nicotine, dopamine is transmitted along two pathways: • *Mesolimbic pathway* to the nucleus accumbens, triggers dopamine to be released into the frontal cortex. • *Mesocortical pathway* to release dopamine directly into the frontal cortex. Both are part of the dopamine reward system – when activated by nicotine creates pleasurable effects (mild euphoria, increased alertness, less anxiety). These effects become associated with smoking through **operant conditioning** (see next spread).
Withdrawal. Resensitised and upregulated.	When not smoking (e.g. overnight) nicotine disappears from the body and nAChRs become functional again – *resensitised* and *upregulated* (more available). nAChRs are now overstimulated by ACh (no nicotine for them to bind with) and at their most sensitive – the first cigarette of the day is best because it strongly activates the dopamine reward system.
Dependence.	Unpleasant withdrawal symptoms are avoided by having another cigarette. But this means there is a constant cycle of daytime downregulation and night-time upregulation and this creates long-term desensitisation of nAChRs (i.e. dependence).
Tolerance.	Continuous exposure to nicotine causes permanent changes to brain neurochemistry (fewer active nAChRs). Tolerance develops because the smoker needs more nicotine for the same effects.

One strength of dopamine explanations is indirect support.

McEvoy *et al.* (1995) found that smoking increased in people with schizophrenia who were taking the dopamine antagonist Haloperidol.

This drug reduces dopamine transmission, so increasing smoking was self-medication using nicotine to increase their depleted dopamine levels.

This supports the view that dopamine has a key role in the neurochemistry of nicotine addiction.

Counterpoint

However, although dopamine is central other neurochemical systems are involved, very complex picture e.g. other neurotransmitters (**GABA**) and endogenous opioids (endorphins) (Watkins *et al.* 2000).

Therefore, the neurochemistry of nicotine addiction cannot be fully understood if looking at only dopamine.

Not the recommended place to stick a nicotine patch.

Another strength is that neurochemistry leads to new treatments.

These include nicotine replacement therapy (NRT), delivering a controlled dose of nicotine that binds with nAChRs and mimics effects of nicotine from cigarette smoke.

This includes dopamine release, so NRT satisfies cravings and a user can reduce withdrawal symptoms by gradually reducing their nicotine dose.

Therefore, a greater understanding of neurochemistry has led to an effective treatment for nicotine addiction.

One limitation is the neurochemical explanation doesn't explain withdrawal.

The explanation claims withdrawal symptoms depend mainly on amount of nicotine in the blood. But these factors are not strongly **correlated**.

Gilbert (1995) argues that withdrawal depends more on environment and personality, e.g. neurotic people experience worse withdrawal symptoms than emotionally stable people.

Therefore withdrawal effects can be explained in other ways without reference to amounts of nicotine.

Evaluation extra: Determinism.

The neurochemical explanation is biologically **determinist**. Chemical events in the brain are beyond our control, including withdrawal. So nicotine addiction is inevitable in someone who starts smoking.

However, addiction may not be inevitable because some people smoke without becoming dependent (Shiffman and Paty 2006), and some find it easier because of personality factors (see Gilbert above).

This suggests that it is inevitable for many people (because of the neurochemistry of nicotine or because of personality) but some people override this.

Revision BOOSTER

Some of the biological terms here are really technical. Don't be intimidated by them, and don't avoid them. Learn them by keeping it simple at first. Use cue cards and quick quizzes to grasp the basics. What is ACh? What is a nicotinic receptor? Only when you feel at home with the terms and concepts are you ready to revise in more detail and depth.

Knowledge Check

1. In relation to nicotine addiction, explain what is meant by 'brain neurochemistry'. *(2 marks)*

2. Outline the role of dopamine in nicotine addiction. *(6 marks)*

3. Evaluate **one** explanation for nicotine addiction. *(6 marks)*

4. Many smokers talk about the cravings they have for nicotine and the pleasure they get out of smoking.

   With reference to these experiences, discuss brain neurochemistry as an explanation for nicotine addiction. *(16 marks)*

Explanations for nicotine addiction: Learning theory

Spec spotlight

Explanations for nicotine addiction: learning theory as applied to smoking behaviour, including reference to cue reactivity.

Lighters can be secondary reinforcers.

Apply it

Janice socialises with a group of friends who all smoke, and she herself has smoked since she was a teenager. Janice and her friends all say they would love to give up, but the hardest part is when they go out together. Seeing her friends in the bar or restaurant with drinks or food seems to trigger her desire for a cigarette.

Use your knowledge of learning theory to explain Janice's nicotine addiction.

Classical conditioning

UCS unconditioned stimulus
UCR unconditioned response
NS   neutral stimulus
CS   conditioned stimulus
CR   conditioned response

Before conditioning:
UCS produces UCR

During conditioning:
NS associated with UCS and becomes CS

After conditioning:
CS produces CR

Chapter 13: Addiction

Operant conditioning

Dopamine system.	Nicotine stimulates the release of **dopamine** in the mesolimbic pathway, part of the dopamine reward system.
Positive reinforcement. Mild euphoria.	If the consequence of a behaviour is rewarding to an individual, then that behaviour is more likely to occur again. Smoking (nicotine) creates feelings of mild euphoria which positively reinforce the smoking behaviour. This explains why people start smoking.
Negative reinforcement. Avoid withdrawal symptoms.	Cessation of nicotine use can lead to an acute withdrawal syndrome including such symptoms as disturbed sleep, agitation, poor concentration and mood disturbances. Therefore addiction is maintained because smoking another cigarette is negatively reinforcing – it stops the unpleasant stimulus (withdrawal symptoms).

The role of cue reactivity

Primary reinforcer. Smoking is intrinsically rewarding.	Smoking is intrinsically rewarding (not learned). It doesn't have to be learned because of the biologically-determined effects of nicotine on the dopamine reward system. The pleasure created by nicotine reinforces the behaviour so an individual is more likely to smoke again.
Secondary reinforcers. Include pubs, friends, lighters, smells, etc.	Any other stimuli present at the same time as (or just before) smoking (and intake of nicotine) become associated with the pleasurable effect of smoking (i.e. **classical conditioning** has taken place). These stimuli become secondary reinforcers (rewarding in their own right). Certain environments (e.g. pubs) and certain people or objects (e.g. a lighter) create a sense of anticipation and pleasure and thus become secondary reinforcers. Even the seemingly harsh feeling of smoke hitting the back of the throat can become a secondary reinforcer because it is associated with the pleasurable impact of nicotine.
Cue reactivity. Cravings are triggered by cues related to smoking.	The secondary reinforcers also act as cues, because their presence produces a similar response to nicotine itself. This is called cue reactivity and is indicated by three main elements: 1. Self-reported desire to smoke. 2. Physiological signs of reactivity to a cue (e.g. heart rate). 3. Objective behavioural indicators when cue is present (e.g. how many 'draws' are taken on the cigarette).

One strength is support for the learning approach from animal studies.

Non-human animal studies confirm the role of **operant conditioning** in nicotine addiction, e.g. Levin et al.'s (2010) study of rats who could lick two water spouts.

Licking one triggered an intravenous nicotine dose (the other had no effect). The rats licked the nicotine-linked spout significantly more often and licking increased over 24 sessions.

This suggests that the effects of nicotine positively reinforce self-administration in rats, implying a similar mechanism in humans.

Levin et al.'s rats self-administered nicotine through water spouts.

Another strength is support for cue reactivity from human research.

Carter and Tiffany (1999) did a **meta-analysis** of 41 studies of cue reactivity. Studies presented smokers and non-smokers with images of smoking-related cues (e.g. lighters).

Dependent smokers reacted with increased physiological arousal (e.g. heart rate) and reported strong cravings to smoke even with no nicotine present.

This shows that dependent smokers learn secondary associations between smoking-related stimuli and pleasurable effects of smoking.

A further strength is there are real-world applications.

Aversion therapy (based on classical conditioning) requires people to associate the pleasant effects of smoking with an aversive stimulus (e.g. electric shock).

Smith (1988) found that, after one year, 52% of people using aversion were still abstaining (compared with 20–25% who just decide to stop smoking).

Therefore treatments based on learning theory can save NHS resources, improve health and ultimately save lives.

Counterpoint

There was no **control/placebo** group and the comparison made was not a valid measure of effectiveness. The benefits of aversion therapy are also short-lived (Hajek and Stead 2001).

This suggests that counterconditioning may not be an effective method of addiction treatment.

Evaluation extra: Animal research.

We use non-human animals in addiction research because conditioning mechanisms are similar to those in humans and there are ethical reasons why animals are preferable.

However, nicotine addiction is more complex in humans who think about reinforcers in a way rats do not (**cognitive** factors) and there are ethical reasons not to use animals.

Therefore, animal studies can help us understand learning processes in addiction but findings must be treated cautiously because human addiction is more complex.

Revision BOOSTER

At A level you can be required to write 16-mark essays. This is split between AO1 and AO3 in a ratio of 6:10. Therefore you're aiming to write 10 marks' worth of evaluation (AO3), which can usually be provided by three or four evaluative points. But these must be thorough (that is, well-elaborated) and ideally show some evidence of 'discussion' (e.g. considering contrasting views).

Knowledge Check

1. In relation to nicotine addiction, explain what is meant by 'cue reactivity'.
   (2 marks)

2. Outline learning theory as applied to smoking behaviour. *(6 marks)*

3. Explain **two** criticisms of learning theory as applied to smoking behaviour. *(6 marks)*

4. Describe **and** evaluate **two** learning theory explanations for nicotine addiction.
   (16 marks)

Explanations for gambling addiction: Learning theory

Spec spotlight

Explanations for gambling addiction: learning theory as applied to gambling, including reference to partial and variable reinforcement.

Watching others winning may be the starting point of an addiction.

Apply it

Tina started playing the National Lottery a few months ago. She won £10 on her third go. Before long she was playing every week and won another £50 after five weeks. It took another 11 weeks before she won anything else, and since then... nothing more. But Tina knows that you have to be 'in it to win it', so she is going to carry on playing the Lottery each week because she knows it's just a matter of time before she wins again.

Using your knowledge of learning explanations, explain Tina's gambling behaviour.

Revision BOOSTER

Always think 'less is more' – writing about fewer things gives you the opportunity to demonstrate your detailed understanding. For 6 AO1 marks we have given you six points but you may need to do fewer to ensure sufficient detail.

Learning theory of gambling addiction

Vicarious reinforcement can be the start of an addiction.	The first component of the learning theory of gambling addiction is through seeing others being rewarded for gambling (e.g. seeing someone else's pleasure when gambling and seeing them sometimes winning money). Vicarious reinforcement can also be experienced through media reports of big wins (e.g. on the National Lottery).
Direct reinforcement can be positive or negative.	The next step is that a person receives direct reinforcement. Positive reinforcement comes from a direct gain (e.g. winning money), and from the 'buzz' that accompanies a gamble (which is exciting). Negative reinforcement occurs because gambling can offer a distraction from aversive stimuli (e.g. the anxieties of everyday life).
Partial reinforcement more effective than continuous.	Skinner's research with rats found that *continuous reinforcement* schedules do not lead to persistent behaviour change. Once the rewards stop, the behaviour quickly disappears (called *extinction*). A partial reinforcement schedule leads to more persistent behaviour change. When only some bets are rewarded there is an unpredictability about which gambles will pay off, which is enough to maintain the gambling.
Variable reinforcement schedule is the most effective.	A variable reinforcement schedule is a partial reinforcement schedule where the intervals between rewards are unpredictable. For example, a slot machine might pay out after an *average* of 8 spins, but not on *every* 8th spin. The first payout might be on the 3rd spin, then the 4th, then the 12th, etc.
Variable reinforcement is very resistant to extinction.	Whilst it takes longer for learning to be established if the reinforcement schedule is variable, once it is established it is more resistant to extinction. The gambler learns that they will not win with every gamble, but they will eventually win if they persist (and then the gambling is reinforced).
Cue reactivity explains how gambling is maintained or reinstated.	Experienced gamblers encounter many secondary reinforcers – things they associate with the exciting arousal of gambling. For example, the atmosphere of the betting shop, the colour of lottery scratch cards, TV horse-racing channels can all cue the arousal that the gambler craves. These low-level reminders are difficult to avoid. These cues can both maintain gambling and cause its reinstatement after a period of abstinence.

One strength is support from research outside the lab situation.

Dickerson (1979) found that high-frequency gamblers in betting shops placed their bets in the last two minutes before a race more often than low-frequency gamblers.

Gamblers find the anticipation exciting regardless of result, dependent gamblers more so. Excitement is rewarding and they delayed betting to prolong it.

This is evidence for the role of positive reinforcement in gambling in a real-world setting rather than in a lab.

Counterpoint

However, gambling behaviour was recorded by one observer, so there was no way to check reliability of observations (no inter-observer reliability).

Therefore, observer bias was not eliminated and the findings of the study may not be valid.

If these bets were very last minute, it is possible they were placed by high-frequency gamblers.

One limitation is learning theory cannot explain some types of gambling.

Learning theory explains addiction to gambling when there is no delay between the bet and the outcome, but not where there is a delay.

In horse racing and most sports betting, the reward (outcome) comes a long time after the behaviour (betting), so conditioning should be less effective.

Therefore, learning theory is limited because it does not provide a general explanation of all gambling addiction.

Revision BOOSTER

Students like to write essays with a beginning, middle and end. It's tempting to 'set the scene' by defining addiction but that won't get you any marks. Focus on the middle. Endings also generally fail to be creditworthy because they are not much more of a summary of what has already been said.

Another strength is learning theory explains why it's hard to stop gambling.

Gambling addiction begins and is maintained through conditioning, an automatic process so a gambler is not even aware they are learning to be addicted.

They are determined to give up but fail again and again – their conscious desire to stop may conflict with conditioning processes that drive their gambling.

Therefore learning theory explains the common everyday experience of most gambling addicts who find it hard to stop gambling.

Evaluation extra: Cycle of addiction.

The gambling addiction cycle is explained by learning theory – initiation by vicarious reinforcement, maintenance by reinforcement schedules and relapse by cue reactivity (Brown 1987).

However, some parts of the cycle are poorly explained, e.g. why many people gamble and experience the same reinforcements but are not addicted. So other factors are involved.

This suggests that the best explanation may involve other concepts beyond just learning theory.

Knowledge Check

1. In terms of learning theory as applied to gambling, explain the difference between partial and variable reinforcement.
   (4 marks)

2. Outline learning theory as applied to gambling. Refer to partial **and** variable reinforcement in your answer.
   (6 marks)

3. Briefly evaluate **one** explanation for gambling.
   (4 marks)

4. Gamblers often report that the enjoyment they get from their addiction comes from the environment in which they gamble, such as the noises and flashing lights of slot machine arcades.

   With reference to this experience, outline **and** evaluate learning theory as applied to gambling. *(16 marks)*

Explanations for gambling addiction: Cognitive theory

Spec spotlight

Explanations for gambling addiction: cognitive theory as applied to gambling, including reference to cognitive bias.

Gambling addicts often believe they are especially lucky.

Apply it

Josh has played poker just about every day for several years. He has won some money, but lost a lot more. He has 'noticed' that he is more likely to win (he thinks) when he wears his lucky underpants. Also, as long as the cards are dealt in just the 'right' way, Josh's current losing streak is bound to come to an end. His next win is just around the corner.

How can cognitive biases explain Josh's gambling behaviour?

Revision BOOSTER

Some description (AO1) questions say 'Describe/explain what research has shown about ...'. In answering such questions you can describe the results of a specific study (such as Griffiths) or describe the more theoretical findings which come from research (e.g. self-efficacy can explain relapse because of the self-fulfilling prophecy).

Cognitive theory of gambling addiction

Expectations. Initiation of gambling.	We all have expectations about the future benefits and costs of our behaviour. People start gambling because they expect benefits to outweigh costs.
	Some people may have unrealistic expectations about how gambling will help them cope with emotions (e.g. provide excitement and alleviate stress).
	Distorted expectations may lead to addiction.
Cognitive biases. Maintenance of gambling.	Gamblers continue to gamble (and progress to addiction) because of their mistaken beliefs about chance and luck (**cognitive** biases).
	Biases influence how gamblers think about their behaviour, what they do/do not pay attention to, and what they remember/forget.
Four different categories of cognitive bias.	Rickwood *et al.* (2010) categorised biases thus: 1. Skill and judgement – gambling addicts have an illusion of control and overestimate their skill against chance. 2. Personal traits/ritual behaviours – addicts believe they are especially lucky or engage in superstitious behaviour. 3. Selective recall – gamblers remember their wins but ignore/forget their losses. 4. Faulty perceptions – gamblers have distorted views of chance (e.g. belief that a losing streak cannot last).
Self-efficacy. Explains relapse after abstaining.	**Self-efficacy** refers to the expectations we have about our ability to achieve a desired outcome.
	A person may have a biased belief that they are not capable of abstaining permanently.
	Self-fulfilling prophecy – they expect to relapse, they do so ('I told you I couldn't stop'), this reinforces their biased belief.

Griffiths (1994) Cognitive biases

PROCEDURE

The study used the 'thinking aloud' method (a form of introspection) to compare cognitive processes of regular slot machine gamblers and occasional users.

Content analysis was used to classify their utterances into rational or irrational.

Interviews were also used to explore participants' perceptions of the skill required to win.

FINDINGS AND CONCLUSIONS

Regular gamblers made almost six times as many irrational verbalisations (e.g. 'The machine likes me') compared to occasional gamblers (14% vs. 2.5%).

Regular gamblers were also prone to *illusion of control* (e.g. 'I'm going to bluff this machine') and overestimated the skill required to win.

One strength is support for the role of cognitive biases.

Michalczuk *et al.* (2011) compared 30 addicted gamblers with a **control group**. The gamblers had more gambling-related cognitive biases (e.g. illusions of control).

Gamblers were also more impulsive and more likely to prefer immediate rewards, even if rewards were smaller than rewards they could gain by waiting.

These findings support the view that there is a strong cognitive component to gambling addiction.

Feeling you can control the dice – a form of cognitive distortion.

Counterpoint

The study above measured cognitive biases using a questionnaire but it is unclear what high scores mean – could mean a gambler has frequent biased cognitions (which was the conclusion) but could reflect a gambler's tendency to use their beliefs to justify their behaviour and their thinking wasn't biased at all.

Therefore, the findings of the study may not reflect a gambler's actual beliefs about gambling.

RED	YELLOW	**GREEN**
ORANGE	BLUE	**GREEN**
YELLOW	BLUE	RED
ORANGE	RED	GREEN
RED	YELLOW	**GREEN**
ORANGE	BLUE	**GREEN**
YELLOW	BLUE	RED
ORANGE	RED	GREEN

The original Stroop task – in addiction research the words are either gambling-related or -unrelated and each word appears several times (in each colour).

Another strength is further support for cognitive biases.

McCusker and Gettings (1997) used a modified Stroop task. Participants identified the ink colour in which words were printed (had to ignore the word meanings).

Gamblers took longer to do this than non-gamblers but only when the words were gambling-related – they could not prevent word meanings from interfering with the task.

This suggests that gamblers have a cognitive bias to pay attention to gambling-related information that does not exist in non-gamblers.

One limitation is the use of 'thinking aloud' in research.

Dickerson and O'Connor (2006) claim that gamblers' off-the-cuff remarks during sessions do not reflect their deeply-held beliefs about chance and skill.

So researchers may get a misleading impression that gamblers' thought processes are irrational when they are not.

Therefore, findings may not be valid because gamblers' utterances do not express their genuine beliefs.

Evaluation extra: The true explanation?

Cognitive theory is the true explanation because cognitive biases explain how gambling behaviour becomes addiction. Addicted gamblers process information differently from non-gamblers.

However, an alternative view suggests that cognitive biases are not the true explanation because they are *proximate* and we have to go further back in causation for the *ultimate* explanation (biological).

Therefore cognitive theory is probably best seen as a description of factors closely associated with gambling addiction but does not explain what causes them.

Revision BOOSTER

What's the Number One route to evaluating an explanation or concept? The answer is – THINK LINK. You've probably noticed that the evaluation sections of this Revision Guide are chock-full of research studies. You need to make sure you use them effectively by LINKING the study back to the point you were trying to make.

Knowledge Check

1. In relation to cognitive theory as applied to gambling, explain what is meant by 'cognitive bias'. *(4 marks)*

2. Explain the role of cognitive bias in gambling addiction. *(4 marks)*

3. Briefly outline **two** explanations for gambling addiction. *(3 marks + 3 marks)*

4. Discuss cognitive theory as applied to gambling. Refer to **one** other explanation for gambling in your answer. *(16 marks)*

Reducing addiction: Drug therapy

Spec spotlight

Reducing addiction: drug therapy.

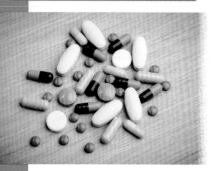

Are drugs the answer to reducing addiction?

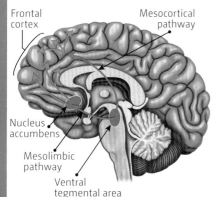

Frontal cortex

Mesocortical pathway

Nucleus accumbens

Mesolimbic pathway

Ventral tegmental area (nicotinic receptors)

You have seen this diagram before (on page 232) but here it is again – the mesolimbic pathway is mentioned on the right.

Apply it

Miah has been desperate to give up smoking ever since she and her boyfriend decided to start a family. She understands the dangers to her and her unborn child's health. She knows that there is no way she can continue to smoke heavily when she is pregnant. She has absolutely decided to give up but she fears that she might not have the 'willpower'.

Explain how drug therapy could help Miah. Refer to why it would be particularly suitable for her.

Drug therapy for addiction

Types of drug therapy.	There are three main types of drug therapy for addiction: aversives, agonists and antagonists. They all work by changing how the person experiences their substance of addiction.
Aversive drugs. Pair addictive drug with unpleasant consequences.	The aversive drug is paired with the behaviour producing unpleasant consequences such as vomiting (**classical conditioning**). For example, *disulfiram* creates the effects of a severe hangover just minutes after alcohol is drunk. The idea is that the addict will associate alcohol and unpleasant effects instead of alcohol paired with pleasant effects.
Agonists. Replace addictive substance by producing a similar effect.	Agonists activate neuron receptors. This produces a similar effect to the addictive substance, satisfies cravings and controls the withdrawal effects. For example, *methadone* is used to treat heroin addiction but has fewer harmful side effects than heroin itself.
Antagonists. Block effects of addictive substance.	Antagonists block neuron receptors. Therefore the substance of dependence cannot produce its usual addictive effects (especially euphoria). For example, *naltrexone* is used to treat heroin addiction.
Smoking – *NRT.* Acts as an agonist, avoid withdrawal symptoms.	Nicotine replacement therapy (NRT) comes in the form of gum, inhalers and patches to deliver nicotine in a less harmful way. Dosage can be reduced over time, decreasing the unpleasantness of withdrawal symptoms. NRT operates neurochemically as an agonist by: 1. Activating *nicotinic acetylcholine receptors* (nAChRs) in the mesolimbic pathway of the brain. 2. Stimulating the release of **dopamine** in the *nucleus accumbens*, just as it does in cigarette smoking.
Gambling – *opioid antagonists.* Reduce release of dopamine.	Gambling addiction taps into the same dopamine reward system as heroin, nicotine, etc. Therefore the same drugs used to treat heroin are used with gamblers (opioid antagonists e.g. *naltrexone*). The process: 1. Enhances the release of neurotransmitter **GABA** in the mesolimbic pathway, which... 2. Reduces the release of dopamine in the nucleus accumbens (and ultimately frontal cortex), which is... 3. Linked to reduced gambling (e.g. Kim *et al.* 2001).

One strength is that research shows drugs are effective.

A **meta-analysis** by Hartmann-Boyce *et al.* (2018) concluded that all forms of NRT helped smokers quit more than placebo and no therapy.

NRT products increased the rate of quitting by up to 60%. NRT also does not appear to foster dependence.

Therefore NRT is an effective therapy which may save lives and reduce costs to the NHS.

Counterpoint

The meta-analysis included only published studies, which have more 'positive' results (**publication bias**). The researchers had a 'poor response' from manufacturers about details of unpublished studies.

This means that NRT may not be as effective as the findings of this meta-analysis suggest.

NRT helps many smokers break their addiction.

One limitation of all drug therapies is side effects.

Side effects may lead to discontinuing therapy. Common side effects of NRT are sleep disturbances, dizziness and headaches.

Side effects for treatment of gambling addiction more serious because dose of *naltrexone* is higher than when used for opioid addiction e.g. muscle spasms and depression.

Therefore side effects should be weighed up against the benefits of the drug therapy and the costs/benefits of other therapies (e.g. psychological therapies).

Revision BOOSTER

Write a very brief essay plan for each possible essay and then practise writing the essay in full from this. Time yourself – 20 minutes for a 16-mark essay.

Another strength is that addiction becomes less stigmatised.

Many people believe addiction is a psychological weakness, so the stigma attached to addiction may lead to self-blame and depression, making recovery harder.

But continuing successful drug therapy (and research into biological basis) is eroding this view because it suggests there is a neurochemical basis to addiction.

Therefore, it could be argued that perceiving addiction as something that can be treated with drugs helps addicts to avoid self-blame and assists recovery.

Not everyone agrees with this conclusion. What do you think?

Knowledge Check

1. Evaluate **one** drug therapy for reducing addiction. *(6 marks)*
2. Outline drug therapy as a way of reducing addiction. *(6 marks)*
3. Explain **one** strength of drug therapy as a way of reducing addiction. *(3 marks)*
4. Some psychologists believe that the most effective way to treat addiction is to address the biological factors underlying the addiction, such as treating faulty brain biochemistry.

   With reference to this argument, describe **and** evaluate drug therapy as a way of reducing addiction.
   (16 marks)

Evaluation extra: Costs and benefits.

Drug therapy has costs because of side effects. It is not a cure for addiction but instead just suppresses cravings/symptoms or provides a substitute.

However, drug therapy can control unpleasant withdrawal symptoms. Side effects are tolerable if the drug is effective. Drugs are also cost-effective and non-disruptive.

Therefore the benefits outweigh the costs – but perhaps only as long as drugs are only used to treat addiction alongside other therapies (e.g. psychological).

Reducing addiction: Behavioural interventions

Spec spotlight

Reducing addiction: behavioural interventions, including aversion therapy and covert sensitisation.

Classical conditioning

UCS   unconditioned stimulus
UCR   unconditioned response
NS   neutral stimulus
CS   conditioned stimulus
CR   conditioned response

Before conditioning:
UCS produces UCR

During conditioning:
NS associated with UCS and becomes CS

After conditioning:
CS produces CR

Aversion therapy

Aversion therapy associates the addiction with unpleasant consequences.	**Aversion therapy** is a behavioural intervention based on **classical conditioning**. The principle is that an addiction can develop through repeated associations between an addictive substance/behaviour and the pleasurable state of arousal caused by it. It follows that the addiction can be reduced by associating the addiction with an unpleasant state (counterconditioning).
Disulfiram used to associate alcohol with severe nausea.	A client is given a drug such as *disulfiram* (UCS) which causes a person drinking alcohol to experience severe nausea and vomiting (UCR). Through association, *disulfiram* and alcohol become **conditioned stimuli** (CSs) producing an expectation of nausea/vomiting (a **conditioned response**, CR).
Electric shocks used to associate gambling with pain.	Electric shocks have been used to countercondition behavioural addictions such as gambling. The gambler selects phrases that relate to their gambling behaviour and others that do not (e.g. 'Went straight home'). They read out each phrase and whenever a gambling-related phrase is read (NS and then CS) they receive a two-second electric shock which they preselect to be painful (UCR and then CR) but not distressing.

Covert sensitisation

Imagined not real.	Traditional aversion therapy has been largely superseded by covert sensitisation, another form of classical conditioning. This is a type of aversion therapy, but *in vitro* rather than *in vivo*, in that the unpleasant stimulus is imagined rather than actually experienced.
Nicotine associated with imagined vomiting.	Clients with nicotine addiction are first encouraged to relax, then imagine themselves smoking a cigarette, followed by the most unpleasant consequences such as vomiting (including graphic details of smells, sights, etc.). The association formed (classical conditioning) should reduce smoking behaviour.
Imagining faeces or snakes.	The client imagines being forced to smoke a cigarette covered in faeces or imagines a slot machine paying out with writhing snakes instead of coins. Towards the end of the session, the client imagines turning away from cigarettes/slot machines and experiencing the resulting feelings of relief.

Aversion therapy could include imagining uncomfortable images while smoking.

Revision BOOSTER

In an exam everyone feels some measure of anxiety – when you are anxious, you forget those things which are not well learned or well practised. So practise, practise, practise.

One limitation is methodological problems in aversion therapy research.

Hajek and Stead (2001) reviewed 25 studies of aversion therapy for nicotine and reported 'glaring methodological problems'.

For example, often no 'blinding' so researchers knew which participants received therapy or placebo, which may have influenced their judgement of success.

Therefore, such inbuilt biases suggest that the research tells us little about the value of aversion therapy.

Another limitation is that aversion therapy has poor long-term effectiveness.

Perhaps he is imagining this cigarette covered in faeces?

Fuller *et al.* (1986) randomly assigned alcohol addicts to receive either *disulfiram* or a placebo, plus weekly counselling for all participants.

There was no significant difference in total abstinence from drinking between the groups after one year – *disulfiram* provided no added benefit to counselling.

This suggests that aversion therapy for alcohol addiction is no more effective than placebo in the long term.

Evaluation extra: Ethical issues.

Aversion therapy is unethical because it uses punishment (so drop-out rates are high) and can cause physical/psychological harm. Could be ethical if effective.

However, it can be considered ethical. Addiction is potentially dangerous and many addicts would rather give themselves small shocks than be addicted. Unethical *not* to use it.

Therefore, aversion therapy is probably best viewed as unethical because the ethical costs are high and the benefits (effectiveness) are small.

One strength is research support for covert sensitisation.

McConaghy *et al.* (1983) compared gambling addicts who received covert sensitisation with addicts who had electric shock aversion therapy.

90% of covert sensitisation participants gambled less (and had fewer cravings) after one year compared with 30% of aversion participants.

This suggests that covert sensitisation is a highly promising behavioural intervention for gambling addiction and probably others too.

One limitation is a lack of suitable comparison groups in studies.

Studies (e.g McConaghy *et al.* above) often make comparison with another behavioural therapy.

Addiction has many non-learning causes (e.g. **cognitive** factors). Non-behavioural therapies (such as **CBT** on the next spread) address these.

This means that the benefits of covert sensitisation may be exaggerated because it is not compared with more effective therapies.

Evaluation extra: Symptom substitution.

Covert sensitisation only suppresses addiction, so clients may appear to recover but issues remain. Some symptoms might disappear but others may appear (symptom substitution).

However, behavioural interventions change behaviour. If new symptoms appear, covert sensitisation can treat those as well.

Therefore, it may still be very helpful to the client to remove the main symptoms of an addiction even if other less serious ones appear.

Apply it

Abby has an addiction to alcohol. She has tried a number of (unsuccessful) treatments but her doctor suggests she might benefit from a therapy that makes her vomit. Abby finds it hard to believe this could work, so she has turned to you, her friend, for some advice because she knows you are a psychology student.

1. Name the therapy that Abby's doctor has suggested.

2. Explain what you would tell Abby about the effectiveness of this therapy.

Knowledge Check

1. Explain the difference between aversion therapy and covert sensitisation as behavioural interventions for reducing addiction. *(4 marks)*

2. Outline aversion therapy as a behavioural intervention for reducing addiction. *(6 marks)*

3. Briefly evaluate aversion therapy as a behavioural intervention for reducing addiction. *(6 marks)*

4. Discuss **two** behavioural interventions for reducing addiction. *(16 marks)*

Reducing addiction: Cognitive behaviour therapy

Spec spotlight

Reducing addiction: cognitive behaviour therapy.

Refusing alcohol with a minimum amount of fuss would be a part of the social skills training element of CBT.

Apply it

Adrian has been referred to a clinical psychologist for cognitive behaviour therapy to treat his addiction to high-stakes gambling machines. He feels compelled almost against his will to start playing on these machines. He has to go into betting shops where the machines are, he can't help it. Unfortunately, because Adrian gambles when he feels happy and also when he feels depressed, he is gambling a lot of the time and losing huge amounts of money.

Explain what Adrian would expect from cognitive behaviour therapy, and how effective it could be in helping him.

Cognitive behaviour therapy for addiction

CBT aims to tackle biased thinking and develop coping behaviours.	**Cognitive behaviour therapy (CBT)** has two key elements: 1. **Cognitive** – identify cognitive biases that underlie the addiction in order to replace them (functional analysis). 2. **Behavioural** – skills-training helps a client develop coping behaviours to avoid the high-risk situations that maintain addictions or trigger relapse.
1. *Cognitive* = functional analysis. Identify biases.	CBT starts with a client and therapist identifying the high-risk situations that lead to the client's substance abuse or gambling. The therapist reflects on what the client is thinking before, during and after such a situation. This process of functional analysis continues throughout the treatment, not just at the beginning of the therapy.
Cognitive restructuring. Confront and challenge faulty beliefs.	The therapist's role is to challenge a client's cognitive biases. For example, a gambler may hold faulty beliefs about probability, randomness and control in gambling. In the initial education phase, the therapist may give the client information about the nature of chance.
2. *Behavioural* = skills training. Replacing poor coping behaviours.	People seeking treatment for addiction may have a huge range of problems but only one way of dealing with them – their addiction. CBT helps to replace this strategy with more constructive ones by developing new skills.
Specific skills are taught (e.g. to deal with anger).	CBT focuses on the wider aspects of a client's life related to the addiction. For example, in the case of a lack of skills to cope with situations that trigger alcohol use: • Assertiveness training – to confront interpersonal conflicts that trigger drinking. • Anger management – often anger triggers drinking so need to learn to control anger.
Social skills training (SST) can help with social situations.	Most clients can benefit from developing skills that allow them to cope in social situations (e.g. trying not to drink alcohol at a wedding). SST helps the client to refuse alcohol in order to avoid embarrassment (e.g. making eye contact and being firm). The therapist may model coping strategies for client and use role play.

One limitation is that CBT may only be effective in the short term.

A **meta-analysis** of 11 studies (Cowlishaw et al. 2012) showed that CBT had medium to very large effects in reducing gambling for up to three months.

But after 9 to 12 months there were no differences between CBT and controls. Also studies may have overestimated CBT effects because they were poor quality.

Therefore, the research picture for CBT is one of benefit in the short term but long-term disappointment.

Counterpoint

However, Petry et al. (2006) in a well-controlled study (e.g. **random allocation**) found that CBT-treated gambling addicts gambled less than controls after 12 months.

Therefore, this one study (which was methodologically better) suggests that CBT is effective in reducing gambling addiction beyond the short term.

Gamblers Anonymous groups plus CBT are effective.

Another limitation is that many clients drop out of CBT.

Cuijpers et al. (2008) note that CBT drop-out rate can be up to five times greater than for other therapies – CBT is demanding.

In addition, clients often seek CBT because of a crisis caused by their addiction, but they drop out when the crisis is less important or resolved.

The high drop-out rate is a major obstacle to the success of CBT in reducing addictions.

Revision BOOSTER

Remember to tailor your description and evaluation of CBT to its role in reducing addiction. Avoid the generic CBT essay. Get detail into your answer by using examples and techniques specific to people with an addiction.

One strength is that CBT is useful in preventing relapse.

CBT presents a realistic picture of repeated relapse in addiction and incorporates it into treatment. It is not a failure but a chance for cognitive restructuring.

Relapse is an inevitable part of an addicted person's life, but manageable as long as psychosocial functioning improves.

Therefore when clients stick with CBT, it can help them to avoid relapse by maintaining a stable lifestyle.

Do you agree with this conclusion?

Evaluation extra: Do we need the C in CBT?

Changing cognitions is necessary to treat addictions. Behavioural interventions may work partly by doing this. Changing cognitions may also avoid symptom substitution.

However, CBT could treat addictions by focusing just on behaviour, e.g. covert sensitisation. Changing cognitions can be counterproductive because it is demanding.

Therefore, overall using a combination of cognitive and behavioural therapy is probably going to be a longer-lasting approach and better for many (but not all) people with addictions.

Knowledge Check

1. Explain the difference between cognitive behaviour therapy and **one other** way of reducing addiction. *(4 marks)*
2. Outline cognitive behaviour therapy as a way of reducing addiction. *(6 marks)*
3. Evaluate cognitive behaviour therapy as a way of reducing addiction. *(10 marks)*
4. Outline **and** evaluate **two** ways of reducing addiction. *(16 marks)*

Applying theories of behaviour change to addiction (1)

Spec spotlight

The application of the following theories of behaviour change to addictive behaviour; the theory of planned behaviour.

Be mindful of intention. Intention is the seed that creates our future

Recovering addicts need more than the best of intentions.

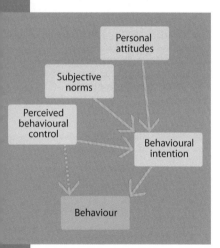

The theory of planned behaviour can be applied to gambling addiction. I intend to stop gambling because I believe gambling has negative outcomes for me (personal attitudes), I perceive that my family and friends disapprove (subjective norms) and I believe I have the ability to stop (perceived behavioural control). Therefore I will put time and effort into stopping (behaviour).

Revision BOOSTER

Have you checked out our revision advice on pages 4 to 9?

Theory of planned behaviour applied to addiction

Intention to change is deliberate.	Ajzen's (1985, 1991) theory of planned behaviour (TPB) suggests we change behaviours in a rational way, evaluating positive and negative consequences.
	Addiction-related behaviour can be predicted from a person's intentions. These intentions arise from three key influences.
1. *Personal attitudes.* Favourable or unfavourable.	An addict's attitudes are a balance of favourable and unfavourable opinions about their addiction, formed by rationally evaluating positive and negative consequences of their behaviour.
	Shifting balance towards unfavourable attitudes should reduce addiction-related behaviour, e.g. associating gambling with outcomes like 'I lose more money than I win' leads to forming an *intention* not to gamble.
2. *Subjective norms.* What is normal?	Addicted person's perceptions about what key people in their life believe to be 'normal' behaviour.
	Would an addicted gambler's family disapprove of their gambling? If 'yes', leads to forming an *intention* not to gamble.
Application.	Aim to change subjective norms to reduce addiction-related intentions and behaviours.
	Many campaigns against substance abuse (e.g. *Talk to Frank*) combat this by providing messages that reveal the true extent of substance abuse in peers (i.e. it's a minority).
3. *Perceived behavioural control.* Self-efficacy.	How much control we *believe* we have over our behaviour (**self-efficacy**), e.g. does the addicted gambler believe they are able to give up?
	Two possible effects of perceived behavioural control:
	1. Indirect influence via *intentions* – the stronger the self-efficacy, the stronger the intention to stop the gambling.
	2. Direct influence – the greater the perceived control, the longer and harder the addict will try to stop. (Note this is the only one of the three TPB elements that has a direct influence on behaviour.)
Application.	Increasing gambler's self-efficacy helps them stop or avoid relapse, e.g. encourage optimistic outlook and confidence in ability to change, also awareness that change requires effort.

One strength is research support for the TPB.

Hagger et al.'s (2011) participants completed questionnaires about alcohol-related behaviours. Attitudes, norms and perceived control all correlated strongly with intentions to limit drinking.

Intentions predicted actual alcohol consumption after one and three months. Perceived behavioural control predicted actual consumption directly.

These findings support predictions derived from the theory which suggests it is **valid**.

Counterpoint

However, the study failed to predict some alcohol-related behaviours (e.g. binge drinking), so the success of the TPB depends on the behaviour being measured.

This suggests that even supportive research indicates that the **predictive validity** of the TPB is limited.

One limitation is that TPB factors have only short-term effects.

A **meta-analysis** (237 tests, McEachan et al. 2011) found that **correlation** between intentions and behaviour varied according to time between the two.

Intention to stop drinking can predict actual stopping but only up to five weeks – evidence that intentions predict behaviour in the longer term is much weaker.

Therefore intentions may not predict changes to addiction-related behaviour in the longer term, limiting the usefulness of the TPB.

Another limitation is the TPB cannot explain the intention-behaviour gap.

Miller and Howell (2005) studied gambling in underage teenagers. Their attitudes, norms and perceived control were all related to *intentions* to stop.

But the key element of the TPB was not supported – the intentions were not related to the actual gambling *behaviour*.

Therefore if the theory cannot predict behaviour change, we cannot use it to help change behaviour.

Evaluation extra: Rational decision-making.

The TPB claims addiction is the result of rational decision-making, e.g. making a cost-benefit analysis by weighing balance of favourable and unfavourable opinions.

However, decisions about drugs/gambling may be irrational (e.g. emotions), not explained by the TPB. TPB data from questionnaires may express rational thoughts but not reflected in behaviour.

Therefore, as an addict may well make real-life decisions under pressure, the TPB is unlikely to consistently explain the (irrational) outcomes.

Apply it

Holly uses cannabis every day and it is affecting her studies at college. A friend has told her what the long-term effects could be, and there is a real danger that Holly could fail all her exams. She has finally realised that she needs to quit or at least reduce her use – she is enthusiastic about doing this, and believes she has the right motivation. Holly thinks that the time is now.

How could the theory of planned behaviour explain Holly's behaviour and the chances of her changing it?

Revision BOOSTER

Evidence is key in psychology. But whether it's description (AO1) or evaluation (AO3) depends on how you use it. Are you outlining what the evidence is? Are you describing the procedures and findings of a study? That's AO1. Are you explaining what the evidence tells us about, say, a theory or concept? Are you linking the findings of the study to the theory. That's AO3. But you need to make this clear to the examiner.

Knowledge Check

1. Outline the theory of planned behaviour as it applies to addictive behaviour. *(6 marks)*

2. Explain how the theory of planned behaviour can be used to change addictive behaviour. *(4 marks)*

3. Briefly evaluate the theory of planned behaviour as it applies to addictive behaviour. *(4 marks)*

4. Simon has been chatting with friends who study psychology and said that he would like to quit smoking. His friends describe the theory of planned behaviour to him and use it to explain how he could quit.

   Discuss the theory of planned behaviour as it applies to addictive behaviour. Relate your discussion to Simon's situation. *(16 marks)*

Applying theories of behaviour change to addiction (2)

Spec spotlight

The application of the following theories of behaviour change to addictive behaviour; Prochaska's six-stage model of behaviour change.

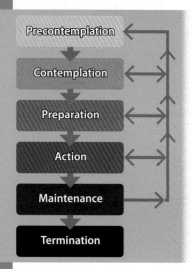

Prochaska's six-stage model.

Apply it

Kayla believes that she will always be an alcoholic, but she hasn't had a drink for several years. To finally get to this point in her life where she has managed to stay away from drinking, she first had to recognise that she had reached 'rock bottom', that she needed to change, that it would be hard and she would frequently 'fall off the wagon' and relapse. Each time she did, Kayla picked herself back up and stayed away from alcohol until the next time.

Describe Kayla's experience in terms of the six stages of Prochaska's model of behaviour change.

The six-stage model of behaviour change

Each stage represents differences in readiness to change.	Prochaska and DiClemente (1983) suggest a six-stage model in which overcoming addiction is a cyclical process.
	Some stages may be reached in the order below but there may be backtracking or even missing out of stages.
	The model is based on two insights:
	1. People differ in how *ready* they are to change.
	2. The usefulness of a treatment *intervention* depends on the stage the person is currently in.
Stage 1 *Precontemplation.* 'Ignorance is bliss'.	People in this stage are not thinking about changing their addiction-related behaviour within the next six months. This could be due to *denial* ('I don't have a problem') or *demotivation* ('I have tried before but had no success, so why bother'). Intervention should focus on helping the addicted person to consider the need for change.
Stage 2 *Contemplation.* 'Sitting on the fence'.	Someone at this stage is thinking about making a change to their behaviour in the next six months. They are aware of both the benefits of change and the costs. *Intervention* should focus on helping the person see that the pros outweigh the cons.
Stage 3 *Preparation.* 'OK, I'm ready for this'.	Now the person believes the benefits are greater than the costs and decides to make a change within the next month. But they don't know how to do this. *Intervention* is support in constructing a plan (e.g. see a drugs counsellor, ring a helpline, see a GP).
Stage 4 *Action.* 'Let's do this'.	People at this stage have done something to change their addictive behaviour in the last six months (e.g. having **cognitive** or behaviour therapy or something less formal such as remove alcohol from the house). *Intervention* should focus on coping skills needed to quit.
Stage 5 *Maintenance.* 'Stay on track'.	The person has maintained some behaviour change (e.g. stopped gambling) for more than six months. *Intervention* should focus on relapse prevention by encouraging application of coping skills and offering support.
Stage 6 *Termination.* Abstinence becomes automatic.	At this stage abstinence is automatic and the person no longer returns to addictive behaviours to cope with anxiety, stress or loneliness. It may not be realistic for everyone to reach this point. *Intervention* is not required at this stage.

One strength is that recovery is viewed as a dynamic process.

In contrast with other approaches, this model doesn't see recovery as a single all-or-nothing event. Time is an important factor and recovery is a continuing process.

Progression through the six stages is always in the same order, but people also recycle backwards and miss stages.

This suggests that this stage model provides a realistic view of the complex and active nature of recovery from addiction.

Counterpoint

However, the stages are arbitrary. Kraft *et al.* (1999) say they can be reduced to precontemplation plus the others grouped. This matters because stages are tied to interventions.

This suggests that Prochaska's stage model has little usefulness both for understanding changes over time and for treatment recommendations.

Another strength is a realistic view of relapse.

'Relapse is the rule' (DiClemente *et al.* 2004), so the model views relapse as part of dynamic behaviour change and not as failure.

But the model also takes relapse seriously because it may blow change off course – recovery can take several attempts to reach maintenance/termination stages.

This means the model has **face validity** with clients and is more acceptable because they can see it is realistic about relapse.

One limitation is research challenging the model.

Taylor *et al.* (2006) conducted a NICE review of 24 reviews/**meta-analyses**, concluding that the model was no more effective than alternatives in treating nicotine addiction.

They also concluded that the key concept of defined stages in behaviour change could not be **validated** by available data.

This suggests the overall research picture is negative, despite over-optimistic claims made for the model by some.

Evaluation extra: Model of behaviour change?

This is a model of behaviour change because it emphasises that change depends on readiness and assumes interventions motivate clients to change their behaviour and move on.

However, it may not be a model of behaviour change because clients move between stages regardless of behaviour changing, so it is about how attitudes/intentions change.

Therefore the model might really be about thinking rather than about behaviour, which may or may not be linked to potentially useful interventions.

Relapse

is a part of Recovery

Recognising this is a key element of Prochaska's model.

Revision BOOSTER

Mnemonic time

The specification includes Prochaska's stages – six of them. That's quite a few, but you should be able to name them all in an exam answer. Create a mnemonic to help you. Make a sentence out of words beginning with the initial letters of each stage:

PC – C – P – A – M – T.

In an essay you won't have time to describe all six in detail so practise an outline version for 200 words maximum.

Knowledge Check

1. Briefly explain **two** theories of behaviour change as applied to addictive behaviour. *(4 marks)*
2. Outline Prochaska's six-stage model of behaviour change as it applies to addictive behaviour. *(6 marks)*
3. Briefly evaluate Prochaska's six-stage model of behaviour change as it applies to addictive behaviour. *(4 marks)*
4. Discuss Prochaska's six-stage model of behaviour change as it applies to addictive behaviour. *(16 marks)*

Glossary

adaptive Any physical or psychological characteristic that enhances an individual's survival and reproduction, and is thus likely to be naturally selected. Such characteristics are passed on to future generations. This is an evolutionary explanation. **18, 19, 33, 41, 71, 94, 138, 139, 150, 158, 188, 189, 190, 191, 198**

androcentric bias Male-centred; when 'normal' behaviour is judged according to a male standard (meaning that female behaviour is often seen as 'abnormal' or 'deficient' by comparison). **103**

antisocial personality disorder A mental health condition where a person has a repeated pattern of manipulating other people or violating the rights of others. Often leads to crimes against people. **210, 230**

APD See antisocial personality disorder. **210, 211, 230, 231**

autonomic nervous system (ANS) Transmits information to and from internal bodily organs. It is 'autonomic' as the system operates involuntarily (i.e. it is automatic). It has two main divisions: the sympathetic and parasympathetic nervous systems. **26, 60, 158, 159, 184**

aversion therapy A behavioural treatment based on classical conditioning. A maladaptive behaviour is paired with an unpleasant stimulus such as a painful electric shock. Eventually, the behaviour is associated with pain without the shock being used. **63, 235, 242, 243**

behaviourist A way of explaining behaviour in terms of what is observable and in terms of learning. **10, 11, 12, 13, 14, 15, 16, 17, 24, 25, 62, 64, 222**

biological A perspective that emphasises the importance of physical processes in the body such as genetic inheritance and neural function. **10, 11, 18, 19, 25, 60, 136, 143, 208, 211**

biological determinism The belief that behaviour is caused by biological (genetic, hormonal, evolutionary) influences that we cannot control. **60, 211**

biological reductionism A form of reductionism which attempts to explain social and psychological phenomena at a lower biological level (in terms of the actions of gene, hormones, etc.). **64, 65**

case study A research method that involves a detailed study of a single individual, institution or event. Case studies provide a rich record of human experience but are hard to generalise from. **11, 31, 38, 43, 46, 47, 66, 67, 103**

CBT A method for treating mental disorders and other conditions based on both cognitive and behavioural techniques. From the cognitive viewpoint the therapy aims to deal with thinking, such as challenging negative thoughts. The therapy also includes behavioural techniques. **24, 41, 131, 132, 133, 136, 137, 149, 176, 215, 224, 243, 244, 245**

classical conditioning Learning by association. Occurs when two stimuli are repeatedly paired together – an unconditioned (unlearned) stimulus (UCS) and a new 'neutral' stimulus (NS). The neutral stimulus eventually produces the same response that was first produced by the unlearned stimulus alone. **12, 13, 138, 140, 141, 234, 240, 242**

cognitive Refers to the process of thinking – knowing, perceiving, believing. **10, 11, 13, 14, 15, 16, 17, 18, 24, 25, 31, 33, 35, 36, 37, 46, 65, 80, 95, 97, 98, 99, 100, 101, 104, 105, 110, 111, 112, 113, 114, 115, 116, 117, 118, 119, 121, 122, 128, 129, 130, 149, 150, 151, 154, 156, 159, 176, 180, 185, 189, 191, 194, 199, 202, 203, 214, 215, 224, 225, 235, 238, 239, 243, 244, 245, 248**

cognitive behaviour therapy See CBT.

collectivist A group of people who place more value on the 'collective' rather than on the individual, and on interdependence rather than on independence. The opposite is true of individualist culture. **23, 59, 73, 81, 85, 89, 95, 167**

concordance rates A measure of similarity (usually expressed as a percentage) between two individuals or sets of individuals on a given trait. **18, 144, 145, 152, 186, 187, 211**

concurrent validity The extent to which a psychological measure relates to an existing similar measure. **49**

confederate An individual in a study who is not a real participant and who has been instructed how to behave by the researcher. **192, 202, 203**

confounding variable (CV) Any variable, other than the independent variable (IV), that may have affected the dependent variable (DV) so we cannot be sure of the true source of changes to the DV. Confounding variables vary systematically with the IV. **33, 41, 44, 117, 155, 161, 195, 201, 203, 209, 221**

control condition The condition in a repeated measures design that provides a baseline measure of behaviour without the experimental treatment (independent variable). **120**

control group In an experiment with an independent groups design, a group of participants who receive no treatment. Their behaviour acts as a baseline against which the effect of the independent variable (IV) may be measured. **33, 34, 35, 49, 115, 120, 137, 141, 150, 157, 160, 179, 192, 198, 199, 209, 213, 218, 225, 235, 239**

correlation A mathematical technique in which a researcher investigates an association between two variables, called co-variables. Correlational studies are studies which have used a correlational analysis. **39, 44, 45, 48, 49, 50, 51, 53, 73, 75, 80, 83, 89, 97, 107, 119, 126, 151, 162, 163, 164, 165, 166, 168, 171, 184, 200, 201, 231, 247**

criterion validity A means of assessing validity by considering the extent to which people who do well on a particular test also do well on other things that you would expect to be associated with the particular test. **125**

cultural bias Refers to a tendency to ignore cultural differences and interpret all phenomena through the 'lens' of one's own culture. **23, 58, 59, 107**

de-individuation A psychological state in which an individual loses their personal identity and takes on the identity of the social group when, for example, in a crowd or wearing a uniform. The result may be to free the individual from the constraints of social norms. **86, 196, 197**

demand characteristics Any cue from the researcher or from the research situation that may be interpreted by participants as revealing the purpose of the investigation. This may lead to a participant changing their behaviour within the research situation. **44, 49, 155, 161, 195**

determinism The view that an individual's behaviour is shaped or controlled by internal or external forces rather than an individual's will to do something. **15, 19, 21, 23, 24, 25, 60, 61, 63, 191, 199, 233**

diathesis-stress model An interactionist approach to explaining behaviour. For example, schizophrenia is explained as the result of both an underlying vulnerability (diathesis) and a trigger, both of which are necessary for the onset of schizophrenia. In early versions of the model, vulnerability was genetic and triggers were psychological. Nowadays both genes and trauma are seen as diatheses, and stress can be psychological or biological in nature. **62, 136, 137, 145, 153, 186, 210, 211**

disinhibited (disinhibition) Normal social constraints against certain behaviours can be weakened by environmental triggers. These behaviours then appear temporarily socially acceptable and therefore more likely. **86, 152, 154, 155, 156, 196, 202, 203**

dopamine A neurotransmitter that generally has an excitatory effect and is associated with the sensation of pleasure. Unusually high levels are associated with schizophrenia and unusually low levels are associated with Parkinson's disease. **29, 126, 127, 130, 131, 136, 143, 144, 145, 152, 153, 229, 230, 232, 233, 234, 240**

DSM The Diagnostic and Statistical Manual of Mental Disorders is a classification system of mental disorders published by the American Psychiatric Association. It contains typical symptoms of each disorder and guidelines for clinicians to make a diagnosis. The most recent version is DSM-5. **69, 108, 109, 124, 125, 150**

DZ twins (dizygotic) Non-identical twins formed from two fertilised eggs (or zygotes). **18, 62, 108, 126, 127, 144, 145, 186, 187, 210, 211**

ecological validity The extent to which findings from a research study can be generalised to other settings and situations. A form of external validity. **49**

EEG Electroencephalograph. A method of detecting activity in the living brain, electrodes are attached to a person's scalp to record general levels of electrical activity. **10, 36, 37, 40, 178**

environmental determinism The belief that behaviour is caused by aspects of our physical or social world that we cannot control, such as rewards/punishments from other people determining our future behaviour (learning theory). **13, 60, 61**

environmental reductionism The attempt to explain all behaviour in terms of stimulus–response links that have been learned through experience. **64**

evolutionary An account of the changes in species over millions of years. Genetic characteristics that enhance survival and reproduction are naturally selected. These characteristics are passed on to the next generation. Animals without such characteristics are less successful at reproduction and thus are not selected. **41, 64, 70, 71, 74, 75, 138, 139, 180, 190, 191, 195, 197, 208**

experiment Involves the manipulation of an independent variable (IV) to measure the effect on the dependent variable (DV). Experiments may be laboratory, field, natural or quasi. **10, 13, 44, 46, 48, 49, 50, 54, 55, 59, 60, 65, 87, 155, 161, 200**

experimental condition The condition in a repeated measures design containing the independent variable (IV) as distinct from the control condition. **120**

external validity The degree to which a research finding can be generalised to, for example, other settings (ecological validity), other groups of people (population validity) and over time (temporal validity). **17, 46, 49, 167, 201**

extraneous variable (EV) Any variable, other than the independent variable (IV), that *may* have an effect on the dependent variable (DV) if it is not controlled. EVs include CVs but also include 'nuisance variables' that do not vary systematically with the IV. Such nuisance variables should not confound the results of research. **41, 60**

face validity A basic form of validity in which a measure is scrutinised to determine whether it appears to measure what it is supposed to measure – for instance, does a test of anxiety look like it measures anxiety? **49, 249**

fMRI Functional magnetic resonance imaging. A method used to scan brain activity while a person is performing a task. It enables researchers to detect those regions of the brain that are rich in oxygen and thus are active. **10, 19, 31, 35, 36, 37, 184**

free will The notion that humans can make choices and are not determined by biological or external forces. **13, 15, 17, 21, 22, 23, 25, 60, 61, 191, 199**

GABA Gamma-aminobutyric acid, a neurotransmitter that inhibits the activity of neurons in most areas of the brain. **145, 174, 233, 240**

gender bias When considering human behaviour, bias is a tendency to treat one individual or group in a different way from others. In the context of gender bias, psychological research or theory may offer a view that does not justifiably represent the experience and behaviour of men or women (usually women). **56, 57, 124, 125, 147, 159, 171, 219**

generalisation In relation to research findings, the extent to which findings and conclusions from a particular investigation can be broadly applied to the wider population. This is made less likely if the sample of participants is unrepresentative of the wider population. **31, 35, 39, 43, 46, 49, 55, 66, 73, 74, 123, 167, 201, 213**

hard determinism Implies that free will is not possible as our behaviour is always caused by internal or external events beyond our control. **24, 60, 61**

holism An argument or theory which proposes that it only makes sense to study a whole system rather than its constituent parts (which is the reductionist approach). **23, 25, 30, 31, 64, 65**

humanistic An approach to understanding behaviour that emphasises the importance of subjective experience and each person's capacity for self-determination. **11, 21, 22, 23, 25, 60, 64, 191**

ICD The International Classification of Disorders published by the World Health Organisation. The most recent version (1993) is number 10 (number 11 is published but will not be used for diagnosis until 2022). ICD is used in the UK and Europe whereas DSM is American. **124, 125**

individualist A group of people who value the rights and interests of the individual. This results in a concern for independence and self-assertiveness. People tend to live in small families unlike collectivist societies. **23, 59, 73, 81, 85, 89, 95, 149, 167**

informed consent An ethical issue and an ethical guideline in psychological research whereby participants must be given comprehensive information concerning the nature and purpose of the research and their role in it, in order for them to make an informed decision about whether to participate. **33, 68**

internal validity A kind of validity, concerned with what goes on inside a study – the extent to which the researcher is measuring what was intended. **49, 167**

longitudinal Research conducted over a long period of time – months or years. **46, 119**

meta-analysis 'Research about research', refers to the process of combining results from a number of studies on a particular topic to provide an overall view. This may involve a qualitative review of conclusions and/or a quantitative analysis of the results producing an effect size. **44, 63, 75, 83, 87, 177, 186, 193, 200, 213, 227, 235, 241, 245, 247**

modelling From the observer's perspective modelling is imitating the behaviour of a role model. From the role model's perspective, modelling is the precise demonstration of a specific behaviour that may be imitated by an observer. **14, 15, 24, 104, 105, 141, 148, 149, 195**

MZ twins (monozygotic) Identical twins formed from one fertilised egg (or zygote). They have exactly the same genes. **18, 62, 126, 127, 144, 145, 152, 153, 186, 187, 210, 211**

natural experiment An experiment where the change in the independent variable (IV) is not brought about by the researcher but would have happened even if the researcher had not been there. The researcher records the effect on the dependent variable (DV). **89, 149, 166, 167, 199**

nature–nurture debate The question of whether behaviour is determined more by nature (inherited and genetic factors) or nurture (all influences after conception, i.e. experience). **24, 62, 63, 97, 99, 106, 107, 119, 121, 187, 197, 209, 211, 217**

oestrogen The primary female hormone, playing an important role in the menstrual cycle and reproductive system. **40, 94, 95, 180, 181**

operant conditioning A form of learning in which behaviour is shaped and maintained by its consequences. Possible consequences of behaviour include positive reinforcement, negative reinforcement or punishment. **12, 13, 15, 24, 134, 140, 148, 178, 179, 194, 200, 222, 232, 234, 235**

operationalise Clearly defining variables in terms of how they can be measured. **44, 48, 49, 65, 201, 217, 222, 223**

oxytocin A hormone which causes contraction of the uterus during labour and stimulates lactation. It is linked to the 'tend and befriend' stress response. **56, 94, 95, 159, 180, 181**

parasympathetic nervous system A division of the autonomic nervous system (ANS) which controls the relaxed state (rest and digest), conserving resources and promoting digestion and metabolism. The parasympathetic nervous system works in opposition to the sympathetic nervous system. One or the other system is active at any time. **26, 27, 158**

placebo A treatment that should have no effect on the behaviour being studied; it contains no active ingredient. Therefore it can be used to separate out the effects of the independent variable (IV) from any effects caused merely by receiving any treatment. **131, 175, 179, 185, 235**

predictive validity A means of assessing the validity or trueness of a psychological test (or explanation) by correlating the results of the test with some later example of the behaviour that is being tested. If the test result is positively correlated with the later behaviour this confirms the validity of the test. **247**

psychodynamic An approach to understanding behaviour that describes the different forces (dynamics), most of which are unconscious, that operate on the mind and direct human behaviour and experience. Freud's psychoanalytic theory is the best known example of the psychodynamic approach. **11, 20, 21, 25, 56, 95, 101, 102, 103, 105, 128, 146, 192, 218, 219**

publication bias The tendency for some kinds of research to be published rather than other types. For example, academic journals may prefer not to publish research that is counter to established principles or research with negative results. **241**

random allocation An attempt to control for participant variables in an independent groups design which ensures that each participant has the same chance of being in one condition as any other. **44, 137, 155, 199, 245**

reductionism The belief that human behaviour is best explained by breaking it down into smaller constituent parts. **17, 23, 24, 25, 64, 65, 95**

replicate Repeating an investigation under the same conditions in order to test the validity and reliability of its findings. **41, 54, 58, 59, 66, 74, 77, 159, 200**

researcher bias The effect that a researcher's expectations have on participants and thus on the results of an experiment or any study. **46**

schema A mental framework of beliefs and expectations that influence cognitive processing. Schema contain our understanding of an object, person or idea. Schema become increasingly complex during development as we acquire more information about each object or idea. **16, 17, 24, 95, 100, 101, 105, 110, 111, 112**

self-efficacy One's confidence in being able to do something. Such confidence generates expectations and these act as self-fulfilling prophecies. **106, 167, 194, 238, 246**

Glossary

serotonin A neurotransmitter found in the central nervous system. Low levels have been linked to many different behaviours and physiological processes, including aggression, eating disorders and depression.   **18, 19, 29, 40, 64, 130, 143, 144, 145, 152, 153, 184, 185, 186, 187, 210**

social desirability bias A tendency for respondents to answer questions in such a way that presents themselves in a better light, i.e. they appear kinder, more intelligent, more attractive, etc.   **49, 169**

social learning theory (SLT) A way of explaining behaviour that includes both direct and indirect reinforcement, combining learning theory with the role of cognitive factors.   **14, 15, 100, 104, 105, 140, 148, 149, 194, 195**

soft determinism The concept that there are constraints on our behaviour but within these limitations we are free to make choices.   **17, 24, 60, 61, 191, 199**

somatic nervous system (SNS) Transmits information from receptor cells in the sense organs to the central nervous system (CNS). It also receives information from the CNS that directs muscles to act.   **26**

standardised (procedures, instructions, conditions) Using exactly the same formalised procedures, instructions and conditions for all participants in a research study.   **48, 49, 54, 66, 222**

sympathetic nervous system A division of the autonomic nervous system (ANS) which activates internal organs for vigorous activities and emergencies, such as the fight or flight response. It consists of nerves that control, for example, increased heart rate and breathing, and decreased digestive activity. The sympathetic branch works in opposition to the parasympathetic branch of the ANS.   **26, 27, 158, 174, 202, 212**

temporal validity The extent to which findings from a research study can be generalised to other historical times and eras. A form of external validity.   **49, 93**

testosterone A hormone produced mainly by the testes in males, but it also occurs in females. It is associated with the development of secondary sexual characteristics in males (e.g. body hair), and has also been implicated in aggression and dominance behaviours.   **94, 95, 180, 181, 184, 185, 212**

validity Refers to whether an observed effect is a genuine one.   **17, 23, 31, 35, 43, 46, 47, 49, 55, 73, 77, 79, 81, 93, 103, 117, 124, 125, 145, 147, 149, 153, 159, 163, 165, 167, 169, 173, 187, 191, 197, 199, 201, 205, 211, 215, 247**

p.11, p.12 (bottom), p.16, p.26, p.32 (bottom), p.40 (bottom), p.45 (bottom), p.82, p.90 (bottom), p.91 (bottom), p.96 (both), p.116 (bottom), p.120 (bottom), p.126, p.130, p.154 (bottom), p.168, p.182, p.184 (bottom), p.188 (bottom), p.232, p.240 (bottom), p.246 (bottom), p.248 © Illuminate Publishing

p.13 © Craig Swanson www.perspicuity.com

p.27 © Cartoonstock

p.31 Barking Dog Art

p.3 and p.256 Stars Aha-Soft / Shutterstock.com; Aleksova / Shutterstock.com; Sashkin / Shutterstock.com; p.6 Kuklos / Shutterstock.com; p.7 OSTILL is Franck Camhi / Shutterstock.com; p.10 CYCLONEPROJECT / Shutterstock.com; p.12 WilleeCole Photography / Shutterstock.com; p.14 Evgeny Atamanenko / Shutterstock.com; p.15 valeriya_sh / Shutterstock.com; p.17 Lukiyanova Natalia frenta / Shutterstock.com; p.18 Katrina Elena / Shutterstock.com; p.19 klss / Shutterstock.com; p.20 RACOBOVT / Shutterstock.com; p.21 Nantz / Shutterstock.com; p.22 Volodimir Zozulinskyi / Shutterstock.com; p.23 Joseph Sohm / Shutterstock.com; p.24 arda savasciogullari / Shutterstock.com; p.25 cunaplus / Shutterstock.com; p28 Fotolia; p.29 joshya / Shutterstock.com; p.30 Blamb / Shutterstock.com; p.32 Chad Zuber / Shutterstock.com; p.33 Oksana Telesheva / Shutterstock.com; p.34 Ocskay Bence / Shutterstock.com; p.35 martan / Shutterstock.com; p.36 Daisy Daisy / Shutterstock.com; p.37 Oleg Senkov / Shutterstock.com; p.38 yomogi1 / Shutterstock.com; p.39 jadimages / Shutterstock.com; p.40 Beauty Stock / Shutterstock.com; p.41 Image Point Fr / Shutterstock.com; p.42 fotofeel / Shutterstock.com; p.43 Javier Brosch / Shutterstock.com; p.44 Fabrik Bilder / Shutterstock.com; p.45 Ivan Kruk / Shutterstock.com; p.46 David Gilder / Shutterstock.com; p.47 eteimaging / Shutterstock.com; p.48 Tony Campbell / Shutterstock.com; p.49 VICHAILAO / Shutterstock.com; p.50 AshTproductions / Shutterstock.com; p.51 studiovin / Shutterstock.com; p.53 JONGSUK / Shutterstock.com; p.54 art_of_sun / Shutterstock.com; p.55 alphaspirit / Shutterstock.com; p.56 Lightspring / Shutterstock.com; p.57 Aleutie / Shutterstock.com; p.58 leungchopan / Shutterstock.com; p.59 Ilike / Shutterstock.com; p.60 inimalGraphic / Shutterstock.com; p.61 sirtravelalot, vklikov / Shutterstock.com; p.62 LeventeGyori / Shutterstock.com; p.63 herjua / Shutterstock.com; p.64 Rocketclips, Inc. / Shutterstock.com; p.65 NEIL ROY JOHNSON / Shutterstock.com; p.66 Andrey_Kuzmin / Shutterstock.com; p.67 Kichigin / Shutterstock.com; p.68 Daniel M Ernst / Shutterstock.com; p.69 AndreAnita / Shutterstock.com; p.70 NDAB Creativity / Shutterstock.com; p.71 pathdoc / Shutterstock.com; p.72 WAYHOME studio / Shutterstock.com; p.73 Maros Bauer / Shutterstock.com; p.74 Flashon Studio / Shutterstock.com; p.75 Halfpoint / Shutterstock.com; p.76 ViDI Studio / Shutterstock.com; p.77 AJR_photo / Shutterstock.com; p.78 CarlosDavid / Shutterstock.com; p.79 Di Studio / Shutterstock.com; p.80 docstockmedia / Shutterstock.com; p.81 wxin / Shutterstock.com; p.83 Jack Frog / Shutterstock.com; p.84 ShotPrime Studio / Shutterstock.com; p.85 DNF Style / Shutterstock.com; p.86 Syda Productions / Shutterstock.com; p.87 Mila Supinskaya Glashchenko / Shutterstock.com; p.88 mooinblack / Shutterstock.com; p.89 Featureflash Photo Agency / Shutterstock.com; p.90 FMStox / Shutterstock.com; p.91 Monkey Business Images / Shutterstock.com; p.92 Tinxi / Shutterstock.com; p.93 Mai Groves / Shutterstock.com; p.94 Knorre / Shutterstock.com; p.95 Zerbor / Shutterstock.com; p.98 UncleFredDesign / Shutterstock.com; p.99 zlikovec / Shutterstock.com; p.100 ESB Professional / Shutterstock.com; p.101 Hugo Felix / Shutterstock.com; p.102 Oksana Kuzmina / Shutterstock.com; p.103 Antonio Guillem / Shutterstock.com; p.104 Unique Vision / Shutterstock.com; p.105 Videologia / Shutterstock.com; p.106 Jamie Hooper / Shutterstock.com; p.107 Stuart Miles / Shutterstock.com; p.108 Twinsterphoto / Shutterstock.com; p.109 TheModernCanvas / Shutterstock.com; p.110 AJP / Shutterstock.com; p.111 Andi Berger / Shutterstock.com; p.112 Purino / Shutterstock.com; p.113 Kidsada Manchinda / Shutterstock.com; p.114 Sorn340 Studio Images / Shutterstock.com; p.115 Boris Bulychev / Shutterstock.com; p.116 gualtiero boffi / Shutterstock.com; p.117 azmaidi / Shutterstock.com; p.118 jeafish Ping / Shutterstock.com; p.119 Africa Studio / Shutterstock.com; p.120 Tomasz Trojanowski / Shutterstock.com; p.121 Syda Productions / Shutterstock.com; p.122 George Rudy / Shutterstock.com; p.123 yifanjrb / Shutterstock.com; p.124 alphaspirit / Shutterstock.com; p.125 Darren Baker / Shutterstock.com; p.127 MriMan / Shutterstock.com; p.128 Sangoiri / Shutterstock.com; p.129 9nong / Shutterstock.com; p.131 Gwoeii / Shutterstock.com; p.132 Photoroyalty / Shutterstock.com; p.133 Monkey Business Images, FrankHH / Shutterstock.com; p.134 Black Salmon / Shutterstock.com; p.135 SvetaZi / Shutterstock.com; p.136 Joshua Resnick / Shutterstock.com; p.137 OSTILL is Franck Camhi / Shutterstock.com; p.138 Photographee.eu / Shutterstock.com; p.139 Anneka / Shutterstock.com; p.140 Nagy-Bagoly Arpad / Shutterstock.com; p.141 Monkey Business Images / Shutterstock.com; p.142 stefan3andrei / Shutterstock.com; p.143 Cathy Keifer / Shutterstock.com; p.144 Phovoir / Shutterstock.com; p.145 Ermolaev Alexander / Shutterstock.com; p.146 fizkes / Shutterstock.com; p.147 fizkes / Shutterstock.com; p.148 Featureflash Photo Agency / Shutterstock.com; p.149 Keith Homan / Shutterstock.com; p.150 Photographee.eu / Shutterstock.com; p.151 ImageFlow / Shutterstock.com; p.152 Kletr / Shutterstock.com; p.153 LuckyStep / Shutterstock.com; p.154 Vlue / Shutterstock.com; p.155 Duplass / Shutterstock.com; p.156 Lamberrto / Shutterstock.com; p.157 Rido / Shutterstock.com; p.158 Cartoon Resource / Shutterstock.com; p.159 Sam72 / Shutterstock.com; p.160 altafulla / Shutterstock.com; p.161 Motortion Films / Shutterstock.com; p.162 Anton Havelaar / Shutterstock.com; p.163 Tyler Olson / Shutterstock.com; p.164 Thinglass / Shutterstock.com; p.165 DJTaylor / Shutterstock.com; p.166 Iakov Filimonov / Shutterstock.com; p.167 G-Stock Studio / Shutterstock.com; p.168 Minerva Studio / Shutterstock.com; p.169 Xiaojiao Wang, Alex from the Rock / Shutterstock.com; p.172 Brocreative / Shutterstock.com; p.173 tomertu / Shutterstock.com; p.174 iofoto / Shutterstock.com; p.175 Image Point Fr / Shutterstock.com; p.176 wavebreakmedia / Shutterstock.com; p.177 wavebreakmedia / Shutterstock.com; p.178 Di Studio / Shutterstock.com; p.179 Andrey_Popov / Shutterstock.com; p.180 Peshkova / Shutterstock.com; p.181 Rawpixel.com / Shutterstock.com; p.182 michaeljung / Shutterstock.com; p.183 Paul Looyen / Shutterstock.com; p.184 SciePro / Shutterstock.com; p.185 SFIO CRACHO / Shutterstock.com; p.186 Dimj / Shutterstock.com; p.187 marcovarro / Shutterstock.com; p.188 Shaiith / Shutterstock.com; p.189 Monkey Business Images / Shutterstock.com; p.190 Yulai Studio / Shutterstock.com; p.191 Monkey Business Images / Shutterstock.com; p.192 pathdoc / Shutterstock.com; p.193 NDAB Creativity / Shutterstock.com; p.194 SpeedKingz / Shutterstock.com; p.195 Oleg Troino / Shutterstock.com; p.196 Alexander_P / Shutterstock.com; p.197 1000 Words, natrot / Shutterstock.com; p.198 Lightspring / Shutterstock.com; p.199 Nejron Photo / Shutterstock.com; p.200 Ekaterina_Minaeva / Shutterstock.com; p.201 Bojan656 / Shutterstock.com; p.202 antos777 / Shutterstock.com; p.203 Aleksei Semjonov / Shutterstock.com; p.204 Javier Brosch / Shutterstock.com; p.205 Opachevsky Irina / Shutterstock.com; p.206 Couperfield / Shutterstock.com; p.207 pingebat / Shutterstock.com; p.208 Zemler / Shutterstock.com; p.210 Chandler McGrew / Shutterstock.com; p.211 Monkey Business Images / Shutterstock.com; p.212 CREATISTA / Shutterstock.com; p.213 Sirswindon at English Wikipedia; p.214 Lucky Business / Shutterstock.com; p.215 marina shin / Shutterstock.com; p.216 En min Shen / Shutterstock.com; p.217 sdecoret / Shutterstock.com; p.218 KK Tan / Shutterstock.com; p.219 Brian A Jackson / Shutterstock.com; p.220 Fer Gregory / Shutterstock.com; p.221 chekart / Shutterstock.com; p.222 TaraPatta / Shutterstock.com; p.223 chrisdorney / Shutterstock.com; p.224 Carlos Caetano / Shutterstock.com; p.225 Master1305 / Shutterstock.com; p.226 StepanPopov / Shutterstock.com; p.227 WindVector / Shutterstock.com; p.228 wk1003mike / Shutterstock.com; p.229 Kunst Bilder, Khosro / Shutterstock.com; p.230 M-SUR / Shutterstock.com; p.231 FabrikaSimf / Shutterstock.com; p.233 fizkes / Shutterstock.com; p.234 moj0j0 / Shutterstock.com; p.235 Tony Wear / Shutterstock.com; p.236 NDAB Creativity / Shutterstock.com; p.237 Icatnews / Shutterstock.com; p.238 Enrique Pellejer / Shutterstock.com; p.239 Photostriker / Shutterstock.com; p.240 Dima Sobko / Shutterstock.com; p.241 Kjpargeter / Shutterstock.com; p.242 ra2 studio / Shutterstock.com; p.243 Sabphoto / Shutterstock.com; p.244 Prostock-studio / Shutterstock.com; p.245 fizkes / Shutterstock.com; p.246 Constantin Stanciu / Shutterstock.com; p.249 Marie1969

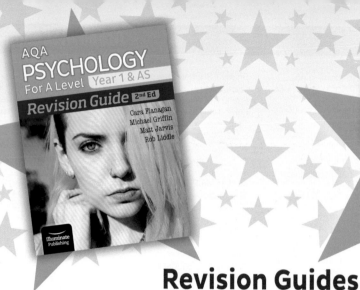

Revision Guides

+

Flashbooks

+

Revision Apps

=

An unbeatable combination for revision!
Visit www.illuminatepublishing.com/aqapsych